The Central Iowa Norwegians

Volume 1

The Central Iowa Norwegians

Histories, Memoirs, and Studies of their Settlement from 1855 to 1905

Volume 1

Arlen Twedt
Author & Compiler

CINP Press/Ankeny, Iowa

The drawing on the cover is Story City in 1875 before the business district was moved a few blocks west when a narrow gauge rail line was completed from Ames to Story City in 1878. The St. Petri Lutheran Church in the foreground was dedicated in 1865, but it originally stood on the other side of the Skunk River. It was moved to this location in 1874 after a second church, the Bergen Lutheran Church, was built on the East Prairie near the present town of Roland. The steeple of the Bergen church is visible on the horizon. Also barely visible on the horizon is a tall object to the right of the Bergen church which may be the artist's way of showing where the town of Nevada, the county seat, is located. Source: *A. T. Andreas' Illustrated Historical Atlas of the State of Iowa*, 1875.

Cover design by Sherry Palmiter

All rights reserved. No part of this publication may be reproduced, distributed, or transmitted in any form or by any means, including photocopying, recording, or other electronic or mechanical methods, without the prior written permission from the author/compiler, except in the case of brief quotations embodied in noncommercial uses permitted by copyright law. For permission requests, write to the author/compiler at the address below:

Central Iowa Norwegian Project
509 NE Stone Valley Dr.
Ankeny, Iowa 50021-4113
Email: atwedt@aol.com

Copyright © 2017 Arlen Twedt
ISBN: 978-0-9985002-0-1

Contents

Preface	ix
The Central Iowa Norwegians: The Settlement Period 1855–1880 by Arlen Twedt	1
Emigration from Skånevik, Etne, and Fjelberg	5
The First Central Iowa Norwegian Settlement: 1855–1860	16
The Second Central Iowa Norwegian Settlement: 1856–1860	36
Making Farmsteads on the Prairie	58
Farming on the Frontier	66
The Frontier Economy	77
Volunteering for War	80
Railway Service Arrives	90
More Glimpses of Pioneer Life	99
Organizing Church Congregations	115
The South Skunk River Watershed	121
"a matter of deliberate colonization"	130
Becoming a Settled Prairie	136
"good loyal citizens"	141
Lisbon, Illinois: A Gateway to the West by Jim Mason	163

Story County in the Early 1850s by Col. John Scott, 1890, William K. Wood, 1900, and William O. Payne, 1911 193

A Brief History of the First Norwegian Settlement of Story and Polk Counties, Ia. 1855–1905 by Oley Nelson, 1905 215

A Little About the First Settlers in Story County by Erik Arnesen Travaas, 1888, translated by Ardis N. Petersen & Arlen Twedt 229

Big Norwegian Settlement, Roland, Iowa by Knut Takla, 1900, translated by Ardis N. Petersen 251

The Early History of the Norwegian Settlement in Howard Township by John M. Mason, 1902 & 1903, and M. O. Rod, 1909 259

The Stavanger and Hordaland Colony in Central Iowa by Hjalmar Rued Holand, 1908, translated by Jacob Hodnefield 271

Notes 287

About the Central Iowa Norwegian Project 337

Illustrations

FIGURES

1	Story County, Iowa, in 1855	3
2	Towns in the central Iowa Norwegian settlement area	4
3	Southwestern Norway	6
4	Lisbon Settlement	8
5	Government land purchased in the Southern Settlement	33
6	Pioneer wagon trail routes from Lisbon to central Iowa	39
7	A section of Joseph H. Colton's 1859 map of Iowa	40
8	Government land purchased in the Northern Settlement	42
9	Norwegians in Iowa, 1870	137
10	1875 drawing of Story City, Iowa	138
11	Ole Apland's barn built in 1875	140

TABLES

1	Year of emigration for Norwegian immigrants who moved to central Iowa before 1861	19
2	Norwegian dwelling houses enumerated on the 1860 Census in the Southern and Northern Settlements	59
3	Value of real estate owned reported for 97 central Iowa Norwegian dwelling houses on the 1860 Census	65
4	Acres of land owned by 52 central Iowa Norwegian families in 1860	69
5	Draft animals owned by 52 central Iowa Norwegian families in 1860	70
6	Grain and hay harvested by 52 central Iowa Norwegian families in 1859	73
7	Average number of livestock owned by 52 central Iowa Norwegian families in 1860	74
8	Agricultural products produced by 52 central Iowa Norwegian families for year ending June 1, 1860	75
9	Deaths during 1855–1865 among the 640 Norwegians who lived in central Iowa before 1861	113
10	Central Iowa Norwegian-Lutheran congregations organized by 1880	117
11	Norwegians who lived in central Iowa 1855–1860: Parishes emigrated from and number of emigrants	131

Appendices

A	1836–1844 emigrants from Skånevik, Etne, and Kvinnherad identified on ship passenger lists	144
B	Why Lisbon, Illinois?	145
C	Did someone plan the 1845–1849 emigration from Skånevik, Etne, and Fjelberg? And if so, who?	148
D	Government land purchased by Norwegians at the U.S. Land Office in Ft. Des Moines, Iowa	155
E	Norwegians living in central Iowa when they volunteered for the Civil War	158
F	Why did families who owned land in Illinois choose to move to central Iowa?	160

Preface

In this book I explore the early history of Norwegian settlement in central Iowa. In June 1855, Norwegian immigrants began settling in southern Story County and northern Polk County, and the following year they founded a second settlement in northern Story County which expanded into southern Hamilton County and southwestern Hardin County. The histories in this book describing the settlements up through 1880 can serve as a resource for family historians and others interested in local history to deepen their understanding of a region that became the third largest Norwegian settlement area in Iowa.

I became interested in local history in 1977 when I started work on a family history. Later as I delved deeper into local history, each resource I discovered made me realize how learning about local history enlarged my understanding of the lives of my ancestors. In 1993, I researched and presented a historical talk on the coming of the Norwegians to central Iowa which further enhanced my knowledge. I started the Central Iowa Norwegian Project in 1995 to collect information to write a history covering the first 50 years of Norwegian settlement in central Iowa.

This is the first of three volumes I will publish about the central Iowa Norwegians. Each book begins with a signature piece by me followed by histories, memoirs, and biographies written by others and studies I have done on special topics. The primary piece in this volume is "The Settlement Period: 1855–1880." Volume 2 will feature "The Early Pioneers 1855–1860: Biographic and Demographic Profiles." It contains short biographies of the Norwegian families living in central Iowa by December 31, 1860, and statistical tables describing the 640 Norwegians who moved to central Iowa or were born there during that time span. The signature piece in Volume 3 will be "The Town Building Period: 1880–1905." The three signature pieces will complete the 50-year history I planned to write when I started the Central Iowa Norwegian Project.

Although I have been a diligent student of central Iowa's Norwegian heritage for over 40 years, it is only recently I have had the feeling that I have exhausted most of the possibilities for researching it and am ready to publish my findings. Perhaps turning 70 had something to do with it, too! In any case, I am confident my 25-year history of the central Iowa Norwegian settlement period is the most complete history available. In it are new answers to the question of why settlers formed two colonies, maps showing the virgin prairie they purchased from the United States government for $1.25 per acre, and information about the 97 log homes and dugouts where they lived when enumerated on the 1860 Census. These records show the amount of prairie broken, livestock owned, and crops produced on 52 of the farmsteads and give an authentic picture of pioneer life for these immigrants.

Lisbon, Illinois, about 60 miles southwest of Chicago, was the original settlement area for many of the early Norwegian immigrants who settled in central Iowa. In the second piece in this volume, Jim Mason discusses why Lisbon was a desirable settlement location for many of these new Americans. Following Mason's article are the earliest histories of the central Iowa Norwegians including Hjalmar Rued Holand's history, the first to be written that combines stories of the two settlement areas.

In reading and analyzing early histories others have written, I have encountered instances of inadequate contextual information and inaccurate facts. I have used endnotes and compiler's notes to address these issues. With these additions to histories others have written and the extensive documentation in my 25-year history, I have sought to strike a balance between two audiences—general readers who may not be interested in sources and ancillary information contained in notes and critical readers who want proof of facts and conclusions and who may want to review the sources for themselves. Careful documentation is important to future researchers, so I hope this is not a distraction for general readers.

The early histories in this volume are reproduced as they appeared in the original source with only minor changes in usage, spelling, and punctuation where it is necessary to better understand the text. I have written short biographies of the authors to recognize the contributions they made to preserving central Iowa's Norwegian heritage.

This book could not have become a reality without the constant support, encouragement, proofreading, and editorial assistance of my wife, Asta. I am grateful for the interest she takes in my research. Others deserving recognition are acknowledged with the appropriate history.

It is my sincere hope that you enjoy reading this first volume of *The Central Iowa Norwegians*, gain a deeper understanding of this important settlement area, and are inspired to learn more about its history.

Arlen Twedt

The Central Iowa Norwegians:

The Settlement Period 1855–1880

The Central Iowa Norwegians: The Settlement Period 1855–1880

by Arlen Twedt

I began learning about the history of Norwegian settlement in central Iowa in 1977 when I started research into the lives of my paternal great great grandparents and maternal grandparents, all Norwegians who emigrated between 1854 and 1910 and who all settled in northern Story County. The first version of this history was a historical talk, "The Coming of the Norwegians to Central Iowa," that I presented in 1993 at the Sons of Norway Lodge in Story City, Iowa. In 1995, I started the Central Iowa Norwegian Project to gather information for a 50-year history of Norwegian settlement in central Iowa. This history incorporates what I have learned about the first 25 years of settlement.

• • •

Central Iowa is the home of the third largest settlement area of Norwegians in Iowa. The settlement area was slightly off the migration route for most Norwegian immigrants who generally moved west-northwest from northern Illinois and southern Wisconsin into Minnesota, northern Iowa, and on to the Dakota Territory. Still, central Iowa became one of the important destination points for Norwegian immigrants to the United States. In *Norwegian Settlement in the United States*, Carlton C. Qualey states, "When the settlers arrived in the new lands on June 7, 1855, they found themselves in central Iowa, in Story County, where they launched one of the largest Norwegian settlements in Iowa and one of the more famous in America."[1]

The most prominent Norwegian-American writer, Ole E. Rølvaag, also took note of the central Iowa Norwegians. In "The Vikings of the

Middle West," he used the 1855 Palestine congregation that settled near Cambridge as an example of the romantic spirit of the immigrants who "threw themselves blindly into the Impossible and accomplished the Unbelievable."[2] The national Norwegian-American press paid attention to central Iowa, too. Between 1893 and 1906, Knut Takla, reporter for *Skandinaven* [*The Scandinavian*] in Chicago, wrote 11 articles about central Iowa. In 1906, Hjalmar Rued Holand published a history of the settlements in *Decorah-Posten* [*The Decorah-Post*] that he used as the basis of a chapter in his 1908 history of Norwegian settlement in the United States. Later, during 1932–1933, Carl G. O. Hansen wrote a nine-part series about the central Iowa Norwegians for *Minneapolis Tidende* [*The Minneapolis Times*].

Most of the early central Iowa Norwegians originally settled southwest of Chicago, Illinois, where in 1834, Norwegian immigrants began settling near the present-day town of Norway. In 1839, Norwegians began settling 10 miles east of Norway near the town of Lisbon. From 1845 up through the 1850s, Lisbon became the most popular immigration destination for new immigrants who later decided to move to central Iowa.

By the mid-1850s, land around Lisbon was becoming too expensive for new immigrants to purchase, so settlement leaders organized scouting parties to find a new area for Norwegians to settle where they could purchase land from the United States government for $1.25 per acre. They found what they were looking for in Story County, Iowa, virgin prairie with ample timber resources. The scouting parties decided to purchase land at the Federal Land Office in Ft. Des Moines, Iowa, for themselves and for friends and relatives also living in the Lisbon Settlement. The first scouting party purchased a large area of government land in southern Story County in September 1854, and the following June, a second scouting party purchased a large area of government land in northern Story County (see shaded areas in Figure 1).

In 1855, two caravans of Lisbon settlers arrived in central Iowa to settle on land purchased the previous year and begin what came to be known as the Southern Settlement in southern Story County and northern Polk County. Their original settlement area was concentrated southwest of Cambridge in Union and Palestine townships in Story County and across the county line in Elkhart and Lincoln townships in Polk County, and it eventually encompassed the towns of Sheldahl, Huxley, Slater, and Kelley. In 1856, another large caravan of Lisbon settlers arrived to begin the so-called Northern Settlement in northern

Story County which quickly expanded into southern Hamilton County and later into southwestern Hardin County. The original settlement area was east of Fairview[3] (present-day Story City) in east central Howard Township where the town of Roland was later founded. The settlement grew to include the towns of Christytown (an unincorporated town), Ellsworth, Garden City, Jewell, Lake Center (an abandoned town), McCallsburg, Radcliffe, Randall, Rosendale (an abandoned town), Story City, and Stanhope. See Figure 2 for a map showing the locations of the towns in the two settlements.

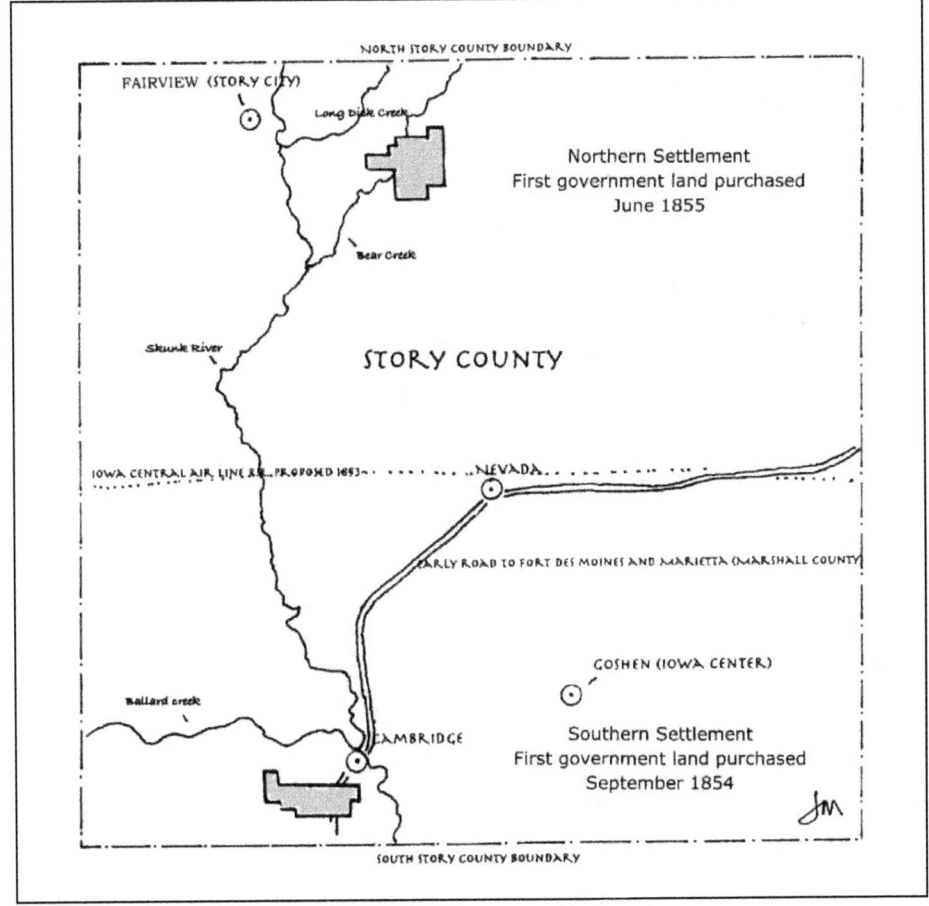

Figure 1
Story County, Iowa, in 1855

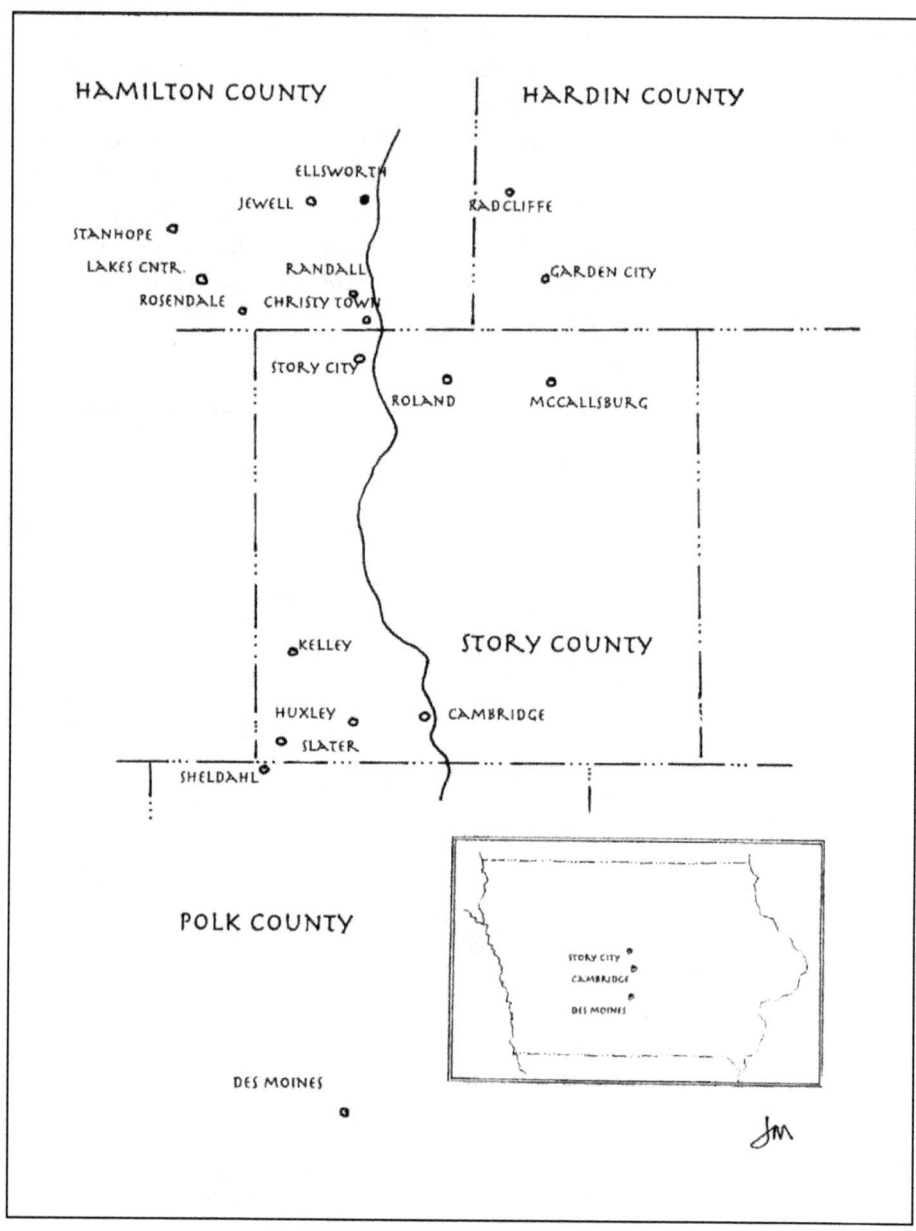

Figure 2
Towns in the central Iowa Norwegian settlement area

Although separated geographically, the two settlements shared a common identity. The Lisbon immigrants and later immigrants who arrived directly from Norway and from Norwegian settlements in Wisconsin and eastern Iowa emigrated almost exclusively from Hordaland and Rogaland, two *fylker* [counties] in southwestern Norway. In addition to their common place of origin, numerous instances of extended family members living in the settlements and marriages between residents in the two settlements created a sense of unity among all Norwegians living in central Iowa.

Today many of their descendants are still living in central Iowa. *Lutefisk* and *lefsa* are served in some homes during the Christmas season, and *kumle*, a heavy potato dumpling cooked with a ham bone, is served throughout the year. There is a Sons of Norway lodge in Story City, and the town holds an annual Scandinavian Days celebration the first weekend in June. As the years pass, though, fewer and fewer people know the story of how central Iowa became an area for Norwegian settlement. Parts of the story are available in local histories, of course, but these accounts are usually written from the point of view of a local church or community and often focus on the very early history of the coming of the Norwegians to central Iowa.

The following account, written from a regional point of view, gives background information on emigration from Norway to Illinois to Iowa and chronicles the 25-year settlement period of the Norwegians in central Iowa from 1855 to 1880. At the end of this period, approximately 6,500 Norwegian-Americans lived in central Iowa. New immigrants continued to arrive up through the turn of the century as additional rail lines entered the region in the early 1880s and new towns were platted bringing products and services closer to the settlements. This next period will be chronicled in "The Town Building Period, 1880–1905," to be published in Volume 3 of *The Central Iowa Norwegians*.

Emigration from Skånevik, Etne, and Fjelberg

Organized emigration from Norway began in 1825 when a group of Quakers and Quaker sympathizers, probably Haugean Lutherans, from near Stavanger, a city on the southwest coast of Norway (see Figure 3), immigrated to the United States. They left seeking greater religious freedom and better economic conditions than they were experiencing in Norway. Their sloop, the *Restauration*, set sail on July 4 and arrived in New York on October 9. There were a few Norwegians already living in the

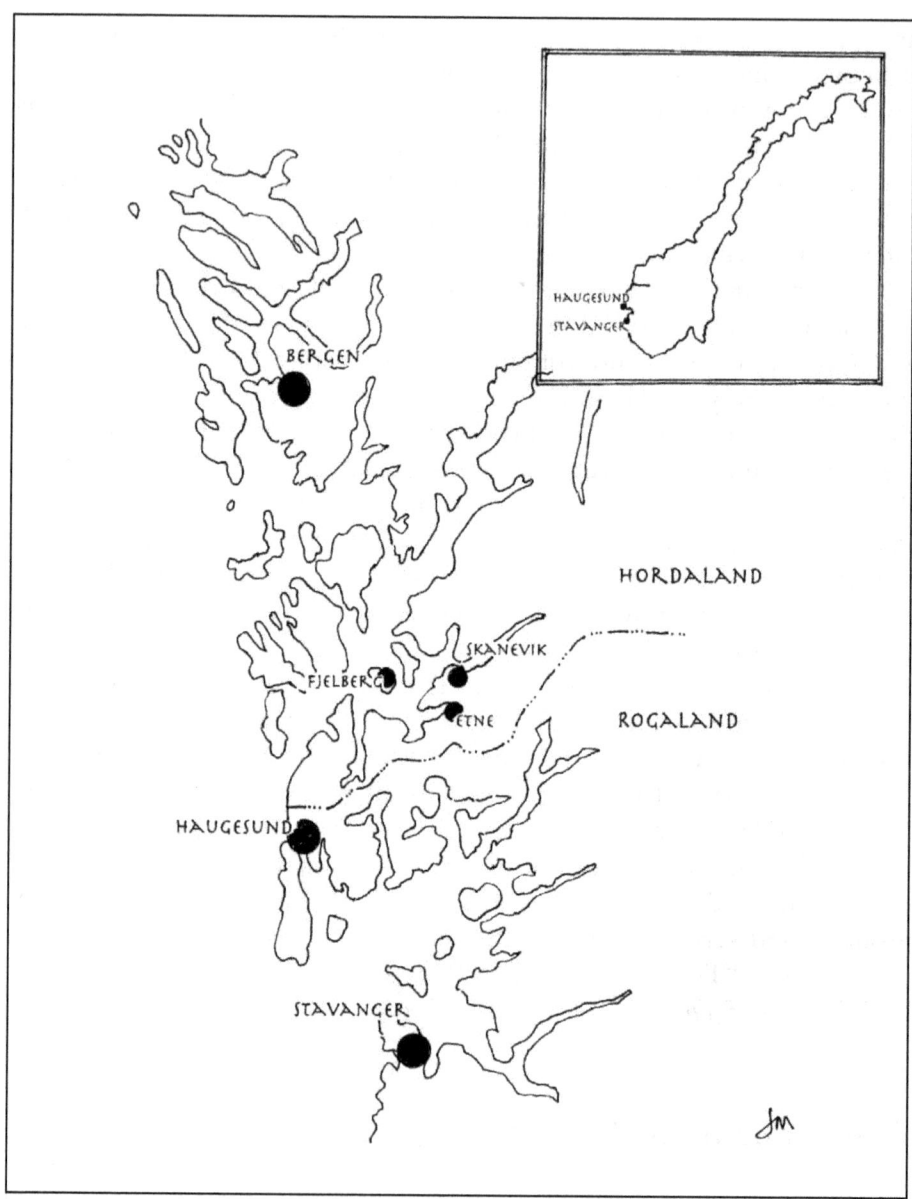

Figure 3
Southwestern Norway

United States, but the arrival of *Restauration* marked the first time a shipload of Norwegian immigrants came, and its 53 passengers became known as the Sloopers.

Four years before their departure, the group sent two representatives to the United States to find a settlement location. One of the representatives, Cleng Peerson, returned to Norway in 1824 with news of a settlement location he had found near Rochester, New York. The Kendall Settlement, as it came to be known, was the first Norwegian settlement in the United States.

Hardships and disappointments in the Kendall Settlement led Cleng Peerson to seek a new settlement area for the Sloopers. In 1833, while walking in a southwesterly direction from Chicago, Illinois, Peerson found what he was looking for near the Fox River in La Salle County, close to present-day Norway, Illinois (see Figure 4). In 1834, six families from the Kendall Settlement moved to Illinois and began a second Norwegian settlement in the United States that became known as the Fox River Settlement.

It was not until 1836 that more shiploads of Norwegian immigrants came to the United States. The brigs, *Norden* and *Den Norske Klippe*, docked in New York in July and August of that year, and they were followed by two more emigrant ships in 1837, *Ægir* and *Enigheiden*, that arrived in New York in June and September.[4] By this time, emigration was reaching beyond the immediate vicinity of Stavanger into *kommuner* [municipal districts] such as Skånevik, Etne, and Fjelberg (see Figure 3), the point of origin for many who eventually settled in central Iowa.[5] Appendix A contains a list of the earliest emigrants from Skånevik and Etne and the adjacent parish of Kvinnherad.

Among the immigrants who arrived in 1836 were Halstein Tørrison Mehus and Guri Rasmusdatter and their two children who emigrated from Skånevik and settled in Chicago. Knud Langeland, author of *Nordmændene i Amerika* [Norwegians in America] published in 1888, states, "... [He] was probably the first Norwegian to settle here in this town."[6] Construction on the Illinois & Michigan Canal had just started, and Halstein was hired to recruit Norwegian workers for the canal. The 96-mile canal, which linked Lake Michigan with the Mississippi River, followed a route southwest of Chicago to Morris, Illinois, and then west to Peru. In 1848, Halstein and Guri moved south of Chicago to Thornton Township, Cook County.

In 1837, Nils Hansen Vettestø and Britha Åmundsdatter and their son emigrated from Etne, and their immigration story involves the first Norwegian settlement in Iowa.[7] The Vettestø family's first settlement location was south of Chicago in Iroquois County. From there they moved west to Calhoun County north of St. Louis and then north to

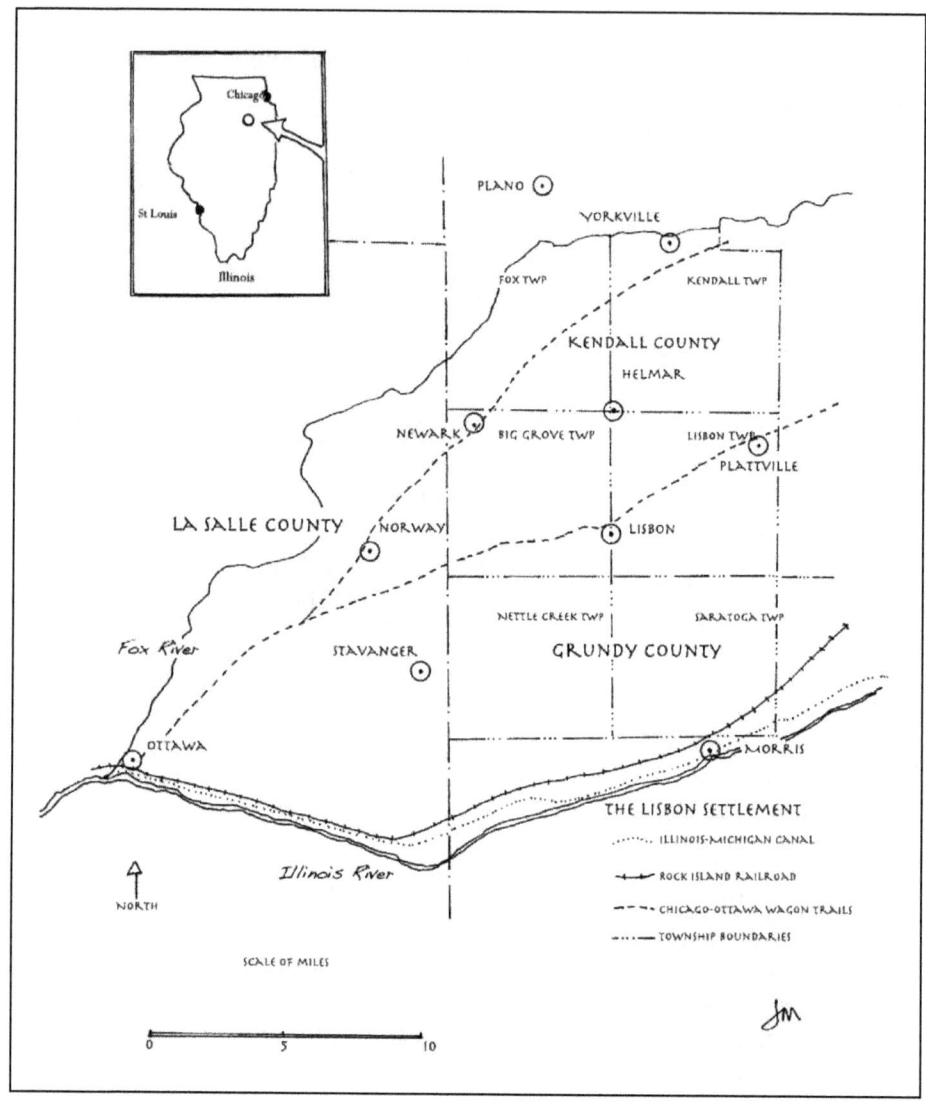

Figure 4
Lisbon Settlement

Shelby County, Missouri, before settling in what became known as the Sugar Creek Settlement in southeastern Iowa.[8] Britha died there in 1843, and in 1846, Nils, who was also known as Nelson Hanson, remarried. They moved to southwestern Iowa where they separated. From southwest Iowa, Nils went to California, and his last known residence was in New Mexico.[9]

The immigration story of the Nils Vettesø family is unusual because northern Illinois and southern Wisconsin were the preferred initial settlement locations for emigrants from Skånevik, Etne, and Fjelberg. More specifically, almost all of the Norwegian immigrants who helped found the two central Iowa Norwegian settlements in 1855 and 1856 or who moved to central Iowa before 1861, lived in northern Illinois before moving to central Iowa. Many of them settled 60 miles southwest of Chicago near the town of Lisbon (see Figure 4). Lisbon is approximately 10 miles east of where the Sloopers established the Fox River Settlement in 1834. It was not until 1839 that a Norwegian settled near Lisbon.[10]

The area around Lisbon became known as the Lisbon Settlement, and it is in this location where the story of the central Iowa Norwegian settlements begins. In 1845, two families who later moved to central Iowa decided to settle near Lisbon. The two families were Rasmus Larson Tungesvik [1803–1873], his wife Margreta [1811–1901], their four children aged two to nine, and Margreta's youngest brother, Osmund Sheldahl [1824–1900] and his bride, Anna [1818–1881]. They were passengers on a ship named *Haabet* [The Hope] that sailed from Stavanger, Norway, and arrived in New York 63 days later on June 21, 1845.

By 1845, southern Wisconsin had already become the preferred settlement area for Norwegians,[11] so why did the Tungesvik and Sheldahl families choose to settle in northern Illinois rather than in one of the Norwegian settlements in southern Wisconsin? Presumably, they had received information about Lisbon being a possible settlement area. The most likely person to have provided this information was Halstein Tørrison Mehus, the 1836 emigrant from Skånevik who was living in Chicago. Appendix B contains more information about Mehus and why the author believes the Tungesvik and Sheldahl families received information about Lisbon from Mehus.

Jim Mason is another historian interested in the question, "Why Lisbon, Illinois?" His paternal ancestors immigrated to Lisbon from the Sandvig farm in Kvinnherad, Norway, in 1861 and later moved to central Iowa. Mason believes there were at least four reasons for choosing Illinois and specifically Lisbon: (1) the religious character of the Illinois settlements, (2) the availability of employment in the Lisbon area, (3) the accessibility of the area to the transportation corridor leading from

Chicago to the southwest and west, and (4) the tall grass prairie environment of Grundy and Kendall Counties.[12] Mason expands on these reasons in "Lisbon, Illinois: A Doorway to the West" written for this volume of *The Central Iowa Norwegians*.

Platted in 1836, Lisbon was a small Kendall County village in 1845, located in both Lisbon and Big Grove Townships (see Figure 4). It became a destination point for many Norwegian immigrants. From Lisbon, they spread out and settled west into Big Grove Township and southwest and southeast into Nettle Creek and Saratoga Townships in Grundy County. When the early settlers referred to Lisbon, they thought of it in the context of this larger settlement area. Within the Lisbon Settlement were the North and South Prairies in Kendall County, the present-day town of Helmar in the North Prairie, and the East and West Prairies in Grundy County, with the East Prairie located southeast of Lisbon in Saratoga Township.[13]

In August 1845, Rasmus Larson, who did not use his Tungesvik farm name in the United States, purchased 80 acres of land two miles west of Lisbon for $540.[14] He was able to buy land soon after his arrival in Lisbon because he left Norway with personal savings plus 500 *Speciedaler* from the sale of his farm,[15] a significant amount considering farm laborers in Norway earned about 25 *Speciedaler* annually.[16] The travel costs for his family at the time were approximately 170 *Speciedaler*,[17] and with an exchange rate of approximately $1.20 for each *Speciedaler*,[18] he may have been able to pay cash for his 80 acres. Osmund Sheldahl obtained his first parcel of land, 40 acres, from the U. S. Government for $1.25 per acre. On September 1, 1849, Sheldahl was issued a patent for this land that was located two miles south of Rasmus Larson's land, across the county line in Saragota Township, Grundy County.[19]

During 1846 and 1847, many people emigrated from Skånevik, Etne, and Fjelberg. Ten families (48 people) left in 1846.[20] Nine of these families were passengers on the *Kong Sverre* that sailed from Bergen and arrived in New York in June 1846 after a 46-day journey. Having apparently heard good reports about this voyage, three men traveled to Bergen to negotiate arrangements for the captain of the *Kong Sverre* to take a full boatload of emigrants from Skånevik, Etne, and Fjelberg the following spring.[21] One of the men was Margrethe's and Osmund's oldest brother, Lars,[22] and another was their first cousin, Torkel Henriksen Kaldestadbakken [1822–1911], a teacher who lived on a farm next to the Skjeldal farm in Etne. Torkel was assigned as the agent to register up to 165 passengers for the voyage, and during that winter, he registered 29 families and 15 single people, 161 passengers in all.[23] They sailed from Bergen on May 11, 1847, and arrived in New York over six weeks later on June 21.

Ståle Dryvik, author of several Etne *bygdebøker* [books which document all inhabitants on farms beginning in the 16th century], has studied the 161 emigrants who left in 1847. He found, "Most of the emigrants from Skånevik came from the east part of Skånevik, and those from Etne from the lower end of the *Stordalsvannet* [Stordal Lake]. It is worth knowing that the easiest place to cross the mountain that separated the two districts was here. Only a mountain and a few hours' walk separated the two districts.[24] They surely knew each other, were friends, and some of them were even related.... Many of the emigrants had their own farms which they had to get off their hands.... The prices recorded show that many of the emigrants were well off when leaving.... At Skånevik, the farms were sold for 400–1,100 *Speciedaler*, in Etne 300–900 *Speciedaler*.... A cotter [tenant farmer] usually owned only the house he lived in, not the site or the land, which he rented on a yearly basis, and/or days of work for the landowner. At that time, the houses were made of logs, could be taken apart, moved, and rebuilt on a new site. Therefore, he could sell his home, which might supply him 20–40 *Speciedaler*."[25]

Ocean travel during this time required extensive preparation. One immigrant recalled, "A journey to America between the years 1840 and 1870—not to mention the Sloopers' voyage in 1825—was an entirely different matter than it is today [1909]. Then direct emigration from Norway to America was exclusively by relatively small sailing ships with only temporary and poor furnishings. The furnishings were intended merely for the voyage across and were to be removed on arrival to make room for other cargo or freight. Now, however, one travels on 'palace liners' more than 700 feet long, and makes the crossing in from eight to 10 days, as compared to six to fourteen weeks, the latter being the longest I have heard about from reliable sources.

"The emigrants in those days had to supply themselves with the necessities of life during the passage and be their own cooks and waiters, families as well as single persons. Several people usually combined their kitchen and food chores and it all occurred, as far as I can recall, without much grumbling or commotion. The only items that were provided without cost by the shipping company were the stove, firewood, and water, as well as fresh air when one stood on deck, though the company did not actually provide the latter. To be sure fresh air was also free below deck, but when so many people had to stay in such a limited space at night and occasionally by day, one may more easily imagine its quality than I can describe it."[26]

Ivar Havneros' history of the St. Petri congregation in Story City contains a brief description of the 1847 immigrants' journey to Lisbon after they arrived in New York: "After ploughing the Atlantic Ocean for six weeks the *Kong Sverre* arrived in New York with its precious cargo, safely and in good condition. From there they traveled up the Hudson River to Albany, then through the canal [the Erie Canal] to Buffalo where they celebrated their first 4th of July. After a day's rest they continued their journey across Lake Michigan to Chicago and from there by oxen to Lisbon, Kendall County, Illinois, where they arrived July 11. They had now reached their destination."[27] The passengers who had sailed on *Kong Sverre* to New York must have made a stop in Milwaukee, Wisconsin, before reaching Chicago because a biography of one of the passengers, Erick Sheldahl [1815–1902], states, "On the 10th of May, 1847, he emigrated direct from his native land to America and landed at New York City, from which place he went to Milwaukee, Wis., afterward moving to Kendall County, Ill."[28]

Mathilde Rasmussen, daughter of Ragnhild Sjursdatter (Haaland) Rasmussen who was an 1846 emigrant from Etne, recalled her mother's memories of the trip from New York to Lake Michigan: "The New York of a century ago was not the New York of today. They were yet far away from their destination, the Middle West. There were no streamlined trains scooting across the country in those days. From New York they traveled by boat up the beautiful Hudson River to Albany. Here they boarded a canal boat drawn by mules to make the trip on the Erie Canal to Buffalo. This was a slow, tedious journey. I remember mother saying that at times the boys would leave the boat and walk alongside the mules. In Buffalo they began their last boat trip on the Great Lakes, en route to Milwaukee. This trip was very rough and stormy—so stormy that they at times despaired of ever reaching their destination. It took seven days to make the trip. At last they reached Milwaukee, then a small town."[29] The trip from Buffalo took them by steamship through the Detroit River to Detroit, Michigan, from there through the St. Claire River to Lake Huron and over to Lake Michigan through the Straits of Mackinac.

In 1848, only two single men emigrated, one from Skånevik and the other from Etne, but the next spring again saw heavy emigration from the three parishes, 32 families and 19 single people, 147 people in all, almost as many as had left in 1847. Again, someone must have arranged for a ship because all 115 passengers aboard *Harmonie* [Harmony] were from

Skånevik, Etne, and Fjeldberg.³⁰ *Harmonie* left Stavanger on May 13, 1849, and arrived in New York on July 3, just in time to celebrate Independence Day. All but one of the remaining 147 emigrants who left in 1849 sailed on *Favoriten* [The Favorite] along with passengers emigrating from communities closer to Stavanger. *Favoriten* sailed from Stavanger three days before *Harmonie* and arrived in New York on June 28, but its passengers were apparently quarantined until July 4 before being released and accompanied by their captain to Troy, New York.³¹

Favoriten and *Harmonie* were new sailing vessels, *Favoriten* having been launched in Stavanger in early 1848 and *Harmonie* completed later that year.³² T. F. Landas, who captained *Harmonie*, composed a song about her 52-day maiden voyage to New York.³³ Theodore Blegen, who discovered the song in a book about the history of Stavanger shipping, quotes the author when he writes, "It was often sung on Stavanger ships in the fifties, sixties, and seventies."³⁴ The title of the song was "Harmonie" and the words to the song follow:

Harmonie

Now that we must leave our country and our sweethearts,
We swear to them that we will never betray the oaths we have sworn.
Many a gale shall we have to weather before
we press once more to our hearts the girls we love.
God give us good luck.

Heave the anchor with joyous shouts.
All our friends are here to see us off.
A loud hurrah for our sweethearts and
for the "Harmony," that is to take us across.

Gaily you dash across the North Sea, good ship "Harmony,"
And many a ship you pass beyond the Shetlands.
Speed on over the Atlantic!
Show them that your timbers were hewn in Romsdal!

But at times the breeze fails; it is not always to be depended on.
And then, equally suddenly, you must buffet the storm.
For ten days and nights you lie there
battling the gale, only your topsail set.

Then a heavy sea breaks over the bow,
and down you go into the trough of it!
Your stays are snapped; there is thundering sound,
and your passengers are thrown in a panic.
At the same moment your bowsprit is ripped off
and your rigging torn to ribbons.

Then in a voice of thunder comes the command:
"Let her ride with the wind!
Keep a stiff upper lip!
Let's see if we can rig the emergency rig before the foremast snaps."
And they did. Hurrah for your Norwegian sailor!
Soon all danger is over, and you sail
on your course proudly over the sea.
Those hundred passengers may indeed shed tears,
for they are leaving Norway forever.
But they too cheer up when the pilot
comes on and we pass Sandy Hook.
You have brought us safely across,
and have won praises everywhere.

At length our "Harmony" is fully repaired,
her hull sheathed with copper,
and once more she swims gracefully on the water.
And so to the West Indies! Gladly we go with you
till you bring us home once more.

In a matter of five short years, Skånevik, Etne, and Fjelberg had sent 366 of their residents to the United States. Why in such a short time did so many families leave this area of Norway? One reason was the excitement caused by the "America letters" that immigrants sent back to Norway describing the available fertile land and the democratic freedoms in the United States. A more fundamental reason, though, was the population growth in Norway at the beginning of the 19th century. From 1777 to 1865, the population in the Skånevik district doubled, creating the need for more food in a mountainous country with limited tillable land resources.[35]

In addition to a strictly economic explanation for emigration, Anders Haugland, author of several Skånevik *bygdeboker*, believes there was a socio-economic reason. His research indicates that 57% of the

Skånevik emigrants from 1836 through 1849 were landowners whose social standing in the community had declined as farms were divided into smaller units to accommodate the increasing population. With enough assets left to purchase tickets to the United States and buy land once they arrived, these Norwegians saw emigrating as an opportunity to regain the socioeconomic status they had once enjoyed. The other 43% of emigrants were tenant farmers who were the poorest segment of the population.[36]

Rasmus Larson is an example of the emigrant Haugland is describing. He was a landowner and could have stayed in Norway. Osmund Sheldahl, on the other hand, was the youngest member of his family with no inheritance rights to a farm as his older half brother had, so it was understandable that he could see the advantages of immigrating to the United States. Osmund and a brother, Rasmus, however, had the advantage of having attended Uppsala University in Sweden. Osmund studied theology and surveying, and Rasmus studied veterinary science.

Emigration from Norway in the 1840s was still in its infancy having increased slowly but steadily since 1825. In 1849, when 147 people emigrated from Skånevik, Etne, and Fjelberg, they were among 3,458 people who emigrated that year, the highest out-migration Norway had experienced.[37] Still, by 1850, only 18,000 people had immigrated to the United States out of the nearly 800,000 Norwegians who would emigrate by 1925.[38]

The departure of the Rasmus Larson and Osmund Sheldahl families in 1845 had apparently ignited the interest in emigrating in the three districts. Just as the Sloopers had sent Cleng Peerson to the United States in 1821 to find a settlement location for them, one wonders if the purpose of the Larson and Sheldahl families' emigration was to find a settlement location for others who wanted to emigrate. See Appendix C for the author's thoughts on this topic.

Many of the 366 people who emigrated from Skånevik, Etne, and Fjelberg from 1845 through 1849 settled in the Lisbon Settlement. When the 1850 Federal Census was taken, there were 413 Norwegians living in southern Kendall and northern Grundy counties (see Figure 4).[39] At least 176 of them emigrated from Skånevik, Etne, and Fjelberg or were born to parents from these districts.[40] Many of them together with friends and relatives who immigrated to Lisbon after 1849 decided to leave their mother settlement and begin two daughter settlements in central Iowa, one in southern Story and northern Polk Counties in 1855 and another in northern Story and southern Hamilton Counties in 1856.

The First Central Iowa Norwegian Settlement: 1855–1860

When I started the Central Iowa Norwegian Project in 1995, one of my goals was to learn about the people who lived in the two central Iowa Norwegian settlements from 1855 through 1860. To accomplish this goal, I identified all the Norwegians enumerated in central Iowa on the 1856 Iowa Census and the 1860 U. S. Census—522 people. For the next five years, I concentrated on learning about them by locating obituaries in newspapers, biographies in county histories, and information in family histories. While looking for information about these people, research that is ongoing, I discovered 118 Norwegians who lived in the two settlements prior to 1861 who were not included in the censuses. This increased the total number of early central Iowa Norwegians to 640.

All the Norwegians who moved to central Iowa prior to 1861 including two children born during their parents' trips are accounted for in this section and in the next section. I determined the spelling of names first by the spelling in the Iowa Genealogical Society's cemetery listings and next by spellings in obituaries, family histories, or through contact I have had with family historians. To the best of my knowledge, all the families and single people who moved to the settlements from the first day of settlement on June 7, 1855, through December 31, 1860, are included. If I have missed someone, I would appreciate receiving this information.

• • •

Excerpts from early histories of Nettle Creek and Saratoga townships provide a glimpse of what life was like for the Norwegians in Grundy County, Illinois: "About 1845, the Norwegian element began to come into the township [Nettle Creek], and it is astonishing to observe how rapidly they have supplanted the original settler. ... About 1847 or '8, the immigration of Norwegians began to appear in this township [Saratoga]. The first came from LaSalle County, with one or two from other sections. They were in poor financial circumstances, but they brought hardy constitutions and abundant energy and were not long in getting upon an equal footing with their more favored neighbors. Their native tastes inclined them to prefer the timber lands, and here and there, where they could buy an acre or two of timber, their sheepskin coats and calfskin vests could be seen all through the northern and middle part of the county. ... The early days of the Norwegian settlement in this country were full of poverty and toil, to which was added the terrible ravages of Asiatic cholera."[41]

The cholera epidemic began the winter of 1848–1849, and from then until 1854, no part of the United States was free from cholera during any 12-month period.[42] Of the 161 people who came in 1847, 23 died before 1850, most of cholera.[43] During 1849, 46 Norwegians died of cholera in the six townships encompassing the Lisbon Settlement (see Figure 4); 11 in Big Grove Township, 22 in Nettle Creek Township, and 13 in Saratoga Township.[44] Cholera was less prevalent in LaSalle County except for Mission Township which bordered Big Grove Township. In Mission Township, 22 people died of the disease.[45] For another LaSalle County township, Freedom Township, the enumerator recorded the following remarks on his census report: "Nearly all the Norwegians who died of cholera had just arrived from Norway at the place where they intended to settle when attacked. Many of their companions died of cholera on their way from New York to Ottawa and at Ottawa. That disease was far more fatal to foreigners including those who had been many years in the country than to natives. Except [for] the cholera, the season of 1849 was healthy in this township."[46]

One of the 1847 immigrants was Carrie Ytterness who immigrated with her parents. Her 1912 obituary describes how cholera affected her life: "The following year, 1848, she was married to John Hansen Olestvedt. Their journey together was of a short duration as he fell victim to the dreaded disease, cholera, which broke out in all its awfulness in their community the following year. She gave birth to a child and with it was left to fight the battles of life alone. ... The cholera raged in all its awfulness. However, she was a brave woman and lost not an opportunity to help care for the sick and dying of her immediate vicinity during a single day but this did not deter her from the duties as she saw them and she continued to render what assistance she could. The conditions were heartrending but she survived them. She later married Ole Fatland who lost his wife during the plague."[47] Another obituary for Carrie states, "In 1849, a cholera epidemic swept over the country which took away her husband, leaving her a widow with one child at this very trying time, when the cholera caused several deaths daily. There were few doctors and no nurses, leaving the burden of caring for the sick and dying to Mrs. Fatland and one other lady who were the only ones in the settlement who escaped the dreaded disease."[48]

Another of the 1847 immigrants who survived was nine-year-old Sarah Jacobson. Young Sarah was the only survivor in her home, which included her father, mother, brother, and six members of another family. She took care of herself for several days after their deaths surviving on a bowl of milk that a neighbor set on the step outside the door of her home each morning. When she was well enough to leave the home, she was united with two other siblings who had been living in other homes in the settlement.[49] The dreaded illness also visited the family of Osmund Sheldahl's older brother, Lars, also an 1847 immigrant. Lars' wife and two of his children died during the epidemic.

Helping out wherever he could was Rasmus Larson. A. M. Henderson, the son of an 1847 immigrant who experienced the cholera epidemic, states, "He [Rasmus Larson] was a cripple from birth. Under this handicap, hobbling about on crutches, he was ever in the forefront during the cholera plague in the Lisbon settlement, ministering both to the spiritual and bodily needs of the afflicted, and much of his time was taken in the making of coffins for the dead."[50] There were so many cholera victims buried in Loughead's Cemetery that it became known as the Nettle Creek Cholera Cemetery.[51]

News of the cholera tragedy is the apparent reason for a significant decrease in the number of the people who emigrated from Skånevik, Etne, and Fjelberg to the Lisbon Settlement during the early 1850s, a time when there was a significant increase in overall emigration from Norway.[52] This decrease can be seen in Table 1 showing the year of emigration for Norwegians who later moved to central Iowa.[53] Only 33 of the 395 early central Iowa Norwegian immigrants left Norway during the years 1850 through 1853.

After concern over cholera subsided, immigrants began coming to the settlement again. In 1854, 81 immigrants who later moved to central Iowa arrived in the Lisbon Settlement. Unfortunately, that same year another widespread cholera outbreak occurred in North America[54] which claimed the lives of 1,424 people in Chicago in 1854.[55] Within the 97 central Iowa Norwegian dwelling houses enumerated on the 1860 Census were 18 homes where occupants had lost parents, siblings, spouses, or children to cholera while they lived in Illinois.[56]

The first central Iowa Norwegian settlement near Cambridge was founded to provide recent immigrants from Norway an opportunity to the purchase inexpensive land.[57] In view of the devastation cholera caused in the Lisbon Settlement, however, one cannot help wonder if another reason it was founded was a desire to find a settlement area free of cholera.[58] At the time, people generally believed cholera was contracted by inhaling contaminated vapors. In 1849, a London physician published a pamphlet proposing contaminated food or water was the cause of the disease, but it was not until cholera struck England again in 1854 that the physician was able to prove his theory that water contaminated by sewage was the cause of cholera.[59][60]

Table 1
Year of emigration for Norwegian
immigrants who moved to central Iowa before 1861

Year	Totals	Year	Totals	Year	Totals
1836	2	1848	3	1855	35
1837	2	1849	63	1856	31
1843	5	1850	8	1857	64
1844	2	1851	1	1858	19
1845	10	1852	8	1859	0
1846	2	1853	16	1860	0
1847	30	1854	81	Unknown	13
				Grand Total:	**395**

When land around Lisbon was becoming too expensive for new immigrants, the Lisbon settlers began discussing finding a new area for settlement for themselves and friends and relatives who wanted to emigrate. People interested in starting a new Norwegian settlement held a meeting and selected four men to be members of a scouting party: Osmund Sheldahl [1824–1900] from Etne, Ole Fatland [1819–1894] from Skånevik, Ole Apland [1827–1879] from Sandeid (near Etne), and Osmond Johnson [1809–1866] from Drangedal in eastern Norway. Ole Apland's son recorded, "These men were selected because they could speak the English language fairly well,"[61] and Osmund Sheldahl's granddaughter remembered, "Osmund Sheldahl was to lead the group of four ... and do the purchasing." They left Lisbon on September 24, 1854, authorized to go as far as Omaha, Nebraska.[62]

Why did the people at the meeting decide to send the scouting party in a westerly direction into Iowa rather than in a northwesterly direction into southwestern Wisconsin, northeast Iowa, and southeastern Minnesota where most of the migration from Illinois had occurred up to the mid-1850s? Hjalmar Rued Holand, author of "The Stavanger and

Hordaland Colony in Central Iowa" published in 1908, credits Erick Nelson Søland with recommending Iowa as a new settlement area. Nelson, an 1839 immigrant who settled in Big Grove Township, was a respected person in the settlement and had traveled through Iowa on a trip to California.[63] Holand states, "Then Erik Nilsen [Erick Nelson Søland] told them about Iowa's wide expanses. ... It was weighed and discussed endlessly, for in the beginning, the idea found little adherence."[64] Later in his history, Holand writes, "This view of the affair [Nelson's view of Iowa] received unexpected support by the chance arrival of Nils Olson Næs, a lay preacher, who had been in northeastern Iowa."[65] Holand's 1908 history is included elsewhere in this volume of *The Central Iowa Norwegians*.

Nils Olsen Næs, also known as Nils Olsen Fjeld [1815–1884], was a fellow emigrant from Skånevik who settled near Lisbon in 1847 with his family. After his wife and four of his five children died of cholera soon after their arrival, Naes became a Bible salesman and lay preacher in southern Wisconsin and northeast Iowa.[66] In Oley Nelson's 1905 history of the Southern Settlement, Nelson states, "In the early fall of the year 1854, ... he [Næs] came to Lisbon, Illinois, and there told them that in Iowa there was government land to be had for $1.25 an acre, fine prairie with timber along the streams—a large area of land. This made a great stir among the emigrants at Lisbon."[67] Nelson's 1905 history is also included elsewhere in this volume of *The Central Iowa Norwegians*.

Another person who played a part in the decision to authorize the scouting party to go as far as Omaha, Nebraska, was Osmund Tøtland, also known as Osmund Tuttle. Tuttle immigrated to nearby Mission Township in LaSalle County in 1836.[68] In the spring of 1854, he made a scouting trip to Iowa and purchased land west of Cedar Rapids, Iowa, in Benton County where the town of Norway was later founded.[69] When the Lisbon settlers met to discuss sending a scouting party to Iowa, they apparently discussed Tuttle's purchase and gave instructions to the scouting party to investigate this area of Iowa.[70]

The state the scouting party was about to explore was named for the Báxoje or Ioway people who had occupied the land between the Mississippi and Missouri rivers for centuries before it was obtained by the United States from France in 1803 as part of the Louisiana Purchase. The Ioway's first contact with Europeans occurred in 1676 when they began trading with the French. In the early 1800s, they were living in what became southeastern Iowa, but then the Sauk and Meskwaki tribes, whose villages were farther north on both sides of the Mississippi River, began hunting in Ioway territory. After a decisive battle with the Sauk and Meskwaki tribes in 1821, the Ioway people resettled west of the Des Moines River. In 1835, as a consequence of the Indian Removal Act of 1830, the Ioway Indians ceded their land in western Iowa, and seven years later, the federal government relocated them on a reservation in northeastern Kansas.

In 1824, the Sauk and Meskwaki Indian tribes relinquished their claim to 119,000 acres in the southeast corner of Iowa, and after the Black Hawk War of 1832, they were forced to cede their land in eastern Iowa thus opening this area for white settlement. In 1842, the Sauk and Meskwaki tribes ceded a large area of land in central and south central Iowa and agreed to move to a reservation in Kansas on October 11, 1845.

When the first territorial census was taken in 1836, there were 10,531 non-native people living in Iowa, but when granted statehood in 1846, Iowa's population had increased tenfold to 102,388 people.[71] A state census completed two months before the departure of the four-member Lisbon scouting party enumerated 326,013 people in Iowa with most of these new Iowans living in the eastern part of the state.

Anfin Apland's history states, "They [the scouting party] rode in a two-seated spring wagon drawn by a span of horses"[72] which would have required them to take a well-traveled route across Illinois. Their likely route followed present day U.S. Highway #6 to Rock Island, Illinois, where they ferried across the Mississippi River to Davenport, Iowa. In his early history of Scott County, Willard Barrow describes Davenport at this time: "The year 1854 was one of the most distinguished and busy years in the existence of Davenport. The foundations of her prosperity were laid this year. The immense immigration that had settled in the county for the two years previous now began to exhibit the fruits of their industry. The city had kept pace with the backcountry in her improvements, and added to her population 3,000 while the county contained about 15,000. The onward progress of both city and county for three years had been such that all looked for better times. The 'great river' was to be spanned this year by a bridge! The increase of population created a great demand for dwelling houses, stores and workshops. Labor of all kinds was in demand. The railroad westward was to go on with increased exertions. Money began to be plenty. Immigration began to pour in at the opening of spring and the streets of Davenport seemed thronged with strangers."[73] The bridge Barrow refers to, a railroad bridge completed in 1856, was the first bridge completed across the Mississippi River.

After leaving Davenport, the scouting party probably continued on the main trail to Iowa City before beginning to explore possible settlement areas. Ole Apland's wife's obituary records, "They took a thorough survey of the country near Cedar Rapids,"[74] which indicates either at Iowa City or shortly thereafter they left the main trail and headed northward to see the area in Benton County where Osmund Tuttle had purchased land earlier in the year. Anna Apland's obituary further states, "It was not exactly to their liking and they pressed farther west."

What they did not like about the Cedar Rapids area is unknown, but perhaps while they were in Davenport they heard about or read "Letters on the West" published in the *Davenport Commercial*, a new newspaper started during the spring of 1854. The newspaper's publisher, Nathan H. Parker, who included excerpts of the letters in his first edition of *Iowa as it is in 1855; a gazetteer for citizens, and a hand-book for immigrants*, states, "These letters are from the pen of Willard Barrows, Esq.; than whom, probably, no individual in the State possesses more thorough information on the topics he speaks of; he having spent some eighteen years as Government and General Surveyor."[75] Among Barrow's observations about Iowa that might have influenced the scouting party are: "Central Iowa is the best body of land in the State; and, in all probability, the State of Iowa is the best in the United States,"[76] and "The immigrant who is willing to penetrate unsettled portions and endure the privations incident to a frontier life, can lay, for himself and his children, the foundations of a fortune and a home that will make glad the hearts of his children's children; for Iowa is destined to be the most densely populated State in the Union."[77]

According to Osmund Sheldahl's granddaughter, the scouting party found land in Story County by accident. After leaving Newton, Iowa, the scouting party became confused in their directions and took a road that headed them toward Story County instead of continuing along the main road to Ft. Des Moines.[78] The road they took by mistake led them through Peoria City and Iowa Center, then across the Skunk River to a small store and a saw mill where the town of Cambridge may have already been platted.[79] In the unsettled virgin prairie southwest of Cambridge, near where the Palestine Lutheran Church sits today a mile southeast of Huxley, the scouting party decided they had found what they were looking for—a large area of land available at the government price of $1.25 per acre.[80] From there they proceeded to the Federal Land Office at Ft. Des Moines where they purchased land for themselves and others on October 9, 1854.

Normally, immigrants in search of land to purchase in a new territory visited the nearest Federal Land Office first to find out where government land was still available, but perhaps someone living near Cambridge told them about the availability of land southwest of Cambridge. It is also possible the scouting party inspected the area thoroughly at that time, so when they arrived at the land office they were ready to make their purchases of 1,657 acres of land for themselves and others back in the Lisbon Settlement. A biography of Osmund Sheldahl states, "He carried on his body, in a belt, the cash needed to pay for that land."[81] The land office required specie payment, gold or silver, but the cash the scouting party brought with them was undoubtedly bank notes, a safer and more easily hidden form of cash that for a fee they exchanged for specie at one of four banking houses in Ft. Des Moines in 1854.

Another factor which could have influenced the scouting party to decide to begin a new settlement near Cambridge is that Swedish immigrants had settled fifteen miles west of Cambridge near Swede Point, now Madrid, Iowa. They began settling near the Des Moines River in Boone County in 1846, and 10 years later there were only 70 people of Swedish descent enumerated in the county on the 1856 Iowa Census,[82] but knowledge of their presence may have made the decision to settle near Cambridge easier.

When the scouting party returned home a month later, Osmund Sheldahl reported, "We have fulfilled our mission and found a land that far exceeded our fondest expectation in beauty and fruitfulness. It is a land of level, sunny hills without any roads; of rich green pastures without danger of floods. It has good water and sheltering woods along all watercourses. It is surely a land like Caleb's Canaan, flowing with milk and honey, but unlike that renowned land, there are no enemies to make us fear. There are no Jebusites and Amorites nor powerful sons of Anak, who barred the entrance of God's chosen peoples into the Promised Land. At one time, no doubt, red Indians galloped over the prairie, hunting buffaloes, but have now gone to more distant hunting grounds. Now the land is lying in quiet peace, waiting for us to come. Brothers! It is the land that the Lord has prepared for us. From Norway's mountain passes we came, where we had to break stony ground on steep hills between floods and slides, where our pastures lay in ice-bound and shady hills. Here we can comfortably stretch our limbs in peaceful pursuit, following plough and scythe and the rich soil will abundantly repay us for our work. From the Government we have secured papers which will secure our rights to the land for all time to come."[83]

Oley Nelson's description of the scouting party's return to the Lisbon Settlement after their trip to Iowa implies all scouting party members were in agreement with Osmund Sheldahl's glowing report of the settlement location they selected in central Iowa. One member of the scouting party, though, must have been concerned about beginning a new settlement so far out on the frontier. Hjalmar Rued Holand wrote about him in his 1908 history of the central Iowa Norwegians: "Ole Fatland and Ole Apland fully agreed to this. Osmund Johnson on the other hand was a little doubtful. While he would not deny the correctness of what Sheldahl had said, he would nevertheless doubt that the land ever would be settled that far west. It was after all 300 miles from Lisbon. It would in any case take four or five hundred years. In the meantime there would not be any railroad, and it would be a long time before any kind of Government and civilized manners would find their way that far. He believed, therefore, that he would not go."[84] The fact that Osmund Johnson purchased 331 acres of land during his trip to central Iowa in 1854 and that he and his wife decided to leave the comforts they had in Illinois in 1859 for life on the frontier suggests that Holand embellished the information he had been told about Osmund Johnson's concern, but his assertion does provide an interesting insight into how some people viewed central Iowa at that time.

During the winter of 1854–1855, families made preparations for their journey. They repaired and purchased wagons and white canvas cloth to cover them, selected strong oxen or horses and sold excess livestock, and landowners found buyers for their land. One of the future Iowans, Oscar Larson, supervised the construction of some of the wagons which was later recorded by his granddaughter: "Early in youth, he joined his father in the field of blacksmith. This was a popular field to be in and became even more so to him as he reached America. ... Under his direction in late 1854, he organized a group of unskilled men to build covered wagons—wheels and all."[85]

The soon-to-be Iowans also pared down their personal possessions to the most essential items to take along, made and repaired clothing, and prepared food for the journey. Anfin Apland, a son of scouting party member Ole Apland, and who later became interested in recording recollections from his mother and others who made the trip, writes, "Women folk had prepared an abundance of food to eat on the way such as *lepsa, flatbroe, kavring, krengla, fatost, gammelost, sotort, dravela, primost*, and they had their camp stoves so they could make *raspa, komla, hagleta*, and *mossor* and *paatete kaka*."[86]

While these families were making their preparation, others in the Lisbon Settlement were clearly thinking about moving to Iowa. Thor and Erik Ericson immigrated to Lisbon in 1854, and the following year, they wrote their brothers in Skånevik that land in Kendall County was selling for $8 to $20 an acre, but in Iowa it was only $1.25 per acre. "To build up a farm it is necessary to have 2 horses approximately 300 dollars or 2 oxen approximately 100 dollars, a cow approximately 30 dollars, a wagon approximately 80 dollars, and a plow approximately 12–14 dollars." At the time, they were working for local farmers for $16 per month. They concluded their letter with this plea: "Dear brothers, If you emigrate, and are just as lucky as we are, you will never be sorry that you left."[87]

Concerned, apparently, that there would not be cheap government land available near Cambridge after the caravan arrived in central Iowa, a second scouting party made a trip to Iowa in April 1855. Led by the leader of the first scouting party, Osmund Sheldahl, they were able to purchase more government land at the land office in Ft. Des Moines. Knud Bauge and John Severson each purchased 160 acres in Union Township, Story County; Brit Olson purchased 120 acres in Elkhart Township, Polk County; and his brother, Ole Heggen, purchased 40 acres in Lincoln Township, Polk County.[88] Osmund Sheldahl also purchased additional land during the trip from a private owner, 80 acres of timberland north of Cambridge along the Skunk River.[89]

On Wednesday, May 16, 1855, 23 families and five single men, a total of 108 people, met at Holderman's Prairie west of Lisbon in LaSalle County.[90] The next morning, May 17th, *Syttende Mai*, Norway's Independence Day, they said good-bye to friends and relatives who came to wish them well and began their trip in 24 covered wagons along with a large herd of cattle.[91] They had also organized themselves into a church congregation, the Palestine congregation, electing Ole Anfinson as pastor, Knute Bauge as teacher, and Erick Sheldahl as chorister.[92]

The families and single men in the caravan are listed below:[93]

Rev. Ole and Enger Anfinson and two children
Knut and Kari Bauge
Knud and Kari Ersland and nine children
Ole* and Carrie Fatland and four children
Severt and Alice Gravdahl and two children
Ørjan and Ragna Hauge and three children
Ole and Anna Heggen
Solamon and Sarah Heggen and three children

Peder Christian and Anna Serina Heggem
Barney and Sarah Hill[94] and daughter
Oley and Valbor Houge and son
Thomas and Magdela Houge and two children
Oscar and Golla Larson and three children
Brit and Sarah Olson and daughter
Torger and Gjertru Olson and three children
Mrs. Torres Olson and two children[95]
John and Betsy Severson and three children
Julia Shaw and three children
Erick and Margreta Sheldahl and four children
Osmund* and Anna Sheldahl and five children
Lars and Martha Tesdahl
Iver and Malinda Twedt and daughter
Weir and Martha Weeks and seven children
Single men: Ole Apland,* Erick Johnson, Even Olson, Ole Tesdall, and Lars Thompson
* Members of the September 1854 scouting party

A 1955 newspaper article commemorating the 100th anniversary of the Palestine congregation includes a photograph of an 1853 map owned by Osmund Sheldal that is believed to have been used by the leaders of the caravan.[96] An enlarged portion of the map also shows the route the caravan may have taken through Iowa.[97] Assuming this information is correct, the caravan would have taken the road from Holderman's Praire to Ottawa, Illinois, where they joined other caravans of immigrants heading west.[98] At Rock Island, Illinois, they hired a ferry to take their wagons and cattle across the Mississippi River to Davenport, Iowa.

A day or two before the caravan likely arrived in Rock Island, Spencer, Robinson and Company began operating a new ferry between Rock Island and Davenport. The May 23, 1855, edition of *The Weekly Rock Island Republican* contained the following news item about the ferry the caravan hired to take them to Iowa: "The new ferry boat, *Davenport*, is running today, and the *Wilson* is laid up for repairs. The *Davenport* is the largest and best ferry boat on the Mississippi, being still an improvement on the 'Wilson.' She is 115 feet long, 49 feet wide on her guards, and measures a carrying capacity of 130 tons. Her hull was pronounced by the inspector at Cincinnati, the best he had ever examined, being complete, staunch, and a perfect model. She is furnished with two engines, each 75 horsepower, with 17-inch cylinders and 5-feet stroke. She is also furnished with a 'doctor' to keep the boilers supplied with water. She can carry 20 teams at a trip, and taken altogether is quite a large affair for a ferry boat. Her entire cost was about $15,000."[99]

After ferrying across the Mississippi River to Davenport, the caravan traveled through Iowa City and Marengo to Newton where they left the main road and headed for Peoria City in northwestern Jasper County on their way to their final destination, Cambridge, Iowa. Their 300-mile trip took 21 days including three Sundays when they did not travel so they could worship and rest their animals. Caravans driven with oxen hoped to make 15 miles a day, and their average of almost 17 miles a day was due to good weather.

As intentional as the planning for their trip was, one would think someone in the caravan would have kept a journal, but the only accounts the author has found were written later. A 1926 biography of Peter Christian and Anna Serina Heggem contains a brief description of the trip: "The roads were dimly laid out, so they followed the stage road, fording the streams and rivers. The Mississippi River was crossed on a ferry."[100] Another account recorded in 1929 describes the prairie: "Mrs. [Kari] Bauge, who was one of the party and who died only a few months ago, used to tell how the blue grass of the prairie was so tall that it would almost conceal the caravan, except for the tops of the covered wagons. Bells were fastened on the necks of the cattle so that they might be located in the grass. The teams had to be changed about in order to take turns breaking the paths."[101] And Anfin Apland, whose mother, Anna (Ersland) Apland was a member of the caravan, recorded this in 1945: "These emigrants followed what was called the California trail—the same trail that the four delegates had followed. They were lucky; they had good weather on the whole journey. The worst difficulty they had was in crossing the streams. One time one wagon got in a little too deep and they needed help. Another time, the cattle went down the stream and they had quite a time to round them up. But all the men were raised right along the ocean in Norway and could swim like fish.... They had a bunch of cattle with them, some milk cows, so they had milk for the children."[102]

Without the benefit of having diaries and letters written by the early settlers, one is left to imagine daily events and the thoughts and feelings members of the caravan might have had during their journey to Story County. They were familiar with the prairie from living in the Lisbon Settlement, but except for members of the scouting party, they had not experienced the vastness of the prairie nor could they fathom what life would be like for them in what was considered frontier country. Some of the immigrants they met on the trail who were moving to Iowa from the eastern United States were even less informed about the prairie. In *Iowa as it is in 1855,* Nathan Parker, who was born in Massachusetts, included a short but eloquent chapter, "General Appearance of the Prairies," describing the prairie landscape from early spring to late fall. He began his description of the prairie: "The novelty of the prairie country is striking, and never fails to cause an exclamation of surprise from those who have lived amid the forests of Ohio and Kentucky, or along the wooded shores of the Atlantic, or in sight of the rocky barriers of the Allegheny ridge. The extent of the prospect is exhilarating. The outline of the landscape is undulating and graceful. The verdure and the flowers are beautiful; and the absence of shade, and consequent appearance of a profusion of light, produces a gaiety which animates every beholder."[103]

The caravan arrived in central Iowa on Thursday, June 7. They circled their wagons one last time on Osmund Sheldahl's land south of Ballard Grove.[104] Apland states, "They [the women] had prepared enough food so that nearly one half of it was left when they reached their destination and that came in very handy."[105] At their church service the following Sunday, they gave thanks for their safe journey to Iowa and asked God to bless them in the days ahead. One of the hymns their song leader, Erick Sheldahl, led them in singing at their first church service in Story County was, "Now Thank We All Our God." The English translation of the first verse of that familiar hymn reads:

> *Now thank we all our God*
> *With hearts and hands and voices,*
> *Who wondrous things has done,*
> *In whom this world rejoices;*
> *Who, from our mothers' arms,*
> *Has blest us on our way*
> *With countless gifts of love,*
> *And still is ours today.*

The area southwest of Cambridge where the scouting party purchased land and which the members of the caravan were about to settle was part of a much larger area of unsettled virgin prairie described later by Anfin Apland: "When they came in 1855, there were quite a few families in Des Moines, a flour mill, a few stores, a blacksmith shop, and some sawmills.[106] [There was] a store and a sawmill at Swede Point [Madrid],[107] a small store at Cambridge,[108] and when you started north from Des Moines and got about four miles north of where the State House [Iowa State Capitol Building] stands now, there was not a house or building of any description until you got to Ballard Grove [the grove north and east of Huxley, Iowa]. And when you started east from Swede Point, got east four miles, there was not a house or a stick of any kind until you got to way past Skunk River."[109]

In the summer of 1855, a second but smaller caravan of families and single people left Lisbon to join these new central Iowa Norwegian pioneers. Apland states, "This colony was ready to start on May 17th with the rest but could not start that day on account of having to wait for Simen Johnson, who was born a few weeks after. So they started on August 25th."[110] The members of this caravan who left to settle near Cambridge were:

Nels and Kari Christoferson and two children
Wier and Kari Johnson and seven children
Gunder and Kari Madskeer and two children
Ole and Margaret Nernes and son
Erick and Barbro Tesdahl and five children
Benjamin and Enger Thompson and four children
Single woman: Anna T. Larson[111]
Single man: Thomas Berhow

One account of their trip describes their journey and arrival in the settlement: "... [They] arrived in Cambridge after six weeks of hard travelling. The roads had been softened by much rain and were often impassable, and the water in the creeks was so deep that it came into the wagon boxes. Upon their arrival in Union Township, they found all available space in the houses occupied and were forced to camp in the open. Unlike the Americans, who settled in the timber, the Norwegians preferred to locate in the open prairie and to haul the timber they needed from the bluffs down to their own land."[112]

Another family, Lars and Herbor Sheldall and four children, and a single man, Thor Hegland, were also members of this caravan. Their destination was land further north along the Skunk River that Lars had purchased in southern Hamilton County. Many years later, Lars' son, Rasmus, who was a young boy at the time, recalled the journey in more detail: "Fifteen wagon outfits started out from Lisbon at one time, together with a herd of about 150 head of cattle."[113] Erick Sheldall [Rasmus' older brother] and John [Johnson] Bjerkestrand drove the cattle, accompanying the cavalcade on horseback. Among those in the party were Viar [Johnson] Bjerkestrand and wife, and the two sons John and Ole; Gunder Matskaar and wife, and a man remembered by Sheldall as 'Haringe Nils' [Nels Christoferson], also his wife, were in the company. Some of the owners of the wagons drove oxen, other horses, and some of them possessed both oxen and horses. Many of the cows were in milk, and in the morning after milking, the cans holding the milk would be hung under the top of the 'Prairie Schooners' and by evening the motion from the moving vehicle had transformed the contents into butter and buttermilk. The travelers were often detained on the way, sometimes because of floods, at other times on account of inferior bridges. On Sunday they would always come to a halt, and all would then gather to hear God's Word.

"They reached Iowa Center during a snow-storm and were obliged to stay there for several days as they could not get across the swollen Indian Creek. They finally rafted their wagons across, carrying the freight by hand over a foot-log. In order to get the cattle over, the bell cow was wheedled into crossing first, and then only were the rest willing to come. Gunder Matskaar was taken sick with typhoid fever and died while they were at Iowa Center."[114]

The pastor ministering to many of these immigrants before they left the Lisbon Settlement was Pastor Ole Andrewson. Andrewson, an 1841 immigrant to Wisconsin, was issued a call by Norwegians living near Mission Point, Illinois, northwest of Lisbon in LaSalle County, to be their pastor.[115] Pastor Andrewson and his family moved to Mission Point in 1847, and during the next four years, he organized Norwegian Lutheran congregations in Leland, Fox River, and Lisbon. In 1851, Pastor Andrewson accepted a call to Wisconsin, but two years later returned to Mission Point to serve the Fox River congregation again as well as other congregations in the area.[116] In a September 14, 1855, report to a society providing financial support for his ministry, Pastor Andrewson wrote about the departure of the Lisbon immigrants to Iowa stating, "In the field where I now laboure, things seems about the same. I have formerly informed you of the more awakened interest in the preached word of God, but the main difficulty is now, that the people moves out to Iowa. Oure whole congregation in Lisbon has left, consisting of between 30 to 40 families & by next spring I suppose a good number will start from this settlement [the Lisbon Settlement]."[117]

At an Old Settlers Picnic in Cambridge, Iowa, in 1920, a son of Benjamin Thompson, K. B. Thompson, who was a child when he came in the fall of 1855, recalled that the second caravan arrived in the settlement on September 30, 1855.[118] Thompson also told about the first year on the Iowa prairie. The day after the first caravan arrived on June 7th, the first order of business was to help those without land locate property to purchase. Most of them purchased government land, but some bought land from speculators for $2–$2.50 per acre.[119] Osmund Sheldahl helped identify property lines by using the rear wheel of a wagon to measure from the section markers set when the U. S Government surveyed Story County. Building materials for their log cabins and livestock sheds came from timber tracts purchased in Ballard Grove [plus timber lots beside the Skunk River and in White Oak Grove south of Cambridge].[120] Some of the cabins were 12 by 16 feet and others were 14 by 18 feet. They were one-room cabins with a door, a window, and roofs made from clapboards. The sheds which were open to the east and south were pole sheds covered with slough grass.[121] Apland states, "Lars Tesdahl, Knute Ersland, and John Severson were the first to erect their own homes."[122]

The building materials for log cabins and livestock sheds not only came from the woodlands beside Ballard Creek, but also came from the Skunk River woodlands north of Cambridge including the 80 acres Osmund Sheldahl purchased on April 13, 1855. Osmund also purchased two 40-acre timber tracts after the caravan arrived on June 7, one in Ballard Grove on July 16 for $500 and another beside the Skunk River on June 19 for $175.[123] John Severson purchased 40 acres of timberland north of Cambridge in July for which he paid $800.[124]

During the next three years, the settlers purchased additional parcels of land at the Federal Land Office in Ft. Des Moines, but by early 1856, immigrants and land speculators had purchased most of the government land sold through the land office.[125] Figure 5 shows the location of all but 546 acres of the government land purchased in Ft. Des Moines by Southern Settlement Norwegians,[126] and Appendix D contains a list of the owners of the land. These purchases represent the heart of a settlement area known as the "District of Norway"[127] according to a newspaper correspondent from Cambridge and what others called the "Ballard Grove Colony."[128]

The other families and individuals who moved to the settlement after 1855 and before 1861 were:[129]

1856—Osmund and Balinda Anfenson and two children
1856—Oliver Dobbe

1856—Osmund and Inger Siverson and son
1857—Simon and Malinda Arntz and three children
1857—Severt and Engeborg Helland and two children
1857—Ole Johnson
1857—Ole and Stine Loe and two sons
1857—Amos and Marie Thompson
1858—Thor and Malinda Olson aka Hill and daughter and a son born during the trip
1858—John Thompson
1858—Ole Thompson
1858—Torres and Sarah Scott and five children
1858 or 1859—Knud and Anna Lenna and two children
1859—Osmond and Thone Johnson and son
1859—Thomas and Kari Larson and son
1859 or 1860—Barney and Engebor Charlson and two daughters
1859 or 1860—Erick and Britha Egland and two children who were members of a caravan who came to the Northern Settlement in 1858[130]
1859 or 1860—Peter Egland and mostly likely his brother, Henry (brothers of Erick Egland and Engebor Charlson)
1860—Ole and Bertha Berhow and two children
1860—John and Ingeborg Hemmingson and four children
1860—Ole K. and Johanne Johnson
1860—Hemming Romsa and son
1860—Torkel and Martha Romsa and three children
1860—Thomas and Elizabeth Simonson and three children
Year of arrival unknown—Ole Alsovader, Thor Fatland, Oliver Mattzona, John Olleson, Julee Oleson, and Thomas Thompson

In total, there were at least 314 Norwegians who lived in the Southern Settlement from 1855 through 1860. One hundred and eighty-five of them were born in Norway, two were born at sea on the way to Quebec, Canada, 55 were born in Illinois, three were born in Wisconsin, and 69 were born in Iowa. The immigration stories of all of the families and single people are contained in Volume 2 of *The Central Iowa Norwegians*. The stories of a few of the families who moved to the settlement after 1855 conclude this account of the founding of central Iowa's first Norwegian settlement:

In 1856, Osmund and Inger Siverson and their two-year old son sailed from Bergen, Norway, on May 12 and arrived in Quebec, Canada,

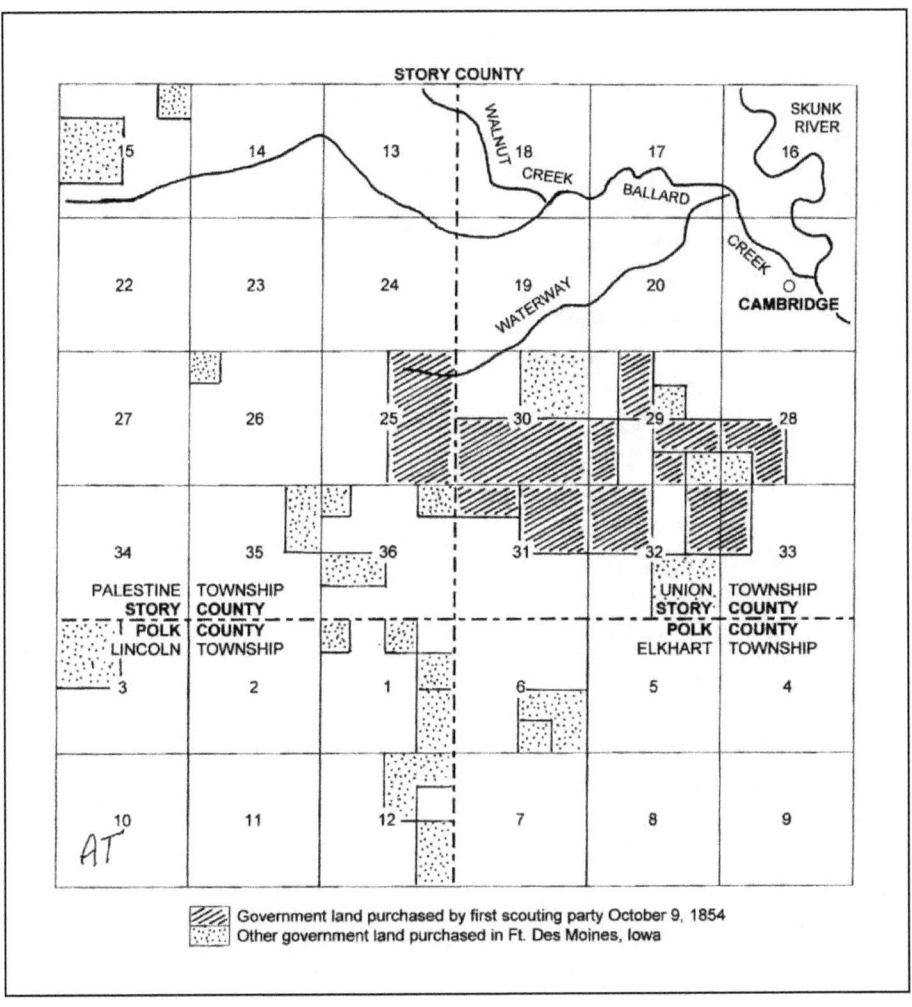

Figure 5
Government land purchased in the Southern Settlement[131]

on June 14.[132] After reaching Chicago, Illinois, they likely traveled on the Illinois & Michigan Canal for the rest of their journey to Morris, Illinois, where they expected to find Osmund's brother and sister-in-law, John and Betsey Severson. Unbeknownst to Osmund, however, John and Betsey and their three children had moved to Iowa in May 1855. Osmund and Inger's daughter, Margretha, who was born near Cambridge, Iowa, in 1858, later described her parents' immigration experience: "In the year 1856, Osmund and his wife and their two-year old son left Norway for

America. In those days, there being no steamships, they set sail in old style sailing ships. The name of the ship was 'Hebe.' They had nice weather all the way so it took only three weeks to cross the ocean, but another three weeks went by before they reached their destination.

"There being no railroads in the early days, sometimes they were transferred on a little boat in the canal that was drawn by oxen or team on the dry land. One could not travel very fast in those days in contrast with the present mode of travel. When they left the ship all went together thinking if they did not find their relatives right away, they would surely meet them at the church, but they found out America was much larger than they anticipated.

"Osmund did not find his brother, John, so he wrote to Norway for his address and then he wrote him that he was in America. His brother, John, hitched up his oxen and lumber wagon and went to get him and the trip took many days. They stayed with him the first year, then they bought eighty acres of land close to his brother, near Cambridge, where they lived for about 46 years."[133]

Margretha's account of her parents' immigration experience does not mention the fact that her mother was pregnant and that her brother, John O., was born in Story County on December 17, 1856. It is also interesting that after the family arrived in Grundy County, Illinois, approximately mid-July, Osmund was able to correspond with relatives in Norway, then correspond with his brother, wait for his brother to come and get them, and still get to Story County before John was born. The nearest railroad depot at the time was in Iowa City, so it is possible that Osmund's brother met them there with his lumber wagon.

In 1857, Norwegian immigrants from Wisconsin began moving to central Iowa. The first three families were Simon and Malinda Arntz and their three children, Sivert and Engeborg Helland and their two children, and Amos and Maria Thompson who moved from southwestern Wisconsin (Crawford County) to Story County. Sivert Helland's sister, Sarah, who settled southwest of Cambridge in 1855 with her husband, Salamon Heggen, may have encouraged them to move to central Iowa. It is quite likely that all three families had originally settled in Illinois because two of the children, Andrew Thompson (Arntz) and Ole Helland, were born in Illinois.

It is also likely that Sivert Helland's parents, Ole and Esther Helleland, came to the settlement in 1857. They emigrated from the Helleland farm in Etne that same year along with their daughter, Ane, and their niece, Alice Mikkelsdatter. Their initial destination was probably

Crawford County, Wisconsin, where they reunited with their son and his family and traveled with them to central Iowa. Ole and Esther, their daughter, Sarah, and her husband, and their son, Sivert, and his wife all established farmsteads southwest of Cambridge in northeast Lincoln Township, Polk County. The Arntz and Thompson families settled immediately north of the Helland family in Story County.

The Hemming and Torkel Romsa families emigrated from the island of Romsa in the Fjelberg parish to Illinois in 1857 and moved from Illinois to Iowa in the spring of 1860, but only one of the families was enumerated on the 1860 Census. Torkel, his wife, Martha, and their three children were enumerated in Story County, Palestine Township, as the Thomas Jacobson family, but Hemming, who was a widower, and his son were not enumerated. It is clear the two families traveled to Iowa together because during their trip from Lisbon, Illinois, to Story County, Iowa, they had a photograph taken of their families in their two covered wagons.[134]

Also arriving in the settlement in 1860, but later than the Romsa families, was another member of the Berhow family, Ole, and his wife, Bertha, and their two children. Their arrival is illustrative of how parents, siblings, aunts, and uncles were transplanted from Norway to Illinois to Iowa. In 1849, two of Ole's maternal aunts emigrated from Skånevik to Lisbon with their families, and in 1854, their brother, Benjamin, joined them in Lisbon with his family. Ole's oldest brother, Thomas, also emigrated in 1854. The next year Thomas and his uncle's family, Benjamin and Enger Thompson and their four children, were in the second caravan of settlers that left the Lisbon Settlement for central Iowa on August 25, 1855.

In 1857, Thomas and Ole's parents, Ola and Elsa Berhaug (Americanized to Berhow), and their five youngest children ranging in age from five to 17, immigrated to Lisbon leaving their son, Ole, in Norway with his wife, Bertha. In 1859, Ole and Bertha immigrated to Lisbon with their daughter, Elsie. Apparently, Thomas and his parents, Ola and Elsa, and three of their children moved to central Iowa in 1858 or in 1859 because marriage records show their daughter, Sarah, was married in Story County on January 1, 1860.

The reunion of Ole with his parents and siblings took place August 12, 1860, after Ole and Bertha and their daughter arrived in central Iowa. The reunion may have taken place near Swede Point (Madrid) where Ola and Elsa and their children, Thomas, Halvar, and Mikel, were enumerated in Douglas Township on July 13, 1860. Living in a nearby dwelling house were Elsa's brother, Benjamin, and his family. Ola, his son, Thomas, and Ola's brother-in-law, Benjamin, were working as carpenters, but in the early 1860s, they moved to the Norway District southwest of Cambridge and began farming. Ola and Elsa and their children went by the surname, Berhow, while Benjamin used the Thompson surname, an Americanized version of his Norwegian Christian name, Bjørne Tomasson.

A recap of the important events so far is helpful before continuing the story of how central Iowa became the third largest settlement area for Norwegians in Iowa:

1845—Rasmus and Margreta Larson from Skånevik and their four children and Osmund and Anna Sheldahl from Etne immigrate to Lisbon Illinois. A few families from Skånevik, Etne, and Fjelberg had emigrated prior to this time, but their emigration had been sporadic.

1846—48 more people emigrate from Skånevik and Etne.

1847—Osmund Sheldahl's cousin, Torkel Henryson, recruits 161 people from Skånevik, Etne, and Fjelberg to emigrate on the sailing vessel, *Kong Sverre*.

1848—The cholera epidemic begins which proves fatal to many immigrants and drastically slows emigration from Skånevik, Etne, and Fjelberg between 1850 and 1853.

1854—Mass emigration resumes, but now land around Lisbon is too expensive for new immigrants, so a scouting party is elected to find a new settlement location.

1855—On June 7, 1855, a caravan of 23 families and five single people leaves Lisbon, Illinois, to begin the first central Iowa Norwegian settlement southwest of Cambridge. Six families and two more single people join them on September 30, 1855.

1856 to 1860—Additional families and single people arrive in the settlement.

The Second Central Iowa Norwegian Settlement: 1856–1860

The 1854 scouting party's glowing report of central Iowa and the preparations being made to move to the new settlement area were, undoubtedly, topics of never-ending conversation in the Lisbon

Settlement during the winter of 1854–1855.[135] Two of the Lisbon settlers who discussed these matters thoroughly were Lars Sheldall, an 1847 Etne immigrant to Lisbon, and Jonas Duea, an 1849 Skånevik immigrant to Lisbon. Anxious to see the settlement area Lars' younger brother, Osmund, helped select, they decided to go to central Iowa in March 1855.

Considering the time of the year, perhaps Lars and Jonas chose to travel to central Iowa by stagecoach rather than in their own wagon. The first railroad bridge over the Mississippi River was not completed until the following year, so they may have ridden on the Chicago and Rock Island Railroad to Rock Island, Illinois, ferried across the river to Davenport, Iowa, and traveled on a Western Stage Company stagecoach from Davenport to Ft. Des Moines, a three-day trip.[136]

If Lars and Jonas took the stage coach, they went directly to Ft. Des Moines. If they traveled in their own wagon, they may have gone to look over the settlement area before going to Ft. Des Moines to visit the Federal Land Office. In Ft. Des Moines, they discovered settlers and land speculators were buying land at a hectic pace and had purchased most of the land southwest of Cambridge that was near timber resources. However, large areas of virgin prairie near the Skunk River were still available farther north, land that would soon be purchased. A Ft. Des Moines newspaper editor who witnessed the land office business later wrote, "Business was so furious that the great rush was over by 1856."[137]

Before leaving Ft. Des Moines, Lars and Jonas visited the banking house of Maclot, Corbin & White where they met Miles White, a wealthy Baltimore businessman. White came to Iowa anticipating a rise in real estate values as a result of the discovery of gold in California.[138] While he resided in Iowa, Miles White made 755 purchases at federal land offices, the largest number (445) at the Ft. Des Moines office.[139] White or one of his agents may have taken Lars and Jonas to Story County, as was customary for land agents to do, because on March 30, 1855, White sold them land located northeast of Fairview, Story City's name before it was changed to Story City in 1878. The property was located north of the Story County line in the southwest corner section of what was later named Norway Township and still later became Scott Township in Hamilton County.[140]

Soon after Lars and Jonas returned to Lisbon, others interested in moving to Iowa organized a meeting. According to Paul Thompson who was selected to be a member of a scouting party, "A mass meeting was called and the matter was drifted thoroughly, resulting in the naming of a committee that should take a trip into Iowa and investigate the prospects for getting good government land at a figure, which they hoped they would someday be able to pay."[141] The scouting members chosen were:[142]

Jonas Duea [1824–1910]
Jacob Erickson [1812–1881]
Mons Grove [1830–1903]
John M. Johnson [1831–1902]
John Nelson [1820–1899]
Lars Sheldall [1804–1881]
Oliver Thompson aka Ola Øine aka Ole Aine/Eino [1837–1917][143]
Paul Thompson [1829–1917]

According to Hjalmar Rued Holand, author of a 1908 history about the central Iowa Norwegians, the scouting party waited until the Palestine congregation left Holderman's Prairie on May 17th before beginning their journey.[144] Driving two span of horses each pulling a wagon,[145] they may have started their journey on the same route the Palestine caravan followed which took them southwest of Lisbon to Ottawa, Illinois, and from there to Davenport, Iowa, where they crossed the Mississippi River. An alternative route would have taken the scouting party in a northwesterly direction from Lisbon to Fulton, Illinois, where there was another major Mississippi River ferry crossing to Lyons, Iowa, now a historic district in Clinton, Iowa. Figure 6 shows the route the first caravan of Lisbon settlers took to Story County in 1855 and the routes from Rock Island/Davenport and Fulton/Lyons (Clinton) that the 1855 scouting party might have taken to Story County.

Nathan Parker, the author of *Iowa as it is in 1855*, recommended the Lyons (Clinton, Iowa) to Story County route for immigrants interested in exploring central Iowa. After he had traveled from Lyons to Boonesboro (Boone, Iowa) and up to Ft. Dodge, Iowa, in 1855, he included the following description of his journey from Marietta to Nevada in his *Iowa Handbook for 1856*: "Leaving Marietta, we pass into Story County, which we find as yet but sparsely settled. Pursuing our course westward, we pass over extended prairies, dotted here and there with groves of timber. Occasionally, a red deer bounds away over our pathway, and seeks the nearest ravine for shelter from our dreaded presence. Our eyes sometimes wander over the sea of billowy green before us, four hours without seeing anything to indicate the presence of mankind save the worn track or trail across the prairies. As we advance we see broken fields, and a blue smoke curling up from a settler's rude cabin. Bending our course southward we arrive at Nevada."[146] In describing the Skunk River that flows through the western side of the county, Parker states, "This river extends through the county in a diagonal direction, and the banks are covered with a good quality of timber."[147]

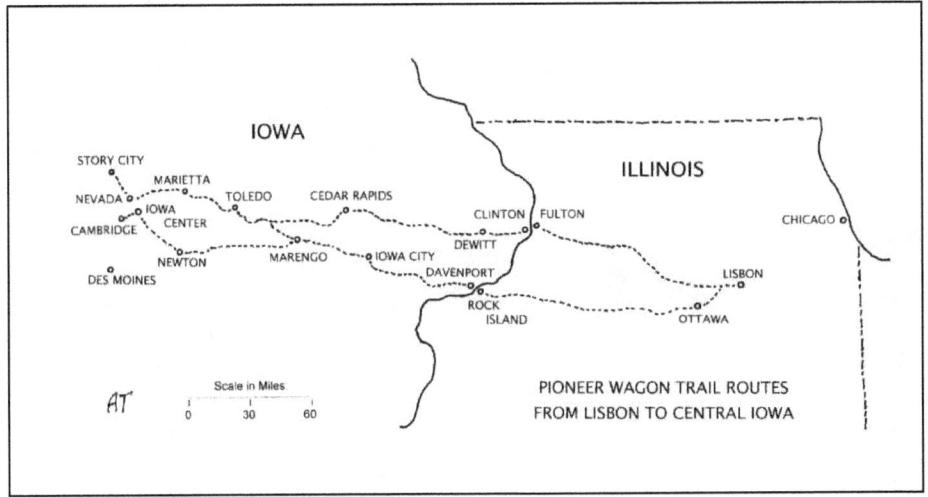

Figure 6
Pioneer wagon trail routes from Lisbon to central Iowa

Whichever route the scouting party members took to Story County, they apparently reached their destination on one of the first days of June because on June 5, 1855, a justice of the peace wrote a deed for the sale of a five-acre timber lot from James C. and Sarah Smith of Story County to one of the scouting party members, John Nelson. Ivar Havneros writes that during the time the scouting party explored northern Story County and southern Hamilton County, "They ... made old Mr. Smith's home their headquarters. This man had a hut right by the timber one mile east and one mile south from the present Story City."[148] The hut, most likely a log home, was near Long Dick Creek and was the home of James C. and Sarah Smith, born in Virginia and Maryland respectively in the mid-1790s. They lived in Indiana before moving their family to Appanoose County in southern Iowa.[149] In 1852, their son, John, along with other Appanoose County families including George Prime, began settling alongside the Skunk River in northern Story County, and John's parents came the following year.

Figure 7 shows the road from Marietta in Marshall County to Nevada, the county seat of Story County. Also shown is the route of the Iowa Central Air Line Rail Road proposed in 1853[150] and an accurate drawing of the Skunk River on the western side of Story County and the creeks flowing into it. The northern most creek flowing into the Skunk River from the east is Long Dick Creek, and the next creek is Kiegley Creek flowing in from the west followed by Bear Creek flowing in from the east. Story City, although not shown on the map, was located on the east side of Lafayette Township in the northwest corner of the county. In southern Story County, Ballard Creek flows in from the west on the north side of Cambridge.

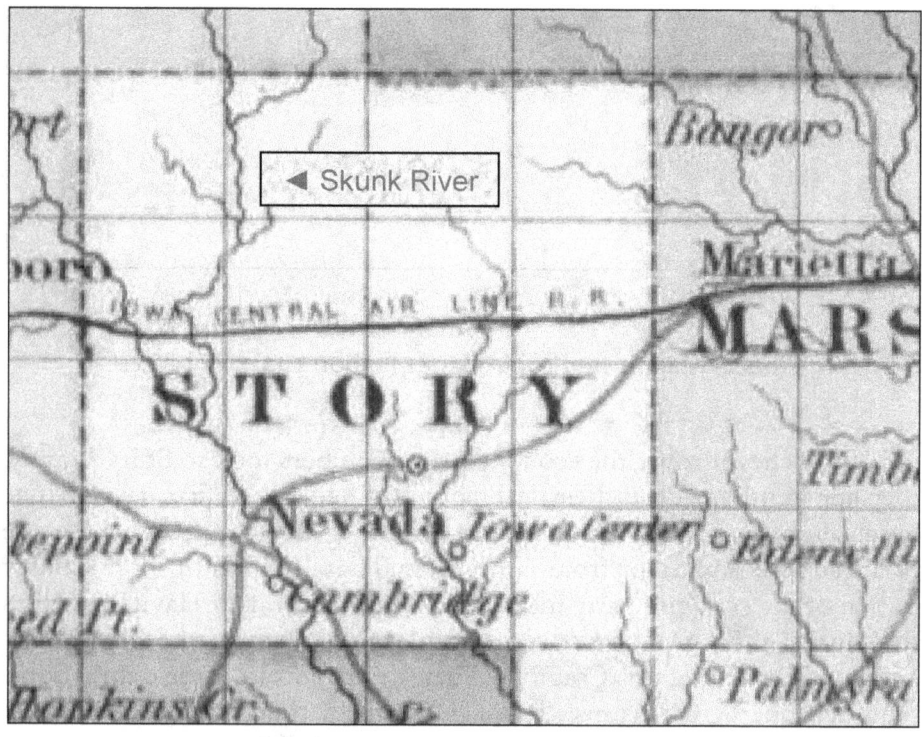

Figure 7
A section of Joseph H. Colton's 1859 map of Iowa

When the scouting party arrived in Iowa in early June 1855 to look for a large amount of land available for sale at an affordable price, they relied on information gained by Lars Sheldall and Jonas Duea during their trip to Iowa almost three months earlier. When Sheldall and Duea explored northern Story County and southern Hamilton County, the timberland alongside Skunk River and most of the prairie land within one to two miles of the river had already been purchased by immigrants and land speculators. Therefore, in order to find an area of government land large enough to begin a new settlement, the scouting party knew they would have to purchase land farther away from the river.[151]

Figure 8 includes all the purchases made by the scouting party, and, presumably, the members agreed the area near Bear Creek in Howard Township was the best location to purchase land (see Appendix D for a list of the owners of the land). While the quality of timber alongside the creek was poorer than that alongside the Skunk River, obtaining timberland nearby was nevertheless an important consideration in deciding where to purchase land. In addition to being a source of wood for cooking, the creek provided a natural drainage system for the flat prairie landscape.

The only factual information known about the scouting party's visit to central Iowa is where they stayed in Howard Township and when and where they purchased land. The rest of their visit can only be surmised from another important event that occurred during this time—arrival of the Palestine caravan at Cambridge on Thursday, June 7, 1855, the same day Lars Sheldall purchased a timber lot near Story City. That day or the next, the scouting party traveled to Ft. Des Moines where one of its members, John Nelson, purchased 200 acres of government land in Howard Township on Friday, June 8. One wonders why they purchased only a small amount of land then, but perhaps the main purpose of the scouting party's visit to the land office was to be certain a large area of government land was still available in the township considering the robust demand for land. Their next destination was likely Cambridge to see if their friends and relatives from Lisbon had arrived, and finding them camped on Lars' brother's land south of Ballard Grove, the scouting party may have decided to stay with their friends and relatives a few days to hear about their trip to Iowa, to worship with them on Sunday, and to further discuss the matter about where to purchase land. On Monday, June 11, or the next day, the scouting party likely returned to Howard Township to inspect the area one more time before returning to the Federal Land Office in Ft. Des Moines on Thursday, June 14, where they purchased an additional 2,160 acres in Howard Township and 200 acres in Lafayette Township. From Ft. Des Moines, they headed back to Lisbon to report about the land they had purchased and to report that the Palestine caravan had arrived safely in Iowa.

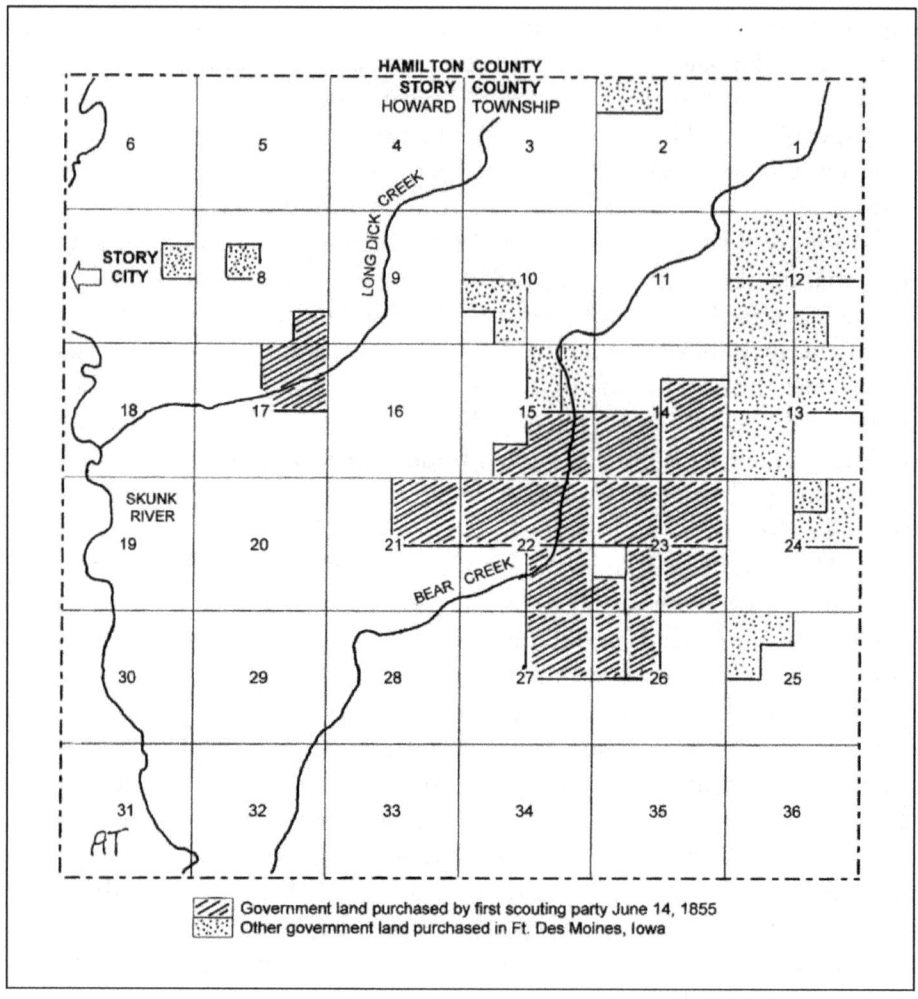

Figure 8
Government land purchased in the Northern Settlement

Lack of sufficient desirable government land in southern Story County was a factor in the decision to begin a second Norwegian settlement in central Iowa, but there were other possible considerations. In his history of both settlements, Hjalmar Holand assumes members of the Palestine congregation were Synod-Lutherans who believed in maintaining the traditions and practices of the state church of Norway and that the Howard Township settlers were Haugeans, followers of the Norwegian lay preacher and evangelist, Hans Nielsen Hauge, who believed in more informal and personal "low church" practices and in lay preaching. Holand states, "The first group was Synod-Lutheran, while the other was Haugian [Haugean]. Moved by the same kind of cordial love which separated Lot and Abraham, and with thoughts of peace in matters of the church, they put a distance of 25 miles between them."[152] Facts, however, do not support this statement by Holand. Synod-Lutherans called pastors with university seminary training to their congregations and would not, as the Palestine congregation did in 1855, elect a lay preacher, Ole Anfinson, to be their first pastor and in 1859, elect another lay preacher, Osmund Sheldahl, as their second pastor. Holand was correct in his belief that there were many Haugeans among the founders of the Howard Township settlement, but the Palestine congregation's decision to elect lay preachers reflects a Haugean influence in this settlement, too.

If there were religious reasons for founding two settlements, they were most likely related to affiliations with the pastors who were ministering to them rather than with synods. As stated previously, Pastor Ole Andrewson was apparently ministering to some or all of the members of the Palestine congregation before they moved to Iowa. The pastor ministering to many of the families who moved to northern Story County was Pastor P. A. Rasmussen and before him, Pastor Elling Eielsen. Holand, who apparently interviewed one or more of the first settlers in the Howard Township settlement, states Pastor Eielsen discouraged his parishioners from moving to Iowa believing that, "Such unsteady desire to wander and desire for worldly gain was only an outcropping of the old heathen Viking blood. He warned against tempting the Lord by resorting to the wilderness, where, far removed from the loving communion with the believers and with those rich in grace, the faith of their childhood might suffer wreckage. Fallen to the lusts of the flesh and to Mammon's greed, they would be surrendered to the devil, who goes about like a roaring lion seeking whom he may devour."[153]

Ivar Havneros, author of the 1907 history of the St. Petri congregation founded in the Northern Settlement in 1857, also believed there was a religious basis for founding separate settlements. He states, "In the southern part of the county there was already a nucleus of a Norwegian settlement who church-wise belonged to the Swedish Augustana Synod. Being the new emigrants were members of Pastor Rasmussen's congregation, they would rather establish their homes farther north in the county." However, the fact is the Palestine congregation did not affiliate with any synod until 1860, and then it was with the Augustana Synod. Havneros' reference to their relationship with

Pastor Rasmussen certainly supports the idea that pastoral loyalty could have influenced Lisbon settlers to found a second Norwegian settlement.

Another possible reason for choosing to settle in northern Story County involves the Skunk River and what was then known about the future route of a rail line into central Iowa. The Skunk River was infamous for being a difficult river to ford during wet seasons, especially near Cambridge and further downstream.[154] By locating on the east side of the Skunk River, settlers had one less river to ford to obtain supplies 120 miles away in Iowa City, the end of one of four rail lines that had started across the state. One of the railroad companies, the Iowa Central Air Line Rail Road, was planning a line through Story County. Iowa maps published in 1854 and 1855 show the route from east to west through the exact middle of the county,[155] but after Nathan Parker's 1855 trip through the county, he wrote, "The route of the railroad lies through the northern part of the county, which, though but recently organized and sparsely settled, to the present time, is now rapidly filling up."[156] An 1857 map and Joseph H. Colton's 1859 map in Figure 7 also show the planned route going through the northern part of the county.[157] Rail service was critical to the future growth of the settlement, and Lars and Jonas and the other members of the June scouting party may have considered the future location of a rail line in their decision to begin a second settlement in northern Story County.

All but one of the members of the June scouting party moved to central Iowa. John M. (Mehus) Johnson, an 1849 immigrant from Skånevik, and the only member of the party who purchased land outside of Howard Township, stayed in Kendall County, Illinois. While he was in Iowa, Johnson purchased 200 acres of government land southwest of Story City in Lafayette Township. Later in the year, he purchased another 160 acres of government land west of Story City alongside Kiegley Creek, a purchase likely made for him by someone else. During the next few years, Johnson made additional purchases in Lafayette and Howard townships, suggesting his purchases were made for investment, not settlement reasons since he never moved to Iowa.

Early in the fall of 1855, a second Lisbon scouting party came to investigate land opportunities in northern Story County.[158] The members of this scouting party were Rasmus Ask aka Rasmus Erickson [1801–1876], Erick Nelson, Jacob Nilson (Brue) [1816–1894], Hans Pederson [1820–1908], and Torkel Henryson [1822–1911].[159] Torkel Henryson was the person who recruited 161 passengers for *Kong Sverre* who emigrated in 1847, and Erick Nelson was the Lisbon settler who had suggested Iowa as a location for a new Norwegian settlement. All but Pederson purchased government land at the Ft. Des Moines Federal Land Office for themselves and others back in Lisbon on September 27, 1855. Rasmus Ask, Erick Nelson, and Jacob Nilson purchased land in Howard Township, and Torkel Henryson purchased land in Lafayette Township for himself and his twin brother, Lars. Lars moved to central Iowa in 1857, but in 1858, Erick Nelson sold his land to Henryson after apparently deciding to stay in Kendall County, Illinois. Torkel Henryson moved to Lafayette Township in 1865.

While this scouting party was in central Iowa, they also investigated land in the southeast corner of Ellsworth Township in Hamilton County immediately north of Lafayette Township (see Figure 2). Ask, Henryson, Erick Nelson, and Pederson purchased land there, too, their purchases being made from previous owners. With these purchases and the purchases Duea and Sheldall made northeast of Story City in Scott Township, Hamilton County, during their March 1855 scouting trip, Norwegians were beginning to claim land on both sides of the Skunk River in southern Hamilton County, too. Henryson also purchased land west of Story City alongside Kiegley Creek.

Hans Pederson may not have returned to Illinois with the other members of the scouting party as evidenced by his purchases of land in October and again in January 1856 when he purchased more land in Hamilton County, this time in Scott Township immediately north of Howard Township. The January purchase was 320 acres of government land for $1.25 per acre purchased at the Federal Land Office in Ft. Dodge, the only government land purchased by Norwegians in either Ellsworth or Scott Township. Sometime after his January purchase, Pederson must have returned to Illinois because he is included on lists of members of the first caravan of settlers who arrived in Howard Township June 1856.[160]

There was yet another scouting party that came to northern Story County later in the fall of 1855. Lars Larson [1836–1904] and Torkel Opstvedt [1806–1878] purchased land at the Federal Land Office on October 29, 1855, along with Thor Hegland who had just moved to the area with the Lars Sheldall family. They purchased land in Howard Township, but they also made a purchase in Lafayette Township for Osmund Henryson, the younger brother of Torkel and Lars Henryson. Lars Larson, his parents and five siblings, and the Torkel Opstvedt family were in the caravan of Lisbon settlers that came the following year to found the new settlement. Lars' parents were Rasmus and Margreta

Larson who along with Osmund and Anna Sheldahl immigrated to Lisbon in 1845.

Upon his return to Illinois as a member of the June scouting party, Lars Sheldall began selling his property in Grundy County and making preparations to move his family to central Iowa in the fall. As previously described by his son, Rasmus, the Lars Sheldall family and a recent immigrant, Thor Hegland, were members of the caravan who arrived in the Cambridge settlement on September 30, 1855. Once they reached their final destination near Story City, they lived in a cabin on the land Rasmus Ask purchased in June and later moved into an existing log home, presumably on the property Lars purchased in Hamilton County in March.[161] Lars and Herbor Sheldall, their five children, and Thor Hegland thus became the first Norwegians to settle in what came to be known as the Northern Settlement.

The following spring, 1856, a caravan of 17 families and three single people left the Lisbon Settlement to begin the second Norwegian settlement in central Iowa.[162] Two of the heads of families, Jacob and Ellen Erickson, 1849 immigrants, and Hans and Abella Twedt, 1854 immigrants, are great great grandparents of the author:

> Rasmus and Methe Ask and four children
> Shur and Martha Britson and four children
> Jonas* and Martha Duea and two children
> Jacob* and Ellen Erickson and seven children
> Elias and Randy Henrickson
> Erick and Bertha Jacobson and daughter
> Jacob B. and Nille Jacobson and six children
> Rasmus and Margreta Larson and six children
> Betsy Ness and four children
> John* and Sarah Nelson and three children
> Jacob and Laurensa Nilson and seven children
> Torkel Opstvedt and three children
> Ole and Anna Rasmusen and daughter
> Erick aka E.R. and Betsy Sheldahl
> Rasmus and Ingebor Sheldahl and daughter
> Haavar and Anna Thompson and three children
> Hans and Abella Twedt and son, and daughter born during the trip
> Single woman: Siri Olson
> Single men: Lars Hegland and Hans Pederson
> * Members of the June 1855 scouting party

In his history of the St. Petri congregation, Ivar Havneros gives the following account of the preparations made by this group and their journey to central Iowa: "In the winter of 1855 and 1856, the most essential preparations were made and in May 1856 the first large company moved westward. The caravan consisted of 18 covered wagons drawn by 18 span of oxen and 2 horses. They had a fairly large herd of cows and young cattle, also a flock of chickens. Besides the most needful articles as bedding, household furniture and utensils, these emigrants did not forget—in the case of most of them—the only heritage they had from their childhood home in Norway, namely their Bibles, hymnbooks, books of sermons, other devotional books, and Luther's books for children, including the Catechism. These people were from childhood brought up in the Christian faith, having been diligently taught the Word of God. Church attendance, the singing of hymns, and the worship of God were indispensable to them. During their early days in a new land, in the absence of church or pastor, they more diligently than ever made use of their Bibles and devotional books.

"On the trip to Iowa they were blessed with beautiful weather. Having reached Cedar River [or the Iowa River[163]] where they camped over Sunday, a beautiful baby girl was born to the Hans Tvedts [Twedt]. Here also, tragedy struck in the drowning of John Naes [Ness]. After the long difficult journey from Lisbon, some of the boys decided it would be wonderful to have a bath in the river, and John was the first one to jump in. Immediately the other boys noticed something was wrong. He got Lockjaw and was unable to move hand or foot. The stream washed him down the river. Hans Pederson hurriedly mounted a horse and galloped down along the river hoping to rescue him, but his efforts were in vain. His body was found the next day. They wrapped him in a sheet and buried him by the riverside.

"No traveling was done on Sunday, and after they were somewhat organized, the families would get together for devotional meetings. Their Bibles, hymnbooks, and devotional books were in use. Here in God's free nature on the western prairie, worship services were held. Here was the House of God, the gate of heaven from whence a ladder created by the Word, ascended from earth to the kingdom of heaven. How beautiful the chiming of the following verse must have sounded as they worshiped here:

Lord send Thy holy angels down,
Let Thy voice by me be heard.

Light over me a holy peace,
And may the foe not touch me.
As a poor wanderer,
Lead me to my Fatherland,
And save me by Thy grace.

"The collect and epistle for the day were read and one of the members would lead the group in prayer. The rough dry hands were folded in prayer, the furrowed and weather beaten faces were turned toward heaven, the words spoken, though simple and childlike, were warm and sincere and surely reached the throne of grace. Heaven's blessings, God's love, and the Father's concern and protection rested upon them—all made possible by the merits of Jesus. The worship service continued with a hymn from Kingo, a devotional from Luther, a sermon from the Book of Sermons, another hymn, and finally a short closing prayer.

"About the middle of June, the caravan journeying to the northern Story County stopped at Long Dick Creek at the same spot where the land company had been the previous year. Here by the beautiful oak timberland, they pitched camp for the last time and then spread out over the prairie, each family seeking their future home."[164]

According to an obituary for the oldest son of Jacob Erickson, Mikel Erickson, the caravan arrived at their destination on June 14, 1856.[165] Soon after their arrival, the 1856 Iowa Census was taken, and the census enumerator found the families camped in four smaller groupings of wagons throughout Howard Township where they lived until the first log homes were constructed.

Of the 17 families and three single people in the 1856 caravan, only three families and one single person did not settle in the township. In October 1856, Rasmus Larson purchased 200 acres in Lafayette Township, and some of this land included the village of Fairview (Story City).[166] In December 1856, Haavar Thompson purchased 40 acres of virgin prairie in Scott Township, but after a prairie fire destroyed his log home, Haavar moved his family west of the Skunk River into Ellsworth Township to a location protected from prairie fires.[167] Although Hans Pederson already owned land in Scott Township when he arrived in June, after he married Lars Sheldall's stepdaughter, Taaron Peterson, in December 1857, they established a farmstead in Lafayette Township. Elias Hendrickson did not purchase land until 1878, 68 acres in Warren Township east of Howard Township.[168]

On January 8, 1857, the first Story County newspaper began publication. Three weeks later, the editor, R. R. Thrall, published a history of the young county that had been organized only four years earlier on April 4, 1853. It contained the following account of living conditions for the Norwegians living east of Story City: "A colony of Norwegians in the northwestern part of the county is in a very thriving condition, being composed of industrious settlers. They expect a considerable addition to their numbers in the coming spring."[169]

During 1856, additional scouting parties came from Illinois to central Iowa to investigate land opportunities, and this is the reason R. R. Thrall was able to report that more settlers would be coming in the spring. Two of the people who traveled to Story County with the intention of purchasing land were Lars Henderson [1825–1908] and Peder Larson [1826–1863], known to their friends as *Tallige* Lars [Patient Lars] and *Storre* Per [Big Peder].

Tallige Lars emigrated from the Håvig farm in Bømlo in 1847, went back to Norway where he married Anna in 1850, and returned to Illinois in 1856 with Anna and their three children. In 1852, *Storre* Per and Malena Larson emigrated from the Tjernagel farm in Sveio to Waupaca, Wisconsin. Their next destination was the Koshkonong Norwegian Settlement east of Madison, Wisconsin, and by the end of 1852, they were in the Fox River Settlement southwest of Chicago where Malena's brother settled in 1849. *Storre* Per died in 1863, but *Tallige* Lars lived a long life and was fond of reminiscing about his early years.[170] Fortunately, an account of their scouting trip was recorded in 1888 by Erik Travaas, a Norwegian immigrant living in Story City. Travaas' historical narrative, "A Little About the First Settlers in Story County," is included elsewhere in this volume of *The Centeral Iowa Norwegians*. It is the earliest history the author has discovered about the central Iowa Norwegians. An excerpt about the scouting trip follows:

"Lars drove the oxen while Per stared out over the landscape whistling an old sad tune. It is so lovely, so refreshing, to breathe the fresh air, so stimulating to look out over the fertile fields. He thinks about his poor home in Norway, makes comparisons, but finds that it is infinitely poorer than the rich earth he can see here. Even though he feels a good deal of loneliness in his heart, he cannot but feel thankful that Providence has brought him so well and so surely to this fertile land whose richness, by diligence and work, will be inherited from generation to generation.

"The further west they come, the wilder and more desolate the country looks. Often it seems they never will arrive at their destination. The obstacles caused by the difficulties of travel have already lengthened their trip, but Lars and Per are still in good spirits. From their earliest childhood they have gotten in the habit of waiting for everything with patience, and that helps them. A trip over the wild prairie demands patience like nothing else.

"Finally they reach as far as the border of Story County. Here the wild prairie begins to show its impressive expanses. When one looks out over the endless plains, it appears as a troubled sea where the waves begin to subside after a storm. They were very surprised about all the uncultivated land which lay here waiting to be changed to productive acres and meadows. . . .

"A little before the sunset they had reached the area where Roland was later built. Also, here the same empty landscape was spread before them.

"Here they began to look around really well. The country was beautiful and had a deep rich soil. If they could just find some wood for fuel, for building a house and such, they thought then they might be all right."[171]

Tallige Lars and *Storre* Per did not purchase land during their scouting trip, although they certainly must have returned to Illinois with thoughts about where they would like to settle and build their homesteads. There were two other future central Iowans, however, who did purchase land in 1856. In late June, John Pierson purchased 193 acres in the most northwest section of Howard Township which included timber land along the Skunk River.[172] Then on October 13, Sivert Knutson purchased 40 acres and a two-acre timber lot in the section directly north of Pierson's section[173] in the southwest corner of Scott Township where the Lars Sheldall family settled. Since *Tallige* Lars had just returned to Illinois with his family that summer, he likely did not come to Iowa until fall which means Sivert Knutson could have also accompanied him and *Storre* Per to Iowa.

The following spring, 1857, the Henderson, Knutson, Larson, and Pierson families were in a wagon train of settlers who moved to the new Norwegian settlement near Story City. Three other members of the group; John Christian, Samuel Haaland, and Osmund Henryson, had purchased land without making scouting trips to Iowa. According to a Ritland family history, "There were 17 covered wagons, drawn by oxen, in the caravan."[174]

The list below includes the families and single people who were in the wagon train plus others known to have arrived in the settlement during 1857:

Elling and Brita Braland and five children
Anders and Helga Christenson and son
Samuel and Anna Haaland and daughter
Ole T. and Britha Hegland and five children
Knudt and Engeborg Helvig[175]
Lars and Anna Henderson and three children
Osmund and Anna Henryson
Sivert and Siri Knutson and three children
Peder and Malena Larson and two children
John and Bertha Pierson and seven children
Lars B. and Ubjor Olson and four children
Halvor and Enger Opstvedt and two children
Ole and Sarah Ritland and six children
Osmund and Maren Weltha and daughter
Single women: Gjore Ersland and Rakkal Thompson
Single men: Lars Boyd,[176] John Christian, Christ Peterson, and
   Bernett Reinertson

It took the wagon train three weeks and two days to complete its journey to northern Story County, indicating they had good weather. They must have arrived at their destination on or before June 3, 1857, because on this date, Lars B. Olson purchased 80 acres two miles north of Story City in the same section of land in Ellsworth Township, Hamilton County, where the September 1855 scouting party purchased land.[177] Other members of the caravan who did not already own land in central Iowa did not begin making their purchases until July, but Lars' brother-in-law, Haavar Thompson, who settled in Hamilton County the previous year, could have made arrangements for Lars' land purchase. It was to the west side of the Skunk River that Haavar moved his family after the prairie fire destroyed his log home on the open prairie east of the river.

One of the 1857 arrivals, Christ Peterson, likely came to the settlement after June 3. His 1902 biography states, "He made his way by rail from Illinois to Iowa City and thence proceeded on foot to Story County."[178] His brother, Hans Pederson, had come the year before, and both brothers were, no doubt, anxious to see each other again.

Again, according to the Ritland family history, "They [the members of the caravan] lived in their covered wagons along the Skunk River on the outskirts of Story City until they secured temporary shelter in a log cabin."[179] Temporary shelter usually meant living with another family until a log home or dugout could be constructed, but some of the families may have lived with other families for a year or longer because they did not purchase land until 1858 or later. The Anders Christenson family, for example, was enumerated on the 1860 Census in the dwelling house of Bernett Reinertson. Anders' 1889 biography states, "When Mr. Christenson came to Iowa he had not money enough to pay the expense of bringing his family from Illinois. He worked for others at farm work for some time before buying his land and also worked a farm on Section 3 belonging to Albert Hall, on shares, and in 1864 bought his present farm."[180]

With the arrival of the 1857 caravan, more families began settling in Hamilton County. After he married in 1858, Christ Peterson joined Lars B. Olson in Ellsworth Township, and the Braland, Christenson, Knutson, Larson, and Henderson families along with Bernett Reinertson settled in Scott Township. The rest of the 1857 arrivals settled in Story County. The Henryson family settled in Lafayette Township, and the Haaland, Hegland, Helvig, Opstvedt, Pierson, Ritland, and Thompson families and John Christian settled in Howard Township. There are no land purchases in county land deed index records for Lars Boyd. Lars likely returned to Illinois sometime before August 1862 when he enlisted in the 91st Illinois Infantry.

In 1858, two more caravans of Lisbon settlers arrived in the settlement. Concerning the larger caravan, Havneros states, "This company left Kendall County the first part of May and it required six weeks to reach their destination. The weather was bad that spring with much rain which caused many of the rivers to overflow. They had to wait a whole week by Rock River in Illinois before they dared cross the flooded river. Each Sunday they rested and had devotional services conducted alternately by Paul Thompson and Johannes Matre [John Larson]."[181]

There were 10 families and a single man in this caravan:[182]

Baar and Margrethe Beroen aka Henryson and six children
Charles and Borgilde Charlson and four children
John and Bertha Charlson and five children
Christen and Britha Erickson and four children

Lars and Anna Henryson aka Henderson and four children
Thor and Malinda Olson aka Hill and daughter and a son born during the trip. Upon arriving in Story County, they went to the Southern Settlement where Thor had purchased land two years earlier.
Knudt and Brita Johnson and daughter
John and Elisabeth Larson and six children
John and Betsey Michaelson and two children
Paul* and Enger Thompson
Single man: Mons Grove*[183]
* Member of the June 1855 scouting party

Many years later, Paul and Enger Thompson told the story about their journey to Iowa for a newspaper article about their 60th wedding anniversary in 1911. The author of the article, likely the *Roland Record* owner and editor, M. O. Rod, recorded, "... [They] left Illinois in the spring of 1858 arriving at their destination in July. There were ten families in the company and they had twelve covered wagons in which was stored all their earthly belongings, except their cattle, which they drove in a herd after the wagons. Slowly they wended their way westward crossing the Mississippi River on a ferry, and fording other streams which they were obliged to cross. They traveled every day except Sunday, when they would go into camp and would conduct religious services, they being brot [*sic*] up in the Lutheran religion in their mother country, and they were loyal to it wherever they were."[184]

John M. Mason, a grandson of John Michaelson, published yet another account of their trip. Mason, who was then editor of the *Roland Record*, wrote, "The spring and summer was terribly wet. Lars Henderson [Henryson] and John Michaelson had horses while the others had oxen. Mr. Michaelson's team was used times innumerable to pull others less fortunate out of the mud and mire. In crossing the Wapsipinicon River, the water was high on account of the heavy rains. A yoke of oxen became entangled in crossing and sank. John Michaelson swam the river to save the oxen and went down with them but managed to save himself and the oxen, a feat he has always considered the work of God Almighty."[185] The fact that they forded the Wapsipinicon River means this caravan ferried across the Mississippi River from Fulton, Illinois, to Lyons (Clinton), Iowa, at a place called "The Narrows" where a ferry service was started in the late 1830s (see Figure 6).

The other notable event of the trip occurred near the end of the caravan's journey to northern Story County. According to Havneros, Thor Hill's (aka Thor Olson) wife gave birth to a child east of Nevada, Iowa, on June 26. If the journey had taken the expected three weeks to accomplish, Malinda would have delivered their baby in Palestine Township where Thor had purchased land in 1856.[186]

John and Elizabeth Larson's son, Sam, who was a young boy of age 12 when his parents arrived in Scott Township in 1858, later recalled, "Aside from a few log cabins scattered along Skunk River, the country was practically unsettled. The nearest trading post was Iowa City. They were practically without funds, but were rich in hope, energy and determination of purpose, firmly believing in the great possibilities of this great land where so many of their countrymen had fared well."[187]

The second caravan that arrived in the settlement in 1858 included members of two families, the Christenson and Egland families plus a single man:

>   Mary Christenson and three children
>   Erick and Betsy Egland and son
>   Knud and Maria Egland and three children
>   Single man: Ola Øino aka Oliver Thompson*
>   *Member of the June 1855 scouting party

Mary Christenson's son, Anders, and her step-daughter, Malena Larson, and her husband, Peder Larson, were already living in Scott Township, where the Knud and Marie Egland settled, too. Erick and Britha Egland moved to the Southern Settlement in 1859 or before June 1860. Mr. Øino is likely the Oliver Thompson who was a member of the June 1855 scouting party. After his trip to Iowa in the caravan of 1858, he may have returned to Illinois the following year or the next because he was married in Illinois in 1862 and the following year moved to Story County where he purchased his first 40 acres in Howard Township in 1864.

Nehemias Tjernagel published an account of this caravan's journey to Iowa in his 1922–23 series of articles in *The Story City Herald*, "Little Stories of Pioneer Days." His description of their trip includes an encounter with Indians in Tama County. In their 1842 treaty with the United States, the Sauk and Meskwaki tribes agreed to move to a reservation in Kansas in 1845, and most members of the Sauk tribe complied. Many members of the Meskwaki tribe, however, either hid in unsettled lands along the Cedar, Iowa, Skunk, and Des Moines rivers in central Iowa or resettled with the Potawatomi Indians in southwestern Iowa.[188] In early 1856, Meskwaki leaders decided to use their annuity payments to purchase land in their former settlement area, but they discovered they were not permitted to purchase land because they were not legal citizens of the United States. Through the help of friendly white residents in Tama County and Iowa's Governor James Grimes, a special legislative session passed a law later in the year allowing them to purchase land.[189] When the small caravan of Norwegian immigrants encountered them in 1858, they had just begun to return to their former homeland along the Iowa River, an area known today as the Meskwaki Settlement.

Nehemias writes, "In the year 1858 Endre [Christianson] crossed the prairies from Illinois to Iowa in the company of his mother, his two sisters, Helen (married Haaver Thorson) and Bertha (married Knute Nelson, soldier), also Erick and Knud Egland and Mr. Øino. They drove oxen and it took them three weeks [six weeks[190]] to make the trip. Lars Henryson, Paul Thompson, Tjerand Halsnes (Charles Charleson), Christen Skarhaug (Erickson), Mons Grove and others came at the same time, but Endre's party preferred to travel separately and kept themselves a few miles ahead of the others during the whole journey. It rained much during the trip and they had great trouble in fording swollen streams and crossing make-shift bridges.

"At the Indian reservation near Tama, where they camped, they were joined by three grocery-haulers, who had four oxen with two bulls in lead on each wagon. In the evening Endre and others, together with the grocery-haulers went over to the river to explore into the Indian domiciles there. In the edge of the timber they were met by some ferocious Indian dogs which sent them scurrying back, all except the oldest grocery-man who succeeded in escaping the fangs of the canines and whistled for the others to return. This they did and were met face to face with some Indian braves who escorted them to a place in the deep timber where they were holding a dance and pow-wow. The visitors were invited to seat themselves on straw mats and witness the performances. While sitting thus one of the dancers snatched Endre's hat off his head and he feared he had seen the last of it and would be obliged to go bareheaded the rest of the journey. His companions laughed at him, but it was his turn to laugh when the whirling dancers dexterously picked off the hats of the rest of the party. They drew rapidly away with them as if to hide them, but suddenly returned them as deftly and unexpectedly as they had removed them.

"While watching the Indians in their dancing contortions the head grocer suddenly divested himself of his hampering garb, jumped into the ring and joined the dancers. This gave them great glee, the squaws especially. He took one on each arm, swung them around, and hoisted himself to their shoulders and performed many other antics for their entertainment. Suddenly a stentorian call came from out of the wood and as a mist, quietly as a whisper, the vast throng faded out of sight and our party was left utterly bewildered and alone. The chief had spoken, and the merriment was over for the night."[191]

In 1859, two more families came to the settlement, George and Margrethe Boyd and their four children and Abel and Jorine Olson. The Boyds settled in Ellsworth Township, and the Olsons, who were married in Chicago the same year, arrived in the fall and settled in Howard Township. Ingebrit Chelsvig may have come this year, too, because his name was added to the 1859 call letter to Pastor Amlund. In 1861, he married Britha Erickson whose husband, Christen, died of injuries from a wood cutting accident the year they came to central Iowa.

In 1859 or 1860, the parents of Knud Egland, Erik and Guro Egland, moved to the settlement along with their three youngest daughters.[192]

More families came in 1860. In a biography of Thomas and Helen Lein, their daughter recalled, "In 1860, he moved with his family [including two children] to Iowa in a prairie schooner drawn by a yoke of oxen.... There were twelve other families in the same crowd with them from the same community.[193] There was also danger of highway robbers in those days. I have heard father tell about the wife having what little money they had sewed between her dress and the lining, so it would be safe if they were held up. These families settled in Story County, some in the same community and were neighbors.... Father bought land and settled one mile west of where Roland now is, and a timber claim two and one-fourth miles southwest of there so they would have logs for building their log cabin and stables and wood for fuel. Iowa City was the nearest town; later Boonesborough [which became part of Boone, Iowa, in 1887], where there was a mill."[194] Three of the other families in the 1860 caravan with the Lein family were Ole and Valjer Wierson and their three children, Knudt and Christena Thompson and their three children and his mother, Kjesti,[195] and John and Malena Evenson who settled in Howard Township.[196] The author has not been able to identify the other nine families, some of which appear to have settled in the Southern Settlement according to the Lein biography.

By the end of 1860, the settlement that began in east central Howard Township had spread north into southern Scott Township, and a few families had settled on the west side of the Skunk River in Lafayette and Ellsworth townships.

In total, there were at least 326 Norwegians who lived in the Northern Settlement from 1855 through 1860. Two-hundred and eight of them were born in Norway, 66 were born in Illinois, one was born in Wisconsin, and 51 were born in Iowa. The immigration stories of all of the families and single people are contained in Volume 2 of *The Central Iowa Norwegians*.

Below is a summary of the events marking the beginning of what became known as the Northern Settlement:

1855—Lars Sheldall and Jonas Duea travel to central Iowa in March to see where Lars' brother's scouting party purchased land the previous fall west of the Skunk River near Cambridge in southern Story County and northern Polk County in what became known as the Southern Settlement. Lars and Jonas decide to purchase land farther north near Story City but on the east side of the river in southwestern Scott Township, Hamilton County. Lars and Jonas return to central Iowa in the summer as members of a scouting party sent to investigate purchasing land. On June 14, 1855, the scouting party purchases a large amount of government land east of Story City along Bear Creek in Howard Township. In the fall, the Lars Sheldall family and a recent immigrant, Thor Hegland, move to central Iowa and become the first Norwegians to settle in the area.

1856—The first caravan of immigrants from Lisbon, 17 families and three single people, arrive and begin what became known as the Northern Settlement.

1857–1860—Additional caravans of Lisbon settlers arrive, and the settlement expands into southern Scott Township and west of the Skunk River into Lafayette Township in Story County and Ellsworth Township in Hamilton County.

Making Farmsteads on the Prairie

Central Iowa was mostly unsettled when Norwegian immigrants founded their settlements in 1855 and 1856. Nathan Parker's *Iowa As It Is in 1855* includes reports from the Federal Land Offices regarding vacant lands in the state. Story County was reported as three-fourths vacant, Polk County still had 20,000 acres vacant, and Webster County, which included townships organized into Hamilton County in 1856, was nine-tenths vacant.[197] A biography of Brit Fatland whose parents settled two miles west of Cambridge in 1855 describes the unsettled prairie: "... the country was in a very virgin condition, the prairies not being settled at all, and only a few homes along Skunk River."[198] A biography of Christ Peterson who settled two miles north of Story City on the west side of the Skunk River in 1859 adds to this description of central Iowa: "When Mr. Peterson took up his abode in Hamilton County, he found that the entire district was almost an unbroken prairie. Plenty of wild game abounded and wolves were also frequently seen."[199]

The settlement of Story County began in 1848,[200] and when its first census was taken in 1852, there were only 214 people enumerated in the county.[201] By 1854, the population had grown to 822,[202] and by the time a special Iowa Census was taken in 1856, Story County's population had surged to 2,868.[203] Two years later the population was 3,826,[204] and when the 1860 U. S. Census was conducted in June, 4,051 people were enumerated in the county with 388 of them being of Norwegian descent.[205] There were also 43 Norwegians enumerated in Polk County, 14 near Swede's Point in eastern Boone County, and 95 in southern Hamilton County. Table 2 lists the township locations of the 97 dwelling houses where Norwegian families were enumerated in the two settlements on the 1860 Census and the post offices where the occupants received their mail.

Foremost on the minds of immigrants arriving in central Iowa during late spring in the 1850s was breaking a few acres of prairie before the end of July so the thick roots of the prairie grass and other plants could completely decompose and a crop could be planted the following spring. The tall grass prairie of central Iowa contained numerous sloughs or prairie potholes, so only the high ground was plowed. Immigrants needed to choose sites for homes and cattle sheds, but building them would have to wait until later because they needed to cut prairie grass during the summer to have ample feed for their cattle during the winter months. They also needed to harvest trees and haul logs to building sites to construct their homes, furniture, sheds, and fences.

Table 2
Norwegian dwelling houses enumerated on the
1860 Census in the Southern and Northern Settlements

County	Township	Southern Settlement Dwelling Houses	Northern Settlement Dwelling Houses	Post Office
Boone	Douglas	2		Swede Point
Hamilton	Scott*		18	Story City & Lakins Grove
Polk	Delaware	1		None listed
Polk	Lincoln**	6		Polk City
Story	Howard***		28	Story City
Story	Lafayette		4	Story City
Story	Palestine	15		Cambridge
Story	Union	23		Cambridge
Totals		**47**	**50**	

* Originally named Norway Township until it was changed to Scott Township in 1860
**Lincoln Township was part of Madison Township until 1870 when it was organized as a separate township.
***Howard Township was part of Lafayette Township until 1860 when it was organized as a separate township.

While the important tasks of choosing a building site, breaking prairie, and harvesting prairie grass and trees were completed, families in the caravans who arrived southwest of Cambridge on June 7, 1855, and east of Story City on June 14, 1856, lived in their covered wagons. The census taker for the 1856 Iowa Census found recent arrivals, E. R. and Betsy Sheldahl, camped with his parents and youngest sister, two other sisters and their husbands, his first cousin who was single at the time, and Betsy's mother. A family historian for E. R. and Betsy states, "They traveled to Iowa with 17 families in covered wagons in which they lived all summer, five families using one stove. In the fall, Mr. Sheldahl built a small one-room log cabin which was their home for 11 years, when they built a new home."[206]

Most of the families in the caravan who arrived in the Southern Settlement on June 7, 1855, had already purchased land from the federal government. For others, finding land to purchase was their most pressing need. If they could find property quickly, they, too, could still break some prairie that summer. A few were able to purchase government-owned land up through mid-1856, but after that the only government land that could be purchased for $1.25 per acre was swamp or overflow land. This was land the federal government designated unfit for cultivation and deeded to the state of Iowa under the Swamp Land Act of 1850. The state of Iowa in turn deeded the land to the counties who sold it to people who agreed to drain the land and convert it to agricultural and other uses. In 1858 and 1859, the Simon Arntz, Oliver Dobbe, and Severt Helland families and Ole Tesdall, were able to purchase government land this way. For those who were unable to purchase swamp land and had to purchase property privately from previous owners, the average price per acre for virgin prairie was $2.53.[207]

In the Northern Settlement, most of the families who arrived on July 14, 1856, had also purchased land from the federal government, but the families who arrived in 1857 through 1860 had to purchase land from previous owners as there was very little government or swamp land available in Howard Township and southern Scott Township where most of them settled. They paid prices ranging from $1.25 to $18.75 per acre depending on how close the land they purchased was to the Skunk River and if the land had been improved, i.e., any of the prairie had been broken and farmed.[208] Those who purchased land two or more miles away from the river paid an average of $3.09 per acre while the average cost of land purchased within a mile from the river was $6.67 per acre.[209]

The Lars B. Olson family paid the high price of $18.75 per acre.[210] Soon after they arrived in the settlement in June 1857, they purchased 80 acres two miles north of Story City on the west side of the river. Lars had immigrated to Illinois in 1836, and for the 1850 Census, he reported owning real estate worth $500[211] which explains how he could afford to pay this high price. For the 1860 Census, Lars and Ubjor reported their 80 acres as all improved land which also may have meant they did not have any prairie to break when they purchased it and that it also came with a home and set of farm buildings.[212]

Essential for every family who moved to central Iowa during its early years of settlement was wood for fuel and constructing buildings.

According to John Scott, an 1856 immigrant to Story County and author of three chapters in Goodspeed's 1890 history of the county, "The native timber on Skunk River and in adjacent groves ... was of fair quality, and in furnishing the early population with fuel, fencing and building material, was of great value."[213] He added, "A large portion of the best timberlands was sold off in small tracts to those who lived on the adjacent prairie. The best trees were taken as logs to the sawmills; others were cut and split into posts and rails for fencing; others were dressed down for framing timbers for dwellings and barns; and from the tops of these, and from standing and fallen trees in the timber, there was obtained most of the fuel used for the first fifteen or twenty years of occupation."[214]

Some of the families purchased timber lots or had scouting parties buy them prior to moving to central Iowa. If they did not own a timber lot prior to coming to Iowa, purchasing a lot was another immediate priority upon their arrival. For those who bought privately-owned land, a timber lot was occasionally part of the land purchase, but it was normally purchased separately. The average size of a timber lot owned by early central Iowa Norwegians was 5–7 acres, and the average price per acre was $13.78 with the better quality timber lots costing up to $30 per acre.[215]

Soon after the caravan of families arrived in Howard Township on June 14, 1856, some of the property owners requested the county surveyor to locate their land and timber lots. Eight of the requests during June and July 1856 were for land surveys, and the rest were for timber lot surveys. The first person to have a timber lot surveyed was Rasmus Ask whose lot in the northwest corner section of the township was surveyed on June 18, 1856.[216] Others who had timber lots surveyed by the county's surveyor that summer were Shur Britson, Jacob Erickson, Thor Hegland, Erick Jacobson, John Nelson, and Torkel Opstvedt.[217] Several of the surveys included a drawing of the area surveyed with the species of trees and their quantity. Among the trees species listed were ash, black walnut, cottonwood, elm, hickory, linden, maple, oak (black, red, and white), and willow. In addition to the county surveyor, there were five other Story County surveyors enumerated on the 1856 Iowa Census, and other families may have hired one of them to survey their land or timber.

The arrival of immigrants to Story County in the early '50s created a need for sawmills so settlers could have wood milled if they could afford it. East of Cambridge, Chandler's water-powered sawmill began operation on the Skunk River in 1854, and a short distance downstream another water-powered mill, Nellis' Mill, also began operating in the mid-

1850s.[218] During 1856–1857, J. C. Sladden, the owner of a small store in Cambridge who had been helpful to the Norwegians when they arrived in 1855, opened a steam-powered sawmill in Ballard Grove in Palestine Township.[219]

In Fairview, the first sawmill, a water-powered sawmill, was constructed in 1854 or 1855, but it was a failure.[220] A steam-powered sawmill was constructed in 1856, but it was moved to another location a year later and replaced by another steam-powered sawmill, Messer's Mill, in 1857.[221] This mill operated until 1865 when it was sold and moved away, and then the nearest railroad depot was the only place settlers could obtain milled lumber.

At least one family was able to have a considerable amount of wood milled when they moved to central Iowa. This was the Ole T. Hegland family who emigrated from Skånevik in 1857 and settled in Howard Township the same year. Ole and Britha's two oldest sons, Thor and Lars, immigrated to Lisbon, Illinois, in 1854, and in the fall of 1855, Thor moved to central Iowa with the Lars Sheldall family. Many years later, their youngest son, Michael Hegland, related the following story about his family's trip to Story County: "The Hegland family upon coming west took the train to Iowa City, whence they and their belongings were hauled in covered wagons, drawn by ox teams, to their destination. They were entertained at the home of Rasmus Larson Tungesvig the first few days after their arrival, and later they lived with the Jonas Duea family for a few months till their own home could be built and made ready for them. ... During the stay at the Duea home the elder Hegland and his boys rushed the building of their own dwelling with might and main, and soon had a large frame house built from lumber fetched from Harden's sawmill [Harding's sawmill also known as 'Messers Mill'[222]] on the Skunk near Story City. This was the first large frame house built for many miles around and was often used as an inn for travelers, for purposes of worship, and for meetings of other kinds."[223]

The Hegland frame home was not only an unusual sight in northwest Story County in the late 1850s, but also it was unusual to see a frame home in other parts of the county because almost all immigrants were living in log cabins or dugouts during this time. With a plentiful growth of trees beside the Skunk River on the western side of the county and Indian Creek in the southwest part of the county, immigrants had an abundant source of building material. Julian E. McFarland, a life-long student of the history of central Iowa, described cabin-raising in *A History of the Pioneer Era on the Iowa Prairies*: "With the help of neighbors, it took only a day or two to raise a cabin, but for a 'loner' it would be a more formidable task."[224] McFarland continues, "The site of the cabin was chosen by reason of the accessibility of wood and water, or by reason of suitability of terrain. Often the presence of a spring dictated the site, and even a rudimentary spring could usually be converted to a well which would provide water for the family and for the livestock."[225]

K. B. Thompson's reminiscences of the first year in the Southern Settlement southwest of Cambridge describe their one-room log cabins as being either 12 by 16 feet or 14 by 18 feet with a door and one window.[226] Thompson does not, however, mention any of the settlers living in dugouts, but there was at least one family whose first home was a dugout and surely there were others. The Osmund Siverson family moved to the settlement in 1857. They lived with his brother's family, the John Severson family, the first year before moving into their dugout. Their daughter, Margretha, recalled, "We lived in this dug-out for seven years. While living here my father dug a little square hole under the floor for the water to come in and my mother dipped water out of this when she washed clothes. One day when she was washing she left the lid off, and being a little girl, I fell in and got all wet. I had some of my clothes in the wash and did not have any dry ones to put on so mother put me to bed— I had to stay there until my clothes got dry."[227]

Dugouts were common in the Northern Settlement near Story City. Carrie Knutson was seven years old when her parents moved to southern Hamilton County in 1861. In a memoir written many years later, she remembered, "So many lived in dugouts—just one room and some did not even have a floor—usually one small window although some had two and some sealed them and had floor. They were very warm in winter and cool in summer. They never were afraid of storms in them—most were dug in a hillside."[228]

Some of the families who founded the settlement in June 1856 must have built dugouts. Havneros states, "The settlers worked diligently to build sheds for their livestock, and dwelling houses and caves for themselves."[229] H. B. Henryson, who moved to the settlement with his parents in 1857, referred to the dugouts as caves when his pioneer story was recorded: "The settlers lived mostly in log cabins, the dimensions of these primitive abodes being as restricted as possible merely to accommodate their inmates temporarily until a better day dawned. Often they were only 12 by 14 feet, but snug and warm as you please. Many dug caves in the hills to live in. These were sod-roofed. Into these rude dwellings there would sometimes enter the most unwelcome company such as snakes, toads, lizards and the like, which would run in for longer or shorter visits."[230]

A biography of Ole and Margaret Nernes who settled near Cambridge in 1855 states, "They tell of how three families lived together in a log house about twelve feet square ...,"[231] but except for married children living with their parents or other extended members of the family, multiple-family living arrangements appear to have been infrequent and temporary during the first five and one-half years of settlement. An examination of the special state census taken during June 1856 shows all but two of the families who settled near Cambridge in 1855 were enumerated in separate dwelling houses.

The Knud Bauge and Erick Tesdahl families were two of the Southern Settlement families enumerated in June 1856 living in the same dwelling house. Erick's wife, Barbro, died soon after they arrived in the settlement,[232] so perhaps this is why Erick and his five children were living with Knud and Kari Bauge. The Barney Hill and Iver Twedt families, also founders of the settlement, were also enumerated in the same dwelling house in June 1856. Barney and Iver lived on farms next to each other in Norway and emigrated together in 1849. Barney purchased a three-acre timber lot in Ballard Grove in August 1855, and trees from there were likely used to construct their dwelling house because neither family purchased land until the summer of 1856.

John and Betsy Michaelson moved to the Northern Settlement in 1858 and lived with the Erick (E.R.) Sheldahl family their first year in central Iowa.[233] Moving to the settlement together with the Michaelsons were Knudt and Brita Johnson and their daughter, Hattie. An obituary for Brita recorded, "For the first year they made their home at the John Michaelson home southwest of here [Roland, Iowa], then moved north of Story City for a few years, after which they moved to the farm that was the home at the time of her death."[234] The author of Brita Johnson's obituary was probably correct about the Johnson and Michaelson families living together and did not know both families were living in the Erick Sheldahl family log home. In 1859, the Michaelsons purchased an existing log house from a nearby neighbor, Dr. Moses Ballard, and moved it to their 80 acres. When the 1860 Census was enumerated, they were sharing their home with John and Malena Evenson. The Evensons may have lived there more than a year because they did not purchase a timber lot until December 1861 and did not purchase farm land until 1863.

On the 1860 Census, there were six dwelling houses where more than one family was living. In addition to the Michaelsons, Knud and

Kari Bauge were again sharing their home with Kari's mother and her two young children and Kari's sister and her husband and their one-year old child. Three other families had either adult married children living with them or a brother and his family. The sixth dwelling house where multiple families were living was owned by Bernett Reinertson who lived in southern Hamilton County. Anders and Helga Christenson and their young children and Anders' mother and sister were living with Bernett. They had all emigrated from the same parish and may have known each other in Norway.

When census takers visited dwelling houses for the 1860 Census, in addition to enumerating each person living in the dwelling house, they also collected information about the full market value of real estate owned by the occupants. Table 3 summarizes the value of real estate owned reported at the dwelling houses within each Norwegian settlement. It provides an overview of the general economic well-being of the settlements and the progress families were making in establishing farmsteads on the prairie in Story, Polk, and Hamilton counties.

Table 3
Value of real estate owned reported for 97
central Iowa Norwegian dwelling houses on the 1860 Census

Value of Real Estate Owned	Southern Settlement		Northern Settlement		Totals
	Dwelling Houses	Average Value	Dwelling Houses	Average Value	
$0	8	$0	8	$0	16
$1–499	16	$279	11	$265	27
$500–999	15	$564	19	$663	34
$1,000–1,499	6	$1,066	7	$1,029	13
$1,500–1,999	0	$0	3	$1,533	3
$2,000–2,500	2	$2,100	2	$2,000	4
Totals	47	$449	50	$547	97

Occupants in 16 of the 97 dwelling houses did not own real estate indicating these families were still trying to gain a foothold in central Iowa. They were mostly families who immigrated to the United States in 1854 or later.[235] The families in the next two categories who owned less than $1,000 worth of real estate representing two-thirds of the total were families who had been able to purchase land and begin farming. They were a mixture of families who immigrated in the late-1840s and the mid-1850s or later. With the exception of two families,[236] the 20 families who owned $1,000 or more worth of real estate were those who had immigrated to Illinois by 1850 and moved to Iowa with financial resources and apparent successful farming experience in the tall grass prairie environment of Illinois.[237]

Nine of the scouting party members who selected the locations of the two central Iowa Norwegian settlements were established farmers in Illinois, and yet they and other families who owned land chose to move.[238] What caused them to "pick up stakes" as it were and move to the edge of the American frontier where the nearest railroad depot was 120 miles away when they already had built up a pioneer farmstead and were close to a town with a railroad depot where they could purchase supplies and sell their products?[239]

Was their motivation, as early histories assert,[240] to help recent immigrants purchase land they could afford, or did they have other reasons for moving to central Iowa? Answers to the question of why they chose to move are still a mystery because information about their specific reasons for this decision has not been found. Without it, historians are left with only questions. Appendix F contains further thoughts regarding why established farmers chose to move to Iowa.

Farming on the Frontier

Prior to the invention of a steel moldboard[241] in 1833, breaking the strong roots of the prairie grasses usually required land owners to hire someone with a large breaking plow pulled by three to six yoke of oxen. These plows cut furrows 20 to 32 inches wide and one and one-half to two inches deep: "Three yokes of good-sized oxen drawing a 24-inch plow with two men to manage the work would ordinarily break about two acres a day."[242] Prairie breakers usually received $2.50 to $4.50 per acre, the wage differential depending on whether or not they received meals or lodging or feed for their oxen.

Until plows with steel moldboards became available, the prairie soil constantly clogged settlers' wooden and cast iron plows requiring them to stop plowing to clean the moldboard with a wooden paddle: "In 1833, John Lane, an Illinois blacksmith, cut three lengths of steel from an old saw and fastened two to the moldboard and another to the share. This worked quite effectively, but Lane did not apply for a patent."[243] This set the stage for John Deere."[244] Deere made his first plow in his blacksmith shop in Grand Detour, Illinois, in 1837. In 1848, he moved his factory 75 miles southwest to Moline, Illinois, by a railroad alongside the Mississippi River. In 1857, John Deere produced 10,000 plows.[245]

Prairie historian, Daryl D. Smith, asserts, "The tough prairie sod was an almost insurmountable obstacle to the early prairie settlers. ... Much of the initial prairie breaking was done with massive unwieldy breaking plows pulled by several yokes of oxen and operated by custom crews. Subsequent technological developments changed the problems of plowing prairie sod from formidable obstacles to temporary inconveniences." Citing the Deere plow and the Oliver Chilled Plow manufactured by James Oliver, Smith continued, "These plows proved to be very effective for breaking prairie."[246]

In spite of the steel plow being available, the wooden plow was still being used in central Iowa as late as 1862. A biography of Frank A. McLain, an early immigrant to Story County who settled near Nevada, states, "He came to Story County, Iowa, in May, 1854, and the following year, in partnership with J. R. Lockwood, he bought four yoke of oxen and broke prairie at $3 per acre, after which, for some time, he was engaged in teaming to the river."[247] After Ole and Sarah Ritland moved their family from Lisbon, Illinois, to northwest Story County in 1857, two of their sons broke prairie. Their family history records, "The two oldest sons, Ole O. and Jens, were in partnership farming and breaking the prairie at a certain price per acre using a huge breaking plow drawn by eight oxen. They were so occupied until Jens volunteered for service in the Civil War ...."[248] Another person in the Northern Settlement who broke prairie was John Christian whose biography also mentions breaking prairie: "He came to the United States [in 1847] when a lad of fifteen and passed his early youth in Kendall County, Illinois. In 1857, he moved to Story County. His employment at first was teaming, and he also engaged in cultivating new prairie land ...."[249]

When Thor and Erik Ericson, 1854 immigrants to Illinois, wrote to their brothers in Norway in 1855 to encourage them to emigrate and to inform them about the $1.25 per acre land in Iowa, they listed a plow among the items necessary to move to Iowa. They wrote that the plow would cost $12–14.[250] Although plows are not mentioned in the histories of the Lisbon area settlers' migration to central Iowa, Jacob Erickson likely brought a plow with him in 1856. An obituary for his oldest son, Mikel, states when they arrived in Howard Township they, "... at once proceeded to break the sod on which to raise a crop."[251]

The 1856 Iowa Census reported that families living in 502 Story County dwelling houses had broken 8,484 acres of the 60,529 acres they owned. They grew spring and winter wheat, oats, and corn on the broken acres and harvested hay (prairie grass) from the unbroken land.[252] They also sold 879 hogs and 382 cattle and produced 11,302 pounds of butter, 169 pounds of cheese, and 740 pounds of wool. The 1860 Federal Census also required enumerators to collect agricultural product information. They obtained this information at 52 of the 81 Norwegian dwelling houses where the occupants owned real estate.[253] The following tables present some of this information and provide a glimpse into frontier farming—the acres of improved and unimproved land owned, the tools and implements used to farm and the crops grown, and the livestock owned and other products produced after the first five years of settlement.

Table 4 shows the average number of improved acres i.e., plowed land, and unimproved acres and the average total number of acres owned by farmers in each settlement. The 52 farmers owned a total of 7,111 acres of land in 1860, slightly over 11 sections of land. Almost 30% of it, 2,095 acres, was improved land suitable for growing corn and small grains like wheat and oats.

Histories describing the caravans that brought Norwegian families to central Iowa reveal most of the covered wagons were driven with ox teams. Oley Nelson states the families who founded the first central Iowa Norwegian settlement southwest of Cambridge in June of 1855 were "... transported by eighteen covered wagons drawn by ox teams; six covered wagons drawn by horses and one single spring wagon."[254] In August 1855, a second caravan of families left the Lisbon Settlement to join them. Rasmus Sheldall's account of this caravan recalled, "Fifteen wagon outfits started out from Lisbon at one time .... Some of the owners of the wagons drove oxen, others horses, and some of them possessed both oxen and horses."[255] Ivar Havneros states the caravan of families who founded the settlement east of Story City in June 1856 "... consisted of 18 covered wagons drawn by eighteen span of oxen and two horses."[256] In describing his trip to the Northern Settlement in 1857, H. B. Henryson remembered, "There were twelve wagons in the party, two being drawn by horses and the rest by oxen."[257]

Table 4
Acres of land owned by 52 central Iowa Norwegian families in 1860

Type of Land	29 Farmers in the Southern Settlement		23 Farmers in the Northern Settlement	
	Range	Average	Range	Average
Acres of improved land	6–50	24	20–160	62
Acres of unimproved land	17–360	96	8–290	101
Total acres of land owned	42–400	120	40–330	163

Table 5 shows draft animal ownership among the 52 Norwegian families during the summer of 1860. By this time, over one-half of the families (27) were farming exclusively with horses, 13 families were farming with both horses and oxen, and 12 families were farming with only a pair of oxen. Overall, horses outnumbered oxen owned by the 52 families by a margin of 72 to 49, a sign that they were prospering but not quite at the level of farmers in general in the state who owned 3.2 horses and mules for every ox.[258]

The trend of replacing oxen with horses and mules would continue, but using oxen was a wise choice for immigrants moving to unsettled areas. While they were slower than horses and mules, they were cheaper to purchase, could pull heavier loads for longer periods of time, and could live by eating prairie grasses. Their pulling power and better traction made oxen the preferred draft animal for immigrants to drive across the wet prairie and to break prairie sod with John Deere or similar plows: "After the land was opened up and could be plowed more easily and more advanced riding farm tools were developed, horses frequently replaced the oxen."[259]

Table 5
Draft animals owned by 52 central Iowa Norwegian families in 1860

Draft Animals	Families in Southern Settlement	Number of Animals	Families in Northern Settlement	Number of Animals
Oxen only	9	2 each	3	2 each
Oxen and Horses	6	2 oxen and 1–4 horses	7	2–4 oxen and 1–5 horses
Horses only	14	1–4	13	2–4
Totals	29	26 oxen & 35 horses	23	23 oxen & 47 horses

Among the food, cooking utensils, clothing, bedding, and other supplies packed in the covered wagons of these families when they moved to central Iowa were tools and equipment for building homes and beginning farming. Typical tools and equipment included: "set of augers, gimlet, ax, hammer, hoe, plow, shovel, spade, whetstone, oxbows, axles, kingbolts, ox shoes, spokes, wagon tongue, heavy ropes, and chains."[260] Some or all of the following harvesting tools were likely in their wagons, too—scythes, cradles, flails, screens, husking pins, and corn knives.

The value of farming implements and machinery was another topic census enumerators inquired about when they visited dwelling houses in 1860. In the Southern Settlement, the value of farming implements and machinery ranged from $10 to $145 with an average of $43, and in the Northern Settlement the range was $30 to $150 with an average of $69.

Farming on the frontier was labor-intensive. Implements used in field preparation consisted of a plow and harrow made from a V-shaped branch of a tree. Grain was sown and planted by hand and the hoe was the primary tool for weed control. The scythe and cradle were used for harvesting wheat and other grains and prairie grass, and the flail and screen were used for threshing grain. Corn was picked by hand with the help of husking pins or cut with a knife and shocked for drying.

Census takers visited seven dwelling houses where the value of implements and machinery reported was $100 or more. The Ole Apland, Lars B. Olson, John Pierson, and Paul Thompson families owned implements and machinery worth $100, and the value of the Jacob

Erickson, Erick Sheldahl, and Osmund Sheldahl families' implements and machinery was $145–150. Iowa farmers used threshers, mowers, and the McCormick and Manny reapers in the 1850s[261] but mainly in the settled part of the state. The cost of the latest two-horse McCormick Reaper and Mower in 1860 was $140, and that was the cost if a farmer purchased it in Chicago where it was manufactured,[262] so with the exception of the plow and harrow, farming for the 52 families was done with hand tools.

Frontier farmers who were able to break prairie in April could plant sod corn and expect half the crop that would be produced on sod fully decomposed. Sod corn was planted by using an ax to cut a gash in freshly broken prairie sod, dropping kernels of corn into it, and covering them. Immigrants arriving at the beginning of summer, however, had to wait until the following spring to plant their first crop. Hay was the only crop they could harvest their first year on the prairie.

In 1857, the year after Norwegians began settling east of Story City in Howard Township, Dr. Moses Ballard purchased an 80-acre improved farm in the southwest part of the township and a 12-acre timber lot beside the Skunk River all for the price of $11 per acre.[263] His son, H. D. Ballard, later recalled, "I remember the prairie grass was much higher than I had ever seen before. ... That year I with my brothers put up nearly 100 tons of wild hay for our stock and did it with a common scythe. We did not consider it very great hardship to do this. Grass was fully three feet high and stood thick on the ground and often we cut grass more than four feet high.[264] We let it lie in the swatch one day and then piled it up into a 'hay cock' as it was then known.

"With the amount of work we had on hand, the summer soon passed and when the autumn came corn in the field had to be husked. Father was an eastern Yankee and he insisted that every husk and silk should be taken off from every ear.... Such work was slow and we did not crib half as many bushels per day as the ordinary man does now. Corn then was not nearly as large as it is now. A yield of 25 and 30 bushels [per acre] was considered a good crop and it was often discussed and decided that we were on the north line of the Corn Belt which seems a laughable circumstance now. We raised wheat, oats, corn, potatoes, buckwheat, etc., the next year and were happy."[265]

Wheat and oats were sown by grabbing a handful of grain from a bag and scattering it while walking across the field at a steady pace, and a harrow was dragged across the field to work the seed into the ground. John Michaelson's obituary states, "The spring and summer [of 1858] was terribly wet. ... He had $6.00 when he came and no work to be had. This year was a bad one. Many were sorely disappointed. Erick Sheldahl sowed eight bushels of wheat in the spring and reaped eight bushels in the fall. This first summer Mr. Michaelson plowed up the sod on his eighty, and in the fall he and Mr. Sheldahl husked corn here for one John Smith southwest of here for which they received each a bushel of corn a day and one bushel for the use of the team. They divided the salary and so they each had a bushel and a half a day for their labor. ... Grandpa Michaelson has told us that when he bought the farm ..., he broke up the sod south of the creek and sowed wheat for which he received $2 a bushel and the first crop paid for the land."

Corn could be planted by placing kernels of corn on the ground and covering them by hand or with a stick or by using a home-made stab planter. After the stab planter was pushed into the ground, the blades of the planter were opened and the kernels were dropped. Stepping on the hill of corn completed the planting process. Sina Kloster Moran's grandparents, Severt and Kari Nass, immigrated to Lisbon, Illinois, in 1857 and moved to the Southern Settlement in 1866 or 1867. Sina's biography of her grandparents describes how her mother planted corn: "Corn was planted by hand and mother told about how grandpa put three kernels of corn in each hill and how she as a small girl followed behind and spaced the corn evenly (using a small stick), so that the kernels should not be too close together, and then she covered the hills, and what back breaking work it was and how glad she was when that job was finished."[266]

Table 6 shows the grain and hay harvested in the two settlements by the 52 Central Iowa Norwegian families in 1859.[267] Corn was the main crop used not only to feed hogs and cattle, but also as a food staple for families. Oats were grown for horse feed, and wheat and rye could be used for livestock, too, but their main use was for baking or selling or trading for other items a family needed. Their hay was the prairie grass they cut from the unbroken sections of their land.

In addition to the oxen and horses yoked and harnessed to the covered wagons that brought Norwegian families to central Iowa, families brought cattle and chickens with them. Oley Nelson's 1905 history of the settlement founded southwest of Cambridge on June 7, 1855, does not mention the families bringing cattle, but Apland's 1945 "re-compiled, corrected and added to" version of Nelson's history does mention cattle: "Another time, the cattle went down the stream and they had quite a time to round them up."[268] Rasmus Sheldall was eight years old in late summer 1855 when he traveled with his parents, Lars and Herbor, to Iowa. Years later, he related his experiences to local historian, Nehemias Tjernagel: "Fifteen wagon outfits started out from Lisbon at one time, together with a herd of about 150 head of cattle."[269]

Table 6
Grain and hay harvested by
52 central Iowa Norwegian families in 1859

Grain, Potatoes, & Hay Harvested	29 Farmers in the Southern Settlement		23 Farmers in the Northern Settlement	
	Range	Average	Range	Average
Corn, bushels of	20–800	249	50–800	196
Wheat, bushels of	1–180	49	20–80	53
Oats, bushels of	0–200	26	0–50	11
Rye, bushels of	0–20	2	0	0
Hay, tons of	0–40	20	4–50	23

A history of the caravan of families who settled in northern Story County in 1856 states, "They had a fairly large herd of cows and young cattle, also a flock of chickens."[270] Another account of a caravan that came to the Northern Settlement in 1857 records, "There were twelve wagons in the party, two being drawn by horses and the rest by oxen. The other livestock consisted of eighty head of cattle. Two calves were born on the way, and more important still, a child.[271] All fared well."[272]

Accounts of the caravans of Norwegian families moving to central Iowa do not mention bringing swine or sheep with them, but Dr. Moses Ballard had his sons bring his flock of about 40 sheep plus 30 head of cows and heifers when they moved from northeastern Illinois to central Iowa in 1857.[273] The Ballard family, like the Norwegian families, must have purchased swine from local farmers.

Curtis A. Wood, whose parents settled in southeastern Story County near Iowa Center in 1852, recalled, "Cattle and hogs ran at will. The cattle of the well-to-do farmer were rounded up at night into pounds. The swine foraged in the woods till winter, and each owner's were marked. The ear mark known as 'two swallow forks' told that the animal was Mr. Wood's, and the 'one swallow fork and an under-bit' said that it was Lot Morris's."[274] This method of keeping track of who owned the pigs may have worked in 1852 when there were only 214 people living in the county, but as more and more immigrant families arrived, farmers needed to build fences for swine.

H. D. Ballard remembered, "At that time [when the nearest railroad depot was 120 miles away] what the farmer had to sell did not bring much. Dressed hogs hauled to the end of the railroad at Iowa City brought two dollars per 100 pounds if the weight equaled 200 pounds; if 225, $2.25 ...."[275] Rasmus Sheldall told a story about his father: "On one occasion old Mr. Sheldall took a load of dressed hogs to Iowa City, but got so little for them that he was in debt by the time he came back and all the expenses of the trip had been reckoned and paid."[276]

Table 7 shows the average number of livestock owned by the 52 central Iowa Norwegian families in 1860. They owned a total of 214 milk cows, 203 other cattle, 178 swine, and 23 sheep. Every family owned at least one milk cow with over two-thirds of the families owning between two and nine milk cows. The most common number of swine owned was two (19 families) with 14 of the families owning five or more swine. There were only five families who owned sheep, the Salamon Heggen, Thomas Houge, Lars Henryson, John Nelson, and Lars B. Olson families, who owned a total of 23 sheep.

Table 7
Average number of livestock owned
by 52 central Iowa Norwegian families in 1860

Livestock Owned	29 Families in the Southern Settlement		23 Families in the Northern Settlement	
	Range	Average	Range	Average
Milk cows	2–6	3.6	1–9	4.8
Other cattle	0–9	3.1	0–20	4.7
Swine	0–8	3.0	1–10	4.0
Sheep	0–5	0.2	0–7	0.7

Families moving to the frontier country of central Iowa tucked seeds for vegetable gardens and maybe some favorite flowers among their belongings in their covered wagons. Arriving late in the spring, they knew they could not plant crops on prairie that was not broken before June, nor could they plant their garden seeds until the following spring. In the meantime, they had to make do with the provisions they brought with them and the food and livestock feed they might be able to obtain from neighbors with the little money they had or by working for it. Until a rail line reached central Iowa and they could begin to market their agricultural products outside of their local area, they knew they would be living in a subsistence agricultural economy where they were growing only enough food to feed their families and their livestock.

In planning farmsteads, immigrant families needed to choose a building location where they could break prairie close to their log cabins or dugouts, so close that they could literally walk out the door of their homes into their "kitchen gardens" to harvest what they needed. Most of the adults did not read English well enough to understand an article on kitchen, fruit, and flower gardens in the horticultural section of the April 1, 1854, issue of *The Prairie Farmer*, but in designing their vegetable gardens they still may have followed its advice: "The vegetable garden may be laid out in narrow beds or squares, as best suit the form of the grounds, or the convenience of tillage. But bear in mind that protection from blighting winds is of great moment in the production of early vegetables. A close fence, or a well clipped hedge, backed or lined with evergreens, is the best and most appropriate defense."[277]

The only garden products recorded for the 52 families were the bushels of potatoes harvested in 1859. Table 8 shows the average number of bushels harvested in each settlement. Potatoes were stored in a root cellar or buried and covered with straw to keep them from freezing.

Table 8
Agricultural products produced by 52 central
Iowa Norwegian families for year ending June 1, 1860

Products	29 Families in the Southern Settlement		23 Families in the Northern Settlement	
	Range	Average	Range	Average
Potatoes, bushels	0–100	33	1–100	42
Butter, pounds	0–600	176	50–800	377
Molasses, gallons	0–30	6	0–52	7

Butter churns were essential household items families brought with them. Two cows normally produced more milk than the average family needed, so the excess butter could be sold or traded with neighbors. Molasses and sorghum were their only sweeteners. H. D. Ballard's sister, Sarah Boyes, recalled, "In pioneer days, wheat bread was a luxury, as we lived principally on corn bread, but with plenty of vegetables, and all the wild fruit necessary, sweetened with sorghum. Molasses was relished then."[278] Families usually planted one-fourth to one and one-half acres of sugar cane which was processed into molasses in the fall.[279]

In addition to fish from the Skunk River and wild game which was plentiful, families slaughtered or sold their chickens, pigs, or cattle. H. D. Ballard related, "... three year old fat steers off the grass in the autumn brought from $18 to $19 per head, and milch cows from $10 to $12 per head. Butter brought four to five cents per pound and eggs three cents per dozen, and no cash for either, but trade only. ... These are the reasons that people did not make any more than a bare living in those days."[280]

The agricultural production information reported by the 52 families for the 1860 Census provides clear evidence of the progress Norwegians were making in establishing their two central Iowa Norwegian settlements. The families in the Southern Settlement had harvested three crops, and it was the second harvest for the families in the Northern Settlement. Other families living in the two settlements in June 1860 were looking forward to harvesting their first crop, and still others were breaking prairie to plant their first crop the following spring. Yet, for every family living in central Iowa in 1860 and anywhere in frontier America, life would continue to be based primarily on a subsistence economy until rail lines came closer. For families in central Iowa, the nearest train depots were still 120 miles away in Cedar Rapids and Iowa City.

Central Iowa historian, Julian McFarland, was fortunate to have lived during a time when he could listen to pioneers relate stories about their early farming days. McFarland commented, "The labor of getting in the grain crop was extensive. Over in Illinois ingenious blacksmiths were busy inventing harvesting tools and equipment, heralding the revolution, but these inventions hardly touched central Iowa. Here the grain was still cut with a scythe, perhaps with the added cradle, allowed to dry, and put up by hand. It required well-developed farms with large fields to justify the new mowers and reapers as well as large amounts of working capital, and neither was yet available.

"Meanwhile the inventions heralding the farm revolution were all made. The most far-reaching were the steel plow, the various reapers, barbed wire, and clay tile for drainage. But that is another story, and deserves special treatment. None of these improvements except the plow appeared in central Iowa before the Civil War."[281]

The Frontier Economy

Histories and reminiscences of the central Iowa Norwegians refer to the long distances early settlers had to travel to the nearest train depot to obtain supplies. The most frequently mentioned destination was Iowa City which received train service in 1855 and was 120 miles from the settlements. This rail line reached Grinnell in 1863 bringing it within 60 miles of the Southern Settlement. Cedar Rapids (30 miles north of Iowa City) received rail service in 1859, and by 1862, this line had reached Marshalltown, 45 miles away from the Northern Settlement.

During these early years, some supplies that could not be purchased locally were available in Des Moines where the first steamboat arrived in 1843 bringing soldiers and supplies to establish a U. S. military garrison at the confluence of the Raccoon and Des Moines Rivers.[282] In 1859, the year after John and Betsey Michaelson moved to the settlement east of Story City, John traveled 45 miles to Des Moines to buy a new stove,[283] but long trips like this to Des Moines or the nearest train depot were unusual.

When the 1856 Iowa Census was taken, there were 18 merchants enumerated in Story County, and settlers relied on them for many of the supplies they needed. Chapter 17 of Goodspeed's *Biographical and Historical Memoirs of Story County* contains sketches of Story County towns and is an excellent source for a history of the county's towns up to 1890. Historian Rev. B. A. Konkle, author of the chapter, was a careful and thorough researcher, and included in his sketches is information about the county's first stores. In 1856, there were stores in Nevada, Story City, Iowa Center, New Philadelphia (west of Ames), and Cambridge.[284]

Iowa Center's second store was opened by F. W. Baldwin. Konkle recorded, "When Mr. Baldwin began business he hauled his stock from Keokuk [in the southeast corner of Iowa]. By about 1856, the Rock Island Railway had reached Iowa City, and he went there, then Marengo was the next trading point, and finally Kellogg. When the North-Western Railway [it was still the Cedar Rapids and Missouri River Railroad] reached Marshall [Marshalltown], the firm went there and successively followed the terminal point from there to State Center and Colo."[285]

J. C. Sladden, another early merchant in Iowa Center, was probably Cambridge's first merchant.[286] In his history of the Palestine congregation, Andrew Maland states, "Shortly after their arrival [on June 7, 1855] the colonists made the acquaintance of J. C. Sladden, who was operating a small store in Cambridge, then a town of only a few houses. Having lived there a winter or two, first as a squatter, he was of much help to the colonists in making preparations for the winter months, especially in conserving things which nature provided—such as wild crab-apples, grapes, nuts and honey, which were to be found in the woods as well as wild game, which was plentiful on the wild prairie. Mr. Sladden procured his supplies from Iowa City. It took him five days to make the trip."[287]

In the northwest part of the county, three stores opened in Story City in 1856, the same year Norwegians founded a second central Iowa settlement on the prairie east of the village. An early history of the county recorded, "About this time, a store was opened at Fairview [Story City] where a lively trade was carried on between butter and eggs upon one side and groceries upon the other."[288] In July 1857, the editor of the county's first newspaper, *The Story County Advocate*, made a trip to Webster City in northwest Hamilton County: "On this trip, Editor Thrall stopped at Story City where he found his friend, Morganson, at his counter ready for customers …. He appeared to be doing a good, big business in the way of catering to the wants of his customers."[289]

W. O. Payne's 1911 *History of Story County, Iowa* contains numerous references to the first store in the county seat town of Nevada. The following excerpts concerning this store are likely representative of the first general stores established in other Story County towns: "T. E. Alderman was the first resident of the town, as well as the first merchant. He erected the first building … in the autumn of 1853. It was made of roughly dressed logs with split boards for a roof. The boards for the floor were sawed at a mill on Clear Creek in Jasper County, and the sash, doors, etc., were hauled from Keokuk. Esquire Robinson got out and delivered the logs for this building which was 16 by 20 feet. Within weeks another room of the same size and construction was added on the west side with a door between them affording a partial division of space for public and private uses. It served as business house and dwelling, and it afforded space for the general store, post office, parlor, reception room, dining room, kitchen and numerous chambers for sleeping.

"It was a double log house facing the north, and comprising two rooms each about 16 feet square of which the west room was the dwelling and the east room the store, post office, and general business center of the settlement and of the county. … Alderman's store attracted from the country considerable barter trade which helped out town supplies. … Alderman's store at Nevada afforded the settlers small supplies, but for lumber to be used in building and for flour, stoves, and numerous other necessities there had to be trips to Des Moines or some trade center farther away. ... It was the custom of the Nevada neighborhood to bulletin at Alderman's the orders which the stage driver should fill on the occasion of his next weekly trip to Des Moines if he could."[290]

With only 214 people living in the county in 1852, the county had quickly attracted not only farmers, but people in professions, trades, and other occupations to support the frontier economy. In his history of central Iowa, McFarland observed, "Most of the early arrivals were already second generation pioneers; they had grown up in Ohio, Indiana, Illinois, or eastern Iowa, and they had observed that the shortest route to security was to get land and hold on to it. This is not to say they all wanted to be farmers; many planned to be bankers, or merchants, or blacksmiths, or lawyers, or doctors, or what not. But they still wanted land, and if they were shrewd enough to select a future mill site, or town site, or even crossroads, so much the better."[291]

The 1856 Iowa Census provides a picture of the diverse nature of Story County's business community. Among the 2,868 people living in the county when the 1856 Iowa Census was enumerated were 446 farmers, 20 laborers, 24 blacksmiths, 55 carpenters, 2 wagon makers, 2 plasterers, 6 stone masons, 5 engineers, 5 millers, 2 sawyers, 1 millwright, 1 painter, 2 cabinet makers, 1 chair maker, 1 tinner [tinsmith], 1 merchant tailor, 1 tailor, 3 shoemakers, 2 saddle and harness makers, 17 merchants, 1 trader, 1 hotel keeper, 9 physicians, 3 lawyers, 3 clergymen, 3 teachers, 1 musician, 1 teamster, 2 clerks, 2 potters, 6 surveyors, 1 county judge, 1 county clerk, 1 county officer, 1 turner [lathe operator], 1 broom maker, 1 prairie breaker, and 1 hunter.[292]

W. G. Allen's 1887 history of the county contains an 1857 Nevada business directory published in *The Story County Advocate* newspaper. The businesses include five dry goods and groceries merchants one of which also sold hardware, one hardware and stove merchant, one furniture merchant, one boot and shoe merchant, one druggist, one shingle and lathe merchant, one carpenter and builder [there were 20 carpenters enumerated in Nevada Township on the 1856 Iowa Census], four attorney and land agents, three general land and timber sales agents, three surveyors, and one person providing money to loan.[293]

In 1858, the county's population was 3,826.[294] While the rapid settlement from 1854 to 1856 began to taper off, there was a significant increase in the number of improved acres in the county. In 1856, farmers had broken 14% of the 60,529 acres they farmed, and only two years later, they had broken 42% of their 99,689 acres. There were also corresponding increases in the total bushels of wheat, oats, and corn harvested from 1856 to 1858. The county grew even more slowly from 1858 to 1862 when the population increased by only 542 people to a population of 4,368.

Concerning the development of Story County up to 1860, Payne asserts, "It was not yet a great county, but at the beginning of 1860, it had a considerable population and well-defined politics, had made the beginnings from which were to result the first great railroad [a reference to the transcontinental railroad completed in 1869] and the very great institution of practical education [a reference to the Iowa Agricultural College founded in 1858 which is now Iowa State University]; and without knowing what it was really doing it was getting into shape to bear its share of the great struggle for the Union which was soon to come."[295]

• • •

The remainder of this history of the settlement period focuses on the 1860s and 70s beginning with two important events from the early 1860s, central Iowa Norwegians' participation in the Civil War and the arrival of the first train in Story County. These sections are followed by information about events and experiences of central Iowa Norwegians up to 1880.

Volunteering for War

In August 1861, four months after the beginning of the Civil War, Andrew Nelson became the first central Iowa Norwegian to volunteer for the war. Andrew moved to Iowa with his parents, Solamon and Sarah Heggen, in 1855 to help begin the Norwegian settlement near Cambridge, but when he enlisted on August 14, 1861, he had left home and was in Illinois where he reported his age as 19 when he was only 17 years old at the time.[296] On September 23, 1861, Andrew was mustered into the 36th Illinois Infantry in Aurora, Illinois.

Between August 1861 and November 1864, a total of 46 central Iowa Norwegians volunteered for the Civil War (see Appendix E). Thirteen of the volunteers were married ranging in age from 26 to 45 when they were mustered into service. The single men ranged in age from 17 to 43. There were three families in which three sons volunteered, another family where two sons volunteered, and two married brothers volunteered. Twelve of the volunteers died in the Civil War. Eleven are buried in Arkansas, Illinois, Kentucky, Louisiana, Mississippi, Missouri, or Tennessee, and one was able to make it home to Story City before he died. One of the men died in battle, another of over-exertion, and 10 of disease. Six others were discharged early because of disabilities sustained in the war.

10th Iowa Infantry, Company K: In October 1861, seven men, Ole Anfinson, Erick Egland, John O. Johnson, John Birkestrand, Samuel Olson, Torres Scott, and Iver Twedt, volunteered for Company K of the 10th Iowa Infantry. Two months later, Erick Egland's brother, Henry, was mustered into the same company.

Company K joined nine other 10th Iowa Infantry companies that had rendezvoused in Iowa City in August 1861, proceeded to St. Louis, Missouri, to receive clothing and equipment, and were now located at Bird's Point in southeastern Missouri when the eight central Iowa Norwegians joined them. Bird's Point was a strategic Civil War site near the confluence of the Missouri and Mississippi Rivers. While the 10th was assigned to Bird's Point, John Birkestrand was discharged in February 1862 because of a disability.

From Bird's Point, the 10th Iowa Infantry was successively assigned to New Madrid, Missouri; Corinth, Mississippi, another strategic point where important rail lines met; and Iuka, Mississippi, where Henry Egland died of disease in September 1862. A little over a month later, his brother, Erick, was discharged from service, presumably for hardship reasons because of his brother's death. In March 1863, Torres Scott was discharged in Memphis, Tennessee, because of a disability.

The 10th Iowa Infantry's most notable engagement was the Battle of Champion Hill on May 16, 1863, which led to the surrender of the Confederacy at Vicksburg, Mississippi, and was a turning point in the war. Samuel Olson suffered a severe wrist wound during this battle and was discharged for disability at St. Louis, Missouri, in November 1863. A daughter's obituary records, "... he [her father] lost an arm which handicapped him the rest of his life."[297]

Ole Anfinson, John O. Johnson, and Iver Twedt completed their three year enlistments and were mustered out of service north of Atlanta, Georgia, in October 1864. The 10th Iowa Infantry continued to serve until August 1865 when it was mustered out of service. A report of its principal events up through March 30, 1865, concluded: "Summed up, the aggregate distance traveled by the regiment is 8,175 miles, and we have served in 10 states of the Confederacy. The regiment has been in 18 engagements besides skirmishes of lesser note."[298]

23rd Iowa Infantry, Company A: In August 1862, 10 months after central Iowa Norwegians began serving in the 10th Iowa Infantry, nine men from the settlements volunteered for Company A of the 23rd Iowa Infantry: Elias Ersland, Andrew Gravdahl, Thor Hegland, Thor Nelson, Christopher Ness, Torres Opstvedt, Severt Tesdahl, Christ Torkelson, and Oliver Weeks. Their Civil War experiences were reported in letters Severt Tesdahl sent to his father and brothers and sisters.[299]

In Severt's first letter, he wrote about being in St. Louis 10 days where he helped carry 700 sick and wounded soldiers from steamboats to the hospital and guarded rebel prisoners. From St. Louis, Company A was assigned to an area 90 miles southwest of St. Louis where Thor Hegland died of disease in October 1862.

On July 2, 1863, Severt wrote the following from Vicksburg, Mississippi: "I will tell you of two very hard battles which you have undoubtedly heard about." After describing the battles and their heavy casualties, Severt continued, "We are entrenched on the east of Vicksburg with a line of defense fifteen miles long and with gunboats on the other side and have surrounded the town for some time. How long it will take, I have no idea, but we're lying in the trenches in a gully in such a position that they cannot hit us with rifle fire. When we are out in picket duty in front of the line, we are so near the enemy that we can talk with one another, but we are not allowed to shoot at them at such a time. We are having soldiers killed and wounded every day. The enemy is being shot at from all sides. The plans now are to starve them out because it is almost impossible to conquer them in battle." Two days after writing this letter, Oliver Weeks died of disease and later in the month, Elias Ersland also died of disease. In Severt's next letter written August 2, 1863, he relates, "I hope you have heard the enemy surrendered on July 4th and we took all enemy soldiers prisoners there, 27,000 soldiers, 200 cannon, and lots of rifles."

By late August 1863, Severt's company was 90 miles west of Vicksburg in Carlton, Louisiana, where he wrote, "I am still alive and well for which I thank God. We left Vicksburg on the 13th of August by boat on the Mississippi. We got here the 16th. I got a pass from General and went to New Orleans by train to see the town. It is quite large and has many ships." On November 2, 1863, Severt reported, "I took sick at Brasier City, 80 miles west of New Orleans and was sent to New Orleans by train to a hospital for six days. Andrew Gravdahl and Christian Sande [aka Christ Torkelson] have also been sick and returned also. I'm due to go back to the regiment but don't know where they are. I think they may be in Texas." Later in November, Andrew Gravdahl died of disease, and the next month Torres Opstvedt was discharged for a disability.

Company A left Carlton on November 18, 1863, traveling to New Orleans by rail and then 800 miles by steamboat in "bad weather and rough sea" to Fort Expranza near Matagorda Island on the coast of Texas. On December 18, Severt expressed conflicted thoughts between going home on furlough or staying with his company: "I can go [home] ten days from now, but it is so far from home that I couldn't stay more than two weeks and it would cost me $40 ... and I feel I should stay with the Company. ... Many of our Company are sick now. Seven have died lately and five were discharged." Christopher Ness was discharged for sickness during this time and died after returning home to Story City.

Severt's 16th letter, written at Spanish Fort, Alabama, near Mobile, on April 20, 1865, reports, "Since I wrote, we fought with the enemy for 13 days before we took this fort. On the 9th of this month, we stormed the right wing of the fort and chased the Rebels out and took a lot of prisoners and shortly after, we took [Fort] Blakely and approximately 5,000 prisoners, lots of cannon, both large and small, bomb shells and ammunition." He concluded, "It seems like the war will soon end if rumors are true."

Severt's 17th and last letter was written in Columbus, Texas, on June 28, 1865. Now he could look to the future: "I see by your last letter that you could have sold my six best oxen at $50 apiece. Go ahead and sell them for the best you can get. I may not be home for a long time. I think that our time is up September 19, and it will take one month to get home. Try to make a lot of hay so I can buy a lot of cattle to feed."

Severt came home sooner than he expected. He was mustered out of service on July 26, 1865, in Harrisburg, Texas, along with Thor Nelson and Christ Torkelson. They were disbanded at Davenport, Iowa, on August 11, 1865. Company A had been in seven states and "traveled on wheels 1,157 miles, on boat 8,291 miles, and marched 1,497 miles."[300]

32nd Iowa Infantry, Company K: On September 3, 1862, 13 days after Severt and his eight companions were mustered into the 23rd Iowa Infantry, Jonas Duea, Osmund Egeland, Peter Egland, Henry Eliason, Henry B. Henryson, Jacob B. Jacobson, Erick R. Larson, Thomas Lein, John Nelson, Nils L. Nelson, John Ritland, and Erick L. Sheldahl were mustered into the 32nd Iowa Infantry, Company K.

Many years later, John Ritland recounted his Civil War experiences which were published in the local newspaper:[301] "On the last day of our stay in Nevada [Iowa] we were feasted and banqueted in regular wedding fashion. At the tables the soldiers marching to the strains of music were seated first, and directly afterwards those nearest of kin. But there was too much sorrow and weeping at the thought of parting that our appetites were small. Mother could not swallow a morsel. I gave her an apple to take home. Personally I did not feel the pain of parting to be unbearable." The company then proceeded to Dubuque, Iowa, where it was mustered into its regiment on October 6, 1862.

On November 16, 1862, Company K left Dubuque by steamboat for St. Louis, Missouri, and from there it was sent to New Madrid, Missouri, where it again stayed briefly before being sent to Fort Pillow, Tennessee. Ritland continued, "The place was most uninviting. We had to shovel snow off the ground to prepare a place to sleep. Later we built houses there and lived comparatively well. ... From Fort Pillow we were transported to Columbus, Kentucky, where we remained until September 1863. It was here that Mr. Eliason took sick, and who was the first among the Norwegians to pass away.[302]

"Our next stopping place was Island No. 10, where John Nelson Torvastad received his discharge [for disability] and went home. Jonas Duea and I became quite sick while here, but went, nevertheless, into active service in a few days. We had eaten too much fresh meat and had contracted a disease called bloody flux [dysentery]. ... We left Island No. 10 in February 1864 and traveled per steamer some 800 miles, reaching Vicksburg, finally, where we remained a few days pending the collection of a large army. When gathered we numbered about 40,000 men, all under the command of General Sherman. The army, when strung out stretched as far as 15 miles. This was called the Meridian Expedition and was undertaken in February 1864."[303]

On April 20, 1864, George Boyd, Oliver Johnson, and Halvor Opstvedt were mustered into the 32nd Iowa Infantry, and they had likely joined Company K in Vicksburg before Peter Egland died at the end of May.

On June 5, 1864, the 32nd left Vicksburg by steamboat for Memphis, Tennessee. Ritland recalled, "When we were about half way we were ordered off the boats to drive away an army of guerillas who had been bothering transportation on the river of late. In the battle that followed our regiment had four men instantly killed, ... Henry B. Henryson (Beroen) of Story City was killed in this engagement which was called the Battle of Lake Chicot.[304] ... The fighting occurred on an extremely hot day, June 6, 1864. After the battle, we set to work to bury the dead. They were all buried in one grave and some of them had to be carried a considerable distance. My comrade, Osmund Egeland, who was always willing and eager to lend a helping hand got sick immediately after the burying and died in a hospital, or pest-house, in Memphis a few days afterward. The cause of his death was over-exertion, the heart being over-taxed."

After the Battle of Lake Chicot, the 32nd proceeded to Memphis, Tennessee, arriving there on June 24, 1864. Ritland states, "I was taken sick at Memphis and was unable to go with my regiment to Tupelo [Mississippi]. The hospital being full I was taken to what was called Meridian Camp, where there were several hundred others who were sick. It was there I was given my 30-day furlough. ... I stayed home 30 days and had gained in health a great deal but not fully recuperated, so through Dr. Stitzel's (Nevada) aid and intervention, I was allowed an additional 30 days, thus making it a 60-day furlough. By this time I was well again, and started on my way back to the army in September. I found my regiment in Cairo, Illinois." While Company K was in Illinois, Oliver Johnson died of disease in July 1864.[305]

During the fall of 1864, the 32nd was assigned to southeastern Missouri where they pursued the Confederate Army into Kansas before returning to St. Louis. After re-supplying in St. Louis, the 32nd was sent to Nashville, Tennessee, where on December 15–16, it participated in the Battle of Nashville, a Union victory that effectively ended large-scale fighting in the western theater of the Civil War.

On February 9, 1865, the 32nd Iowa Infantry boarded a steamboat for a 1,200-mile trip to New Orleans. After a brief stay in New Orleans, they went to Dauphin Island on the Gulf Coast where they relaxed for three weeks before traveling by steamboat and on foot to near Mobile, Alabama. At Mobile, the 32nd Iowa Infantry along with the 23rd Iowa Infantry and other regiments assisted in the capturing of Fort Blakely in late March and early April 1865. After these engagements, the 32nd was ordered to Montgomery, Alabama.

The 32nd stayed in Montgomery until July 16, 1865, when it began traveling by steamboat, rail, and on foot back to Vicksburg, Mississippi, where George Boyd was discharged for a disability in July. John Ritland, Jonas Duea, Jacob B. Jacobson, Erick R. Larson, Thomas Lein, Nils L. Nelson, and Erick L. Sheldahl, were mustered out of service on August

24, 1865, but Halvor Opstvedt was not mustered out of service until almost a year later in July 1866.

Illinois enlistments: Why did Andrew Nelson enlist in Illinois in 1861 and eight more central Iowa Norwegians enlist in Illinois in 1862? The only information that may shed light on this question for those who enlisted in the 91st Illinois Infantry in August 1862 is that Lars Boyd, Anfin Ersland, brothers Ole O. and Sam O. Hegland, Lars J. Mathre, and brothers Thomas and Wier Weeks reported Lisbon, Illinois, as their residence when they enlisted. The other person who enlisted in Illinois, Jacob Charlson, reported LaSalle County, Illinois, for his residence. The Iowans had friends and relatives living in the Lisbon Settlement who had decided not to move to central Iowa. In spite of the 300-mile distance, travel between Lisbon and the two central Iowa Norwegian settlements was more frequent than one might suspect.

Boyd, Ersland, the Hegland brothers, Mathre, and the Weeks brothers were mustered into the 91st Illinois Infantry, Company E, in September 1862. From then until July 1863, they were assigned scouting and guarding duties in Kentucky and Tennessee before being sent to Louisiana. During part of this time, they were assigned to Benton Barracks, St. Louis, Missouri, where Lars Boyd was discharged in April 1863 because of a disability. In October 1863, they were sent to Texas until late December 1864 when they went to New Orleans. In February 1865, they traveled by steamboat to Mobile, Alabama, where they, too, participated in the capture of Spanish Fort and Fort Blakely. Anfin Ersland, the brothers Sam O. and Ole O. Hegland, Lars J. Mathre, and the brothers, Thomas and Wier Weeks, were mustered out of service in Mobile, Alabama, on July 12, 1865. Jacob Charlson was mustered out of service in Springfield, Illinois, on July 18, 1865.

Other Iowa enlistments: No central Iowa Norwegians volunteered for the Civil War during 1863, but in 1864, eight more volunteered: the previously named George Boyd, Oliver Johnson, and Halvor Opstvedt plus Osmund Anfenson, Oliver Berhow, Thor Fatland, Lars Henderson, and Thomas Shaw. Three of them were in the 44th and 47th Iowa Infantries, two of many Union regiments raised during the summer of 1864 as "Hundred Days Men," regiments assigned to rear area garrison duty to release veteran troops for General Sherman's Atlanta Campaign to end the Civil War in 100 days. All the 1864 volunteers returned home except for Thor Fatland who died of disease eight days before his unit was mustered out of service.

The home front: While central Iowa Norwegians were away from home fighting for their newly adopted country, their families were enduring sacrifice and hardship along with everyone who had husband, son, or brother in the war. Stories about the sacrifice and hardship of wives and families are absent from the histories of Story County and from many histories about the Civil War. Their experiences are mostly contained in letters wives and parents sent to their loved ones. Fortunately, there are historians who have written about this aspect of the Civil War, too. Glenda Riley's book, *Frontierswomen: The Iowa Experience*, and Joseph L. Anderson's journal article, "The Vacant Chair on the Farm: Soldier Husbands, Farm Wives, and the Iowa Home Front, 1861–1865," draw from letters exchanged with men serving in the war and memoirs written after the war.

Anderson comments, "Women had always been partners and, to varying degrees, decision makers in the farm enterprise. But confronted with the absence of husbands, they often made significant decisions about farm affairs on their own, sometimes in consultation by correspondence with husbands or other male kin. Some women performed new tasks in fields and farmyards, although relatively few women conducted the kinds of physical farm labor that their husbands had performed before the war. Farm women were busy with other farm work and childrearing and, in what appears to be a common occurrence, left the farms they operated in partnership with their husbands and moved in with the husband's or wife's parents."[306]

Among the concerns discussed in letters were the inability to hire local men for field work and decisions about whether or not to sell livestock or to find someone to care for them. Some families decided to rent their land out before the husband was mustered into service and others decided to have a trusted relative or friend manage the farm in the husband's absence. "One of the most vexing wartime issues for couples was how to provide firewood for women who lived without an adult male in the household."[307] In the Cambridge settlement, Torkel Romsa kept his neighbors supplied with wood until he died of a wood cutting accident leaving his wife and four children alone.[308]

Torkel Romsa's death was a tragic war-related story from the home front. Most stories of everyday life in the central Iowa Norwegian settlements in the absence of 46 men who were serving in the war are not that dramatic, but all are important when considering the contributions families made to the total war effort.

The four husbands who entered the 10th Iowa Infantry in October 1861 had young families. Erick Egland's wife, Britha, had just given birth to their third child in January. Erick's sister and her husband were living close by and could help Britha until Erick was discharged one year later. Ole and Enger Anfinson had four young children, and Ole's brother, Osmund and his wife, could assist Enger. Iver and Malinda Twedt had three young children, and they did not have any relatives in the settlement. Iver emigrated with Barney Hill who lived nearby, and, perhaps, he and his wife helped Malinda. Malinda died before Iver was mustered out of service in October 1864. The oldest child among the four families was Thomas Scott who was 14 years old when his father, Torres, left. Thomas' obituary states, "…young Tom had to take his place as the head of the family during his [father's] absence, which meant heavy work in those days for young shoulders."[309] Two and one-half years after beginning his enlistment, Torres was discharged for a disability and returned home to his family.

The nine volunteers who entered the war in August 1862 were among the 33 unmarried central Iowa Norwegian men who volunteered from 1861 through 1864. All but three of these men were in their late teens and twenties, and their absence placed additional burdens on their families and other families who planned to hire them as farmhands.

In September 1862, five husbands entered the 32nd Iowa Infantry, Jonas Duea, Henry Eliason, Jacob Jacobson, Thomas Lein, and John Nelson. Except for Henry Eliason whose wife, Maria, was expecting a child, the other husbands had young families. Jacob Jacobson, who had three teenagers at home, was the only man who had children old enough to help with the farm work. Jacob and his wife also had a brother and a sister living nearby who could help the family. Jonas Duea's parents-in-law and his wife's brother lived close to their farm. Thomas Lein's oldest brother and his wife lived in Howard Township and could help Thomas' wife, Helen. John and Sarah Nelson did not have relatives living in the settlement, and Sarah had just given birth to a son five months before John left. Sarah had three older children to care for, too. Henry and Maria Eliason had just moved to Howard Township and had been there less than two months when he volunteered for the war.[310] Maria gave birth to a son in March 1863, and a few months later she learned her husband had died of disease in a hospital in Columbus, Kentucky. Maria stayed on their farm and was assisted by Henry's cousin, Erik Evans, who had just immigrated.[311] In July 1864, Maria invited a family who had just moved to the settlement to live with her which they did until 1866 when Maria and Erik Evans were married.³¹²

In 1864, four more husbands volunteered for the war, Osmund Anfenson, George Boyd, Lars Henderson, and Halvor Opstvedt. They also had young families, and along with their wives were faced with how to provide for the family in the face of their absence and a shortage of men in the community to lend assistance.

In the fall of 1864, the men who were able to complete their three-year enlistments began coming home. John Ritland was mustered out of service one year later in August. His reminiscences describe his last three months in the 32nd Iowa Infantry and his joy in being able to return home to central Iowa. "We had been through a good many battles by now and we had taken several forts, but to be honest we dreaded what was now before us, viz. the contemplated siege of Ft. Montgomery. It was a large fort and we realized fully what it would mean to take it. I had seen so many of my intimate friends with whom I had fought shoulder-to-shoulder, killed, wounded and maimed for life, and as we had only three months left on our enlistment, and there were so few of us left, I wanted this remnant to be spared and get home. But there was no sympathy or sentiment, all we had to do, or think about, was to obey orders and go to Montgomery [Alabama] and take that fort.

"When we were nearing the fort on our last day's march we would occasionally be halted, and then we would hear a mighty hollering and cheering far ahead of us. Soon it was whispered that good news was coming. The cheering came closer and shortly a man on horseback drew up opposite our regiment, halted us, got off his horse, and officially announced that General Lee had surrendered to General Grant, and that the war was now ended.

"Then came our turn for cheering, which we did most lustily and from the bottom of our hearts. Amidst the cheers there were hats and handkerchiefs thrown aloft, and some had been propelled so swiftly and went so high that they caught in the tree tops and had to be left here— but who cared for hats or handkerchiefs at such a time? It was the happiest moment of my life! Never before or since have I felt such raptures of joy and happiness. The cruel war was over, and those who were left of us were safe and had the best prospects of getting back to our dear ones again."

John, his Norwegian friends, and the others from the 32nd Iowa Infantry who were able to complete their three-year commitments were mustered out of service in Clinton, Iowa. John had already taken the train from Clinton to Nevada when he was home on furlough, but there were certainly others for whom the sight of a steam locomotive in Story County would be another new experience.

Railway Service Arrives

One of the oldest railroads in the United States is the Baltimore and Ohio Railroad. It was chartered in 1827 and completed its first line in 1830. "It came into being mostly because the city of Baltimore wanted to compete with the newly constructed Erie Canal which served New York City and another canal being proposed by Pennsylvania which would have connected Philadelphia and Pittsburg."[313] In 1852, the Baltimore and Ohio was the first eastern railroad to reach the Ohio River, and railroads would continue to replace canals for transporting goods and people.

Rail service was still in its infancy in 1843 when Osmund and Thone Johnson and their two children arrived from Norway to New York Harbor. From New York, they likely took another ship up the Hudson River to Albany where they boarded a canal boat for their trip on the Erie Canal to Buffalo. From Buffalo, they traveled by ship again on the Great Lakes to Milwaukee, Wisconsin. A few months after settling in Muskego, Wisconsin, the Johnson family walked over 130 miles to the Lisbon Settlement southwest of Chicago.[314] Ole and Astri Fatland and their two children took the same route to Chicago when they immigrated in 1847, but instead of walking the 60 miles to Lisbon, they traveled in a wagon driven with oxen.[315]

When Ole Apland's emigrant ship docked in Quebec, Canada, in 1854, people could travel from there by rail, canal boat, and steamship to Detroit, Michigan, and from Detroit by rail on the Michigan Central Railroad to Chicago.[316] Prior to the arrival of the Chicago Rock Island Railroad in Morris, Illinois, in 1853, people traveled by canal boat from Chicago to Morris on the Illinois & Michigan Canal which was completed in 1848. By the time Apland came in 1854, he could take a train to Morris and walk the 11 miles to Lisbon.

On February 22, 1854, seven months before Lisbon settlers chose these three men, Osmund Johnson, Ole Fatland, and Ole Apland together with Osmund Sheldahl to investigate land as far as Omaha, Nebraska, in search of a new settlement area for Norwegian immigrants, the Chicago Rock Island rail line was completed from Chicago to Rock Island, Illinois, becoming the first railroad to connect Chicago to the Mississippi River. Lisbon settlers had been eagerly waiting for the arrival of rail service so they could market their products, and now that the time had finally arrived, they were about to make a decision to move to a location 120 miles west of the nearest train depot.

The year before the Chicago Rock Island Railroad reached Rock Island in 1854, the Mississippi and Missouri Railroad was chartered in Iowa to complete a rail line from Davenport to Council Bluffs on the western border of Iowa.[317] The purpose of the charter was to extend the rail line after a bridge over the Mississippi River was completed from Rock Island to Davenport, Iowa. The main line of the Mississippi and Missouri Railroad was completed to Iowa City on December 31, 1855, and the bridge, which was the first bridge built over the Mississippi River, was completed in 1856. Iowa City would be the end of the line until 1862 when the line was completed to Marengo, still 100 miles from central Iowa. The rail line reached Grinnell in 1863, Kellogg in 1864, and Des Moines in 1866. For Norwegians living in the Southern Settlement near Cambridge, the nearest depot was now only 20–25 miles away.

In addition to the Chicago Rock Island Railroad, three other rail lines began service in northern Illinois during the 1850s linking its western border to Chicago. In 1856, Congress passed a law authorizing land grants to companies that would complete lines from the eastern Iowa border towns of Dubuque, Lyons (present-day north Clinton), Davenport, and Burlington to the Missouri River on Iowa's western border.[318] Until other bridges were built across the Mississippi River to the Iowa towns, ferryboats carried the freight and passengers from the railroad cars to the cities on the west side of the river in Iowa.

The Illinois rail line ending in Fulton, Illinois, was across the Mississippi River from Lyons, Iowa, and it would eventually bring rail service to Story County and close to both central Iowa Norwegian settlements. In 1853, the Iowa Central Air Line Rail Road Company was organized to build a rail line from Lyons to the western border of Iowa "following as near as near as practicable the 42d parallel, that being the entire center or middle line which divides the state."[319] The company went bankrupt three years later, and the Chicago, Iowa, and Nebraska Railroad Company which was organized in 1856 completed the line to Cedar Rapids in June 1859. In January 1860, a majority of the stockholders in the Chicago, Iowa, and Nebraska Railroad Company organized the Cedar Rapids and Missouri River Railroad to extend the line further. In 1862, this rail line reached Marshalltown, more than 50 miles closer to the settlements than the Chicago Rock Island line to Marengo.

The route of the Iowa Central Air Line Railroad began appearing on maps of Iowa in 1854.[320] On Joseph H. Colton's 1859 Map of Iowa (see Figure 7), the proposed railroad route through Story County runs approximately six miles north of Nevada. The same year the map was published, residents of the county met at the courthouse in Nevada to discuss the proposed route through Story County. Four delegates were appointed to meet with railroad representatives to try to persuade them to change the route so that it would run through Nevada. W. G. Allen, an early resident of Nevada and author of *A History of Story County, Iowa*, reported, "Well, as we old settlers know, after much hard work had been done and money pledged by our citizens, the survey was made, and finally a location was secured and the road built; but the county gave the swamplands [6,712 acres] with the condition the road be built within 3,000 feet of the courthouse."[321]

By the spring of 1864, the Cedar Rapids & Missouri River Railroad Company had extended the rail line from Marshalltown to Colo, only nine miles from Nevada. As the rail line came closer to Nevada, the editor of the *Story County Ægis*, Jno. M. Brainard, reported the historic occasion to his readers: "June 22, **Locomotive**: We were able to see the locomotive attached to the construction train from the door of our office yesterday. The track lacks only a mile and a half of being laid to the depot, and we understand that the material for the building is all prepared to be put together in a very few days. ... July 6, **First Freight**: Messrs. Hambleton and Talbott loaded the first three cars with grain which went out of Nevada depot on the C. R. & M. R. railroad June 30th, A.D., 1864. This marks an epoch in the business of this town. ... July 6, **Hail to the Railroad**: Last Friday, July 1st, is memorable in the annals of Nevada as being the day on which the first train of passenger cars entered the limits of the village. About one o'clock P. M., the scream of the locomotive and the rattle of the train roused old and young from their noon *siesta*, who rushed up to the depot cheering the civilizer. Horses and cattle showed their green-ness by running, snorting, and bellowing over the prairies. Dogs barked and cavorted round like mad, and the *Ægis* people turned out on the 'stoop.' We tried to look dignified, to view matters calmly, to smile at the enthusiasm of our less travelled neighbors, but it was no go and we broke for the track at a pace far from being corrobcrative [*sic*] of our lofty assumptions. A fellow who has been ten years on the frontier is justified in hurrahing when the first locomotive visits his town, and we did it. How are you, Des Moines? Your gas-lit burg must seem tame beside our railroad cities!"[322] During the summer and early fall, the rail line was extended nine miles further west to a location named Ames Station where a depot was built.[323] C. E. Turner's 1871 history of Ames states, "It was finished to Ames in October 1864, but regular freight and passenger trains did not commence running until the following June."[324]

In December 1864, the newspaper ad for train arrival and departure times in Nevada was changed from the Cedar Rapids & Missouri River Railroad Company to the Chicago & Northwestern Railway Company after consolidation of the two companies.[325] In 1867, the Chicago & Northwestern Railway Company became the first to complete a rail line across the state of Iowa. Two years later, this line became part of the first transcontinental railroad in the United States.

In January 1865, a bridge was completed over the Mississippi River from Fulton, Illinois, to Clinton, Iowa,[326] and now Story County had an all-rail connection to Chicago. Completion of the bridge not only meant farmers could begin shipping their cattle and hogs to the Chicago Union Stock Yards which opened the same year, but also meant Norwegian emigrants could make New York Harbor their North America destination again and travel from there by rail all the way to Story County.[327] One of the author's paternal great great grandfathers, Johannes Twedt, brought his children to Story County this way in 1866.

In December 1864, the town of Ames was platted,[328] and the same month the following news items appeared in the *Story County Ægis*: "**Branch Road**: We learn that the Cedar Rapids and Missouri River Company are about surveying a line to determine the practicability of building a branch from Ames Station in this county to Des Moines. Letters say it is the best that could be chosen, being a dividing ridge very nearly all the way. If such a branch should be built from that point, we may look out for a right 'smart speculation' in corner lots. By the way, the company has been securing considerable tracts of land in that neighborhood, which may have meaning."[329]

The Cedar Rapids and Missouri River Company's plan was apparently abandoned because a couple of years later, Col. L. Q. Hoggatt and other leading citizens of Ames met to discuss the possibility of a building a rail line to connect Ames with Des Moines.[330] In 1866, the Iowa & Minnesota Railway Company organized in Des Moines to build a narrow gauge line running north and south from Des Moines to Iowa's borders. Financial problems led to the portion of the line running from

Des Moines to Ames being sold at a sheriff's sale in 1869, and a new company, The Des Moines & Minneapolis Railway, was organized to build this portion of the line.[331] It was not until January 12, 1874, that the company laid its first rail during ceremonies in Des Moines where Col. Hoggatt spoke, and the narrow gauge line was completed to Ames on July 4, 1874.[332]

By 1874, the Norwegian settlement founded southwest of Cambridge in June 1855 had spread west to the border of Boone County, and the route for the narrow gauge railway ran through land in the southwest corner of Story County purchased by Osmund Sheldahl in 1866. On August 4, 1874, Osmund and Anna Sheldahl sold 25 acres of this land for $1.00 "upon condition that the Des Moines & Minneapolis Railway company shall build and maintain a depot at or near the point in Story County where said line of road crosses the line between Polk and Story Counties, Iowa."[333] That same month, an engineer together with Oley Nelson, the Norwegian immigrant who moved from Wisconsin to central Iowa in 1867, laid out a town which was later named Sheldahl. Nelson built a warehouse on the depot grounds, and the next year his brother-in-law, Ole Apland, a member of the 1854 scouting party, had a building constructed that became the first store in Sheldahl which Nelson opened under the name Apland and Nelson.[334]

In his historical sketch of Sheldahl, Rev. Konkel states, "Sheldahl was the outgrowth of the Narrow Gauge railway that appeared from Des Moines in 1874, and of the desire of the Norwegian and Swede population of the southwest corner of the county to have a railway station; for it must be remembered that the Narrow Gauge, now the Des Moines & Minneapolis branch of the North-Western Railway, is a sort of dividing line between a Sweden on the west and a Norway on the east of that region."[335] As noted earlier in this history, Swedish immigrants had begun settling beside the Des Moines River in 1846, the year Iowa became a state.

Sheldahl was the first central Iowa town founded by Norwegians, and its development illustrates how quickly towns were built once railway service reached an area and a train depot was built.[336] In June 1875, periodic reports about the new town signed by "Occasional" began appearing in *The Nevada Representative*. The following excerpts from Occasional's reports during the remainder of 1875 describe the building up of Sheldahl:[337]

"June 3, We have a prospect of a thriving young town. The company has finished their survey, and are [*sic*] now offering lots at reasonable figures. Those wishing first class lots will do well to see about it immediately for they are going off rapidly. Building is going on at a fast rate, our carpenters are all busy, and progress is the order of the day. We don't want the court house, but we do want and expect to have one of the best towns in Story County. We now have two good dry goods and grocery stores, one drug store, one shoe shop, one blacksmith shop, one hotel, one wagon and plow shop nearly completed with about twenty good residences, all built within the last six months. Work will begin on the Swede M. E. Church in a few days. Our citizens are making up a liberal donation for someone who is willing to build a good flouring mill.

"June 15, Our streets have presented a busy scene all day today. Mr. Solbeck & Son have received three cars of hogs and Mr. Seal a like number. ... The large wagon and carriage shop of Walker, Steinberg & Co., is now completed, and work will begin tomorrow. They already have a contract for a number of fine buggies to be delivered by the 10th of July.... The 3rd of July will be celebrated here in good old fashioned style [the 4th was a Sunday]. C. H. Ballet of Nevada, will deliver the oration. Good music has been secured and a general good time is expected.

"June 28, Weather too hot for news items, but not too hot for improvements. The new church was raised last week, and ground broken for several other buildings. ... Mr. John Cassell of Swede Point was in town one day last week talking about building a flouring mill here. Come on Mr. C., we have got a good lot and $300 in cash to give you whenever you say the word. ... People passing over the Narrow Gauge and seeing the daily throng on our streets say we have the liveliest town that they have seen anywhere.

"August 25, The masons commenced laying the foundation for the grain elevator this A. M., it is to be 24 by 36 and 31 feet high having the capacity 15,000 bushels of grain.... September 3, Messrs. Tarplee & Hopkins of Swede Point are contemplating a hardware store at this place, something that is very much needed here, and we hope they will proceed immediately. The addition to the Hotel de Milligan is ready for the roof. It is 18 by 32, two stories high, and already presents a handsome appearance. ... October 30, The elevator will commence receiving grain next week and will give new energy to the grain trade in this place.

"December 8, We learn that Osmund Sheldahl, the founder of this place, is coming here to live. We will be glad to welcome Mr. Sheldahl to our midst and hope that he may live to see the town which bears his name become one of the finest towns in central America."

The completion of the narrow gauge rail line from Des Moines to Ames in 1874 brought rail service closer to Norwegians living near Cambridge. It also brought rail service closer to some of the Norwegians living farther north near Story City—mainly those who lived on the west side of the Skunk River (see Figure 2). However, Norwegians living on the east side of the river near Story City continued to trade in Nevada because of greater availability of products and services and also because of the inability to ford the Skunk River when the river was full.

In January 1877, the following news item was published in the *The Nevada Representative*: "**Narrow Gauge from Ames to Story City**: A correspondent from Ellsworth Township in Hamilton County writes to the Hamilton *Freeman* that the citizens of that vicinity are talking over the propriety of voting a five per cent tax in aid of a narrow gauge railroad from Ames to Story City. Here is what the writer says:

"Ed. Freeman;--We are enjoying ourselves with railroad meetings these long winter evenings. The people are talking of getting the narrow gauge from Ames to Story City by voting a five percent tax in the township of Ellsworth and Scott, in Hamilton County, and Lafayette in Story County. We have held several meetings already to see what the people think of voting this tax. But it is hard telling whether it will carry or not. Now, I advise you not to shade yourself, Mr. Voter, but give this thing a fair thought if we get an election. I think we who are so far from market—15 to 18 miles—ought to do something now. I think we have suffered enough these cold winters taking our produce to market. We have worn out horses, harness, wagons, and ourselves, besides enough to pay even ten per cent tax. We have sold our corn long enough for 18 and 20 cents a bushel to our stock-feeders, who now stand with outstretched arms crying: 'Don't vote a tax, it will ruin you! It will do you no good!'

"Now fellow citizens, look into this matter, study on it, and you will find that you will lose more in two years than paying a five per cent tax. Don't take any stock in this Tilden [an Ames merchant] kind of preaching; we've had enough of it to last a hundred years. SUBSCRIBER."[338]

In March 1877, Lafayette Township voters passed the tax increase by a majority of four to one. The measure stipulated, "The company should have a train run into Story City not later than 12 o'clock noon of January 1, 1878."[339] An observer of the event, L. J. Tjernagel, recalls, "I remember very distinctly that the New Year service at the church was cut short that day so we could be at the station to see the first train come into Story City. It was a great event, and we were all there."[340]

The rail line ran a mile west of Story City's original town, a 13-acre town called Fairview close to the Skunk River (see Figure 10), and so a new town had to be platted. The town was platted on land purchased by Rasmus Larson in 1856, the same year he moved to Story County. Rasmus' sons, Lars and Erik, helped plat the new town just before the first locomotive arrived.[341] As soon as the new town was platted, businessmen began moving their stores from the Fairview business district to Story City's main street. Now Norwegians living in the Northern Settlement had nearby railway service.

In July of 1878, the following letter from Story City appeared in *The Nevada Representative*: "Mr. Editor: A few items from this place may be interesting to some of your readers. Our little town, new as it is, has some very attractive features. First, we have altogether one of the handsomest depots on the D. M. & M. R. R., the best water tank and stock yards on the line. Under the supervision of Mr. R. E. Hurley, the Chief Engineer of the road, all of the improvements of the road about here are of the best quality. Unusual care has been taken by him in platting the town and giving grade, building height, etc., all of which was done, as well as grading, ditching, and tiling the streets before any lots were offered for sale. A handsome or more convenient town plat cannot be found in any country village in this State or any other new state. People settling here are assured of good cellars, dry and fine, at small cost. We have a fine main street through the town direct to the depot, graded and drained, upon which there is [*sic*] already some fine buildings, and many more in progress of construction.

"Our business directory embraces the names of H. Larson & Co., John Swan & Co., general merchants, John Swan, hardware, Helvig & Ellingson, grocers. A new building 22 by 40 feet, with cellar, under the direction of a Mr. Vold, is going up, probably for groceries; B. F. Allen drugs, medicines and paints, S. H. Brown, a neat tasty and prosperous meat market, A. O. Orin hotel; Mr. Hipshire for G. Sowers, live stock merchant; Sam Larson, also live stock, both live men [*sic*]; W. A. Wier, agricultural implements has done a spendid business in the line, and deserves all the patronage received, for his machinery is first class. Amlund & Bro., wagon and buggy manufacturers, make as straight an article in their line as is made anywhere. Ole Espies plow works will be in operation in the fall. L. Dale, merchant tailor, Johndall Brothers, cabinet makers and furniture dealers. Many others engaged in business here who will be reported, as well as anything new, at another time. In the meantime we would say that there is plenty of patronage awaiting many enterprising men. A first class grain buyer would find a profitable location. A lumber dealer would find a splendid opening and fine grounds can be secured for either or both enterprises on satisfactory terms. Signed, 'More anon, STORY CITY'."[342]

The Des Moines & Minneapolis Railroad company planned to complete the narrow gauge line all the way to Webster City in northwest Hamilton County. The five per cent tax measure in the spring of 1877 was passed by voters in the four southwest townships of Hamilton County, Ellsworth, Lyon, Scott, and Lincoln, but in the townships that would have completed the line to Webster City, the measure failed by 14 votes.[343] Work on extending the line from Story City began early in 1878, and in April, a town named Callanan was platted seven miles north of Story City on the east side of the Skunk River. Now Norwegian families living in Scott and Lincoln Townships had a nearby depot. Subsequent attempts to extend the line from Callanan to Webster City failed, and so Callanan became the end of the Des Moines & Minneapolis line.[344]

The Skunk River runs south through the middle of the four townships in southwest Hamilton County, and it may have been because the river was difficult to ford that the railway company decided to build another depot north of Story City to serve the families living in Lyon and Ellsworth Townships. L. J. Tjernagel states, "At Randall, a switch-station was established in 1878 so corn could be shipped from there, as also livestock."[345] The depot was built on land owned by Lars Henryson who moved his family from Lisbon, Illinois, to southwest Scott Township in 1858. In 1863, a post office named Randall was established on the Henryson farm in southwest Scott Township[346] which was later moved to the town of Randall after it was platted.[347]

By the summer of 1878, families living in both central Iowa Norwegian settlements could now market their grain and livestock at depots at Nevada and Ames on the east-west Chicago & Northwestern rail line and at four depots on the Des Moines & Minneapolis narrow gauge rail line running north from Des Moines to Callanan; one at Sheldahl and three north of Ames in Story City, Randall, and Callanan. The two railway lines were the only lines completed in or near the two settlements before 1880. Previous attempts to complete lines from towns south of Nevada and from there in a northwesterly direction to Webster City and beyond had failed primarily because of the difficulty in building a railroad bridge across the Skunk River. This part of Story County's settlement history will be discussed later in the section on the South Skunk River Watershed.

• • •

On a winter walk in 1989, I began thinking about my great great grandparents, Hans and Abella Twedt and Jacob and Ellen Erickson, who helped found the settlement east of Story City in June 1856. I recalled reading about the harsh winter their first year in Howard Township, and this thought led me to wishing I knew more about their life in Iowa. I had not found any letters, diaries, or memoirs about my ancestors' lives for the family history I completed in 1985, and I decided the only way I could learn about what life was like for them was to look for what other people had written. Each account I have found has helped me better understand my ancestors' lives. I hope the following glimpses of the early settlement period also broaden your insight into pioneer life.

More Glimpses of Pioneer Life

Erik Travaas wrote the earliest known history of the central Iowa Norwegians in 1888 when he recorded Lars Henderson's recollections of his 1856 scouting trip to central Iowa. In 1902, Knut Takla published a history of the settlement near Story City, and that same year John M. Mason became publisher of the *Roland Record* and began including local historical information in some obituaries of Howard Township settlers. In 1905, Oley Nelson published a history of the settlement southwest of Cambridge, and in 1908, Hjalmer Rued Holand incorporated information about both settlements into a general history of Norwegian settlement in central Iowa. These histories are elsewhere in this volume of *The Central Iowa Norwegians*. They are primarily accounts of scouting parties purchasing land in central Iowa, immigrants moving from Illinois to found the settlements, and some information about life in the settlements after they were established.

In 1907, Ivar Havernos published the first church history of the central Iowa Norwegians, a history of the St. Petri congregation organized near Story City in 1857. There are many other histories of congregations organized in the two settlements. These histories contain some glimpses of pioneer life, too, but it was not until Nehemias Tjernagel began publishing articles in *The Story City Herald*, often under the title of "Little Stories of Pioneer Days," that a fuller description of pioneer life was recorded. During 1922–23, Tjernagel published over 80 articles in the newspaper. Later, he also published articles in Iowa's historical journals, *The Palimpsest* and *The Annals of Iowa*.

Other glimpses of pioneer life are preserved in biographies published in local newspapers and county histories and obituaries. A few of the early settlers wrote memoirs,[348] and family historians have recorded other stories passed down to descendants. Sometimes these stories are mere fragments of information, but when combined with others, they shed light on the daily life of these pioneers.

In 2009, Nehemias' pioneer stories were published in *The Passing of the Prairie by a Fossil*,[349] but the other stories of pioneer life are scattered in many different sources making them difficult to find. A major goal of the Central Iowa Norwegian Project is to locate such stories. Through the years, many stories about people and events have been found, but others, most certainly, await discovery. Together with the stories Nehemias preserved, they provide a more complete description of what life was like for Norwegians who decided to settle in central Iowa.

The settlement area: In 1909, Nehemias' older brother, Peder Gustav Tjernagel, wrote a memoir about life in his neighborhood northeast of Story City. The title of the memoir, *The Follinglo Dog Book: From Milla to Chip The Third*,[350] combines the name of his parents' farm, Follinglo Farm, with a chapter for each of the 13 dogs who lived on the farm. It is the earliest known historical account of life in a central Iowa Norwegian settlement.

Peder Gustav and Nehemias' parents, Ole Andrias and Martha Tjernagel, moved from Illinois to Iowa in 1864 and settled on land in southwest Scott Township, Hamilton County, a farm they named Follinglo in honor of Martha's parents. Their first child, Peder Gustav, was born in 1865, and their second child, Nehemias, was born in 1868.

Peder Gustav states, "The country around here in those days was known as the east prairie and the west prairie, the Skunk River being the dividing line. The west prairie extended without a break clear out to the Des Moines River. ... Farther south were the everglades of Story County, a most ideal place to get stuck. ... The east prairie on our side reached from the Skunk River woods on east, I do not know how far, broken only by creeks such as Long Dick and Bear Creek but, thanks to Providence, minus the swamps.

"This then, was the arena upon which we were to do some of our acting, and mighty glad am I that I have had the great privilege of living through that era that has wrought such great changes on central Iowa from the winding cattle paths to the modern highways on every section line, from the scrub cow that could travel twenty miles a day in quest of choice tufts of grass (and in the evening not feel any the worse for it) to the grand Shorthorn cow of today."³⁵¹

Jacob B. Jacobson's obituary contains another description of the settlement area. Jacob and his wife, Nille, and their six children were among the families who founded the settlement in June 1856. Jacob's obituary states, "... in the spring of 1856 the little band of settlers arrived in Story county and scattered themselves on Howard Township. Jacob B. Jacobson settled on the farm one mile east of Roland and Jacob Nilson [Jacob's brother-in-law] took the one adjoining his on the north. These were at first the [eastern] outpost of the little settlement and there were no others east nearer than Johnsons Grove [six miles southeast of the Jacobson farm]. ... Many instances of hardships have been told, of going to Iowa City to trade or to Marengo or Des Moines to mill, driving oxen and consuming a week of time and much labor. No one thought of going alone, and they usually went in a train [convoy] so as to help each other over bad places."³⁵²

The settlement area described above by Peter Gustav and the author of Jacob B. Jacobson's obituary is the so-called Northern Settlement that encompassed northwest Story County where the settlement was founded east of Story City, southeast Hamilton County where Peder Gustav lived, and southwest Hardin County (see Figure 2). The headwaters of the Skunk River are in Hamilton County, and the river draws its water from a shallow valley containing many small wetlands or sloughs which Peder Gustav states were "a most ideal place to get stuck." The wetlands were especially prevalent in Lafayette Township where Story City is located.

The first Norwegian settlement in central Iowa was the Southern Settlement founded southwest of Cambridge in 1855. The prairie in southwest Story County and northwest Polk County was poorly drained and full of sloughs, too. Osmund and Inger Siverson came to the settlement in 1857, and their daughter, Margretha (Siverson) Severeid, remembered getting stuck in sloughs: "It was not so easy to travel in those days. We had no gravel and paved roads. When we went to Des Moines or other places, we often had to unhitch our oxen or our horses from the wagon, let them wade over the sloughs full of water, and get them on the other side on dry land, and then take the log chain which we always had to have along in those days to fasten to the loop of the tongue to draw the wagon across the sloughs as the water was so high at times it almost lifted the wagon box from the wheels."³⁵³

Anfin Apland's father, Ole Apland, was a member of the 1854 Lisbon, Illinois, scouting party who decided to purchase land for the settlement southwest of Cambridge. Ole helped found the settlement the next year along with others who moved to central Iowa in 1855. Anfin Apland states, "Look at the picture: one hundred and forty-one souls, fifteen horses, forty-four oxen, and another bunch of cattle on the raw prairie, and too late to plant anything that year. How could they live until they reaped their harvest the next year facing a long cold winter? Some of them had a little money, but there was not much that you could buy with money. They had a little groceries and some foodstuff at the little store at Cambridge, also at the store at Swede's Point [Madrid, Iowa], and at the few stores at Des Moines (but that was far to go). They got some grain from the settlers around Swede Point and probably a little at Ballard Grove [immediately east of Cambridge], and maybe they had to go to Des Moines for some. But sometimes they got down so low that they had to grind corn on the coffee mills to get corn meal to make corn bread and corn mush. And if they had plenty milk, that would keep them from starving for a while. But the children had to have their milk first. But they were like people are in all new colonies, friendly and helpful, and divided the best they could. There was an abundance of good upland wild hay, but the stock could not live on hay alone. They had to have a little grain with it."[354]

Building homes: When the settlers arrived in June 1855 and 1856, the first priority was to break a few acres of prairie in order to be able to plant a crop the following spring. Knut Takla's history of the Northern Settlement states, "The land or the farm often came first, and the prairie schooner had to be, for the time being, kitchen, dining room, living room, and bedroom, for some clear into November. Concerning the house building, they followed the good old custom of helping one another. Most of the first settlers bought a larger or smaller piece of wooded land which they could buy the first year for $10.00 an acre. ... On this land they got timber for a log house and whatever else was needed. When five or six neighbors had gotten a house built for one, they would go to the next, and that way all around. ...."[355]

Peder and Anna Heggem, who helped found the Southern Settlement in June 1855, found life on the prairie so difficult they moved to Des Moines in the spring of 1857. Des Moines was a growing city of over 4,000 people, and Peder used his team of horses to haul produce to the steamboats that came up the Des Moines River from Keokuk, Iowa. They found a small, 10-foot square shanty to live in near the Old Brick

Capitol.[356] That fall their 20-month old daughter became sick and died. In 1860, they moved back to their 240-acre farm in Palestine Township and began breaking more prairie on the high ground, around sloughs that could become ponds of many acres during periods of heavy rain.[357]

Years later, Peder and Anna's daughter, Malinda Ann Heggem Thompson, began her memoir with a description of the log home she lived in as a child: "The story of our pioneer home starts in 1855, for then the farm was bought. But my personal remembrance of the home begins in 1860 when the family moved back to the farm from Des Moines. First the log cabin was built and then the little shelter for the horses, for Father had a team. This shelter was built of slough grass, making it a warm house also for cattle and a hog or two. The chickens ran at large, roosting wherever they could. There were no fences and only a few rails for the hog corral or cattle at night. The stable consisted of a framework of poles and rails covered with wild prairie hay and banked with the same. The hay was put up in long stacks or rickets, for there was an abundance of prairie hay. The home was built near a creek [Ballard Creek] for the convenience of water; then later a shallow well was dug, placed about halfway between the house and stable. They drew water with a well sweep. Later came the oaken bucket which was still later replaced by a wooden pump. This was the beginning on a farm of 240 acres of government land bought at $1.25 per acre, northeast of where Slater now is.

"Our house of hewed logs consisted of one room about 12 by 12 feet in size. The roof was shakes split from black walnut three-fourths of an inch thick and 26 inches long which had been smoothed off to fit with a draw knife. These shingles were laid 10 inches to the weather. The floor was laid with wide rough boards. In time the wear, and also the mopping and sweeping, did the planing, so that it became white and smooth. In the northwest corner of the room was a homemade cord bed with a trundle bed for the children which was run under the bed in the daytime. There was a small window in the south end of the room. I remember the little table Father made stood under the window. Little other furniture except a flat lid hardwood chest set in [sic] southwest corner of the room. The cook stove was placed at the north end of the room with the wood box. The entry from the outside was in the east side."[358]

Immigrants moving to the settlements after they were founded sometimes lived with families who had already built homes. Sina Kloster Moran's grandparents, Severt and Kari Nass, immigrated to Illinois in 1857 where Kari washed, ironed, and mended clothes for unmarried men, and Severt worked as a farm laborer until they had saved enough money to purchase land in the Southern Settlement in 1865. Sina states that after moving to central Iowa, "They were so happy to have a place to stay while their home was built, and though all houses were small and many times there were large families, they were always happy to help out someone else. Later on, my grandparents had families stay with them in the same way as they knew how nice it was to receive help when it was needed."[359]

Mrs. Erick (Julia) Johnson was an infant when her parents, Erick and Jane Erickson, moved from Lisbon, Illinois, to Howard Township in 1864. Julia remembers her parents telling her, "Well, our journey to Iowa lasted three weeks. Having no home to go to at first, we found shelter with some friends, who had gone west the year before. We stayed with them thru the winter. In the spring father bought a 40-acre farm. ...."[360]

Early living conditions: With few supplies available locally and little or no cash to purchase them, settlers made and grew most of what they needed and bartered for the rest by exchanging labor, services, or commodities. In 1857, Michael Hegland came to the Northern Settlement with his parents, Ole T. and Britha Hegland. Michael was 12 years old at the time, and he later described frontier living conditions this way: "At first we raised only enough to supply the family needs. Everything used was made by hand on the farm and the fare was principally cracked corn and pork. We had no market and in fact we had nothing to sell and practically nothing with which to buy anything."[361] In another conversation, he elaborated on their diet: "We never suffered for want of food in the family, though the one-sided ration of cornmeal early, and cornmeal late, sometimes gave rise to a fervent desire for a change of menu. Salt pork was fished out of the brine to give variety but it, too, grew monotonous. Wild game was not wanting, and fresh fish could be hooked when farm work was not too pressing, so that between times, the table invited other feasts besides mush and milk and swine meat."[362] Michael Hegland's memory of the monotonous diet lies in contrast to Anfin Apland's more glowing report, but Apland's memories would have been from the 1870s and on: "There were lots of wild grapes, plums, and berries; all kinds of nuts in the timber, and strawberries to the glory of all on the prairie. All kinds of game—reindeer, wolves, coyotes, groundhogs, skunks, rabbits, squirrels, mink, and what not. There was also an abundance of wild geese, ducks, prairie chickens, and quail—lots of fish in the streams."[363]

Margretha Severeid's memoir about her family's first years in Iowa in the Southern Settlement echo Michael Hegland's description of frontier living conditions in the Northern Settlement: "Osmund [her father] worked a whole summer for 50 cents a day from seven in the morning until sundown and never got more than 50 cents in cash. The man he worked for had no money, so he had to take butter and eggs from him to get his groceries and sometimes had to wait for that. They did not get money for what they had to sell. Many a time they traded one bucket of butter for a bucket of salt and was glad to get that. Osmund and his family lived a year on just 50 pounds of medling (course meal). No flour in the house for a whole year. We had to eat potato cakes made out of corn meal. We ate sour milk or molasses on our mush when we did not have milk. Otherwise, it was corn cake and corn meal. We got tired of this at times but had to live thru it. We only got coffee on Sunday mornings; otherwise it was coffee made of burnt cornmeal with a little molasses in. Some burned wheat and oats and others used potato and cornmeal mixed to make coffee. The eggs sold at two or three cents a dozen. We never received any cash so were unable to buy a cow, only if we could work for it. The butter we had was salted lard most of the time."[364]

H. B. Henryson's parents settled near the Hegland family in 1858. H. B. recalled, "They had nothing but corn to live on at first.... When the pet porker had been pampered sufficiently to be slain for food, there was more variety on the table, but the main 'eats' consisted usually of pork and cornbread, or cornbread and pork, served without frills about three times a day. In summer a certain kind of weed was found on the prairie which was dried and used in place of tea. In lieu of coffee they concocted drinks made from roasted corn, wheat or rye."[365]

The grist mill on Long Dick Creek was Smith's Mill, a water-powered mill in operation from 1856 through 1863.[366] Before 1865 when a flour mill was built in Nevada, families living in the Northern Settlement milled their wheat in Marshalltown, a three-day trip in a wagon driven with oxen.[367] In 1857, a saw mill six miles south of Story City, Sopher's Mill, was converted to a grist mill, and in 1871, it began milling wheat. In 1880, Swan's Mill, a steam-powered mill, began milling wheat in Story City. In the Southern Settlement, Chandler's Flour Mill began operation in Cambridge in 1856, and although the distance to Cambridge was shorter, families in the Northern Settlement continued to mill wheat in Marshalltown until 1865 when they could mill it in Nevada.[368] In 1874, a steam-powered flour mill, Snyder's Mill, began operation in Sheldahl, and families in the Southern Settlement could get their wheat milled there.

The harsh winter of 1856–57 is mentioned often in historical accounts of central Iowa. During a historical talk presented at a 1920 Old Settler's Picnic, K. B. Thompson recalled, "The winter of 1856 was one of the most severe winters the settlers can remember. The snow was so deep that they could not get to the mill at Swede Point [10–15 miles west of where they were living]. Some had to grind corn in the coffee mills to get some meal to make corn bread."[369] K. B. was only three years old when his parents, Benjamin and Enger Thompson and their four children immigrated to Lisbon in 1854. The next year, they moved to central Iowa and helped found the Southern Settlement.

Lee's 1912 *History of Hamilton County, Iowa* contains a much more detailed description of the winter of 1856–57: "All of the old settlers will yet remember the winter of 1856, the longest and most severe that has yet been seen here. In the fall the weather up to about 3 o'clock in the afternoon of December 1st had been unusually fine, when the sky became overcast with black clouds; the wind rose almost to a hurricane and by night the snow was falling, blowing, drifting, and the storm lasted for three days, during which time it was dangerous, and most of the time impossible to leave the house. The air was so full of flying snow, that objects at only a few feet distant could not be seen. Many were unable, during those three days, to even feed or care for their stock, and when at last the wind died down and the snow had ceased to fall or fly, stables and houses had, many of them, to be dug out of the snow. In places drifts of snow were twenty or thirty feet high, and especially was the drifting to be seen around the houses and stockyards, where it seems all the snow had been collected. So hard had the wind blown and so solidly was the snow packed, that horses and cattle could walk over the highest drifts without any danger of breaking through, and many farmers fed their stock on top of the drifts clear above the stake and rider fence that enclosed the yards. … This storm was only the beginning of a series of blizzards lasting all winter and until late in the spring. There seemed to be very little 'let up' to the storms and it kept the settlers busy between storms to provide fuel and keep their stock dug out of the drifts and fed. The roads were almost impassable, and it was dangerous to go out of the sight of the settlement for fear of getting caught in a blizzard and freezing. Flour became scarce, indeed, in many instances nothing like flour or meal was to be had, and whole families subsisted for days upon corn ground in a coffee mill and made into coarse mush or bread. Others varied the monotony of such a diet with what is known as lye hominy, and these delectable viands, this attenuated menu of Johnnie cake, hog and hominy was a compulsory diet, though we cannot say that the settlers came out any thinner in flesh on account of it. But when the storms let up, flour was produced and wheat bread was again upon the table, what a luxury, indeed, it seemed."[370]

Another memory of frontier living conditions is going barefoot and wearing wooden shoes. Margretha Severeid remembered, "Mother said for three years she did not have any other shoes, she wore them where ever she went, even to church. They did not stay home from their church in those days on account of their clothing. I think it was all right too. The men-folk in the summertime went to the church in overalls and a blue-striped hickory shirt and a straw hat and many of them were barefooted, too, and we children never went to church in the winter, not having the necessary clothing."

Carrie Knutson wrote, "Our shoes wore out and another problem was how he [Father] should buy more shoes for so many. He got some basswood from this man and sawed it off in lengths according to how long our feet were. He chopped the chunks smooth on all four sides, put two pieces close together and fastened them on something that had four legs and was about two and half feet high. They had to be fitted in real tight so they did not move while he worked on them. He used a big auger first to bore many holes, then he had another auger that looked like a spoon on the end. It was very sharp on the end and sides. He shaved out the wood with that and when he had them hollowed out, we put our feet in to see if they were big enough or if they hurt our feet any place. When they were finished, they were very smooth inside and out. He scraped them with a piece of glass to make them look better. Then he turned the stove lid upside down and wet an old piece of cloth and wiped the soot off the lid. He put this on the shoes so they got black, and, oh, how nice we children thought they were! We were so glad we could barely sleep the first night, wishing it was morning so we could put them on. They were comfortable to walk in and not heavy, as the basswood was light in weight, and, oh, so good to skate on the ice with!"[371]

Pioneer farming: The early settlers used primitive farming implements until after the Civil War.[372] Anfin Apland states, "When these settlers first came, they cut all the hay with a scythe; and the small grain with a cradle; planted the corn by hand, plowed it with a one shovel plow and one horse."[373]

H. B. Henryson states, "The farm implements were very much different from what they are now. There were harrows of wood with wooden teeth, breaking plows with wooden mold boards and iron shoes, single shovel plows for tending corn, 12 to 14 inch walking plows to turn over stubble, cradles for the ripe grain, and scythes and rakes to cut and prepare the hay. They husked corn into wagons drawn by oxen. There were often as many as four persons occupied about a single wagon, one man taking the down row, and one on either side of the wagon helping himself to all he could throw in, while the fourth, often a boy, would help behind or before wherever he could manage to get in somebody's way."[374]

In 1860, all of the 52 families who reported agricultural product information for the census owned at least one milk cow, and the average number of milk cows owned plus other cattle was eight head of cattle per family. As soon as new growth appeared on the prairie, the cattle roamed free on the prairie. A cowbell was attached to one of the cows to make them easier to locate when it was milking time, and it was usually the children's responsibility to find the cows and bring them home. In a section entitled "Hunting Cows," Sina Kloster Moran recalled her mother's stories about going to get the cows: "Then there was the problem of knowing where to find the cows when there were no fences anywhere and the cows, perhaps, left in an easterly direction in the morning, but by evening they could be way down by the White Oak neighborhood. Many a time my mother went almost to Cambridge and did not find them so had to strike off in some other direction and altho she ran most of the way it was often 9 or 10 o'clock before she arrived home with the cows as she had gone miles and miles in search of them. Later, when things improved in every way and farms were fenced in, they did not have to go through such hardships."[375]

Julia Johnson recalled the following experience about going to get the cows: "There was prairie all around us, and the cattle could graze to their heart's content, but sometimes they would stray away, and it was the children's duty to see that the cows were home at milking time. This particular evening it was sister and I who should get the cows, but we could not find them. It began to get dark and we were not so brave in the dark, and we would have to walk by the cemetery, and that was the worst of it, and this bothered us—what if we should see a ghost, what then? Well, we clung to each other when we came to the cemetery, and all of a sudden something tall and white stood up right outside of the gate! Well, here is a ghost without a doubt! We clung to each other, and all of a sudden we heard a whistle. We had never heard of a whistling ghost, but what else could it be right outside of a cemetery? We were speechless with fright, but all of a sudden we saw a man coming toward us. He spoke to us, and to our great joy, it was old Mr. McCammon, and the supposed ghost was his big white dog. We did not find the cows that night, but we were convinced there was no whistling ghost: it was Mr. McCammon's whistle to his dog."[376]

During the early days of settlement, farmers traveled as far as Iowa City to sell their products as is described in the following excerpt from a biography of Oliff B. Olson. Oliff was only five years old when his parents, Lars B. and Ubjor Olson, and their four children moved to central Iowa in 1857. The Olsons settled on a farm beside the Skunk River north of Story City, and Oliff's biography mentions having Indians as neighbors. These were Meskwaki families from the settlement in Tama County who came in the fall to hunt and trap. In the spring, they returned to their permanent settlement along the Iowa River to plant corn, beans, squash, and other crops.[377] Meskwaki were a constant presence among Norwegian families living near the Skunk River in both settlements.

Oliff's biography states, "They made the journey from Illinois in an emigrant wagon, as there were but few railroads west of the Mississippi at that time. The Indians still inhabited the forest, and although they were near neighbors and frequent visitors never caused any trouble. There were but few white settlements [settlers] and these were scattered along the river, and where today are highly cultivated farms and thriving towns, stretched miles of unbroken prairie. Market facilities were very poor and there was but little demand for the products of the farmer, butter only bringing four cents per pound at Nevada, Iowa, while dressed hogs commanded two dollars and twenty-five cents per hundred. The first butter that father sold he hauled to Iowa City, a distance of one hundred and five miles. Their nearest trading point at that time was Iowa City, and as the roads were little more than wagon tracks across the prairie they made the journey at rare intervals. The hardships and privations endured by those brave men and women who formed the advance guard of civilization can hardly be imagined by the present generation, as the farm house of today is very often provided with all the comforts and conveniences found in the modern city residence."[378]

Mons Grove was a member of the scouting party that decided to begin a Norwegian settlement east of Story City. Mons moved to the settlement in 1858 and married Anna Sheldahl in 1860. His obituary lists all the towns where the early settlers marketed their products: "The nearest market places were Marengo, Alden, Marshalltown, Boone, Iowa City and Des Moines. To these places they had to haul their butter and eggs and dressed pork where they received but little in return. After a while the county settled up, towns rose up all around, markets became better and were nearer and prosperity came as a welcome guest after years of toil and privation."[379]

Prairie fires, disease, and other causes of death: Prairie fires were a constant threat every fall while pioneers settled on the prairie and turned it into farm fields. Margretha Severeid recalled, "In the early days when people came to settle on the prairie land, they settled quite apart from each other, and the wild grass was thick and tight on the prairie, and in the fall it was very dangerous for the fire on the prairie. Many a night we had to sit up and watch for our places so the fire would not come and burn our homes. When the wind blew, the fire caught on many rods ahead, and as our stable was just made of hay, the horses and cattle were in real danger from the big prairie fires."[380]

Malinda Thompson remembered, "In autumn, the danger that prairie fires might get inside the cultivated area of the homestead was a terror to the first settlers. They turned out to fight it, plowing furrows and burning a fireguard a few rods wide around their homes to prevent the flames jumping over to destroy their homes. Anxious farmers were on the lookout, and sometimes Father and others were called out in the night to fight the flames."[381]

In his *History of Story County, Iowa*, William O. Payne states, "The one successful way to fight one of the fires that was well started was by starting a back fire, and the back fires themselves sometimes proved to be nearly as dangerous as the original fires. It was from one of these backfires that came the first death that is reported in the local paper, as having been occasioned in the county, at least, after the local newspaper had been started. This death was a six-year old daughter of Peder Larson of Lafayette Township, who in November 1859, was caught in a backfire that was started by a neighbor woman to fight a greater fire, which the little girl and her mother had been helping to fight. The little girl was burned to death."[382]

Another threat to pioneer families was disease caused by the wet prairie environment. In "Health Conditions and the Practice of Medicine Among the Early Norwegian Settlers, 1825–1865," the authors quote from Ole Rynning's *True Account of America* published in 1838. Rynning stated, "I shall not conceal the fact that the unaccustomed climate usually causes some kind of sickness among the new settlers during the first year. Diarrhea, or the ague, afflicts almost everyone; but if a regular diet is observed, these sicknesses are seldom dangerous, and Nature helps herself best without medicine. The ague seldom returns unless one has attempted to drive it away by quack medical treatment."[383] Later in the article, the authors state, "Against malarial fever the immigrants were naturally helpless until the insect-breeding sloughs and swamps which surrounded them in the new and undeveloped country had been drained and the soil had been cultivated. Cholera, so called 'bilious fever,' dysentery, typhoid fever, and summer complaint probably spread by contaminated drinking water in many cases; but it seems certain that the unsanitary and crowded conditions in the homes led to more direct infection through various forms of contact."[384]

In Malinda Thompson's memoir, she recalled, "The sloughs were breeders of fever and ague. Malaria fevers were also a very dragging and much-dreaded disease among the pioneers; sometimes more than half of the family was afflicted."[385] In a biography about her grandfather, Osmund Sheldahl who was the leader of the scouting party that selected the settlement location southwest of Cambridge, Carrie Larson describes the land her grandfather purchased one mile north of the Palestine church: "It was not the best land available, but it had a spring of water near the farm yard. This spring furnished water for more than 100 years. The water as it gushed forth became a healing factor for the typhoid victims of the first year in Iowa. How did the pioneers find that this water was a cure? A meeting was called for all families afflicted to determine what caused this illness. Was it food? Could it be the water? Each family was studied, [and] they found that none had been ill on the Sheldahl farm. Why? The only different thing they had was the spring and a fresh water flow. They decided that was it! They soon started to haul drinking water to their homes. Very soon there was [sic] no more typhoid patients among the immigrants."[386]

In January 1856, a Baltimore, Maryland, physician, Dr. Grafton, moved to Cambridge, but he left in 1860 and did not return until ca. 1871.[387] The only other person known to have medical training in the settlement was Martha Romsa who moved to the settlement with her husband, Torkel, in 1860. A Romsa family history states, "Since Martha had worked as a midwife with a doctor in Illinois, she served as a midwife in the new community. She also delivered her own five children born in Iowa."[388]

A history of an area northeast of Story City in southern Hamilton County states, "The health of the early comers was looked after by Dr. Cochran and Dr. Moses Ballard, but when epidemics, such as typhoid and diphtheria, came into the community the toll was generally appalling. In Sivert Knutson's family the wife was stricken, and with[in] a month there were four funerals at their house. The Osmund Weltha family lost three children from diphtheria, the Branjord family lost four—all the children they had at one time—and as late as 1883 four more were carried away;[389] in the Erik Egland family, father and mother died within 24 hours of each other, and inside of 30 days two grown daughters died, all from typhoid."[390] Until the prairie was mostly settled and farmers began tiling out the sloughs, these diseases continued to affect central Iowa families.

According to Anfin Apland, the first deaths in the Southern Settlement were Susana L., daughter of Brit and Sarah Olson (Heggen); Carrie Ersland, wife of Knud; and Barbro Tesdahl, wife of Erick.[391] Susana was a young girl, Carrie was the mother of two adult children and step-mother to seven young children, and Barbro was the mother of five young children. They are buried in unmarked graves the Palestine Cemetery.

Many of the 640 Norwegians who lived in central Iowa prior to 1861 are buried in graves in the Palestine Cemetery established in 1855, in the Roland Cemetery established in 1856, in Boe Cemetery established ca. 1859, and in a family cemetery, the Tjernagel Cemetery, established ca. 1858. The identity of people among the early central Iowa Norwegians buried in unmarked graves has been verified through census records, church records, family histories, and contact with family historians, but there are undoubtedly others, mainly infants and very young children, whose identity will never be known.

The information in Table 9 shows the number of children, women, and men who moved to or were born in central Iowa prior to 1861 and who died between 1855 and 1865. Over one-half of the 81 deaths during this 10-year period were children under the age of 10. There were many more deaths among young children in the Northern Settlement than in the Southern Settlement. One of Nehemias Tjernagel's "Little Stories of Pioneer Days" was about pioneer wells. He began the article stating, "In the early days the people did not know of flowing wells [also known as artesian wells] which now abound in this section nor had they the apparatus with which to drill or to pipe the water supply."[392] This may be the reason there were significantly more deaths among young children in the Northern Settlement compared to the Southern Settlement where families had access to water from a flowing well on the Osmund Sheldahl farm. Overall, though, it is clear that young children were more vulnerable than adults to wet prairie diseases and the harsh living conditions of the frontier.

Table 9
Deaths during 1855–1865 among the 640
Norwegians who lived in central Iowa before 1861[393]

Deaths from 1855 through 1865	Southern Settlement	Northern Settlement	Totals
Children under 10 years of age:	12	31	43
Children 10 years and older:	2	2	4
Women who died in the settlements:	8	9	17
Men who died in the settlements:	4	5	9
Men who died in the Civil War:	4	4	8
Totals	30	51	81

There were 314 Norwegians who lived in the Southern Settlement and 326 Norwegians who lived in the Northern Settlement prior to 1861.

Women also faced a very difficult life on the frontier—preparing food, caring for children, giving birth, washing clothes, keeping the cabin clean, tending the garden, milking the cows, and in some cases, becoming responsible for the farm while husbands were away or after their husbands died. As many as five of the 17 women who died during the 10-year period appear to have died as the result of childbirth. The author's great great grandmother, Abella Twedt, died after giving birth to twins in May 1859. One of the twins lived, Betsey Malinda, and was raised by another family in the settlement. Abella's husband, Hans, hired a young woman, Gjore Ersland, to care for two older children, ages two and four. Hans and Gjore were married in 1861, and had 11 children.

In his introduction to "Angels of the Sick Room," Nehemias Tjernagel states, "... On the American frontier physicians were scarce and trained nurses were unknown. The pioneers had to depend upon their own resources of common sense, household remedies, and generous sympathy for the relief of pain. Every community had its benevolent matrons who looked after the sick."[394] Tjernagel went on to pay tribute to women in his neighborhood northeast of Story City who were always ready to help when people were sick. "Our kind pioneer neighbor, Mrs. Kjetil Knutson, freely gave her services to the sick, diagnosing cases as if by intuition, and caring for her patients devotedly. ... Another woman of broad sympathies and helpful spirit was Mrs. Kristian Karolussen whose intelligent, hearty ways suffused the sick room with an atmosphere of hope and good cheer. ... Other kind helpers in sickness and distress could be mentioned, among them being my Aunt Helga Christenson Tjernagel, Mrs. Catherine Knutson Meltvedt, and Mrs. Haaver Thompson."[395]

Summary: It is over 160 years since Norwegians began settling in central Iowa, and we no longer have the benefit of the strong oral tradition that once passed on stories about frontier life to succeeding generations. Even so, it is clear from these excerpts taken from memoirs, biographies, obituaries, and family and local histories that there are rich sources available to enhance our understanding of the early years of Norwegian settlement in central Iowa. Descriptions of frontier life like the ones included in this section help us grasp the reality of the joys, hardships, and sorrows of everyday life for the early settlers.

Personal narratives such as memoirs, diaries and journals, and letters are cherished family possessions, and at the same time, they are important sources of information for local and regional historians. The memoirs by Mrs. Erick (Julia) Johnson, Carrie Knutson, Sina Kloster Moran, Mrs. E. L. (Margretha) Severeid, Malinda Ann Heggem Thompson, Nehemias Tjernagel, and Peder Gustav Tjernagel contain valuable historical information. While there can, of course, be factual errors in any memory recorded many years later, corroborating information with other memoirs and verifying them with known facts lead to a more complete picture of what frontier life was like. Personal diaries and letters are, similarly, cherished family possessions. They are also exceptional discoveries, but no diary or journal documenting the early settlement period in central Iowa has been found through research conducted for the Central Iowa Norwegian Project. The author is also aware of the existence of only a few letters written by the early settlers.

Since the archival material about the central Iowa Norwegians consists mainly of some memoirs and letters, a large number of church and community histories, several local newspapers that have been microfilmed and in some cases, digitized, and many family histories and biographies, it is important to consider the distinction among different types of archival material: "When they provide an eyewitness account, memoirs [and diaries, journals, and letters] are primary sources. If they record what the writer was told, memoirs must be classified as secondary sources, even when they provide a contemporary account."[396] This author is not ready to concede that there are no diaries or journals written by the first settlers and holds out hope that such sources are only hiding. However, he is grateful for the primary archival material and the abundance of secondary archival material available for researchers and others interested in learning about the early central Iowa Norwegians.[397]

Organizing Church Congregations

In *Norwegian Migration to America* Blegen states, "The Norwegian immigrants who came to America in the earlier years of the migration movement carried with them a deep religious impulse, whether their basic motives for emigration were economic or social and religious or both."[398] This was certainly true for the Norwegians who came to central Iowa. Erik Travaas, who moved to central Iowa after 1870, describes this religious impulse by depicting the thoughts of Per (Peder) Larson, a member of an 1856 scouting party. "Per sat and imagined the beautiful settlement that the Norwegian settlers, in a short time, would establish in this country. He thought about how nice it would be when they could come so far that they could together build a church, call a pastor, and have it just like it was at home where they could go to church and hear God's word, hear the lovely old hymn tunes that could, so wonderfully, dispose one to devotion and holy sadness."[399]

The first group who settled in central Iowa in 1855 decided to organize themselves into a church congregation before beginning their journey to Story County electing Ole Anfinson as their pastor, Erick Sheldahl as their song leader, and Knut Bauge as their parochial teacher. They called themselves the Palestine Congregation, one of only two known groups of Norwegians to organize themselves into a congregation before moving to another area of settlement in the United States.[400] The founders of the Northern Settlement waited to organize a church congregation until their pastor, P. A. Rassmussen, visited them in 1857 and helped them organize the St. Petri congregation. Pastor Rassmussen made several visits to central Iowa until 1860 when the congregation issued a pastoral call to Pastor Nils Amlund to serve them. Amlund was a recent seminary graduate whom Pastor Rassmussen had recruited during a trip to Norway in 1859.

Because of sparse population and isolated locations, some groups had to wait longer to organize congregations. This was the case for 40 immigrants from Sogn, Norway, who settled south of Webster City in

Clear Lake Township in 1869. In 1876, on the occasion of the 60th anniversary of the founding of the St. Paul Lutheran Congregation, a former pastor wrote the following about their church's early history: "... Of course, these first settlers made no immediate move towards organizing a congregation. They had no knowledge of the free-church conditions in this country, and besides there was no minister. But when the days became short, ushering in Christmas, they began to feel an inward urge and longing for connection with 'My church, my church, my dear old church, my father's and my own.' And a rumor had floated to them somehow, that far to the southeast somewhere along the banks of a mighty stream [the Skunk River] should be a Norwegian settlement and a Norwegian Lutheran minister. So shortly before Christmas, Elling Fardal, Hans Satre, Peter L. Hove, and Mons Tynning with Nels Nortes as guide, decided to get in with this Norwegian minister before Christmas. There they go, dressed in their large, hard boots and heavy home-spun of coarse Norwegian weave, huddling through the tall, tangled dry grass on their way to what proved to be St. Petri church at Story City. There they met and talked to the venerable Rev. N. Amlund, who proved to be of such great help to them later on. They had established church connections in America. And they started for home again rejoicing. A kind farmer volunteered to take them home in his wagon. And he did. That was Christmas Eve. As they were sitting in the Fardal home that evening, the stranger took the Bible and read the glorious Christmas Gospel, gave a brief talk and offered prayer. They sang their Christmas hymns and retired. They were happy. It was Christmas in America and they had found the church. That first simple service among this little group was the beginning of a church activity that led up to the organization of the St. Paul Lutheran congregation southwest of Jewell [in 1876]."[401]

The only ordained Norwegian pastors in central Iowa before 1869 were Pastor Ole Anfinson, first pastor of the Palestine congregation, Pastor Osmund Sheldahl, leader of the scouting party who selected the area southwest of Cambridge as a settlement location and who was elected pastor of the Palestine congregation in 1859, and Pastor Nils Amlund who became pastor of the St. Petri congregation in 1860. Anfinson and Sheldahl were laymen who were ordained, and Amlund received his theological education at a university in Norway before immigrating in 1860.[402]

During this time, Pastors Sheldahl and Amlund had occasion to help organize a congregation in each other's settlement and serve it until the congregation was able to call their own pastor. Pastor Amlund helped organize the Fjeldberg congregation in the Southern Settlement in 1865, and Pastor Sheldahl helped organize the forerunner congregation to the Salem and Elim congregations in the Northern Settlement in 1868.[403] They also filled in for each other when they were absent from central Iowa. The growth in the settlements after the Civil War, especially in the early 1870s, and the greater availability of Norwegian pastors at this time made it possible to call eight additional pastors by 1880.[404]

Table 10 lists the Norwegian-Lutheran congregations that were organized in both settlements up through 1880. This listing is helpful in identifying the general boundaries of the two settlements by 1880. Within the greater central Iowa area, Pastor Sheldahl and his successor, Pastor Myhre, as well as Pastor Amlund, helped organize congregations in other settlements, too.[405]

Table 10
Central Iowa Norwegian-Lutheran congregations organized by 1880

Southern Settlement Congregations
1855—present, Palestine Lutheran Church (Huxley)
1865—present, Fjeldberg Lutheran Church (Huxley)
1871—1949, Lincoln Lutheran Church aka Polk City Congregation (Sheldahl & Huxley)
1875—1893, Sheldahl First Norwegian Evangelical Lutheran Congregational (Sheldahl)
1878—present, Bethlehem Lutheran Church (Slater)

Northern Settlement Congregations
1857—present, St. Petri Lutheran Church (Story City)
1868—present, Salem Lutheran Church (Roland) & Elim Lutheran Church (Randall)
1874—present, Bergen Lutheran Church (Roland)
1875—present, Trinity Lutheran Church (Ellsworth)
1876—present, St. Paul's Lutheran Church (rural Jewell)
1880—1903, Ladvig Norwegian Evangelical Lutheran Congregation (Stanhope)

An important aspect of the religious impulse in central Iowa has to do with the influence of Hans Nielsen Hauge [1771–1824], a Norwegian evangelist who began a pietistic movement within the state church of Norway during a time when there was a general religious awakening in

Europe.[406] His followers, called Haugeans, preferred a more simple form of worship and more lay involvement, including lay preaching, than existed in the state church of Norway at the time. Central Iowa attracted more Haugeans than any other Norwegian settlement area in Iowa, and this was especially true of the Northern Settlement.[407] Their beliefs were at the core of the first major church controversy which resulted in many of St. Petri's members leaving and forming a new congregation in 1868. The Lincoln congregation organized in the Southern Settlement in 1871 was another Hauge congregation organized before 1880.

After the Palestine congregation arrived at their new settlement location southwest of Cambridge on June 7, 1855, the first structure they built was a hayshed to use for church services. In his *History of the Palestine Congregation*, Andrew Maland states, "Before proceeding to build their homes, the men erected what was to be their temporary church, a hay shed, the first building in the colony.[408] It was a simple affair with three heavy posts on each side and taller ones through the center. These supported the roof. The roof was made of light logs, covered with long prairie grass. The shed had no walls. Here they held their services through the summer months. When winter came on they met in the different homes and later in the school houses. ... In the summer of 1857, the first schoolhouse was erected in the colony, just across the road from where now stands the church [southeast of Huxley].[409] It was built with public subscriptions. Such as had no money gave freely with their labor. It was the second home of the Palestine congregation."[410]

The author of the *History of the St. Petri Congregation*, Ivar Havneros, states, "In the first year, the meetings of the congregation were held partly in private homes and partly in small schoolhouses, and during the summer they were occasionally held in barns.[411] The schoolhouse south from Lars Henderson [Henryson] became the meeting place for the north circle [northeast of present-day Story City];[412] the schoolhouse by Paul Thompson [south of present-day Roland] was used by the East Prairie people, and the one in Fairview [Story City] became the center for this part of the region. Also, many worship services were held in the roomy attic in Rasmus Ask's home [east of Story City]."[413] Ole and Britha Hegland's home in the East Prairie was also used for church services.[414]

The Palestine and St. Petri congregations both began constructing church buildings in 1861, but due to the Civil War, completion was delayed on both buildings until the end of the war. St. Petri's church building was dedicated in November 1865. It was originally located one mile east of Story City,[415] but in 1874, it was moved to its present location in Story City when a second church was built on the East Prairie near where the town of Roland was platted in 1881. Palestine's church building, built on the grounds of the present Palestine Lutheran Church southeast of Huxley, was dedicated in December 1866.

Parochial school instruction for the children was also an important aspect of religious life in the settlements. As stated previously, Knut Bauge was elected parochial school instructor before the Palestine congregation moved to central Iowa. Parochial school was taught in the Norwegian language and consisted of learning Luther's Small Catechism along with Bible history and group singing. The Fjeldberg congregation organized in 1865 hired its first permanent parochial school teacher ca. 1870,[416] but members of the congregation were most certainly serving voluntarily in this role prior to this time.

Ivar Havneros taught parochial school in the Story City area for 15 years prior to entering seminary in 1905. His parochial school experience and his access to early church minutes are evident in his *History of the St. Petri Congregation*: "School instruction received by the children in those days was not the best; hence the parents with great zeal took hold and began to teach their children at home. After all, the parents are the best teachers for their children, especially in giving them Christian instruction. A father, a member of the Bergen congregation in Roland, Iowa, told how this instruction was given in his home. Every morning, directly after breakfast, his wife gave the children a lesson in Luther's Catechism and every evening the children recited the lesson."[417]

Later in his history, Havneros describes an important aim of the congregation: "One of the things the congregation sought to establish was a Christian Day School for the children. In the early years they had to be content to hire the best man they could find to serve as teacher each year, but they soon realized this was but a makeshift. The children were the congregation's future, and if they were not given the best and most thorough instruction in God's Word, the future of the church would be very uncertain."[418] In 1865, the east district of the parish hired a parochial school teacher, and in 1866, the west district of the parish hired a teacher. The congregation which was organized in 1868 by former members of the St. Petri congregation hired a teacher the next year to teach religion for six months for a salary of $200: "His duties were to instruct the children and catechize the youth of the congregation."[419] The next year the congregation decided to teach religion in the various districts of the congregation.

In addition to being a center for worship and religious instruction, the church provided an opportunity for social interaction. Pioneer life could be lonely, especially for women who often stayed home with the children while their husbands went to town to market products and purchase supplies. Cambridge and Story City were the towns closest to where the families were living until Sheldahl was platted in 1874. Attending church gave families a chance to intermingle. Maland states, "In addition to the preaching and the singing, the meeting also had a social aspect. With the services over, few were in a hurry to go home. They remained for social visits—to talk over the news of the settlement, to exchange views and to find out what the others had heard from home. A Norwegian newspaper, *Decorah Posten*,[420] and others, 'tho several months old,' was often scanned with the greatest interest for news items from the homeland—Norway."[421]

In a similar manner, the country school became more than a place for education, but also served as a facility for church functions and community building. A brief history of the Sheldall School describes the many uses of the country school: "As the only public building in the vicinity, the school was used for public meetings, spelling bees, and debates.... Infants were baptized, couples married and funerals were held here.... Other meetings included musical programs organized by the early pioneers."[422] In 1990, the Story City Historical Society restored and relocated the Sheldall School to its present location in Story City.

In 1902, Pastor G. O. Paulsrud began serving the Elim Lutheran congregation in Randall and the Bethel Lutheran congregation in Story City. In 1917, he also became pastor of the North St. Petri Lutheran congregation northeast of Story City and served these congregations until 1942. During this time, he officiated at funerals for many of the early settlers. In 1931, he conducted a funeral for Ole J. Olson who, in 1863, moved to the settlement where his sisters and their husbands, Jorine and Abel Olson and Malena and John Evenson, had settled in 1859 and 1860. Included in Pastor Paulsrud's sermon at this funeral was the following tribute to the religious impulse of the old pioneers: "I have had and I have great respect for the old pioneers. They were not perfect men and women, neither did they want to be called perfect. They were simple, hardworking, God-loving, church-loving people.

"They were foundation builders. Foundations are hard to build. They grappled with the raw prairie with poor equipment. They had no barns to begin with. Hay and straw had to be dug up from the heavy snow in the winter. The fuel question was serious. Poorly clad, they had to haul the fuel from far off, but they were happy and satisfied in their lot, even though the home was small and the utensils few. But these early settlers did not only think of their daily bread; they knew they and their children had an immortal soul that should be taken care of. So they gave their children a good Christian education, built houses of worship, yea, even schools of high Christian education. They had respect for law and order and the Sabbath day.

"Now as heirs of their toil and labor, what have we done with the inheritance? Maybe we have already destroyed the property inheritance they left. We hope and pray that we will not destroy the spiritual inheritance, the spiritual values they left us.

"Now, as these pioneers leave us one by one, how can we best honor them? We may decorate their caskets and graves, but that is not doing very much. Let us honor them by thanking God for their lives, for the Christian education they gave us, for the churches and schools they built. Let us honor them by serving their God and Savior, by keeping up the church work they started, by reading the Bible they read, by praying to the God they prayed to.

"Today we are following one of these pioneers to his last resting place. He was a foundation builder, a hard working man in his time. He was a man who loved God's church and sacrificed a great deal to build up God's kingdom. He was a man with a big heart for higher Christian education. The Christian education of the young lay heavily upon his heart. ..."[423]

The South Skunk River Watershed

A history of the settlement era for the central Iowa Norwegians would not be complete if it did not include a section about the South Skunk River Watershed, an area that often made frontier life difficult for the early settlers.

Personal reflections: The Skunk River is more than history for me—it played an important part in my life growing up on a farm four miles south of Roland and three and one-half miles east of the river. It is where my father taught me how to fish with a bamboo pole and a red and white plastic bobber, where my friend and I pitched my wall tent in his father's timber north of McFarland Lake, where my cousin and I pitched my tent in back of Mrs. Arrasmith's home which overlooked the location of an early mill (Soper's Mill), where I liked to gaze at the river from a bridge built in 1876[424] and hike upstream from there to my favorite squirrel hunting spot, and where I took my future wife the first time she visited my parents' home. There have been very few years since graduating from high school when I haven't returned to visit my favorite places along the Skunk River.

Why Central Iowa?: The only record of the reasons the 1854 scouting party decided to purchase land southwest of Cambridge, Iowa, is contained in the report Osmund Sheldahl made when the scouting party returned to Lisbon, Illinois: "We have fulfilled our mission and found a land that far exceeded our fondest expectation in beauty and fruitfulness. It is a land of level, sunny hills without any roads; of rich green pastures without danger of floods. It has good water and sheltering woods along all watercourses. … Here we can comfortably stretch our limbs in peaceful pursuit, following plough and scythe and the rich soil will abundantly repay us for our work. From the Government we have secured papers which will secure our rights to the land for all time to come."[425]

In addition to level land, good water, and sheltering woods alongside Ballard Creek and the Skunk River (see Figure 5), the scouting party, undoubtedly, discussed other reasons for deciding to begin a Norwegian settlement in southern Story County. Ft. Des Moines, a city of 650 people in 1853,[426] was 20–25 miles away from where the scouting party purchased land, and steamboats were bringing supplies up the Des Moines River to its residents. That same year, 1853, the State of Iowa issued a charter to the Mississippi and Missouri Railroad to complete a rail line from Davenport to Council Bluffs, and it would likely be routed through Ft. Des Moines because legislative officials were discussing moving the state capital from Iowa City to Ft. Des Moines.[427] Another topic of conversation could have been the Swedish immigrants who began settling 16 miles west of Cambridge in 1846.

No record has been found describing the reasons another Lisbon scouting party decided to purchase land for a second Norwegian settlement in northern Story County in June 1855 (see Figure 8). This scouting party was likely influenced by two of its members, Lars Sheldall and Jonas Duea, who had traveled to central Iowa earlier that year to see the land Lars' brother, Osmund, and others purchased. While Lars and Jonas were in Iowa in March 1855, they decided to purchase land 25 miles north of Cambridge, and when they returned in June as members of a scouting party, there was still a large amount of government land available east of Story City. There was also an abundant supply of trees beside the Skunk River, and the prospect of another rail line, the Iowa Central Air Line Rail Road, coming through the middle of Story County may also have been discussed by the scouting party. Marshalltown, 50 miles east of Story City, was a new town then,[428] but the possibility of it becoming a source of supplies when the Iowa Central Air Line Rail Road reached it might have been discussed, too.

What is also unknown is how much information either scouting party obtained about the South Skunk River Watershed—a wide, poorly drained watershed with bottom lands that made fording the Skunk River difficult during the rainy seasons. The 1854 scouting party forded the river in the fall when the water level could have been low and the sloughs in the "land of level, sunny hills without any roads; of rich green pastures without danger of floods" could have been dry. The June 1855 scouting party likely saw a much different Skunk River Valley filled with water, but it did not deter them from purchasing land. The immigrants who moved to Story County during its first years of settlement were not only faced with the challenges presented by living on the frontier, they had the additional challenges of contending with the wet prairie environment and the difficulty of fording the Skunk River.

The Wet Prairie: The region of Iowa where the scouting parties purchased land is in the southern part of the Des Moines Lobe, a geological term referring to an area extending from the north central border of Iowa down to Des Moines in south central Iowa. The glacier creating the Des Moines Lobe left behind a level and gently rolling landscape dotted with numerous prairie potholes and kettles which is why the region is sometimes referred to as the Prairie Pothole Region of Iowa.[429]

Within the Des Moines Lobe is the South Skunk River Watershed, an area that begins in northern Hamilton County and ends in southeastern Iowa: "This whole watershed covers parts of 13 counties with most of the area located in Hamilton, Story, and Jasper counties. ... Prior to the installation of subsurface drainage, this region had abundant wetlands, many of which were interconnected prairie potholes, specifically in the Des Moines Lobe."[430]

The area southwest of Cambridge where the September 1854 scouting party purchased land is in the South Skunk River Watershed. However, as the settlement spread further west into the southwest Palestine Township in Story County and into Lincoln Township in northern Polk County, it entered the Des Moines River Watershed. The settlement east of Story City where the June 1855 scouting party purchased land spread in all directions, but it did not extend outside of the South Skunk River Watershed.

The shallow nature of the South Skunk River Watershed in Hamilton, Story, and Jasper counties created serious drainage problems for early settlers.[431] H. D. Ballard, who moved to Howard Township in 1857 recalled, "In coming along the route from Iowa City we had many times been asked where we were going; and when we told them to Story County, they informed us that Story was the wettest county in the state and that we could not get a living in that county."[432]

The first settlers selected land close to its rivers and creeks and avoided the open prairie. H. H. Boyes, who settled on the east side of the Skunk River in Howard Township in 1854 later recalled, "It was not thought at that time that the prairies distant from the timber and streams would ever be settled. It was all covered with tall grass, with no herds or flocks to graze it down, and in the fall would be swept by terrific prairie fires, leaving the landscape black and scorched. Then, when winter came, with nothing to hold the snow, the winds would fill the air with blinding snow."[433]

Col. John Scott, a native of Ohio, settled in Nevada, the county seat of Story County, where he began practicing law and buying and selling real estate in 1856. In the first of three chapters he wrote for an 1890 county history, Scott recalled, "The general surface of this county is that of a comparatively level plain. In the early times the settlers thought much of it too nearly level for general husbandry. It is true that Skunk River flows across the entire length of the county from north to south, and has many miles of tributaries from the east and west, all of which are so far below the general level as to furnish opportunity for the easy outflow of any superabundant moisture. ... but in seasons of excessive rainfall, when the face of the country was covered with the heavy coating of the native grasses as then seen, the wild sod was like a sponge from which the grasses prevented evaporation. There were also innumerable depressions in the general surface, shallow cups of a few square rods in extent, or covering several acres, as the case might be, in which the water would stand throughout the summer. Some of these ponds would have a depth of two or three feet, while others would have but a few inches. But to such an extent did water prevail on the surface that several thousand acres were condemned as swamp and overflow lands, and so certified and granted by the general Government.[434]

"This character of the surface gave the lands of the county for many years an unsavory reputation. Thousands of acres were in reality at that time almost without value for crops of grain or grass. The settlers could see that by the treading of domestic livestock the outlets of these ponds were lowered, and lost their spongy character, and that gradually the surface of the ponds were contracting. But to many an emigrant seeking a home the representation that such were the richest lands, and would in time be more valuable than the lighter soils in other counties, was not heeded, and they went farther, often, perhaps, faring worse. The passing traveler, too, sometimes found himself mired in a pond or slough, and went his way cursing the 'frog ponds' of Story County."[435]

After describing changes that occurred in the county, Scott returned to describing the early settlement conditions: "This different condition of the country in early times, and the sluggish character of Skunk River, had their influences also on the early settlement, and such intercourse among the pioneers as might be practicable. In some seasons, the river bottoms were overflowed from bluff to bluff, and for weeks at a time the smaller streams were not fordable. There were no bridges. If to this are added the difficulties of crossing the flat prairies, meandering the ponds and wading the sloughs, it is not to be wondered that the widely scattered and small settlements should be little known outside of their immediate neighborhoods...."[436]

In 1866, Danish immigrants began settling in Lafayette Township immediately west of Howard Township where Norwegians founded their settlement 10 years earlier. When Danish immigrant, Andrew Frandson, came to Lafayette Township in 1869, the township was sparsely settled compared to Howard Township which had fewer sloughs and better surface drainage. In 1874, Andrew purchased 40 acres of virgin land in the center of Lafayette Township, and his oldest son, Julius, later recalled, "Father often told how he was criticized and razzed by friends and relatives on the river for daring to buy land so far from civilization, so far from timber, neighbors, and roads."[437]

Andrew Frandson's grandson, Phillip E. Frandson, completed a thesis on the geography of Lafayette Township for a Master of Arts degree in geography at the University of Nebraska in 1948. In his introduction to a section about the relationship of settlement to artificial drainage, Frandson states, "Settlement during the 'Hoosier' period (before the Civil War) was along the streams where wood, water, and land that did not need draining could be obtained, but the increase in the number of farms from 31 in 1869 to 137 in 1875 indicates there was an extensive settlement away from the streams on to the prairie during that interval."[438]

In a 1952 article Frandson co-authored with his thesis supervisor, Dr. Leslie Hewes, titled "Occupying the wet prairie: the role of artificial drainage in Story County, Iowa," Hewes and Frandson state, "As late as 1884, the cultivated land of the county amounted to slightly less than forty percent of the total area; now, not including rotation pasture, the cultivated acreage amounts to seventy-five percent. The comparison with 1884 is significant first because very little drainage [tiling] had taken place before 1884, and second, settlement was mature by 1884, ..."[439]

Skunk Bottoms: When Osmund Johnson, Ole Fatland, Ole Apland, and Osmund Sheldahl reached Newton, Iowa, in 1854 in search of land for a new settlement area for Norwegian immigrants, they were in the South Skunk River Watershed. In Newton, they mistakenly took a road that led to Cambridge instead of continuing in a westerly direction toward Ft. Des Moines.[440] Had they stayed on the main road toward Ft. Des Moines, they would have traveled through an infamous part of the California Trail called Skunk River Bottoms: "These boggy mud-holes were known and dreaded by travelers from Maine to California. Emigrants considered themselves lucky if they escaped without being pulled out at least three or more times."[441]

Crossing the Skunk River Bottoms further north in Story County was not easy either. After a stagecoach trip to Nevada in July 1865, a reporter for the *State Register* newspaper in Des Moines sent a letter to the editor of the *Story County Ægis* which began by describing Skunk Bottoms at Cambridge: "Through a combination of very substantial reasons, we, the Junior of the Tripod, celebrated the Fourth at Nevada, Story County. We experienced some perils by flood and field while trying to get there, but through the skill and activity of Mr. McChesney, aided by his corps of assistants, the stage which ran about three feet into the mud of Skunk Valley, was lifted out of its difficulty, and sent on its way rejoicing. No pen of ours is competent to do justice to the aggregation of horrors in this Western County known by the name of Skunk Bottom. And no man who has not made staging a profession or who has not been a traveler for a dozen years among interminable sloughs is capable of comprehending the difficulties which are encountered by the Great Western Stage Company."[442]

In September 1865, the Story County Board of Supervisors voted to spend $400 for a causeway and bridge at Cambridge,[443] but work did not begin until a year later: "This 'Slough of Despond' is now in a far way to be dried up. A subscription page has been circulating among the people of Nevada, Cambridge, and other interested localities, and an amount coupled with the county appropriation of four hundred dollars made over a year ago, is now secured sufficient to build a causeway across the low land and make the road to Des Moines by this route again passable. The lumber is partly on the ground for the sluiceways and everything is moving briskly."[444]

The causeway was still under construction in the spring of 1867 when Oley Nelson and his mother and several other families moved from southern Wisconsin (Dane County) to the Cambridge settlement. In northeast Iowa they began traveling on a road that led to Des Moines. The portion of that road running through Story County is today county road E63: "Upon reaching the Skunk River opposite Cambridge, Story County, Iowa, they found the river bottom flooded, making it extremely dangerous to attempt to cross with a wagon. Accordingly, Oley left his mother upon the bank and hired a pilot for $5 to assist him in crossing with the wagon and animals. After reaching the opposite shore he waded back, the water reaching above his waist, and took his mother on his shoulders, she being a small woman weighing only about 90 pounds, and carried her across safely. The effort practically exhausted him, but after resting a while they resumed their journey and crossed the county line to Polk County, subsequently locating on 80 acres of raw prairie."[445]

The causeway and bridge at Cambridge was not finished until January 1868: "We are informed by Supervisor Finch of Union Township that the crossing of Skunk River at Cambridge is now very good. The causeway is above high water is well graveled and a little widening of the same in the spring is the only improvement deemed necessary. This terror of travel is now no more and the stranger seeking a passage to the Capitol can find it by way of Cambridge without fear of the raging Skunk."[446]

The decision of the Story County Board of Supervisors to appropriate funds for a bridge at Cambridge in 1865 led to building more bridges in the county. In 1866, the board approved expenditures for building bridges over the Skunk River at two other fording places, Hannum's Mill north of Ames and Soper's Mill three miles south of Story City.[447] They also approved a bridge at present-day Story City.[448] Residents of Hamilton County were requesting bridges, too. The June 23, 1866, edition of the *Hamilton Freeman* reported Knud Egland and others living in the Christytown area north of Story City were asking for a bridge which later became known as Grindheim Bridge.[449] Prior to the building of this bridge, settlers had been fording the river a few yards north of where the bridge was built.[450]

Summary: In a history of Howard Township included elsewhere in this volume of *The Central Iowa Norwegians*, John M. Mason, editor of the *Roland Record*, states, "It is a characteristic feature of the Norwegian that he is anxious to have a home of his own. So these people in Illinois heard of the rich prairies of Iowa and in the spring of 1855 Mons Grove, Paul Thompson, Jacob Erickson (Ashe), John Mehus [Johnson], Ole (Aine) Thompson, Erick Sheldahl,[451] Jonas Duea, Lars Grindem [aka Sheldall], and John Torvestad went west to buy land. They came as far west as what is now Howard Township where they decided to locate. They were laughed at for settling in the frog ponds of Story County but their good judgment has since been proved."[452]

Mason does not elaborate about who "laughed at" the scouting party members for choosing a settlement area filled with sloughs, but it would be surprising to find out it was someone who had lived near Lisbon, Illinois. The landscape around Lisbon is quite similar to central Iowa, and this is especially true of the area southwest of Lisbon in Nettle Creek Township where many of the early central Iowa Norwegians lived before moving to Iowa.[453] An 1882 history of Grundy County contains the following description of the township: "The township which bears this name forms the northwest corner of Grundy County and originally consisted almost entirely of level prairie land. Along the creek [Nettle Creek] from the eastern line of the township to the western line of Section 23, there was a considerable growth of oak and black walnut, but the rest was open prairie. A number of prairie runs [waterways], tributaries to the main stream, cross the township in a southeasterly direction, but they have no valleys and the farmers till the land right up to the margin of the streams."[454]

Another description of the township is similar: "Nettle Creek Township gains its name from its principal tributary, which is also known as Little Mazon, which means nettles, this hardly desirable form of vegetation once being found in immense quantities along the rich bottom lands. No longer do they disfigure the landscape, for the present system of drainage has redeemed the land that once was thought of no more use than to grow unproductive nettles, and the home of what gave the township its name is now producing great crops of golden grain or is the rich pasture fields of sleek cattle."[455]

Three members of the scouting party who purchased land in southern Story County in September 1854, Ole Fatland, Osmund

Johnson, and Osmund Sheldahl, had farmed near Lisbon for seven to 10 years. They understood the challenges involved in farming on the wet prairie, and even though they inspected central Iowa in the fall, they must have realized what it could be like during the spring and summer months. Most of the members of the scouting party who purchased land in northern Story County in June 1855 were, likewise, experienced Lisbon farmers. One scouting party member immigrated to Illinois in 1843, and except for one recent immigrant, the others had settled near Lisbon between 1847 and 1850.

Paul Thompson, a member of the June 1855 scouting party, purchased land in Howard Township, and he moved to central Iowa in 1858 with his wife, Enger. On the occasion of their 60th wedding anniversary in 1911, they recalled the days when they lived near Lisbon: "... they were not satisfied to rent land and longed for a time when they would be able to get a home that they could call their own, but as land was already worth considerable in Illinois, they could see no future for themselves there and they began to talk and study plans for moving west into Iowa. Their neighbors and friends were also discussing this question and the more they talked and thot about the matter, the more plausible it seemed, so finally action was taken, looking towards an emigration."[456] Paul and Enger were farming rented land immediately north of Nettle Creek Township when Paul purchased their 160 acres in Story County on June 14, 1855. The wet prairie in Howard Township was not a deterrent to Paul and the other members of the scouting party, and the opportunity to purchase land at the government price of $1.25 per acre meant they could fulfill their dreams of becoming landowners.

In 1873, Paul and three other men opened a Grange store in Howard Township,[457] and by the early 1880s, Paul and Enger were on a list of the 50 largest landowners in Story County.[458] In William G. Allen's 1887 history of Story County, he describes the Thompson homestead south of Roland, Iowa: "We pass from Roland south. Paul Thompson was first to be noticed—his buildings. The dwelling is a beauty. ... Mr. T. has two nice barns; one is class two, the other is class one. The style and finish of his house is surely excellent, and is about one mile south of Roland. It is class one."[459]

There were still "frog ponds" in Howard Township when Allen made his tour of Story County, but based on his assessment of the township, he would agree with Editor John M. Mason that the scouting party's "good judgment has since been proved." Allen observed: "It is one of the good townships in Story County. Howard has many excellent barns and dwellings. Am inclined to believe as to the number of its excellent barns, Howard will lead all the other townships. Howard is a well improved township."[460]

"a matter of deliberate colonization"

In William O. Payne's *History of Story County, Iowa*, Payne states, "Not in the earliest years but in the first decade, there was a movement here that perhaps has counted more than any other one similar movement upon the character of the county and its population. This movement relates to the coming of the Norwegians. Theirs was in the beginning not a straggling movement, nor one in which a number of individuals of family relationship or previous personal association joined their efforts, but it was a matter of deliberate colonization."[461]

Payne's knowledge of Story County came from editing the *Nevada Representative* with his parents from 1882 to 1911 when he published his history and from a thorough reading of previous editions of the county's newspapers including this June 1866 news item: "We hear it reported that four hundred families of Norwegian emigrants are coming to this county to settle and open farms this summer. Correspondence and negotiations towards that end we know were in progress last season and we presume this is the result. It will be quite an addition to our present Scandinavian population. No better settlers come over the seas."[462]

Story County's rapid growth during the 1850s, from a population of 214 people in 1852 to a population of 4,051 in 1860, slowed down during the Civil War. The county's population grew by only 1,837 people from 1860 to 1865, but during the next five years, 5,733 people were added to the county's population. When the 1870 Census was enumerated, 11,651 people were living in Story County.[463]

The Civil War had a similar effect on emigration from Norway. In 1861 there were 8,900 people who emigrated which dropped to a low of 1,100 people in 1863.[464] In 1866, approximately 16,000 people left Norway. Clearly, 400 of these families did not come to central Iowa that year, but the fact that leaders in the two settlements were actively recruiting families certainly supports Payne's assertion that Norwegians' movement to Story County was "a matter of deliberate colonization."

In addition to identifying all the Norwegians who lived in central Iowa by the end of 1860, a major goal of the Central Iowa Norwegian

Project is to identify the farms where the settlers were living before they left Norway. Most of the 395 early central Iowa Norwegians who emigrated came from southwestern Norway, from the *fylker* [counties] of Hordaland and Rogaland (see Figure 3). Nine were from Telemark in eastern Norway.

Table 11
Norwegians who lived in central Iowa 1855–1860:
Parishes emigrated from and number of emigrants

Hordaland		Rogaland		Telemark		Total
Skånevik	129*	Årdal i		Drangedal	5	
Etne	64	Hjelmeland	38	Sannidal	2	
Fjelberg	30	Rennesøy	18	Bamble	1	
Finnås	24	Rennesøy-		Eidanger i		
Kvinn-		Hausken	18	Eidanger	1	
herad	7	Hjelmeland/		sub-total:	9	
Voss	1	Hjelmeland	10			
		Strand	5			
		Strand i Strand	5			
		Tysvær	4	**County &**		
		Vindafjord	4	**parish**		
		Hinderå i		**unknown**	13	
		Nedstrand	3	sub-total:	13	
		Sandnes	3			
		Sand	2			
		Skjold i Skjold	2			
		Vats i Skjold	2			
		Høyland	1			
		Jelsa	1			
		Karmøy	1			
		Sauda i Sand	1			
Totals	255		118		22	395

* includes two children born at sea on way to Quebec, Canada

Listed in Table 11 are the parishes the early central Iowa Norwegians emigrated from and the number of emigrants from each parish.[465] Almost 60% of the early central Norwegians emigrated from four parishes that are adjacent to each other in Hordaland—Skånevik, Etne, Fjelberg, and Kvinnherad. Recruitment efforts were certainly initiated in these parishes, and the fact that many others had relatives and friends already living in central Iowa caused them to settle there, too.

The large increase in emigration from Norway that began in 1866 continued through 1873, a period known as the first great wave of emigration from Norway. During this period over 112,000 people emigrated from Norway.[466] At the end of this period, the newspaper published another news item about Norwegian immigrants arriving in Story County: "A new arrival of settlers from Norway landed at the depot on Saturday last, which they made their headquarters for two or three days. They have by this time scattered over the county and in a few years will become old citizens."[467]

Growing the Southern Settlement: The Central Iowa Norwegian Project has documented 314 Norwegians who lived in the Southern Settlement by the end of 1860.[468] In 1860, this settlement consisted of land purchased southwest of Cambridge in Union and Palestine Townships in Story County and across the county line in northeast Lincoln Township and east into Elkhart Township in Polk County (see Figure 5).

Apland states, "This Norwegian settlement spread out and grew especially after the Civil War. All around Cambridge and west to Kelley and north and west of Kelley, north [south] and west of Slater around Sheldahl, from there to Alleman, and on to White Oak Grove, and from there to Cambridge. Huxley is about in the center of it."[469] Cambridge, Huxley, Kelley, Sheldahl, and Slater are identified on the map in Figure 2. Alleman is six miles south of Huxley in Polk County and White Oak Grove is three miles south of Cambridge, also in Polk County.

A settlement area Apland does not mention is Walnut Grove four miles northwest of Cambridge.[470] The first Norwegian family to settle in this area may have been Erasmus Lewis and his bride, Anna Margreta, and Erasmus' brother, Jonas, who moved from southern Wisconsin to Story County, Iowa, in 1864.[471] Jonas' obituary states, "He immigrated to America in 1864 staying a few weeks at Rock Prairie, Wisconsin [in Rock County], and came to Cambridge June 8, 1864 ...."[472] The Tobias and Johanne Severson family came the next year,[473] and in 1866, more Rock County families moved to Iowa according to a biography of the Jonas T. Larson family which states, "...in the spring of 1866, Jonas and Sina packed their earthly possessions into a covered wagon including their two little boys, Lewis and Fred. ... There were five or six other wagons in this caravan. Together, they crossed the Mississippi River at Clinton, driving their wagons and the livestock onto a flatboat, and thus were ferried across since there were no bridges at that early date."[474]

Within families and extended families, it was common for one or two people, often single or recently married, to emigrate and be followed by others as exemplified by the Landa family from Skånevik. Eight unmarried Landas immigrated to Lisbon, Illinois, from 1855 to 1861. Gjert became ill during the voyage and died in Quebec, Canada; Thor died of a fever in Mobile, Alabama, just as he was ready to return home from the Civil War; and the other early Landa immigrants moved from Lisbon, Illinois, to central Iowa in the spring of 1866. That same year, 34 other members of the Landa extended family in Norway immigrated directly to Story County arriving by train in Nevada, Iowa, on June 22, 1866. Apparently, there was a misunderstanding about their arrival date because there was no one there to meet them at the train station. They spent the night in the basement of a new hotel being constructed and the following day made the trip in three wagons to Elkhart Township in Polk County where the rest of the family was awaiting their family reunion.[475] There was, apparently, still room in Elkhart Township in 1879 for a large group of immigrants because that year *The Nevada Representative* reported, "A large accession to the Norwegian settlement in Elkhart Township, Polk County, is expected this summer."[476]

During the 1860s, the settlement also spread further west in Lincoln Township. In 1867, several families from southern Wisconsin settled east and southeast of where the town of Sheldahl was later platted.[477] These families came from southern Dane and northern Green Counties which border Rock County from where the Lewis, Severson, and Larson families had moved during 1864–1866.[478] According to a biography of Malinda Queensland, daughter of Ole and Anna Halverson, and who was eight years old in 1867, "...these pioneers filled seven covered wagons. The wagons were drawn by oxen. A herd of cattle was also taken along."[479] Oley Nelson and his mother who were also in the carvan decided to move to central Iowa after hearing "that the soil was richer and the corn grew taller in Iowa than in Wisconsin."[480]

There were, undoubtedly, caravans of families leaving the Lisbon Settlement for central Iowa after 1860, too, but after railway service reached Nevada in July 1864, some husbands drove wagons to central

Iowa loaded with family possessions, and their wives and children came by train.

Growing the Northern Settlement: The Central Iowa Norwegian Project has documented 326 Norwegians who lived in the Northern Settlement by the end of 1860.[481] In 1860, this settlement consisted of land purchased primarily in Howard Township (see Figure 8) and some land purchased west of Howard Township in northeast Lafayette Township and across the county line in southern Ellsworth and Scott Townships in Hamilton County. From the settlement's founding location where the town of Roland was later platted, this settlement spread mainly north, west, and east of Roland (see Figure 2).

One of the more interesting stories about encouraging people to move to central Iowa is contained in Carrie Knutson's memoir about her family moving to central Iowa in 1861 or 1862: "An elderly man who had walked from Iowa to Illinois came to Father's house, and he told my father he thought he would do better by coming to Iowa as he believed the country at that point would soon be settled, and it was a very good place to raise cattle because there was so much grass there. ... Well, I must tell you what Father did. We got two oxen, which made a good team. ... He bought an old wagon, made a cover on it, loaded up what we had, and started out on the journey. We also had two cows and two young yearlings, and when we left Illinois, we had one dollar and four cents in money to go on."[482]

In Ivar Havneros' history of the St. Petri congregation, he states, "In the years 1865–1875 the settlement here had a significant increase when almost 200 Norwegian families arrived during those years. Some came as emigrants from Norway, others from Clinton Co., Iowa, still others from Kendall Co., Illinois, or other places in the country. ... But the period of greatest importance as far as the coming of emigrants was concerned, are the years from 1871–1876. In these six years there were 175 families who came over and established homes inside the borders of this settlement."[483] Havneros names many of the families that came during this time, but a more complete list of the early pioneers was compiled by Nehemias Tjernagel and published in *The Story City Herald* in 1922.[484]

The families who came from Clinton County, Iowa, were from a Norwegian settlement founded near Calamus, Iowa, in 1853. Additional families who originally settled in two other eastern Iowa Norwegian settlements also moved to central Iowa. They came from Norway in

Benton County and Conroy in Iowa County where Norwegian settlements were founded in 1854.

In June 1869, a group of 40 immigrants arrived in Webster City which was the end of the Iowa Central Railroad. They were from Sogn, Norway, a county north of Hordaland from where the majority of central Iowa Norwegians emigrated. They made the trip from Chicago in a boxcar, sitting on planks spread across kegs. They had wanted to go to Decorah, Iowa, where they had relatives, but they were persuaded to go to central Iowa where they were told there was plenty of good land. After living in a cabin in Webster City for two weeks, the group traveled 20 miles south of Webster City where they had purchased land in Clear Lake Township. Their nearest trading places were Webster City and Boone, and it would be December before they would meet any of the Norwegians living in Story City.[485]

In addition to immigrants from the Lisbon Settlement, other Norwegian immigrants who originally settled northwest of Lisbon, Illinois, in Lee County began moving to central Iowa. In his history of Trinity Lutheran Church, John Ringstad recalls, "As early as 1871, a few families moved from Lee County, Illinois, among whom were Nils Eitreim and Knut Severson who settled in southeastern Hamilton County. In the fall of 1873, John Thorson and John Ringstad made a trip from Illinois to visit their friends. They first came to Nevada, Iowa, where large stretches of uncultivated land were in evidence. They proceeded afoot to Hamilton County where they were well received by their former neighbors. They were so well pleased that they bought land. When they moved to Iowa, they were accompanied by J. A. Rytter and wife and Tollef O. Cragwick. Thorson and Cragwick sent for their families. Henry Larson and family also came the same year. These persons soon brought others of their friends and acquaintances from Illinos to settle in the vicinity. A number came from other places."[486]

The author's first local history project was a study of 60 members of an extended family who emigrated from the Helvik farm in Kvinnherad between 1852 and 1892. They helped found the Iowa towns of Calamus, Roland, Thor, and Ruthven as well as towns in Minnesota and South Dakota. Twenty-four Helviks settled near Roland and Story City, some changing the spelling of their name to Helvig and others dropping their farm name and using their Christian names of Olson, Sampson, and Iverson. In 1860, Abel Olson, the first Helvik immigrant, moved to Howard Township where his sister, Abella and her husband, Hans Twedt, had settled in 1856. Abel and Abella's last siblings to leave

Norway were two of their sisters who immigrated to Roland in 1878 along with their mother who was then 94 years old. Steamships were replacing sailing ships by then, so the trip was not as arduous, but it was still quite a trip for a person of her age. She lived almost two more years before dying in 1880.[487]

Most of the Norwegians living in central Iowa in 1880 moved there from northern Illinois or directly from Norway. A review of the 1880 Census shows only 53 families moving to central Iowa from other states: 39 from Wisconsin, nine from Minnesota, three from South Dakota, and two from Kansas.[488]

Becoming a popular settlement region: Almost 3,000 Norwegians were living in central Iowa when the 1870 Census was taken. This was a five-fold increase from 1860 based on the 640 Norwegians documented by the Central Iowa Norwegian Project. There were 1,882 Norwegians in Story County, 531 in Polk County, 447 in Hamilton County, and 62 in Hardin County.[489] By 1870, central Iowa had become third most popular settlement region in Iowa as can be seen on a map of Norwegian settlement in Iowa in 1870 (see Figure 9).

The most popular area in 1870 was northeast Iowa where Norwegians began settling in Clayton County in 1846. In 1850, Norwegians settled northwest of there in Winneshiek County, and Decorah became the center of this settlement area. In 1853, Norwegians began settling west of Winneshiek County in Mitchell County and then in Worth and Winnebago counties which became the second most popular settlement region in Iowa for Norwegian immigrants.

Becoming a Settled Prairie

In early August 1866, the editor of *The Story County Ægis*, John M. Brainard, included a description of the Northern Settlement in a report of a trip he made to Webster City, Iowa: "**The Beautiful Prairies**: Our ride to Webster City took us through some of the finest lands in Iowa. It is quite enough that we say we were until this trip totally unprepared to do justice to an Iowa prairie in the full generosity of its harvest. In this county we have just as good land and as full crops as can be produced in the teeming west. We have seen no corn which will compare with a field belonging to Mr. Griffith on Long Dick [a creek southeast of Story City]. All the way along the Skunk the fields were crowded with wheat shocks, much thicker than we have been accustomed to see them. Returning through the Norwegian settlement we were delighted with the evidences of thrift there manifest. Good fences, heavy crops. Barns and other convenient outhouse buildings, farming implements in abundance, and the 'cattle upon a thousand hills,' the long rows of willow hedges, all conspired to make a picture of rural beauty and thrift, which we are sorry not to have witnessed sooner. (It was our first visit in that part of our county.) If heavy crops, inexhaustible soil, water, grass and energy make banner counties, please enroll Story. She is much more of an average county than we took her to be, and we are pleased that our lines have fallen in her pleasant places."[490]

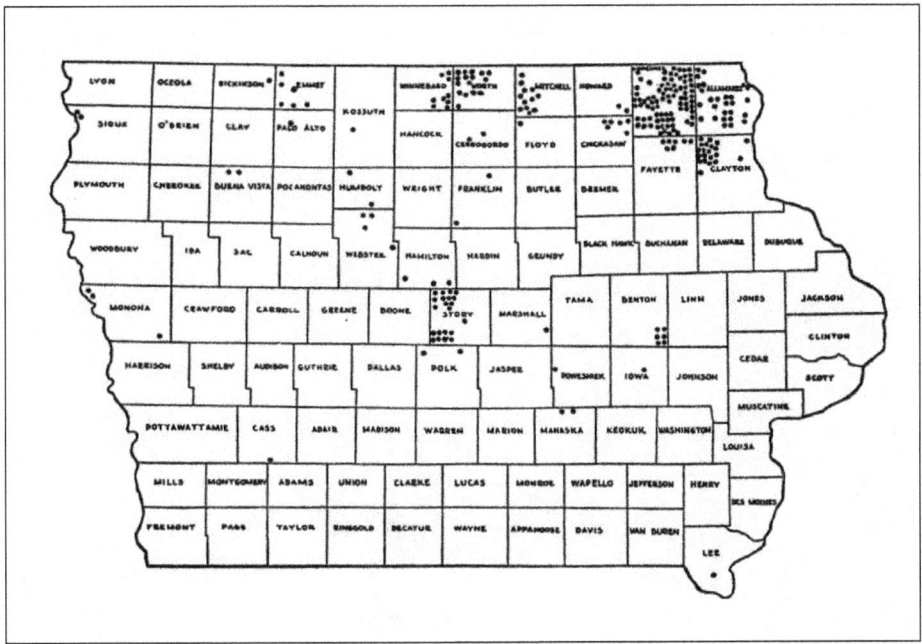

From *Norwegian Settlement in the United States* by Carlton C. Qualey, 1938, reprinted with permission from the Norwegian-American Historical Association

Figure 9
Norwegians in Iowa, 1870

Editor Brainard's description of the Norwegian farmsteads portrays a prosperous settlement. By 1874, Howard Township had become so settled that the St. Petri congregation built a second church building in the middle of the township and moved the church building completed in 1865 from the east side of the Skunk River into Story City. Both church buildings are shown on an 1875 drawing of Story City (see Figure 10).[491] The church built in 1865 is in the same location where the St. Petri Lutheran Church sits today. The drawing shows the steeple of the new church building visible on the horizon at the location where the town of Roland was platted in 1881. The business buildings shown in the drawing were moved one mile west when the narrow gauge rail line was completed to Story City in 1878.

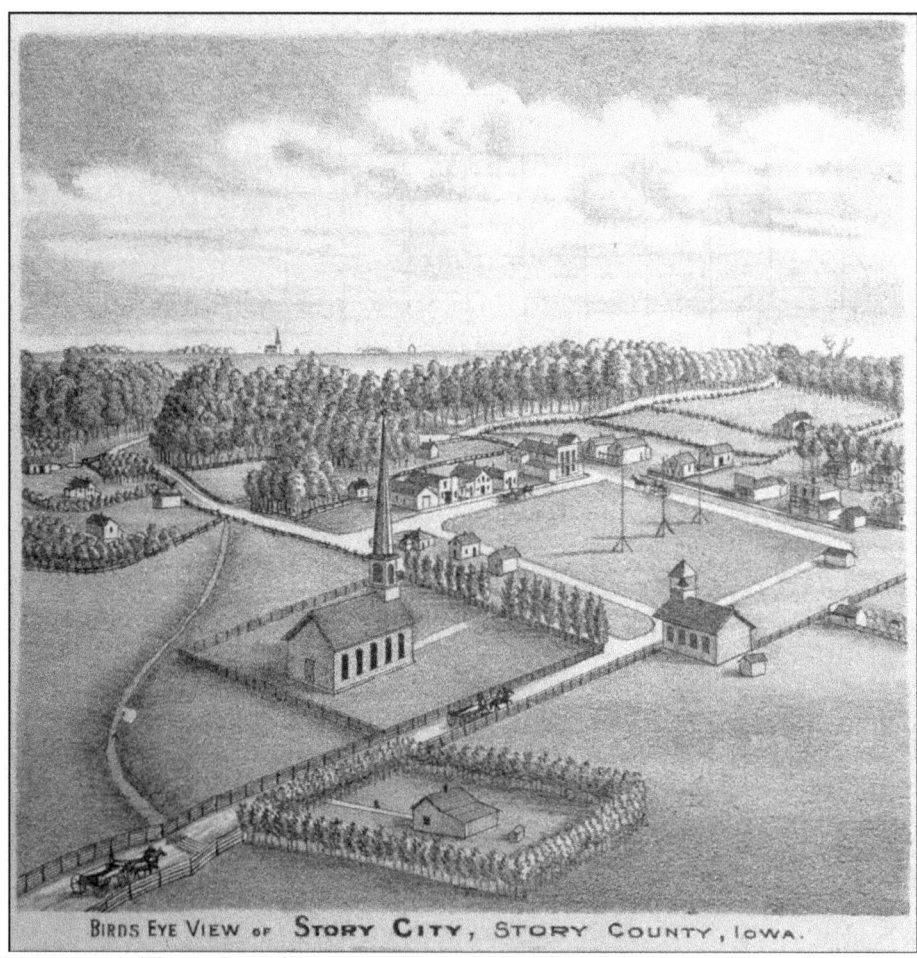

Source: *A. T. Andreas' Illustrated Historical Atlas of the State of Iowa*, 1875

Figure 10
1875 drawing of Story City, Iowa

Also on the 1875 drawing of Story City is a portion of the land Rasmus Larson purchased in 1856 which is shown adjacent to the open area with the three tall poles. The importance of Rasmus Larson and his brother-in-law, Osmund Sheldahl, and their families settling near Lisbon, Illinois, in 1845 and encouraging other families to settle there is discussed in the section on "Emigration from Skånevik, Etne, and Fjelberg." Osmund Sheldahl's subsequent roles as leader of the 1854 scouting party and as second pastor of the Palestine congregation are also discussed previously. Rasmus continued to play an important role, too, until his death in 1873, especially in providing advice to other immigrants. His daughter, Caroline, states, "While he [Rasmus] owned a farm he did not personally engage in agricultural pursuits. He was a mechanic and while in Norway engaged in watch-making. After coming to the new world he followed carpentering, shoemaking, and the tinsmith's trade, and in fact could do anything in mechanical lines. He was a man of unswerving integrity and possessed sound judgment. People came for miles around to ask his advice, especially in matters concerning building or buying."[492]

Norwegian immigrants also sought advice from Ole Apland. He immigrated to Lisbon, Illinois, in 1853, and the next year he was chosen as a member of the 1854 scouting party. Ole purchased land southwest of Cambridge in October 1854, and on June 7, 1855, he helped found the settlement. In August 1855, he and Anna Ersland became the first Norwegian couple married in Story County. They lived in a dugout until 1868 when they built a frame house, and in 1875, they built a new barn (see Figure 11).[493] An 1890 biography of the family states, "Mrs. Apland is the owner of 240 acres of land, has it all under cultivation, and has the largest and finest barn in the township."[494]

Ole Apland died of cholera in 1879, and at the time of his death, he was the second largest landowner in Story County.[495] His obituary states, "He was a Norwegian by birth, a very careful business man, who had by strict economy and close attention to business, amassed a large property."[496] More than three-fourths of the land Ole owned represented deeds he was holding as collatoral for loans he made to Norwegian immigrants seeking to become landowners and business owners in town.[497]

In a letter sent from Howard Township to the Kvinnherad parish in Norway in January 1876, Paul Haugland wrote that the Norwegian farmers were doing well, but stated, "the land is quite bought up around here."[498] The prairie was becoming more settled in the township north of Howard Township, too. After reminiscing about his days of herding cattle

Photograph courtesy of Dan Apland, descendant of Ole Apland

Figure 11
Ole Apland's barn built in 1875
Ole Apland standing beside his four sons ca. 1877–78

out on the open range in Scott Township and about other events from his boyhood, Peder Gustav Tjernagel concluded his memoir of life in the Christytown neighborhood northeast of Story City: "These scenes or settings from the prairie of central Iowa, or you may even call them little dramas, had sooner or later to come to an end. The squatters were rapidly decorating the hillsides with their thatched roofs, sod houses and even frame houses. This spelled only too plainly that this would be the last season [*circa* 1879] on the prairie for the milk cows belonging to the settlers along the Skunk River."[499] Later he recalled seeing his first roll of barbed wire in a hardware store in Ames. The scarcity of virgin prairie land and the end of open range grazing were signs that the frontier era in central Iowa was coming to an end.

In 1880, Story County published a promotional publication, "Resources and Wealth of Story County,"[500] describing its favorable farming conditions and the services available in its towns. The purpose of the publication was "to convince those in the east that this is one of the best, and destined to become one of the wealthiest counties in the State."[501] Nine-thousand copies were printed, and a newspaper announcement about it said, "Every resident of Story County should have a few copies to send to eastern friends."[502]

The document also included information about the availability and cost of land in each of the townships. In the two townships in southern Story County where the first settlement was founded, there was still land available with the price ranging from $5 to $15 per acre. However, in Howard Township where the second settlement was founded in northern Story County, the document states, "No acres vacant land." It goes on to say, "This is one of the finest, best settled and improved townships in the county—principally occupied by an industrious and prosperous class of Norwegians. Prices, $12 to $15 per acre."[503] West of Howard, Lafayette Township was also fully settled and selling for $6 to $10 per acre, but there was still vacant land to the east, 10,000 acres in Warren Township for $6 to $10 per acre and 3,000 acres to the south in Milford Townshp for $12 to $15 per acre. In the Southern Settlement, both Palestine and Union Townships were also fully settled with land selling from $5 to $15 per acre.

When the 1880 Census was enumerated, there were 6,480 Norwegians, foreign-born and their children, living in central Iowa: 3,555 in Story County, 816 in Polk County, 2,109 in Hamilton County, and 146 in Concord Township in southwest Hardin County.[504] With the arrival of rail service to both Sheldahl and Story City, the marketing of agricultural products became easier, supplies became more readily available, and there became less need to make the long trip to Nevada. By 1880, Sheldahl had a population of 322, comparable to Story City which had a population of 331 and larger than Cambridge with its population of 223.[505]

"good loyal citizens"

In "Early Days in Howard," H. D. Ballard reminisced about the contributions the Norwegians made to the development of central Iowa. Ballard was born in New York in 1842 and moved from Illinois to Howard Township with his parents in 1857. His father was the first physician near Story City. Ballard states, "Numerous families of Norwegians soon came and their industry soon made the wild prairie blossom like a rose, and yield up gold that was used to build the fine houses and barns which stand where the wolf used to burrow and roam unmolested. What a blessing foreigners have been to the country! They have made good loyal citizens, have subdued the earth and are benefactors because they have made two blades of grass and grain grow where there was before only one or none. They soon imbibed the spirit of the republic and helped to make it great by civilizing and bringing forth from the earth something that benefits all nations as well as our own. The fruits of their patient, persistent labor, they now enjoy as they could never have hoped to, had it not been for the American republic. The rich soil they made better and dug out of its storehouse the things that make life worth living. It is the foreigners from all nations that make us great, for we have the spirit of every clime and the talent making a cross that the highest individual can spring from, and possessing the vitality needed to battle successfully with life. When the war of 1861 came, families who had sons were distressed to see their boys, husband, father or uncles, shoulder the musket and go to the front to do battle for the life of this republic. It was then our foreign born population showed their loyalty to the country of their adoption. It cemented the whole as one family, with one purpose, under the same flag, making this republic stronger than it ever was before. Long may they live to enjoy it."[506]

• • •

A sequel to this history, "The Town Building Period: 1880–1905," will be published in Volume 3 of *The Central Iowa Norwegians*. Topics to be covered are: Building Towns, Educating Children, Mills and Markets, Communication and Travel, Political Involvement, Farms and Agriculture, Businesses on Main Street, Amusement and Culture, and The Turn of the Century. Volume 3 will also contain an extensive bibliography of resources for learning more about the central Iowa Norwegians.

The author is interested in learning more stories illustrating life in the central Iowa Norwegian settlements for these topics. To contact the author, write to him at the Central Iowa Norwegian Project, 509 NE Stone Valley Dr., Ankeny, Iowa 50021-4113; phone him at 515-964-4160; or email him at atwedt@aol.com.

Acknowledgments

I am profoundly grateful to authors of early histories of the settlements; authors of church, community, and county histories; people who wrote memoirs, biographies, and obituaries; and compilers of family histories who provided resources that have been invaluable in researching and writing this history. I am thankful, too, to those responsible for microfilming local newspapers, another extremely valuable resource.

I wish to thank my wife, Asta Twedt, for her constant support of my historical research and for the incalcuable number of hours she has sat at our kitchen table or in the passenger seat of our car on road trips proofing and editing material to make it clear and understandable. Her mother, Ardis Nielsen Petersen, also assisted me by translating Erik Travaas' narrative, "A Little About the First Settlers in Story County," and Knut Takla's "Big Norwegian Settlement, Roland, Iowa," both of which are included in this volume of *The Central Iowa Norwegians*.

Tusen takk (a thousand thanks) to my friend, Steve Sheldahl, for his careful editorial review of each section of the history as it was completed and for his suggestions for revising and reorganizing material. Steve has paternal ancestors who settled northeast of Story City, the Lars Sheldall family in 1855 and the Lars Henryson family in 1857. Steve is an avid family historian and author of *Searching For Roots: A Study of Ancestors* originally published in 1997 and updated in 2010.

Tusen takk, also, to my friend, Jim Mason, for his analysis of an early version of this history, for sharing his extensive knowledge of the general history of Norwegian immigration to the United States, and for drawing four of the maps included in this history. Jim has paternal ancestors who settled near Roland, the John Michaelson family in 1858 and the Mats Mason family in 1876. Jim is the Mason family historian and is the author of "Lisbon, Illinois: Gatway to the West" contained elsewhere in this volume of *The Central Iowa Norwegians*.

Appendix A:
1836–1844 emigrants from Skånevik, Etne, and Kvinnherad identified on ship passenger lists[507]

Year	Parish	Ship	Emigrant(s) and Settlement Location
1836	Skånevik	Den Norsk Klippe	Halstein Tørrison Mehus and Guri Rasmusdatter and two children. Settled in Chicago. In 1848, moved south of Chicago to Thornton Township, Cook County.
1836	Kvinnherad	Den Norsk Klippe	Erick Johannesen Sævig and Ingeborg Johannesdatter. Settled in Mission Township, Illinois, in 1837.
1837	Etne	Ægir	Nils Hansen Vettestø and Britha Åmundsdatter and son. Lived in Illinois and Missouri, and by 1840 were living in southeastern Iowa where Britha died. In 1846, Nils remarried and moved to southwest Iowa, then California, then to New Mexico.[508]
1837	Etne	Ægir	Jacob Fredrik Weltzin. Served in the Civil War and later returned to Etne.[509]
1837	Etne	Ægir	Halvor A. Sæbø and Kari Johannesdatter and six children. Settled in Mission Township, Illinois, in 1837.
1843	Kvinnherad	Juno	Anders Eriksen Hjortås. Settlement location unknown.
1843	Etne	Haabet	Helje Johnsen Osvåg and Ingebor Abrahamsdatter and two children. Settlement location unknown.
1843	Skånevik	Haabet	Torbjørn Larsen Tungesvik and Kari Eriksdatter and daughter. Moved to Stavanger parish in 1842 and emigrated in 1843. Second child born in Wisconsin, but by 1847 had moved to Lisbon, Illinois. In 1870, homesteaded land in Clay County, Kansas.[510]

Appendix B:
Why Lisbon, Illinois?

Why did Rasmus Larson, also known as Rasmus Larson Tungesvik, and Osmund Sheldahl decide to settle near Lisbon, Illinois, in 1845? This is a question to which I have been seeking an answer since 1993 when I prepared a historical talk on Norwegian settlement in central Iowa presented at the Sons of Norway Lodge in Story City, Iowa.

For some years, I thought I had found the answer to Why Lisbon, Illinois? in George T. Flom's *A History of Norwegian Immigration to the United States* where he states, "The first Norwegian settler at Lisbon was John Hill (Hidle) from Fjelberg in Sonhordland, Norway," and "In 1838, he [John Hill (Hidle)] settled at Lisbon, Kendall County, being thus the first Norwegian to settle in that county (for Ole O. Hetletvedt did not come till 1839)."[511] In the 1840s, the Fjelberg parish bordered the Skånevik and Etne parishes where the Larson and Sheldahl families emigrated from, so I reasoned John Hill might be the person who encouraged them to settle near Lisbon. Learning John Hill was not from Fjelberg[512] eliminated him as a possibility unless Rasmus and Osmund talked to him while investigating the Lisbon area.

The next possible answer I found to the question, Why Lisbon, Illinois?, was in Martin Ulvestad's *Nordmændene i Amerika* where he states, "The first Norwegians in the area of Lisbon were Erick Larsen Grove and Henry Munson from Voss, John Hill (Hilde) from Fjelberg, and Severt Anderson (Sjur Arentson) from Øvre Severeide [Sævareid] in Skånevik."[513] The Øvre Sævareid and Tungesvik farms are close to each other, so I reasoned perhaps Rasmus learned about Lisbon from Severt Anderson, also known as Sjur Arentson. However, Severt Anderson did not emigrate from Øvre Sævareid until 1854,[514] so he could not have been the source of information about Lisbon.

Next, I began thinking about people who emigrated from Skånevik and Etne before the Larson and Sheldahl families emigrated in 1845, specifically Halstein Tørresson Mehus and Guri Rasmusdatter who emigrated from Skånevik in 1836 and Nils Hansen Vettestø and Britha Åmundsdatter who emigrated from Etne in 1837. When I discovered Rasmus' younger brother, Torbjørn Larsen Tungesvik, also known as Thomas Larson, and his wife, Kari Eriksdatter, who was Osmund's sister, emigrated in 1843, I realized they could have been the ones who informed Rasmus and Osmund about the Lisbon settlement area. The discovery of Thomas and Kari's emigration in 1843 led to further research in collaboration with Steve Sheldahl and Jim Mason.[515]

Halstein Tørresson Mehus and Guri Rasmusdatter settled in Chicago in 1836. Construction on the Illinois & Michigan Canal had just started, and Halstein was hired to recruit Norwegian workers for the canal. The 96-mile canal, which linked Lake Michigan with the Mississippi River, followed a route southwest of Chicago to Morris, Illinois, and then west to Peru. In addition to the incentive of obtaining immediate work on the canal, Halstein likely used the availability of land as an incentive to encourage people to work on the canal. This required knowledge of land prospects in the area, especially land prospects near the canal route. In 1836, most of the Norwegians were living near Norway, Illinois, in LaSalle County, but by 1850, many had settled 10 miles east of Norway near Lisbon in Kendall County and south of Lisbon in Grundy County (according to the 1850 U.S. Census, there were 949 Norwegians living in LaSalle, 211 in Kendall, and 202 in Grundy). Even if Rasmus and Osmund did not correspond with Halstein before they emigrated in 1845, they likely knew he was living in Chicago and may have sought him out for advice on where to settle.

Nils Hanssen Vettestø, also known as Nils Veste and Nelson Hanson, and Britha Åmundsdatter immigrated to Chicago in 1837. They initially settled south of Chicago in Iroquois County before successively moving to Calhoun County north of St. Louis and from there north to Shelby County, Missouri, before settling in southeastern Iowa (Lee County) where Britha died in 1843. Nils remarried in 1846, and they moved to southwestern Iowa where they separated, his wife moving to a Morman community in Utah and Nelson to California.[516] Britha's sisters, Ragna, and her husband, Torkjell Larsson Ve, and Barbro, and her husband, Erick Sjursson Tesdahl, immigrated to Lisbon in 1850 and 1855 respectively. It is possible the Larson and Sheldahl families received information about Lisbon from Nils and Britha or their relatives in Etne, but it seems more likely they would have received information from Halstein Tørreson Mehus.

Thomas and Kari Larson and their daughter moved from the Skånevik parish to near Stavanger in 1842. The next year they were passengers on *Haabet* that arrived in New York during July 1843. Their second child, Randi, was born in Wisconsin on November 3, 1843,[517] but it is not known if Wisconsin was Thomas and Kari's original destination or if they went to Wisconsin after arriving in Chicago. Thomas' obituary states, "In 1843, he emigrated to Illinois which was at that time a new country,"[518] and Kari's obituary states, "They emigrated to America in 1843 and settled in Illinois.... After living near Morris, Illinois, for twenty-seven years they moved to Clay County, Kansas [in 1870]."[519] Living in Illinois for 27 years indicates they moved to Illinois soon after Randi was born on November 3, 1843; however, an obituary for Thomas and Kari's daughter, Margaret, states they settled in Nettle Creek Township, Grundy County, Illinois, in 1847, suggesting they either lived elsewhere in Illinois before that time or in Wisconsin.[520]

In 2010, after completing the research with Sheldahl and Mason on the question, Why Lisbon, Illinois?, I discovered a new piece of information concerning Thomas and Kari's possible whereabouts from 1843 to 1847. In 1847, Kari's brothers, Lars, Rasmus, and Erick and their families were among the 161 passengers from Skånevik, Etne, and Fjelberg on *Kong Sverre* that sailed from Bergen on May 11 and arrived in New York Harbor on June 24, 1847. A biography of Erick states he "went to Milwaukee, Wisconsin, afterward moving to Kendall County, Illinois."[521] His brothers went directly to Kendall County where their sister, Margreta Larson (Rasmus' wife), and brother, Osmund Sheldahl, had settled in 1845. Lars and Rasmus settled southwest of Lisbon in Grundy County, Nettle Creek Township, and Erick settled in Saratoga Township which shared its western border with Nettle Creek Township. Erick's reason for disembarking at Milwaukee while his brothers continued on to Chicago and from there to Lisbon, Illinois, may have been to find Thomas and Kari and encourage them to move to Lisbon.

Of course, one final possible answer to the question, Why Lisbon, Illinois?, is: The Larson and Sheldahl families discovered the Lisbon area on their own. This is a plausible answer to the question, too, if upon arriving in Chicago, they decided to follow the Chicago Trail, also known as the High Prairie Trail, to look for a place to settle. This trail headed in a southwesterly direction from Chicago through Plainfield, Plattville, Lisbon, Holderman's Grove, and on to Ottawa, part of a main travel route between Chicago and St. Louis. However, I suspect the Larson and Sheldahl families had prior information about Lisbon, and the most likely person to have provided it was Halstein Tørresson Mehus.

Appendix C
Did someone plan the 1845–1849 emigration from Skånevik, Etne, and Fjelberg? And if so, who?

The dramatic upsurge of emigration from Skånevik, Etne, and Fjelberg during the late 1840s has always intrigued me. The registration of 161 passengers to sail on *Kong Sverre* in 1847 was obviously deliberately planned as evidenced by the fact the ship was reserved for passengers from the three districts. But what about the seven families and two single men who emigrated in 1846 and the Rasmus Larson and Osmund Sheldahl families who emigrated in 1845? Were their decisions to emigrate responses to an evolving interest in emigration (see Appendix A) or were they beginning steps in a strategy to accommodate large numbers wanting to emigrate?

During my many years of research into the history of the central Iowa Norwegians, I have looked for a letter or diary to substantiate my belief that the departure of the Larson and Sheldahl families in 1845 was the first step of a plan, but the only evidence I have discovered is in secondary sources describing who may have provided the encouragement and leadership for so many families and single people leaving the three districts in the late 1840s. Despite the lack of conclusive proof, I remain convinced the Larson and Sheldahl families left Norway with the intention of finding a settlement location for others wanting to emigrate, and they found that settlement location southwest of Chicago near Lisbon, Illinois (see Appendix B).

Hjalmar Rued Holand begins his 1908 history of the "The Stavanger and Hordaland Colony in Central Iowa" stating, "Old Fox River in Illinois has always been the great gathering place for emigrants from Stavanger, Hordaland, and Hardanger. In the forties and fifties many hundreds of these came hither every year. But Fox River was only the portal to America. They stopped here for a short time and worked for their acquaintances, whereupon they later journeyed farther west in order to found their own homes.

"Among these early immigrants may be mentioned the brothers Sheldahl. Their names are Lars, Rasmus, Erik, Haldor, and Osmund Sheldahl. They were sons of a bailiff in Norway and all were schoolteachers. They went to America in 1846[522] and became leading men in Illinois and Iowa among the people from their home districts, and they did much to promote emigration. Another man, also from Etne, who deserves to be mentioned, is Torkel Henryson, who occupies a position of special esteem among his fellow countrymen in the vicinity of Story City, Iowa. In 1847 he, together with Lars Sheldahl [the oldest brother who Americanized his farm name to Sheldall], and on the encouragement of the Sheldahl brothers, organized an emigration society of 165 persons, hired a ship on his own account in Bergen, and arrived safe and sound in New York."[523]

Carrie Larson, granddaughter of Osmund Sheldahl, visited the farm her grandfather emigrated from in Etne in 1936. Her 1980 family history contains this description of her great grandfather, Erik Heinriksson Skjeldal: "Erik served as sheriff, whose duties were law and order and the collector of the area taxes. The community taxes must be collected and paid in full by the sheriff whether the individual citizens paid it or not. Bad times came, followed by years of depression in the 1830s. He had educated his sons but found himself 'broke.' ... [Erik Heinriksson Skjeldal], a governmental employee, a shrewd businessman, lost his fortune. He saw no future for his five sons [from his second marriage] whom were already equipped to take up their life's work. He urged his family to go to the new country, the U.S.A., to seek their fortune."[524] Erik sold the Skjeldal farm in 1829 to his eldest son, the only son from his first marriage, and in 1834, Erik died. The father's advice to his children from his second marriage about emigrating came, therefore, at a very early stage in emigration from Norway. One of the sons, also named Erik, must have been thinking about emigrating in 1839 because that year he received military permission to emigrate.[525]

Holand and Larson do not mention another son, Torbjørn, also known as Thomas Larson, who was the first member of the Skjeldal/Sheldahl family to emigrate. Thomas and his wife, Kari, who was Rasmus Larson Tungesvik's sister, and their first daughter, Ingri, emigrated in 1843. Thomas and Kari's second child, Randi, was born in Wisconsin in November 1843. Whether they continued to live in Wisconsin is unknown, but they apparently did not settle near Lisbon, Illinois, until 1847. Thomas and Kari later moved to Kansas while the rest of their siblings settled in central Iowa, so perhaps this is the reason they are not mentioned in Holand's history (see Appendix B for more information about Thomas and Kari).

Organized emigration from Norway began in 1825 when a shipload of Norwegian immigrants settled near Rochester, New York. In 1834, some of these immigrants moved to Illinois to begin a second Norwegian settlement near the Fox River southwest of Chicago, Illinois. Letters from these immigrants and others who emigrated the next few years were shared locally, but widespread distribution of "America letters" did not occur until Gjert Hovland emigrated in 1831. His letters were copied and distributed throughout southwestern Norway.[526] If it is true, as Carrie Larson states, that her great grandfather, Erik Heinriksson Skjeldal, was encouraging his children to emigrate before his death in 1834, his advice to his children took place during the very early stage of emigration from Norway.

In an article written for the 150th anniversary of emigration from Skånevik, local historian Ingvald Skålnes identifies Rasmus Larson as another promoter of emigration. Skålnes states that Larson "was a central person in the emigration, and accelerated it. A large part of his and her people [the families of Rasmus Larson and his wife, Margreta Skjeldal] traveled over the sea the following years."[527] Skålnes does not elaborate on his last sentence, but what he is alluding to is that two years after the death of Erik Heinriksson Skjeldal in 1834, Erik's widow, Rannevig, married Lars Sjurson Tungesvik from Skånevik, the father of Rasmus Larson. Lars' first wife died in 1831, and with his marriage to Rannevig in 1836, the Tungesvik and Skjeldal families became inextricably linked, so much so that three of Rannevig's children (Lars, Margrethe, and Kari) married Lars' children (Magdela, Rasmus, and Thomas).[528] This strong connection between the two families bound them together in the beginning stages of emigration from Skånevik and Etne.

Skålnes goes on to discuss the qualities necessary for emigrating at that time. He states, "Good opportunities were not the only motivating force to get one to take such a risky journey. There were people with initiative, a little sense of adventure, and a need to try out new ways under more tolerant conditions than here at home. Rasmus Larson probably had some of these characteristics since he abandoned a good farm and traveled to a more or less unknown land." Additionally, Skålnes describes what is known about Rasmus' parents, that his father was a member of the local school board in 1820 and could write, a skill normally possessed only by pastors and sheriffs, and that his mother was a daughter of a noteworthy man from Etne. Skålnes then asks the question, "Had Rasmus [Larson] Tungesvik received a part of these characteristics?"

Assuming there was a calculated strategy behind the large emigration from Skånevik, Etne, and Fjelberg during 1845–1849, was sending an advance party to the United States to investigate settlement locations part of the strategy just as the Sloopers had done in 1821? If so, how did they decide whom to send? And were they volunteers or were they chosen? The answer to the latter question could very well be "Yes" in either case because both Rasmus Larson and Osmund Sheldahl possessed special qualities and skills for such an assignment, so they could very likely have volunteered *and* have been chosen.

The best description of Rasmus Larson I have found is from a biography of one of his daughters, Caroline, that contains a short paragraph about her parents. It states, "While he [Rasmus] owned a farm he did not personally engage in agricultural pursuits. He was a mechanic and while in Norway engaged in watch-making. After coming to the new world he followed carpentering, shoemaking, and the tinsmith's trade, and in fact could do anything in mechanical lines. He was a man of unswerving integrity and possessed sound judgment. People came for miles around to ask his advice, especially in matters concerning building or buying."[529] It would have been difficult for Rasmus to farm as he was disabled and had to use crutches to walk.[530]

Osmund Sheldahl had studied theology and surveying at Upsala University in Sweden.[531] His knowledge of surveying certainly would be useful, but his accomplishments after he immigrated provide the best insight into why he would have been a good choice for an advance party. These include being the leader of the 1854 scouting party that selected central Iowa as a new location for Norwegian settlement, being elected the second pastor of the Palestine congregation in 1859, and being the first Story County Norwegian elected to a county position, that of county drainage commissioner in 1859.

Holand's 1908 history of "The Stavanger and Hordaland Colony in Central Iowa" first appeared as a newspaper article in *Decorah-Posten* [The Decorah Post] on February 6, 1906. This was shortly after central Iowa Norwegians celebrated their 50th anniversary of settlement at Cambridge, Iowa, on June 7, 1905, and again at the fourth triennial convention of the Norwegian Pioneer Association of America held in Story City, Iowa, on October 11–12, 1905. The following report about the convention appeared in a Des Moines newspaper on October 13, 1905: "STORY CITY, Ia., Oct. 12—Special: The triennial convention of the Iowa Norwegian Pioneer Association was held at this place Wednesday and Thursday. The city has been thronged with visitors nearly all week. Representatives from nearly all the northern states are in attendance, especially from Wisconsin, Illinois, Minnesota, and the Dakotas. Although the weather was very unfavorable the exercises were carried out in full. An immense tent had been provided and addresses were made by

Prof. Rasmus B. Anderson of Madison, Wis., editor of *America*, known as the 'father of Norse literature in America,' and former minister to Denmark; Attorney Oscar M. Torrison of Chicago; Prof. O. G. Fielland of Northfield, Minn.; Prof. Pettersen of Minneapolis, and Halle Steensland of Madison, Wis., president of the association. A banquet was given at the opera hall in the evening in honor of the pioneers. Two hundred guests were present and many well-known Norwegian-Americans responded to toasts, among them Nicolai Grevstad, editor of the *Scandinavian* of Chicago; Prof. A. A. Veblen of Iowa City; B. B. Haugen, editor of *Vor Tid*, a leading Scandinavian paper published at Minneapolis. The pioneer convention meets every three years, and only Norwegians who have lived in the country forty years are eligible to become members."[532]

Rasmus B. Anderson, author of *The First Chapter of Norwegian Immigration (1825–1840): Its Causes and Results* published in 1895, gave the opening address. Other speakers not mentioned in the Des Moines newspaper report were George T. Flom, professor of Scandinavian Studies and Literature at the State University of Iowa, and The Honorable Oley Nelson from Slater, Iowa. Flom later published *A History of Norwegian Immigration to the United States From the Earliest Beginning down to the Year 1848* (1909), and Nelson had just published *A Brief History of the First Norwegian Settlement of Story and Polk Counties, Ia. 1855–1905* for the June celebration at Cambridge.

Given Holand's keen interest in immigrant history and the fact that his newspaper article about the central Iowa Norwegians appeared in *Decorah-Posten* four months after the convention, he must have been a convention attendee. I have reviewed the Story City and Roland newspapers for evidence of Holand's presence and have not found him mentioned, but it is clear from his February 1906 article that his information about the Cambridge settlement came from Oley Nelson's recently published history.

It is also clear from the contents of Holand's newspaper article that he talked to people familiar with the history of the Norwegian settlement founded east of Story City in 1856. The Sheldahl brothers were no longer living in 1905 and neither was Rasmus Larson, but Torkel Henryson was living in Story City. Henryson was a Sheldahl cousin who was born in 1822 on a farm next to the Skjeldal farm in Norway. Growing up, he may have heard conversations about emigration, and he became intimately involved in emigration in 1846 when he went to Bergen with Lars Sheldall to arrange for a passenger ship and was assigned as agent to register passengers on *Kong Sverre*. Holand's statement, "Another man, also from Etne, who deserves to be mentioned, is Torkel Henryson, who occupies a position of special esteem among his fellow countrymen in the vicinity of Story City, Iowa," indicates Holand was referred to Henryson by more than one person attending the convention and, presumably, personally interviewed Henryson.

Another person still living in 1905 who lived in nearby Roland was Jonas Duea who was born in Skånevik in 1824 and emigrated from Etne in 1849. In March 1855, Duea and Lars Sheldall traveled to central Iowa to see the area southwest of Cambridge where a scouting party headed by Lars' brother, Osmund, had purchased government land in September 1854. Jonas and Lars decided to purchase land 25 miles north of this area in the southwestern corner of Scott Township, Hamilton County. Four months later, they returned to central Iowa as members of an eight-member scouting party that purchased government land east of Story City in Howard Township, Story County, for a second central Iowa Norwegian settlement. Lars moved his family to central Iowa late in the summer of 1855, and Jonas Duea came the next year with his wife, Martha, and their two children. Martha was the daughter of Erick Sheldahl, Lars' brother. Jonas Duea's familiarity with emigration from Skånevik and Etne and his close relationship with two of the Sheldahl brothers made him another person from whom Holand could have obtained information about the Sheldahl family's role in promoting emigration from Skånevik, Etne, and Fjelberg.

In view of Ingvald Skålnes' belief, and mine, too, that Rasmus Larson played a significant role in the early emigration from Skånevik, it is interesting that Holand did not mention him. There were people living in Story City in 1905 who knew about Larson's role in emigration whom Holand could have interviewed. Unfortunately, Rasmus and Margreta's oldest son, Lars, who was a prominent citizen in Story City, had died the previous year; however, their daughter, Margaret, lived in Story City, and another daughter, Caroline, lived nearby in the Roland community. Their second oldest son, Erick, lived in southwestern Minnesota, but the possibility of seeing his relatives and some of his old friends may have been enough of an enticement for him to have attended the convention, too.

I may never find documents like letters or diaries that substantiate (or refute) my belief that the departure of the Rasmus Larson and Osmund Sheldahl families in 1845 marked the beginning of an effort to promote and organize emigration from Skånevik, Etne, and Fjelberg and that these two families left Norway with instructions to find a settlement location where others who wanted to emigrate could settle, too. There were, undoubtedly, other people in Skånevik, Etne, and Fjelberg who played important roles, also, but I have not discovered any mention of them in my extensive study of the families who settled in central Iowa prior to 1861. The only sources I am aware of that contain information directly related to who could have planned and provided the leadership for a mass emigration from these three districts in the latter part of the 1840s are those written by Hjalmar Rued Holand, Carrie Larson, and Ingvald Skålnes.

Appendix D
Government land purchased by Norwegians
at the U.S. Land Office in Ft. Des Moines, Iowa

The information below is from microfilm of the land entry tract books documenting the transfer of public land from the U.S. Government to private ownership.[533] Similar information is available online on the Bureau of Land Management (BLM) Web site. One important difference between the two sources of information is the date the land was purchased is recorded in the tract books, and the BLM Web site shows the date the patent or warrant was issued to the purchaser. When people purchased land at a U.S. Land Office, they received a receipt of their purchase, but it often took several months before they received their official patent or warrant for the land.

Southern Settlement Land Purchases

Purchase Date	Name	Township	Section	Acres
October 9, 1854	Ole Apland	Union	32	160
October 9, 1854	Knut Ersland	Union	28	120
October 9, 1854	Ole Fatland	Union	31	160
October 9, 1854	Severt Gravdahl	Union	29	80
October 9, 1854	Osmund Johnson	Union	30	331.45
October 9, 1854	Wier Johnson	Union	29	80
October 9, 1854	Oscar Larson	Union	31	85.36
October 9, 1854	John Severson	Union	32 & 33	160
October 9, 1854	Lars Tesdahl	Union	29	40
October 9, 1854	Wier Weeks	Union	29	80
October 9, 1854	Erick Sheldahl & Osmund Sheldahl	Palestine	25 & 36	360
April 15, 1855	Brit Olson	Elkhart	6	120
April 16, 1855	Ole Olson Heggen	Lincoln	1	40
April 18, 1855	Knut Bauge	Union	30	160
April 18, 1855	John Severson	Union	32	160
June 29, 1855	Erick Johnson	Lincoln	12	80
June 29, 1855	Osmund Sheldahl	Palestine	35	80
October 9, 1855	Ole Fatland	Lincoln	1	80
October 9, 1855	Osmund Sheldahl	Palestine	36	80

Date	Name	Township	Section	Acres
Nov. 6, 1855	Peter Apland	Palestine	26	40
February 1, 1856	Erick Tesdahl	Lincoln	1	40
April 17, 1856	Lars Tesdahl	Union	29	40
April 17, 1856	Wier Weeks	Union	29	40
April 18, 1856	Osmund Sheldahl	Palestine	10	80
April 18, 1856	Osmund Sheldahl	Palestine	36	80
April 23, 1856	Erik Sheldahl	Lincoln	3	145.98
May 14, 1856	Brit Olson	Elkhart	6	40
May 22, 1856	Ole Anfinson	Palestine	15	160
June 6, 1856	Barney Hill	Palestine	21	40
June 6, 1856	Barney Hill	Palestine	21	120
June 6, 1856	Thomas Houge	Lincoln	12	120
October 9, 1856	Knud Ersland	Union	28	40
Feb. 11, 1859	Erick Sheldahl	Palestine	36	40
August 30, 1866	Thomas B. Erickson	Lincoln	1	40
		Total Acres:		3,523

Northern Settlement Land Purchases

Purchase Date	Name	Township	Section	Acres
June 8, 1855	John Nelson	Howard	8 & 17	200
June 14, 1855	Sam Christian	Howard	23	80
June 14, 1855	Jonas Duea	Howard	22 & 23	480
June 14, 1855	Nels Egeland	Howard	26	80
June 14, 1855	Jacob Erickson	Howard	14	160
June 14, 1855	Mons Grove	Howard	22 & 23	200
June 14, 1855	John Hill**	Howard	14	240
June 14, 1855	Hans Johnson Twedt	Howard	23	160
June 14, 1855	Ole Johnson	Howard	21	160
June 14, 1855	Samuel Johnson	Howard	23	160
June 14, 1855	John Michaelson	Howard	26	80
June 14, 1855	Lars Sheldall	Howard	15	200
June 14, 1855	Paul Thompson	Howard	27	160
June 14, 1855	John Johnson**	Lafayette	23	200
Sept. 27, 1855	Andrew Anderson	Howard	12	160
Sept. 27, 1855	Jacob B. Jacobson	Howard	13	160

Date	Name	County	Section	Acres
Sept. 27, 1855	Rasmus Ask	Howard	7	40
Sept. 27, 1855	Knute Halvorson**	Howard	15	80
Sept. 27, 1855	Erick Nelson**	Howard	12	160
Sept. 27, 1855	Erick Nelson**	Howard	15	80
Sept. 27, 1855	Jacob Nilson	Howard	13	160
Sept. 27, 1855	Ole Rasmusen	Howard	10	120
Sept. 27, 1855	Ole Rasmusen	Howard	12	160
Sept. 27, 1855	Lars Henryson	Lafayette	5	160
Sept. 27, 1855	Torkel Henryson	Lafayette	4	80
Sept. 27, 1855	Torkel Henryson	Lafayette	4	80
Sept. 27, 1855	John Johnson**	Lafayette	5	80
Sept. 27, 1855	John Johnson**	Lafayette	5	80
Oct. 27, 1855	Osmund Henryson	Lafayette	4	115.89
Oct. 29, 1855	Thor Hegland	Howard	24	120
Oct. 29, 1855	Lars Larson	Howard	25	120
Oct. 29, 1855	Lars Larson	Howard	24	40
Oct. 29, 1855	Torkel Opstvedt	Howard	13	160
Jan. 12, 1856*	Hans Pederson	Scott	20	320
Oct. 15, 1856	Thor Hegland	Howard	24	40
January 20, 1858	Jonas Duea	Howard	2	65.8
August 22, 1861	Ole Ritland	Howard	12	40
Dec. 1869[534]	Enoch Johnson	Howard	8	40
		Total Acres:		5,222

* Purchased at the U.S. Land Office in Ft. Dodge, Iowa.
** Did not move to Iowa.

Appendix E
Norwegians living in central Iowa when they volunteered for the Civil War

Name	Age	Marital Status	Mustered In	Mustered Out
10th Iowa Infantry, Company K				
Ole Anfinson	39	M	10-11-1861	10-11-1864
Erick Egland	41	M	10-11-1861	10-17-1862
Henry Egland	28	S	12-26-1861	Died in CW
John O. Johnson	21	S	10-11-1861	10-11-1864
John Birkestrand	19	S	10-11-1861	2-24-1862
Samuel Olson	22	S	10-11-1861	11-7-1863
Torres Scott	37	M	10-11-1861	3-4-1863
Iver Twedt	26	M	10-11-1861	10-11-1864
13th Iowa Infantry, Company G				
Osmund Anfenson	45	M	11-6-1864	7-21-1865
16th Iowa Infantry, Company I				
Lars Henderson	41	M	11-18-1864	7-19-1865
23rd Iowa Infantry, Company A				
Elias Ersland	18	S	8-16-1862	Died in CW
Andrew Gravdahl*	26	S	8-21-1862	Died in CW
Thor Hegland	31	S	8-21-1862	Died in CW
Thor Nelson*	30	S	8-21-1862	7-26-1865
Christopher Ness	22	S	8-21-1862	Died in CW
Torres Opstvedt	18	S	8-21-1862	12-18-1863
Severt Tesdahl	20	S	8-21-1862	7-26-1865
Christ Torkelson*	21	S	8-21-1862	7-26-1865
Oliver Weeks	26	S	8-21-1862	Died in CW
32nd Iowa Infantry, Company K				
George Boyd	33	M	4-20-1864	7-15-1865
Jonas Duea	37	M	9-3-1862	8-24-1865
Osmund Egeland*	26	S	9-3-1862	Died in CW
Peter Egland	26	S	9-3-1862	Died in CW
Henry Eliason*	33	M	9-3-1862	Died in CW
Henry B. Henryson	19	S	9-3-1862	Died in CW
Jacob B. Jacobson	40	M	9-3-1862	8-24-1865
Erick R. Larson	21	S	9-3-1862	8-24-1865
Thomas Lein	32	M	9-3-1862	8-24-1865

Oliver Johnson*	43	S	4-20-1864	Died in CW
John Nelson	43	M	9-3-1862	1-10-1864
Nils L. Nelson	18	S	9-3-1862	8-24-1865
Halvor Opstvedt	43	M	4-20-1864	7-10-1866
John Ritland	24	S	9-3-1862	8-24-1865
Erick L. Sheldahl	18	S	9-3-1862	8-24-1865
44th Iowa Infantry, Company H				
Oliver Berhow	18	S	6-1-1864	9-15-1864
47th Iowa Infantry, Company F				
Thor Fatland	18	S	6-4-1864	Died in CW
Thomas Shaw	19	S	6-4-1864	9-28-1864
36th Illinois Infantry, Company H				
Andrew Nelson	17	S	9-23-1861	9-13-1864
91st Illinois Infantry, Company E				
Lars Boyd	28	S	9-8-1862	4-29-1863
Anfin Ersland	22	S	9-8-1862	7-12-1865
Ole O. Hegland	24	S	9-8-1862	7-12-1865
Sam Hegland	21	S	9-8-1862	7-12-1865
Lars J. Mathre	23	S	9-8-1862	7-12-1865
Thomas Weeks	24	S	9-8-1862	7-12-1865
Wier Weeks	22	S	9-8-1862	7-12-1865
Henshaw's Independent Battery Light Artillery				
Jacob Charlson	21	S	12-3-1862	7-18-1865

* Moved to central Iowa after 1860.

Appendix F
Why did families who owned land in Illinois choose to move to central Iowa?

Nine of the scouting party members who selected the locations of the two central Iowa Norwegian settlements were established farmers in Illinois, and yet they and other families who owned land chose to move. What caused them to "pick up stakes" as it were and move to the edge of the American frontier where the nearest railroad depot was 120 miles away when they already had built up a pioneer farmstead and were close to a town with a railroad depot where they could purchase supplies and sell their products?[535]

Was their motivation, as early histories assert,[536] to help recent immigrants purchase land they could afford, or did they have other reasons for moving to central Iowa? Answers to the question of why they chose to move are still a mystery because information about their specific reasons for this decision has not been found. Without it, historians are left with only questions.

Was moving to the frontier an opportunity to leverage their economic success in Illinois?

Were they thinking about the future of their children who would want to purchase land some day or other relatives and friends in Illinois and Norway who wanted to become landowners? Did they believe their farming experience in Illinois' tall grass prairie environment would be needed in order for the central Iowa settlements to succeed?

Were they thinking about the cholera epidemic that reappeared in 1854 after causing many deaths in the Lisbon Settlement when it broke out in 1849? Did they believe moving 300 miles west of Lisbon was a way to be free from the scourge of this disease?

Was the adventuresome spirit that led them to emigrate from Norway tugging at them again? In *Concerning Our Heritage*, Ole E. Rølvaag states, "Our people are a restless folk. They are strongly rooted, and yet they are restless. Their spirit ranges far and wide. The call of the unknown and the lure of adventure are stronger in our kin than they are in most other peoples. We are easily captivated by risk-taking. The Norwegian people can stand gazing at the impossible until they can't resist the challenge any longer; they simply have to try. The attempt is often brilliant and frequently it succeeds."[537]

Was Lisbon a temporary settlement area for them where they could learn American farming methods before moving on to another area? In a chapter entitled "Changing Frontiers," Theodore Blegen wrote, "The scene in America, after the emigrants have broken old ties and crossed the seas, is one of continuing dispersion. Immigration becomes migration and merges with the American westward movement. ... The Fox River settlement in Illinois [which expanded to include the Lisbon Settlement in Kendall and Grundy counties], is important less for its priority than because it generated a social ferment in the immigrants' world, served as a center for the play of religious ideas and forces, harbored such leaders as Elling Eielsen, symbolized to Norway the destiny of its emigrated sons and daughters, and became a fertile mother colony."[538]

Were there religious reasons for deciding to move to central Iowa? Many of the immigrants in the Fox River Settlement area were influenced by Hans Nielsen Hauge [1771–1824], a lay minister who led a spiritual and social movement in Norway.[539] One of his followers was Elling Eielsen [1804–1883] who, after Hauge's death in 1824, became one of the "most active and widely known" Haugean lay preachers in Norway.[540] When Eielsen immigrated in 1839, the largest colony of Norwegian immigrants lived in the Fox River Settlement, and Eielsen continued his evangelistic ministry there.[541]

In *The Lutheran Church Among Norwegian-Americans*, Nelson and Fevold state, "A characteristic feature of Hauge's outlook was his concept of a person's daily work as a divine calling. He was of a practical bent of mind and urged his followers to be diligent in their everyday work. When he stayed at the home of a farmer during his travels, Hauge assisted with the farm work and advised his host how he could improve his farming methods and equipment. He wanted his followers to be economically independent so that the progress of God's Kingdom could be facilitated. He assisted several of his friends in getting established on farms and in various business enterprises."[542]

When the nine scouting party members were chosen, did they consider it a divine calling? By accepting the responsibility, were they agreeing to move to the area they selected and help others get started in farming? All nine purchased land before returning to Lisbon, and the last part of Osmund Sheldahl's scouting party report is consistent with Hauge's concept of divine calling. Sheldahl exclaimed, "... Brothers! It is the land that the Lord has prepared for us. From Norway's mountain passes we came, where we had to break stony ground on steep hills between floods and slides, where our pastures lay in ice-bound and shady hills. Here we can comfortably stretch our limbs in peaceful pursuit, following plough and scythe and the rich soil will abundantly repay us for our work."[543]

Moving to frontier America was a difficult decision,[544] and these questions may have been among the many questions Lisbon families discussed before deciding to move to Iowa in the 1850s.

Lisbon, Illinois: A Gateway to the West

by Jim Mason

Why Lisbon? Why did Rasmus Larson Tungesvik and Osmund Sheldahl, among the early arrivals from the Norwegian fjord communities of Skånevik and Etne, who later became pioneers in the Norwegian settlement of central Iowa, choose the vicinity of Lisbon, Illinois, as their first destination in the United States? How did it happen that this patch of Illinois prairie, 60 miles by coach road from Chicago became a destination for so many Norwegians in the early decades of immigration from Norway?

I've asked this question many times, listening to the tales told of my Norwegian forebears who were among those who found their way to the Lisbon settlement in the mid-1800s. For my grandparents and great grandparents, the stories do not dwell on the precise reasons as to why they went to Illinois rather than Wisconsin, the preferred destination of many more Norwegians during the first decades of the migration. Nor will we ever know exactly what circumstances led Rasmus Larson Tungesvik and Osmund Sheldahl to choose the prairie countryside of the Yankee village of Lisbon, Illinois, as their first destination in the United States. But we can uncover a few of the considerations that were likely to have played a part in their decisions by looking more closely at the social and cultural landscape the two pioneers encountered when they came into the Upper Illinois River countryside in the mid-1840s.

Chicago – 1845

On their way to create a new home in the midlands of North America, Osmund Sheldahl, together with his wife of a few months, and his sister Margaret and her husband, Rasmus Larson Tungesvik, with their five children, arrived in the youthful city of Chicago during the summer of 1845. The hard times that had followed the Panic of 1837 had finally passed, and the frontier settlement was once again a bustling town. Already in its second decade, Chicago was a city with a future, spread out on the shores of Lake Michigan, a cluster of residences and business places, churches and schools, warehouses, barns, stables and shops, sprawling south, west, and north onto the encircling prairie. Everywhere new enterprises were appearing, with more in the works. Streets were being improved. Horse and oxen-drawn wagons, and horses with coaches and carriages were coming and going throughout the day. Schooners and steam boats loaded and unloaded at Chicago's crowded harbor. Plank roads and railways were being planned and financed. Workers were once again engaged in the city's most celebrated project, the Illinois and Michigan Canal, 96 miles in length, 60 feet wide, connecting the Chicago River and Lake Michigan with the Illinois River and the Mississippi. Twelve thousand people resided in Chicago in 1845, including French-Canadians with roots in the city's trading post beginnings; Yankees and New Yorkers, who dominated Chicago's business, political, and cultural life; one hundred and forty African-Americans; over a thousand Germans; and nearly as many Irish, with a majority working as laborers on the canal. Also counted in 1845, according to the J. W. Norris City Directory, were over five hundred Norwegians, the city's third largest immigrant group, and probably most of them with words of advice for newcomers from their homeland, like Rasmus Larson Tungesvik and Osmund Sheldahl.[1]

It is likely that these two summer arrivals in Chicago would be given the latest news of Fox River, the oldest Norwegian settlement in the Midwest, lying southwest of the city near the termination of the canal that was then under construction. But probably they were also told of newer settlements of Norwegians that were then underway, including Muskego and Koshkonong, both in Wisconsin; Long Prairie in Boone County, Illinois; Jefferson Prairie on the Illinois-Wisconsin state line; and the Lisbon settlement, on the road to the Fox River community. Meeting another group from Norway that arrived in Chicago during the summer of 1845, Norwegians in the city told them "to go north, preferably to Koshkonong in Wisconsin, where there (is) said to be an abundance of fertile land at low prices." Their advice to Rasmus Tungsevik and Osmund Sheldahl may have been the same: "Go to Wisconsin; a new land awaits you!"[2]

Surely there were also Norwegians in Chicago who would extend an invitation to the newcomers to settle in their city, already the home of what was to become a major urban colony of Norwegian-Americans. But there is no evidence that Tungesvik and Sheldahl were interested in remaining in Chicago. Like most of their compatriots, they would be inclined to envision themselves as living in a farm community in America, not in an emerging metropolis. As Svein Nilsson, the first collector of the histories of the Norwegian immigration, wrote in 1869:

"Most of the Norwegian emigrants have preferred farming to any other occupation in life. This was especially true during the early years, when the emigrant ranks were filled almost exclusively with people from the mountain regions who from early childhood were accustomed to regard tillage and cattle-raising as the surest source of food and income. The turmoil and instability of city life did not agree with their conception of well-being. They left the old country in order to find a plot of ground on this side of the ocean which they could call their own. With great reluctance a few of them did take temporary jobs in the cities as servants or day laborers but only in order to earn enough money to buy a little land in regions which the red men had abandoned for new hunting grounds in far western wilds still untouched by civilization."[3]

Tungesvik and Sheldahl also were likely to have heard tales of the city's Norwegian community as being a wild and wooly lot, prone to drinking and fighting. As one Norwegian visitor to the United States, Ole Munch Raeder, noted in 1847, "it seems probable...that in such a harbor city, where people are employed as quay porters and at odd jobs, it is easier to fall into all sorts of vice than among the simple, thrifty populace in the rural communities, especially, if...a nucleus of bad company already has been formed, where drinking, gambling, and fighting are the order of the day."[4] Reflecting a similar judgment, the pioneer churchman from Norway, Johannes W. C. Dietrichson, visited the Norwegian colony in Chicago during the summer of 1844 and found members of that community to be "drinkers who, by their disturbances and fighting, have brought our people into bad repute among the Americans. Under the nickname 'the Norwegian Indians,' they are frequently lampooned in the newspapers." While some members of the Chicago colony may not have met the pastor's standards of dignity and decorum, he did find at least one Norwegian to be "an industrious man, orderly and well thought of by the Yankees." Dietrichson was referring to Halstein Torrison, one of the earliest Norwegian settlers in Chicago, having come to the city in 1836 from a district of Norway close by the home communities of Rasmus Larson Tungesvik and Osmund Sheldahl.[5]

If a single voice was responsible for Tungesvik's and Sheldahl's choice of Lisbon as their destination, Halstein Torrison could have been a likely candidate. Torrison worked as a gardener for Walter Newberry, a prominent member of the city's business community, who had come to Chicago from Connecticut in 1833. In addition to his work on the Newberry estate, Torrison is said to have been employed as a recruiter of Norwegians to work as laborers in the building of the Illinois-Michigan canal. In such a capacity, he would have been informed of the movement of Norwegians through the larger region, especially the canal corridor. He also may have had knowledge of temporary lodging and work opportunities, and may even have been familiar with the question of farm land availability along the waterway.[6]

With Chicago behind them, the Tungesvik and Sheldahl party moved on, but not to Koshkonong or other settlements north and northwest of Chicago (see Figure 1). Their destination was the community of Norwegian settlers who had settled on the eastern side of the lower Fox River, northeast of Ottawa, Illinois. Their route was likely to have been the "high prairie trail," the ancient path sometimes known as the Potawatomi Trail that ran southwesterly from Chicago to the Upper Illinois River valley.[7] The road traversed an open land with expansive horizons, like no place these Norwegians from the rugged north Atlantic coast had previously experienced. No doubt they had heard of the boundless prairie, of the fertility of its soil and the beauty of its summer flowers and wind-blown grasses. But they had also heard the stories of disease and fever that were said to lurk in the untilled grasslands, and of prairie fires, droves of insects, springtime floods, summer's heat, and winter winds that swept the plains. Now they had finally arrived in such a landscape, following a road through open country, broken only by a few bottomland woods that traced the course of rivers and creeks, and an occasional hardwood grove on an upland site where a few newly established farmsteads lay among its trees. It was a different world they were about to enter, and the Fox River settlement and Lisbon, Illinois, would be its doorway.

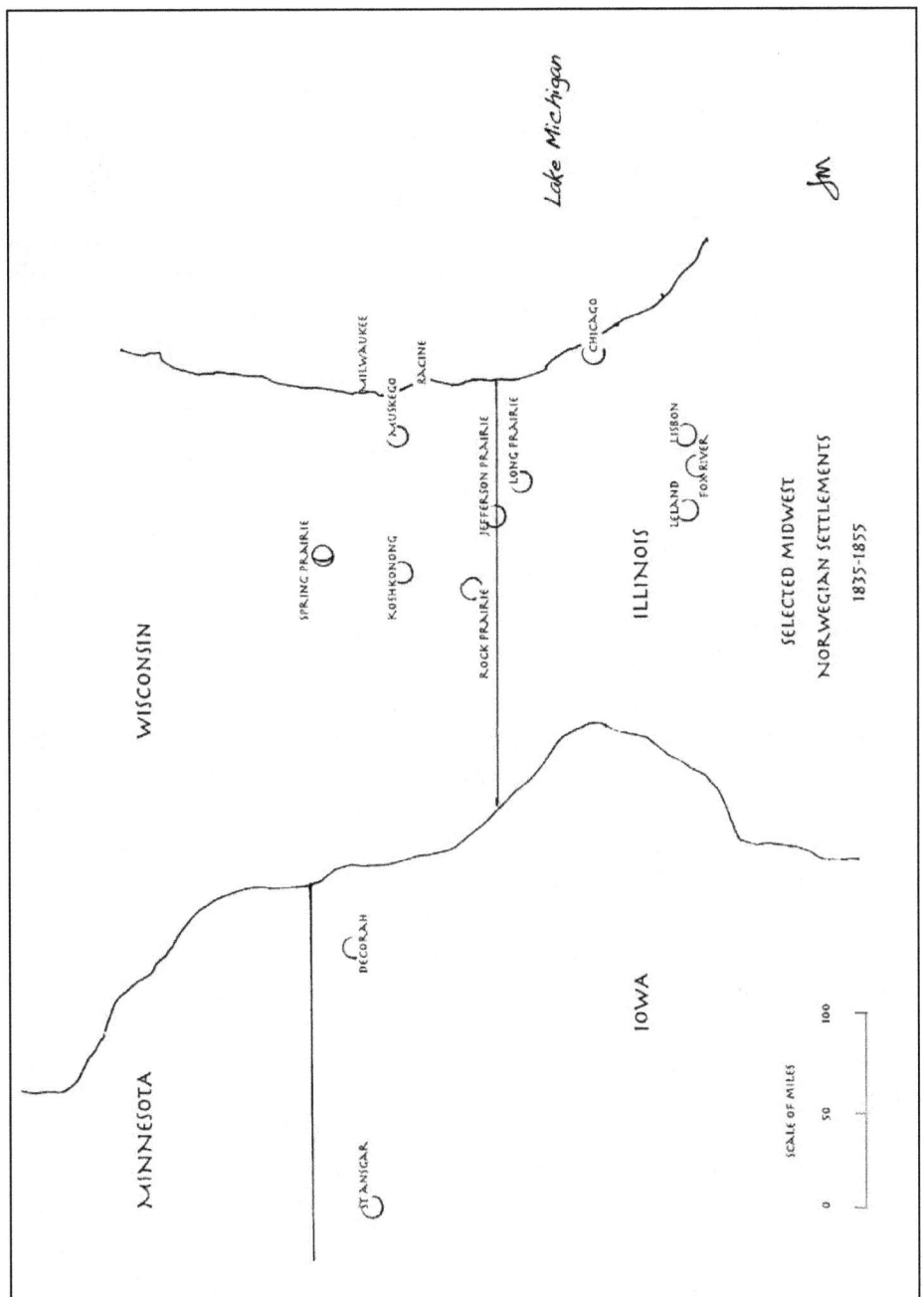

Figure 1
Selected Midwest Norwegian Settlements 1835–1855

Lisbon, Illinois: a Yankee colony

The "Lisbon settlement" was a rural Norwegian community near the small prairie village of Lisbon in south Kendall County, Illinois. In its earliest years, the settlement consisted of no more than a sprinkling of Norwegians who made up an easterly extension of the more substantial Fox River settlement, located in the rolling prairie landscape between the Illinois River and its tributary, the Fox River in La Salle County, Illinois. With the passage of time and a swelling of its Norwegian population, Lisbon developed more of its own identity, especially after 1855, fostered in large part by the reputation of the Lisbon Evangelical Lutheran Church and the leadership of its pastor for 40 years, Peter Andreas Rasmussen. For new immigrants and travelers on the main road heading west out of Chicago, the small rural community of Lisbon was the first Norwegian settlement to be encountered beyond the expanding borders of the city. It would not be surprising that the Lisbon settlement would come to be recognized both as a gateway to the west and a seedbed for the establishment of Norwegian colonies and congregations in northern Illinois, Iowa and the Upper Midwest.

In 1845, when Rasmus Tungesvik and Osmund Sheldahl and their families arrived in the Lisbon area, they would have found only a few Norwegians living in the vicinity. What they encountered was a predominantly Anglo-American community comprised largely of families who had arrived from northeastern United States ten years earlier. The beginnings of the village of Lisbon lay in the continental shifts in population that took place in northern Illinois in the early years of the nineteenth century. Leading this transition was the dispossession and removal of the indigenous nations of the region, culminating in the short-lived Black Hawk War of 1832 and the 1833 treaty at Chicago with representatives of the Potawatomi and allied peoples, the last in a series of negotiations and land acquisitions surrounding lower Lake Michigan that had begun following the War of 1812.[8] Giving impetus to this movement was the internal migration of population entering the region first from the lower Midwest and southeastern United States, but soon overtaken by the larger move of Yankee immigrants from New England and New York. Encouraged by the completion of the Erie Canal in 1825, connecting the Hudson River with the Great Lakes, and opening a northern water route to the middle of the continent, the Yankee invasion of the upper Midwest, including northern Illinois, was a move of thousands, transforming the prairie landscape and shaping a society that would dominate the economic, political, and cultural features of the Midwest for more than a century. Like the "America Fever" that swept through the farms of southwest Norway, "Illinois Fever" found a welcome response among the farmers and townsfolk of New England and New York. "Whether the discontent was for social, political, or religious conditions, the same idea underlay it all," wrote the historian of the New England migration, Lois Kimball Mathews, in 1909, "and that idea was that greater advantages might be gained for one's self and one's children in the new home than in the old...Yet even in their ambition, the frontiersmen from New England have not been unmindful of the moral and religious side of life...Therefore, the emigrants carried with them their school, their church, and their town-meeting; certain that their own institutions were best..."[9]

Minor groups accompanying the movement of New Englanders and New Yorkers into the region were Irish, German, Scandinavian, English and Scotch immigrants, who tended to form enclaves within the larger quiltwork of settlement. Adding to this diversity were religious colonies, most notably Mormons who settled at Nauvoo, Illinois, on the Mississippi River in 1840, leaving after the murder of Joseph Smith in 1844; and the Swedish followers of Eric Jansen, who arrived at Bishop Hill in Henry County, Illinois, in 1846.

A feature of the migration from New England and New York was the "colony" settlement—the organized move of a group of families from a single community, forming a nucleus of settlement in a particular locale in the Midwest. Typically, a colony would send a few members ahead to act as a scouting party, delegated to select a location and acquire land for members of the group. The goal of most colonies was to establish a town. Some had religious or social reform purposes and were led by a member of the clergy; a few sought to create a college or academy. The intention of all colonies was to improve the economic situation of its members. At least twenty-two Yankee colonies were established in Illinois during the 1830s, including Lisbon, which resulted from the move of families and single individuals from Oneida County, New York, in 1835.[10]

Years later, Mathilde Rasmussen, the daughter of Peter Andreas Rasmussen, the pastor of the Norwegian Lutheran Church at Lisbon for nearly a half-century, noted the coming of the Oneida colony and the beginnings of the town of Lisbon in her memoir of her father and mother. "When Lisbon was a prairie," she wrote, "a group of fine, cultured, educated Christian people from New York State—traveling westward in covered wagons—found this to be the Goshen of their search for a new home. Evidently they were people of means. They built the village of Lisbon. Stores were built. A good-sized stone church and a two story stone school house were erected.... (T)hese are still standing, as are the homes they built. Many were comfortable frame buildings, but a few were smaller mansions...The farm homes were also large and comfortable. In my mind I can see them as they were, with the names of the owners, Knox, Wilcox, MacEwen, Langdon, Kelsey, Tuttle, etc., not to forget the two Moores—the Lisbon merchants..."[11]

The core of the Lisbon colony was a group of families who had been associated with the Oneida Institute of Science and Industry, an educational academy in Whitesboro, New York, near Utica. Featuring a curriculum that combined work and manual education with classical learning and evangelicalism, the school favored an anti-slavery sentiment that led toward the positioning of abolition as a central element of the school's educational mission. Closely allied with Galesburg, Illinois, founded by another colony with ties to the Oneida Institute, the Lisbon community was among the stronger supporters of Knox Manual Labor College, which was opened at Galesburg in 1838. Herman Muelder, an historian of the colony movement and its role in the establishment of Knox College, noted that the Big Grove Congregational Church, the original church of the Lisbon colony, was the mother church of congregations in Ottawa, Aurora, Newark, and Lisbon village, "all of which took a lead in the resurgence of Congregationalism and were identified with the reform 'causes' of the day. This concern with reform was especially a characteristic of the Lisbon church that was founded in 1838."[12] With abolitionists in Galesburg, Princeton, and other northern Illinois communities, members of the Lisbon church were linked with the regional Underground Railroad network during the 1840s and 1850s.[13] Ole Olson Hetlevet, a lay preacher and Bible salesman, and one of the first Norwegians to move into the Lisbon settlement, joined with his Yankee neighbors in providing sanctuary for escaping slaves and their families. Olson's oldest son, Porter Olson, was a teacher in the Lisbon Academy, a school for older youth founded in the mid-Forties. During the Civil War, Porter served as an officer in a company of the 36th Illinois Infantry, made up largely of volunteers from the Fox River communities.[14]

For the Yankees from the forested hills and rocky fields of eastern New York and New England who moved into the Lisbon area in the 1830s, the prairie landscape was as much a "new world" as it would be for the Norwegians who followed a few years later. The first farm sites to be taken by the easterners were in or adjacent to timbered tracts—woodlands along the watercourses of meandering creeks and the Fox and Illinois Rivers; and hardwood groves located on the terminal moraine that ran diagonally from northeast to southwest, west of the future location of the village of Lisbon. Woodlands offered familiar surroundings for the settlers, but more importantly, they provided fuel, timber for buildings and fences, wild honey, maple syrup, walnuts and hickory nuts, shade from the summer's heat, and shelter from the winter winds. The largest grove, the site of the first settlement in the area, was known as Big Grove, later becoming the name of the township in southwest Kendall County, which until 1841 was part of La Salle County, Illinois. Other wooded areas on the moraine often took the name of an early settler, like Holderman's, or Hollenback's, two other groves in the Lisbon countryside.[15]

"We are now living on the prairie"

As wooded farm sites in southwest Kendall County were taken up and as Yankees and other early arrivals became more familiar with the advantages afforded by the midwestern prairie, settlers began moving into the treeless open country. An early historian of Lisbon told the story of the first families that moved from the security of the trees of Big Grove out into the open prairie to build their homes on the future site of the village in 1836: "Great was the astonishment" of the community, she wrote, to see dwellings appear on the grass covered plain stretching for miles south and east of the woods where the first settlement had been made. One of those making the move wrote to her parents in New York in the summer of 1836: "We are now living on the prairie, three miles from timber...We moved on to the prairie the 27th day of April and commenced ploughing the middle of May." Continuing, she wrote, "suppose the meadow we used to own (in New York)...contained hundreds of acres all as handsome as that and the grass tall enough to mow and spangled with a great variety of flowers, and growing on a deep rich soil and plenty of good water, all in the state of nature—would you call it good or not?"[16] Within a couple of years, the open prairie site of Lisbon village was platted and named, and contained its first residences, a store, a station on the road from Chicago to Ottawa, and the first school converted from a log granary. In 1838, the Congregational church was organized in the village and work was begun on a new frame school house, and in 1844 Lisbon Academy was underway. Four years later, the Illinois-Michigan Canal was completed, opening a prairie passage just eight miles south of Lisbon village, transporting goods and people, accelerating the commercial and agricultural development of the Upper Illinois valley, and stimulating the growth of cities along the waterway, including Morris, the county seat of Grundy County, positioned directly south of Lisbon. In the fall of 1851, work began on the Chicago and Rock Island Railroad to provide an overland link between Chicago and the Mississippi, via the Upper Illinois. Laid parallel to the Illinois-Michigan Canal, the construction of the railway reached Morris and Ottawa in the winter of 1853, arriving at the Mississippi River one year later.[17]

"All the land was full of people"

Throughout this early period of Lisbon history, the New York journalist and poet, William Cullen Bryant, witnessed the changes taking place along the stage road from Chicago to the Illinois River valley on his occasional trips west to visit his brothers who had first come to northern Illinois in 1831. A member of his family had moved west with the Hampshire Colony from western Massachusetts, settling on the prairie near what was to become the town of Princeton, Illinois.[18] Bryant visited his brothers several times, providing opportunities for him to record his travels in verse or newsworthy prose. Soon after his first trip west, which took him through the northern Illinois landscape, Bryant shared his initial impressions in his poem, *The Prairies*, written in 1833. He wrote of the prairie's "unshorn fields, boundless and beautiful," and likened the "airy undulations" and "verdant swells" of the grassland to the ocean, writing expansively of the "magnificent temple of the sky—with flowers whose glory and whose multitude rival the constellations!" Turning to the human history of the prairie, Bryant wrote of the succession of indigenous nations that had "ranged so long" on the "blooming wilds" of the midwestern plains, and how in recent years they moved on, looking westward where they "sought a wilder hunting ground." After expounding on the passing Native American occupancy of the Illinois prairie, Bryant concluded the poem with a foretelling of yet another people moving into the midlands:

*"The sound of that advancing multitude
Which soon shall fill these deserts. From the ground
Comes up the laugh of children, the soft voice
Of maidens, and the sweet and solemn hymn
Of Sabbath worshippers."*[19]

Years later, Bryant recorded the fulfillment of that poetic reverie in a narrative of travel on the same prairie trail in 1846. With its ruts, bumps, and deep pockets of mud, the road was much the same as on his earlier ventures. But its surroundings witnessed to the transformation from a few frontier outposts in a prairie landscape to a settled countryside in less than a generation. "I was struck with the difference." he wrote, "Frame or brick houses in many places had taken the places of log-cabins; the road for long distances now passed between fences, the broad prairie, inclosed [*sic*], was turned into immense fields of maize, oats, and wheat, and was spotted here and there with young orchards, or little groves, and clumps of bright-green locust trees, and where the prairie remained open, it was now depastured by large herds of cattle, its herbage shortened, and its flowers less numerous."[20] The echoes of Bryant's "advancing multitude" were heard by dozens of his contemporaries—poets and writers, who mourned the demise of a noble people, yet cheered the inevitable arrival of thousands with old world roots. Perhaps most familiar was the New England poet, Henry Wadsworth Longfellow, who in 1850 concluded his epic poem, *Hiawatha*, with his hero paddling off into oblivion in his birch canoe, envisioning

*"...the westward marches
Of the unknown, crowded nations,
All the land was full of people,
Restless, struggling, toiling, striving.
Speaking many tongues, yet feeling
But one heart-beat in their bosoms."*[21]

Ole Munch Raeder, a Norwegian government official who toured the early Norwegian settlements in the United States in 1847 and 1848, offered a similar perspective on the uprooting of the indigenous peoples of mid-America and their displacement by the "the westward marches" of settlers from abroad. "Silently the Indians came to this country," he wrote in his letters home, "and silently but restlessly they roamed about the plains and valleys here hundreds or thousands of years, only to vanish as the spirits of midnight at the rising of the sun, when the light of civilization and Christianity rose upon this continent."[22] For a deeply rooted people, as were many Norwegians in the first decades of the migration, leaving a centuries-old attachment to a farm and parish to seek a new place in a new land, the dislocation of Native Americans could have been a troubling matter for reflection and concern. But the prevailing evidence indicates that the attention of the early immigrants from Norway was given more to improving the circumstances of their own lives, establishing and sustaining their families, and practicing their faith in a new environment, and not to the preservation of indigenous homelands or questioning the part they were playing in American expansionism. To use Raeder's figure of speech, "at the rising of the sun," while Native Americans seemed to vanish from the landscape, the bearers of the "light of civilization"—Yankees from New England and New York, other Americans from the mid-Atlantic states and the eastern Midwest, and immigrants to follow, from Ireland and Britain, Germany, Canada, Scandinavia, and the Low Countries—were on their way to becoming a prairie people.

Norwegians were a minority

Although never more than the lesser of the predominant ethnic elements in the social landscape of Grundy and Kendall Counties, Norwegians provided a continuing presence in the counties since the two adjoining jurisdictions were created by the Illinois state legislature in 1841 (see Figure 2). As noted above, immigrants from Norway came into the Upper Illinois River area during the boom years of the 1830s, settling ten miles west of Lisbon, near the Fox River. Beginning with a few families, Norwegians soon settled in the vicinity of Big Grove, Lisbon, and the nearby village of Newark, another Yankee community, originally named Georgetown. During the depressed economy that followed the Panic of 1837, there was a slowing of the in-migration flow, and work on the canal came to a standstill. The growth of the area picked up again in the 1840s, especially after 1845, and the completion of the canal in 1848. In the forefront of the mid-century emigration to Lisbon from Etne, Skånevik, Matre, and other Sunnhordland communities, Osmund Sheldahl and Rasmus Tungesvik arrived at an opportune moment in the agricultural and economic development of the area, and the emergence of a small, but thriving Norwegian settlement.[23]

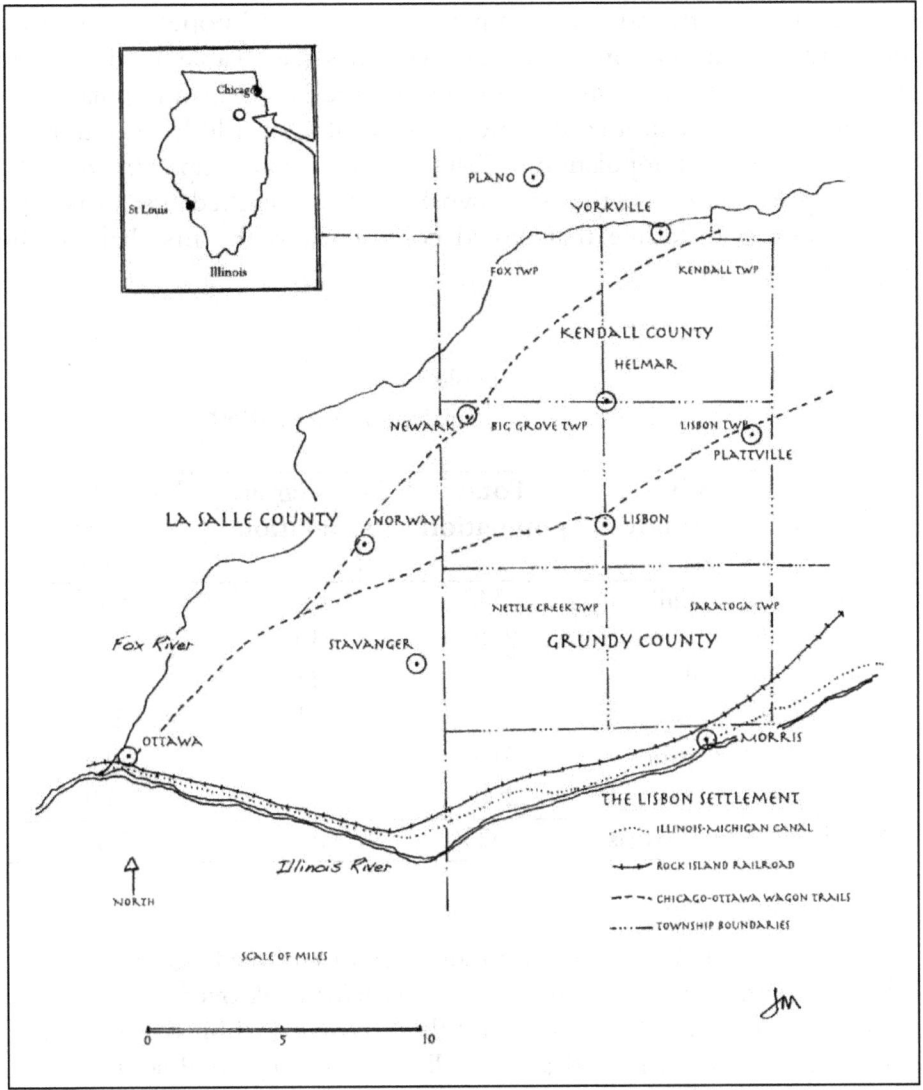

Figure 2
The Lisbon Settlement

By 1850, the population of persons born in Norway, including their children born in the United States, residing in the Lisbon settlement area of the four townships in the southwest corner of Kendall County (Fox, Kendall, Big Grove, and Lisbon) and two townships in northwest Grundy County (Nettle Creek and Saratoga) had grown to number 391, which amounted to a little less than ten percent of the total population of four thousand in that portion of the two counties (see Table 1). Ten years later, the 1860 federal census recorded that the Norwegian population in the Lisbon settlement area had increased to 983, or a little over thirteen percent of the total population of 7,400 in the six townships. By 1870, the overall population of the six townships had reached its peak and was beginning a decline that would continue into the first half of the twentieth century.[24]

Table 1
Population, Lisbon settlement area, 1850[25]

Township in Kendall or Grundy Counties	Total population	Norwegian population	Norwegian percent of total
Big Grove, Kendall	1,343	132	9.8
Fox, Kendall	846	40	4.7
Kendall, Kendall	797	23	2.9
Lisbon, Kendall	519	13	2.5
Nettle Creek, Grundy	318	97	30.5
Saratoga, Grundy	200	86	43.0
Total, Six Townships	4,023	391	9.7

As the original Yankee community aged or moved on to the upper Midwest, central plains, or far west, Norwegians took over their farms or moved west to Iowa, Minnesota, and the Dakotas. Lisbon was a portal to the west, but also remained as a small but enduring rural settlement of Norwegian Americans in the Chicago region. My own forebears were typical of many Norwegian immigrant families. The parents of one of my grandmothers came to the Lisbon area in the early 1850s, moving west to settle in northern Story County, Iowa, a few years later, while the family of her husband, my grandfather, arrived in Lisbon from Norway in 1860, soon to move on, settling successively in Clinton, Benton, and Hamilton Counties, Iowa. Yet another of my Norwegian grandparents was born soon after his father moved his blacksmith trade from Chicago to Lisbon in 1858. Ten years later, his father took over one of the community's original Yankee farms, passing it on to the generations that followed, who farmed the land well into the 1990s.

In 1888, one local observer described the settlement as a well rooted, but separate community. Writing in a special edition of the Morris, Illinois, newspaper, the observer stated:

"The Norwegians of the locality are a very industrious and frugal people, therefore thrifty and frugal. Many of their farms and buildings are models of taste and good judgment. Having acquired title they seldom part with it, or, when a Norwegian buys a farm 'he buys it for keeps,' and never sells if he can avoid it. Though clannish to a high degree, and somewhat exclusive, they add much to the material wealth of the county."[26]

During the 1940s, a century after the first years of the settlement, a research team of the University of Chicago's Committee on Human Development took a look at the Norwegian Lutherans in the historic Lisbon settlement, in a study of social stratification in the city of Morris and Grundy County. "We stand apart," was the team's characterization of the Norwegians as both an ethnic group and a sect.[27] Years later, a member of the study team, Evon Z. Vogt, summarized the research he had undertaken in 1946 in the rural farm area north of Morris:

"The rural area was interesting because it was divided into two basic groups: the Old Yankee Families and the Norwegians. From participant observation in work groups and church socials and from intensive interviewing of both the Yankee and Norwegian farmers, I discovered marked social class divisions in the Yankee population compared to a much more unified and cohesive structure among the Norwegians, who occupied a depressed position in the overall structure. While social class was an organizing principle for the Yankees, the Lutheran church was the core of the Norwegian community."[28]

Since 1946, when Vogt made these observations, while the Norwegian American community became more fully assimilated within the larger society of Kendall and Grundy Counties (which have since been drawn into the southwesterly reaches of suburban Chicago), there continues to be a discernible presence of Norwegian culture in the Lisbon area. As recently as the year 2000, according to the U.S. Census, nearly eight percent of the population of 92,079 residing in Kendall and Grundy Counties identified itself to be of Norwegian descent, ranking them to be the fifth largest ethnic group in the two counties on the outskirts of the

Chicago metropolitan area. More numerous than persons of Norwegian descent were those who identified themselves to be of German, Irish, English, or Italian background. The historic churches of Norwegian Lutheran heritage were still the centerpieces of a Norwegian American presence in the larger community.[29]

During the early years of the settlement, Norwegians did not disperse themselves throughout the greater Lisbon community, but tended to be concentrated in several areas. These included the countryside immediately west of the village of Lisbon, the "North Prairie" in the vicinity of present-day Helmar north of Lisbon, and the open prairie country of the till plain located in the more northerly sections of Nettle Creek and Saratoga Townships in Grundy County. Geographer Michael Gambone's summary of immigrant settlement in 1850 and 1860 in northwest Grundy County speaks to the larger settlement area as well:

"The predominant ethnic groups which settled in Grundy County in 1850 were Irish and English, and Norwegian. Immigrants from England and Ireland could be found scattered in nearly every township. They constituted a majority among new arrivals in all sections of Grundy County except for Nettle Creek and Saratoga Townships. In all, they would constitute 44 percent of the total number of immigrants settling in the county. The next dominant group were those of Norwegian birth...Once they arrived, people of Norwegian extraction tended to gravitate towards individual communities set apart from the remainder of the population. Their prominence in Nettle Creek and Saratoga Townships readily demonstrates this tendency. Extended families were common and the incorporation of a smaller portion of single, landless laborers created remarkably cohesive communities built almost exclusively around agriculture."[30]

Language, dialect, and a shared heritage of life and work in the rural peasant communities that lay among the rocks and waters of the rugged west coast of Norway between Bergen and Stavanger contributed to the cohesiveness of the immigrant communities and their separation from the Yankee dominated society. But probably the most important feature of the heritage that shaped the creation and durability of the Norwegian settlements in rural Illinois was the character of the religious life that was brought by the immigrants from their homeland.

"When there is no one from the church of the fatherland to guide them."

When Osmund Sheldahl and Rasmus Tungesvik and their families arrived at Lisbon, they would have found a lively, but disordered religious scene. During the early years of the Fox River and Lisbon settlements, expressions of organized religion took on a variety of shapes and garments, brought forth by the exhortations of independent itinerant preachers, circuit riders, and missionary representatives of Methodist, Baptist, Mormon, and other religious bodies seeking to arouse the newly arrived immigrants, as well as the initiatives of Norwegian lay ministers among the settlers themselves. Most of the latter, like many of the immigrants coming to the United States in the early years of the migration, had been strongly influenced by the turn-of-the-century religious movement in Norway associated with the lay reformer Hans Nielsen Hauge and his followers, with their emphases on the conversion experience and the commitment of the whole of life to discipleship and a "living faith." Enduring in the histories of the Illinois settlements was the work of Elling Eielsen, a Haugean lay preacher from western Norway, who began meeting with groups of Norwegian Lutherans in the Fox River settlement as early as 1839, and a few years later was ministering to those who were settling in the vicinity of Lisbon.

Mormons, Baptists, Quakers, and the inroads of other Protestant denominations, as well as the preaching of Elling Eielsen and his followers, were all in the mind of Johannes Dietrichson, the clergyman from the church in Norway, when he visited the Fox Valley settlements in the spring of 1845. His troubled impressions of the churchly interests of his countrymen at Fox River were summarized in his travel narrative, published in Norway in 1846:

"In the latter part of April, 1845, I visited this colony, although without much hope of establishing a church, as I had heard reliable reports of much religious confusion among our people...The visit showed all too well what happens to the churchly interests of the unfortunate immigrants when there is no one from the church of the fatherland to guide them. Our dear countrymen, though holy baptism members of the Church of Norway, are with few exceptions scattered among a variety of sects here. Some are Presbyterians, others Methodists, Baptists, Ellingians, Quakers, and Mormons..."[31]

Continuing, Dietrichson went on to write that Fox River was "really the place where Elling Eielsen purports to have been called as pastor...He has erected a building that is used as a place of worship, and he also considers this his principal congregation, visiting it several times a year. The membership, so far as I can learn, has been reduced to only a few."[32]

Eielsen was born near Voss, Norway, in 1804. While in Bergen to learn the blacksmithing and carpentry trades, Eielsen began attending meetings of the "Friends of Hauge," as Hauge's followers were known. At the age of 28, he experienced a religious conversion and felt himself called to become an itinerant lay preacher. During the next seven years, he journeyed throughout Norway, Denmark, and Sweden, preaching, teaching, and ministering to folk. In 1839, Eielsen immigrated to the United States in order to bring his ministry to Norwegian immigrants and their families. He traveled continually, sometimes meeting new arrivals in New York or at ports on the Great Lakes, visiting the settlements, gathering people together, and providing a linkage between one settlement and another. Early in the 1840s, he built a meeting place at Fox River, one of the first religious buildings to be erected in the Norwegian American community.[33]

In the summer of 1843, Eielsen married Sigrid Nelson, whose family had recently arrived in the Muskego settlement in Racine County, Wisconsin. During the same year, he was ordained by a German clergyman in Chicago. Although members of the Muskego community rejected his offer to serve as the pastor of their Lutheran congregation, he and his wife settled in the community near his wife's parents. At the same time, some of the Norwegians at Fox River welcomed his ministries, and while he continued his travels throughout the settlements, he retained a special regard for the faithful congregants in Illinois. A forceful, even charismatic spokesperson for "a living faith," Eielsen was an effective recruiter of followers to assist his work at Fox River and other settlements as teachers or lay preachers. One such person was Ole Andrewson, a teacher in Norway and a lay preacher in Wisconsin, who was ordained to serve as a pastor in Fox River in 1846. Ministerial records indicate that Andrewson and Eielsen also shared in pastoral activities in the early years of the Lisbon congregation, including marriages and baptisms.[34] In 1851, Eielsen recruited Peter Andreas Rasmussen, newly arrived from Bergen, Norway, to teach the young people in the Lisbon congregation. Several years later, members of the congregation asked Rasmussen to become their pastor, which he did, following his ordination after attending the German Lutheran seminary for a few months at Fort Wayne, Indiana. He remained at Lisbon for the next 45 years as pastor of the West Lisbon church, as well as the North Lisbon (Helmar) church, which had been started in 1852. Although Rasmussen and Eielsen soon parted ways, Rasmussen remained a leading spokesperson for mission and lay leadership throughout his career.[35] It should be noted that Osmund Sheldahl was mentioned in the Lisbon church's history as one of the congregation's first lay teachers, coming from Norway in 1845, and that the first services of the Lisbon church were held in 1849 on Tungesvik's land in the house donated by Wier Weeks.[36]

The congregation of the Lisbon faithful, drawn together by Eielsen and Andrewson, was beginning to form around 1845—the year Sheldahl and Tungesvik came to the community. During the decade that followed, the congregation would organize itself as a strong and enduring church presence in the community, but would also find itself in the center of a larger convergence of events, currents, and conflicting personalities that would influence the Norwegian American religious landscape for a century. It was during those years that three synods or organizations of congregations, were initiated, including the Evangelical Lutheran Church in America, or Eielsen's synod, which was organized in 1846; the Northern Illinois Synod, which included Swedish and American congregations, founded in 1851; and the Norwegian Evangelical Lutheran Church in America, an organization formed in 1853 of more traditional Lutheran churches, with pastors trained in the university in Norway. Debates between and among these several bodies and their successors continued for the next half century and after. Much of the debate revolved around the role of the laity, but it also included concerns that reflected the relationship of the immigrant church to American social issues, especially slavery and public education.[37]

"A noticeable difference"

The contributions of Sheldahl and Tungesvik to the emerging life and work of the Lutheran congregation at Lisbon suggests that the reputation of the Illinois settlements at Fox River and Lisbon as a stronghold of the principle of lay leadership may have been one of the reasons for their choice of Lisbon as their initial destination in the New World. A related motivation was the preponderance of Norwegians coming to Lisbon and the neighboring Fox River settlement from the fjord district of the southwest coast of Norway between Stavanger and Bergen, the homeland of Sheldahl and Tungesvik, where the Haugean influence was particularly strong. Writing in the 1920s, J. Magnus Rohne, a professor of religion at Luther College and a historian of the formative years of the Norwegian Lutheran Church in the United States, expounded at length on the "very noticeable difference" that existed between the two major centers of the original Norwegian settlement in the Midwest—the Fox River settlement, Illinois, which included the Lisbon area, and rural Racine County in southeast Wisconsin, also known as the Muskego settlement. "In nothing is this difference more clearly brought out," wrote Rohne, "than in the attitude these settlements took toward Elling Eielsen. Elling Eielsen spent fully as much time at Muskego as at Fox River...At Muskego, Eielsen's invectives against the clergy only aroused disgust among the people...at Fox River, these invectives were a source of strength to Eielsen. Consequently, when Eielsen made a bid for the leadership at Muskego as well as at Fox River, Muskego rejected him, whereas Fox River accepted him." It was not, said Rohne, "a question of Lutheranism, nor even of Haugeanism." Both settlements were Haugean in their religious inclinations. "At the bottom of the cleavage that resulted in two distinct church traditions in America" was the question "of the balance of power between the clergy and the so-called 'laymen'."[38]

Continuing, Rohne wrote that "The fundamental reason for the difference...between the Muskego and Fox River settlers is directly traceable to different religious backgrounds in Norway." The Fox River settlement was recruited chiefly from Stavanger, while the first Muskego settlers were Haugeans drawn largely from Voss, Numedal, and Telemarken. In the former, growing from a strong sense of union fostered through "opposition to the governing classes in Church and State," stated Rohne, laymen's activity meant that "practically all functions are either centered in lay leaders or ignored." At Muskego, while "the impulses...of the social revolution" were retained, so was "their respect and affection for their pastors."[39]

In both settlements, Illinois and Wisconsin, Norwegians were confronted with the question of organizing a church in a nation in which the state played no role in the church's establishment, support, or conduct. The responses of the Fox River and Muskego communities to the question, it was Rohne's judgment, were markedly different, drawing from their respective backgrounds in the social and religious movements in the early decades of nineteenth century Norway.

Along with the affirmation of lay leadership in the life and work of the church, there were other features of the Lisbon and Fox River settlement environment that would have been seen as advantages by emigrants like Osmund Sheldahl and Rasmus Tungesvik, who were competent entrepreneurs as well as dedicated Haugeans. Three of these features should be noted: (1) the availability of employment in the Lisbon area; (2) the accessibility of the area to the transportation corridor leading to and from Chicago, only sixty miles from Lisbon; and (3) the tall grass prairie environment of Grundy and Kendall Counties, Illinois.

The availability of work

Not long after the Sheldahl and Tungesvik families arrived in the Lisbon settlement, a surge of new emigrants from the farms and villages of Norway's southwest coast followed in their path to northern Illinois—brothers and sisters, cousins, neighbors, and friends—all in search of a new beginning in the New World. It was an opportune moment. The Illinois-Michigan Canal was completed in 1848, bringing people and goods, opening new markets, and nurturing new enterprises. Only a few miles south of Lisbon, the Canal needed workers for loading and unloading cargo, building and maintaining boats, and managing the animals that provided towage. Townsfolk in Lisbon and Newark villages or in Morris, Ottawa, Marseilles, and other young cities along the Upper Illinois, and Yankee, British, and Scotch farmers among the prospering farms in the Lisbon settlement area sought laborers, domestic servants, and farm hands for their households and agricultural enterprises. Throughout the growing area, carpenters, blacksmiths, tinsmiths, leather workers, shoe makers, seamstresses, and other skilled craftspersons and their helpers could find work. "When immigrants arrive, the Yankees move on!" was the saying;[40] and the Lisbon community was becoming an example, with some of the original Yankee families, who had settled in Lisbon for just ten years or less, beginning to move out. Selling to the incoming Norwegians and others, the more restless Americans moved on to new pastures in western Illinois, or Iowa and Minnesota, where treaties with Native American tribes were opening new lands for settlement. Yankees, too, would be in the forefront of the expansionist excitement of the Polk presidency, heading for Oregon or California, and the rich, rugged empire of the southwest, taken from Mexico in the Guadalupe Hidalgo treaty of 1848.

A few Norwegians were able to buy land soon after their arrival in the settlement. Around 1840, one of the first Norwegian settlers in the Lisbon area, John Hill, took up land on the boundary of Grundy and Kendall Counties, southwest of Lisbon village. In 1850, the census reported the real estate value of his property to be $1,800, comparable to the value of the farms of many of his Yankee neighbors, but considerably higher than the farms of his fellow Norwegians. Ten years following John Hill's arrival in the community, according to the 1850 census, nearly fifteen per cent of the 369 farms in the Lisbon area—the four southwestern townships of Kendall County and the two northwestern townships in Grundy County—were owned and operated by Norwegian families.[41]

While most of the land in southwest Kendall County had already been taken by the time Osmund Sheldahl and Rasmus Tungesvik arrived in the community, the prairie of northern Grundy County, a few miles south of Lisbon village, was opened up for government sale in the last half of the 1840s. Much of the land was bought for speculation by Yankees and other Americans, anticipating the boom in community development that followed the completion of the canal. A few parcels were claimed by Norwegians in northwest Saratoga Township, Grundy County, including two hundred treeless prairie acres lying southeast of Lisbon village that was purchased by Osmund Sheldahl. By 1850, as recorded by the Federal Census, Saratoga Township had 38 farms, including fifteen owned and operated by Norwegians. According to the census, the average real estate value of the Norwegian farms was $313, while that of the non-Norwegian, predominantly Yankee farms was $1,744.[42]

Most of the immigrants, however, had to wait until suitable farm land became available or until they had bettered their financial means before they were able to make a purchase. Typically, they found temporary employment in the settlement or nearby, and moved in with established settlers until they were able to purchase land of their own. The experience of Wier and Synneva Weeks (Viar and Synneva Tendalsvikjo) of Matrefjord was similar to the story of many immigrants. After being brought to the settlement by Elling Eielsen to meet Rasmus Tungesvik, a previous acquaintance, Weeks was encouraged by Tungesvik to build a cabin on his land. Weeks had been a carpenter and boat builder in Norway, and while he worked on a home for himself and his family, he found employment in Ottawa, Illinois, building canal boats. In addition, he acquired a reputation as a builder of farm machinery. By 1849, Weeks had sufficiently improved his means to make it possible to establish a place of his own. He purchased a farm north of Lisbon and made the cabin he had built on Tungesvik's land available to the Lisbon Norwegian Lutheran congregation as their first meeting place. In a similar story, a neighbor of Wier Weeks and a fellow pioneer in the building of the North Prairie community, Nels Cassem, made his start by working on the towpath of the canal. Lars Nelson, yet another Norwegian pioneer in the North Prairie, began by setting himself up as a teamster, hauling goods to and from Chicago.[43] For years to come, many immigrant families with roots in the Lisbon settlement could relate to such narratives in the telling of their American beginnings.

Immigrants who were able to buy land often found it necessary for themselves and their older children to find other work in the community in order to support a family during their first years on the land. Some, like Wier Weeks, Nels Cassem, and Lars Nelson, found work in the growing transportation infrastructure of the Illinois valley. Others could support themselves through boarding arrangements with established farm families or homes of townsfolk in Morris, Newark, Lisbon, and other nearby communities. The Federal Census of 1850 in the Lisbon area townships reported a number of Norwegians, male and female, some married and some single, living in other households, working as farm hands, domestic servants, and laborers. Opportunities for employment were plentiful during the early decades of the settlement, but for all immigrant families, the process of sustaining one's family and nurturing roots in the prairie earth was an arduous and all-consuming project.

Access to markets and news of the wider world

Closely related to the advantage of the area's employment opportunities were Lisbon's proximity to markets in Chicago and the Upper Illinois valley and its position within the transportation corridor that linked Chicago with travel routes to St Louis, the Upper Mississippi, and the prairies of western Illinois and the upper Midwest. Big Grove community, Lisbon village, and Holderman's grove, all in the Lisbon settlement area, grew up as stopping places on the old coach road that followed the Potawatomie Trail from Chicago to Ottawa on the Illinois River. Running parallel to the coach road came the Illinois-Michigan Canal, completed in 1848, soon followed by the building of the Rock Island and La Salle Railroad out of Chicago, reaching Morris and Ottawa in 1853, and running west to the Mississippi River, which it reached in 1854. Throughout its changing modes of transport, the corridor provided a convenient means for hauling produce to markets in Chicago and the Upper Illinois valley, as well as for travel and shipping and receiving goods. The corridor was also a major source of employment, as has been noted above—hauling goods by wagon to and from Chicago, loading and unloading cargo, working on the canal towpath, handling draft animals, building and maintaining boats, and dozens of other jobs on the canal, coach road, and railway.

Until the railroad reached Morris, the Canal was a primary carrier of passengers on packet boats accommodating 75 to 100 persons (the fare for one person from Chicago to Morris—a 61 mile trip—was $2.50). After 1854, passengers resorted to the railroad, which was faster and cheaper, with the Canal continuing to be used almost entirely for hauling cargo—lumber from the forests of Wisconsin and upper Michigan; corn and grain from Illinois farms; coal, sand, and building stone from the Illinois valley; sugar from the Caribbean via New Orleans; and merchandise from Chicago and St Louis.[44]

There were many advantages to living near this transportation corridor. Not least was access to information provided by travelers heading west, or returning from Iowa, the Great Plains, or California; or from newly arrived immigrants, bearing news from the old country left behind, or making plans for moving on to a "home in the west." For some, living on the edge of the transportation corridor was like having a grandstand seat overlooking the changing drama of families and entire communities heading for the "promised land"—preachers and teachers, hucksters and hustlers, dreamers and poets, runaways and confidence men, surveyors and survivors, and whoever else, coming and going, peddling their wares, sharing their stories, or just passing through—a continuing parade of mid-century, mid-American life.

In the early 1850s, it was the main wagon road from Chicago to trails heading west to California and Oregon, as the *Ottawa Free Trader* editorialized in March 1850:

"Our town has for the past week been every evening so crowded with California teams and emigrants, that the hotels have not been able to accommodate all. We can scarcely look out of the window but we see California teams—some drawn by oxen, some by horses, some by ponies, some by mules—every species of conveyance seems to have been brought into requisition and every known contrivance to get through. On Fox River we

are credibly informed, the emigration will average one out of every six able bodied men; in northern Indiana the proportion is said to be even larger—while in our own county, although not as large as this, the proportion is yet fearfully large—and ten times more so, we honestly think, than it ought to be."[45]

Later in the same decade, the Upper Illinois Valley route became for the Norwegians at Lisbon the main wagon road to trails going west to Iowa and the Norwegian settlements in Clinton or Benton County, central Iowa, or beyond. For Osmund Sheldahl and his companions and relations, the passageway provided dozens of examples of groups of families and entire communities heading west: the Oneida, New York, families traveling west to Illinois in their wagons 20 years earlier, the wagons and carts of Mormons heading for Utah in the mid-Forties, Swedish immigrants on their way to Eric Jansson's Bishop Hill in 1847 to 1849, and the California-bound wagon trains of 1849 and the early 1850s.

An invitation to the midland prairie

Lisbon was a prairie settlement. But it was also a doorway to the immensity of the northern tall grass prairie region that contrasted so dramatically with the homeland landscapes of the Norwegian immigrants and yet was to figure prominently in the Norwegian movement into central and north central Iowa, southwestern Minnesota, the Red River valley, and the eastern Dakotas.

From the beginning, Norwegian travelers wrote of the prairie's advantages. As Ole Rynning wrote in 1838 in one the most influential early guides for emigrants:

"In the western regions, where all the Norwegian immigrants now go, the land is very flat and low...One can go two or three miles over natural meadows, which are overgrown with the most luxuriant grass, without finding a single tree. These natural meadows are called prairies. From earliest spring until latest fall they are covered with the most diverse flowers...The prairies are a great boon to settlers. It costs them nothing to pasture their cattle and to gather fodder for the winter...The soil on the prairies is usually rich, and free from stones and roots...Without being manured, the soil produces corn, wheat, buckwheat, oats, potatoes, turnips, carrots, melons, and other things that make up the produce of the land..."[46]

Or, writing in the early 1840s, Soren Bache, traveling to the Fox Valley settlements:

"The prairies we crossed were still covered with green grass and many varieties of flowers in full bloom. The plains with their patches of woodland appearing in the distance after long hours of travel resembled the sea where, once the land has faded away, there is nothing but sky and water except for occasional islands upon the rim of the horizon...According to our observation, the soil of the prairie really measures up to the high expectations raised by the accounts of Rynning and others. Without manure and with scarcely half the labor we would give to fields at home, it yields abundant crops..."[47]

Or from Ole Munch Raeder, another Norwegian visitor in the 1840s:

"...there is something striking about (the prairie)...to the Norwegians, who are accustomed only to mountains and valleys. As one gazes out over such a prairie, the houses seem like ships on a sea of cornfields, wheatfields, and meadows, gently rolling in the wind...Even its lonely and somber aspect gives it an appearance of grandeur like that of such parts of Norway as are still untouched by the hand of man. Furthermore, the imagination imparts to this new land, only recently snatched from the wilderness, the glamour of a future splendor to which no soil that has yielded to the plough for hundreds of years can lay claim..."[48]

The Norwegians in Illinois were new to the prairie environment and had much to learn as they adapted their farming tools and techniques to the tall grasslands of the Midwest. Fortunately, they could learn from the Yankee, English, and Scottish farmers who were their neighbors in Kendall and Grundy County, and who had found the prairie to be a similar challenge 20 years earlier. Later comers could learn from their fellow Norwegian countrymen, who had settled down on farms in the Lisbon area. Moving west to Lee County, Illinois, or to Clinton and Benton Counties, Iowa, or to central Iowa, or remaining in the open country between the Fox and the Illinois Rivers, the Lisbon Norwegians were the first generation in a long succession of prairie farmers. The map of Norwegian settlement in the upper Midwest during the nineteenth century closely coincides with the northern tall grass prairie region as described by early explorers, travelers, and surveyors. On such a map the Lisbon community—the first Norwegian rural settlement on the way west from Chicago—presented itself as a doorway to a sprawling northern grassland province that extended west to the Missouri and northwest beyond the Red River of the North.

About the Author
by the Compiler

Jim Mason was born in Northfield, Minnesota, in 1928. His father, a high school teacher, and his mother, a nurse, constantly encouraged their children's curiosity about everything in life from taking daily walks in the neighborhood observing birds to reading books like *A Child's History of the World* and *A Child's Geography of the World*. The local librarian thought Jim was too young for the many books he checked out on explorers and adventurers, but she allowed him to have them anyway.

Living only two blocks from St. Olaf College with neighbors who were teaching at the college, Jim decided to attend college there. He wanted to study how plants were used by different cultures (ethnobotany), but listened to his older brother's advice and studied philosophy, history, and English. After receiving his bachelor's degree, he spent a year in the American Studies program at the University of Minnesota before enrolling in Union Theological Seminary in New York where he received a master's degree in philosophy of religion in 1954.

During these formative years, Jim's summers were filled with backpacking trips in the Rocky Mountains and Canada, bicycling and studying in Norway, working in camps and settlement houses near and in Minneapolis and Chicago, and spending time pondering his future life's work. While working in Chicago, he met Sarah Refo who had grown up in China where her parents were missionaries. Jim and Sarah were married in 1952.

Jim became interested in cities while attending the University of Minnesota. He was fascinated with their histories, the ethnic diversity within them, and how people learned to live together. After completing seminary, he and Sarah returned to Chicago where Jim began working at a settlement house with inner-city youth and later in positions researching and writing about neighborhoods, social issues, and urban planning.

In 1963, Jim became director of Pleasant Valley Farm, a camp outside of Chicago, which he converted into an education/conference center modeled after the Highlander Folk School in Tennessee. He hired a very diverse staff and "We became known as a place where groups could find a neutral place to find common ground." In 1977, Jim became director of Wilder Forest north of Stillwater, Minnesota, and developed it into another center where people of diverse backgrounds could meet and learn from one another. Jim retired from Wilder Forest in 1995, and he and Sarah, a historian for the Minnesota Historical Society, moved to a rural farmhouse in west-central Minnesota near Starbuck.

Jim's interest in family history has its origin in boyhood visits to his aunts and uncles and in summer family reunions at the lake where he heard stories about the family and their old days. He always enjoyed the stories told by his uncle, John M. Mason, whose biography is in this volume of *The Central Iowa Norwegians* along with two obituaries he wrote containing stories and general historical information. "If someone were to ask me to write a family history when I was 10 years old," states Jim, "I could do a better job than I do now."

When Jim was about 30 years old and living in Chicago, he discovered pictures of two of his great grandfathers in books about Norwegian immigration to the United States. One was Lars Huus, his great grandfather who emigrated from Norway in 1850, together with his friend, P. A. Rasmussen, who later became the pastor of the church at Lisbon, Illinois. Lars' son, Alfred (Jim's grandfather), married a daughter of Pastor Rasmussen. After Alfred's wife died, he married Malinda Adland who is Jim's grandmother. The other picture was of Mons Adland, who brought his family to Iroquois County, Illinois, in 1837 and later moved to Racine County, Wisconsin. "Looking at those pictures gave me a little assurance that there was some connection in history of my family and [it] gave me kind of a personal connection of my history."

In a manner characteristic of his mother who always looked for the meaning of every life experience, Jim concluded the interview with the compiler by talking about his involvement in family history and his early life and his professional career: "Family [history] was not just piecing together a genealogy or something like that, but it had to do with the connections we have and our rootedness in places and people. For myself, it is more of a fundamental need—I need to have this realization of being part of a human group that extends into all these different people, the extended family, [who] are inter-connected …. There is another dimension to this. I really love the whole idea of place, location, environment—connecting to the whole succession of people who have worked [and lived] here. I think it is just being part of the earth, being a human being, and understanding we are really part of a larger community of people."

Shortly after celebrating their 50th wedding anniversary, Sarah Mason died. Jim continues to live in the rural home she loved and from which he travels to the homes of their four children, to places in search of information about his ancestors, and to destinations where he can keep satisfying his curiosity about the world.

Acknowledgment

The compiler gratefully acknowledges his friend, Jim Mason, for permission to publish his paper which he wrote specifically for this volume of *The Central Iowa Norwegians*. Jim's extensive knowledge of Norwegian settlement in the United States and of the Lisbon Settlement in particular is clearly evident in his investigation of the possible reasons Rasmus Larson Tungesvik and Osmund Sheldahl chose to settle near Lisbon, Illinois. His paper is an invaluable addition to our understanding of the history of the central Iowa Norwegians.

Story County in the Early 1850s

by Col. John Scott, 1890, William K. Wood, 1900, and William O. Payne, 1911

Settlement of Story County began in 1848, and when a state census was conducted in 1852, there were 214 people enumerated in the county. It is difficult to imagine the challenging, even foreboding environment Story County was for these immigrants. The following accounts written by Col. John Scott, William K. Wood, and William O. Payne provide a glimpse into frontier life at that time. Other reminiscences of the early years in Story County are contained in the *Atlas of Story County, Iowa* published in 1902 and in Volume 1 of William O. Payne's *History of Story County, Iowa* published in 1911.

• • •

Col. John Scott settled in Nevada, Iowa, in 1856. He wrote chapters XII-IV of Goodspeed's *Biographical and Historical Memoirs of Story County* which is a general history of Story County. Excerpts from Chapter XII appeared as an article entitled, "How Story County Got Its Name" in the "Nevada—Story County Centennial Edition" of the *Nevada Evening Journal*, June 13, 1953. A member of the Story County Centennial Historical Committee likely selected the excerpts for publication. The following selections from Col. Scott's history are primarily those used by the *Nevada Evening Journal* with some editing by the compiler. The ellipses indicate where the Journal chose to omit material.

• • •

Col. John Scott's History of Story County

The 24 miles square in the heart of Iowa comprised in the 16 Congressional townships, in the numbers 82, 83, 84, and 85 north and Ranges 21, 22, 23, and 24 west of the fifth principal meridian, have the sole honor among the political divisions in America of perpetuating the name of the great jurist and author of standard treatises upon American Law, Joseph Story of Massachusetts....

This name was given Story County Jan. 13, 1846, ... which was given at the suggestion of Hon. P. M. Cassady of Des Moines, who at the date of the christening, was a member of the General Assembly of Iowa....

Birth Is Interesting: The most interesting period of history of any nation or country is that of its birth....

When Iowa was opened for settlement, it required weeks or months of toil and adventure to reach her borders and many weary days to make a choice of location. The emigrant wagon was commonly drawn by oxen. The trail of the buffalo indicated the crossings of the unbridged streams. The sun, the stars, the leaves of the Indian compass, and the prevailing winds, indicated the course to be pursued on the treeless plains. In the early summer, the caravan of the pioneer trod a boundless carpet of green. As the season advanced, the growth of the grass was such as to afford easy concealment except for the tops of the canvass-covered wagons. After the great fires had swept the face of the country in the fall, there was but blackness and desolation everywhere.... Under such conditions, the physical features of the country did much to determine routes of travel and lines of settlement.

Water and timber were prime factors in the problems of pioneer life. The tide of population flowed against the tide of the streams and meandered the groves on their borders.... They were firmly convinced...that the broad prairies would never be occupied for homes.

Thus it followed that in the settlement of central Iowa, the borders of the rivers and groves were first occupied, and for social, as well as natural advantages, the population extended far into the interior along the streams while the great prairies were neglected. The borders of the Des Moines and Iowa rivers were explored before those of smaller streams.

About this time, also, the great California Trail was opened across the State, passing through Jasper and Polk Counties. That tide dropped an occasional emigrant upon its line and sometimes picked up a discontented floater and carried him to the Pacific slope. All these things combined to prepare for the occupation of Story County and the years closely following upon 1850....

Removal of Indians: The removal of the Indians to their Kansas reservation in 1846 opened up the greater portion of Central Iowa to occupancy by the whites, but it was not until 1850, and within the year or two following, that there was any scramble for choice locations in Story County. But about this time, people began to pour in from the direction of Jasper County on the southeast and from Fort Des Moines on the south, the Ballards on one line [on the west side of the Skunk River] and the Parkers on the other [on the east side of the Skunk River] being the advance guard.

The Skunk Divides: Thus for about two or three years, the settlements in the southeastern part of the county and those on the west were separated by Skunk River and an expanse of prairie that was seldom crossed, each party seeking necessary supplies by the route on which he found this way into the county.

Getting Supplies in Early Years: The matter of securing supplies was one of grave consideration.... For several years it was necessary to secure much grain and flour from older settlements. Even as late as 1857, corn was hauled from Marion and Mahaska counties. The trip would require not less than four days, and in mid-winter the time was lengthened indefinitely by storms and accidents, or casualties to the teams.... This was not so much from want of bridges and highways as from the severity of the wintry weather and from the drifting of heavy snows in the unchecked blasts on the great prairies. The cold bridged the streams in those times, and the winds and snows obliterated every sign of travel in a few hours. The higher lands might be bare of snow, while the depressions were drifted many feet in depth. If there had been warmth enough to soften the top, and followed by cold enough to make everything solid, loaded teams could travel on the prairie in every direction, without hindrance; but this would rarely happen. At other times it was necessary for the lone traveler to provide himself with a coil of rope and a large shovel, and he might consider himself fortunate if not called upon to use them many times during the drive. But the usual precaution was to go in companies of from two to ten teams. In that way, obstruction would be rapidly overcome by the larger force, and teams could be doubled or tripled as became necessary.

In this way, trains of corn, flour and bacon were brought from Pella or Oskaloosa or farther east and groceries, iron, nails, hardware, stoves, salt, and many of the necessities and a few of the luxuries of life were brought from Keokuk or other places on the Mississippi River....

Story County In 1853: A birds-eye view of Story County the summer of 1853 would show the physical features still in the condition which the Indian had seen them through all the ages in which it had been his hunting ground. The smoke curled above a cabin here and there, but these were mostly sheltered and partly concealed by the timber which still stood with hardly a noticeable mark of the woodman's ax. The luxuriant grass hid the few cattle of the settler from view, even when the anxious owner might be a few yards from them. ... The head of the solitary horseman would barely appear above the tall grass as he skirted ponds or crossed wide sloughs and low ground, and he could only be seen as he crossed the divides or climbed the prairie knolls to take note of his bearings. If he were miles distant from a grove, without a trail, and the day were dull, or the morning in fog, he might as well have been in mid-ocean without a compass, so far as points of direction could be told. If a man under such conditions were on foot and alone, he might wander indefinitely, and if night were coming on, his situation was one for grave solicitude and not without danger.

Wild Game Found: While wild game was never as abundant here as on the great plains of the far west or among the mountains and great forests, there were some deer, elk, wild turkeys, and grouse. Geese, ducks, and cranes were abundant. Squirrels frisked in the tree tops, and the song of birds filled the groves. The great timber wolf skulked along the streams and made raids upon barnyards and poultry, while the melancholy howl of the coyote or smaller wolf made mournful music far into the night. Amid such surroundings, the wife and children looked anxiously at nightfall for the coming of the absent husband and father, their anxiety being divided between his safety and their own....

Early Mills: The western pioneer, coming from a land of plenty farther east, and never having to resort to whole grain parched or boiled, ... truly believed that fine flour was one of the necessities of life. Appliances for grinding which were later common ... were not known when the ax of the Story County pioneer began to fell trees for his cabin. There was then not a mill in Jasper, Marshall, Boone, or Polk Counties. Mahaska County and the eastern part of Marion County had been settled to a certain extent as early as 1843–45. The country farther to the southeast had corn to spare and presumably mills at which it could be ground. In that direction the early settler turned for bread, often leaving the women and children in dread at his absence and watching impatiently for his return. This state of affairs was not confined to a single family at one time with neighbors from whom one could borrow. It was more frequently the case that borrowing had progressed until all were alike scant as to supplies, and the long weary trip had been postponed to the last day possible. Then would two or more men start together for the Egypt that had corn and flour to spare. In some cases, such were the emergencies that there was an old quilt hung up for a door to the cabin, and the timid wife and children took turns in keeping up the fire as a safeguard against unknown perils concealed by surrounding darkness.

Among the mills visited for custom work in those times were two Parmlee mills, on Middle River, in Warren County. Each arrival with grain waited his turn and carried home what the miller left him after taking substantial toll. Root's Mill at Oskaloosa furnished flour for cash or in exchange for grain. This method enabled the seeker of food to save time. Similar business was done at Iowa City. Thus, it seems that a trip to mill meant a journey of from 50 to 120 miles....

• • •

William K. Wood's recollections of his early days in Story County appeared in Adaline M. Payne's column, "Words From Busy Women," in the *Nevada Representative* on January 24 & 31, 1900.

• • •

William K. Wood's Reminiscences of Pioneering
transcribed by Adaline M. Payne

Mr. William K. Wood of Iowa Center is now nearing his seventy-seventh birthday. Nearly fifty-one years of his life have been passed in Iowa. The memory of such an old resident is a storehouse of local happenings which may well be drawn from to fullest limit. The writer has recently been privileged to gather from the lips of Mr. Wood some reminiscences of his early days in Iowa, and they are presented in these columns as of interest to our readers and valuable to history. In order to keep as close as possible to Mr. Wood's own expressions, the narrative is given in the first person. Following is the story, beginning with:

The Pilgrimage to Cory Grove: In our party making the trip from Kosciousko County, Indiana, in the early summer of 1849, there were thirteen adults and several children. The heads of families were Father Jeremiah Cory, and his three sons-in-law—Lemuel Venneman, Abraham Byers, and myself. Father and Mother Cory rode in a comfortable covered carriage. The rest of us, all young and vigorous, came in true emigrant style. Five covered wagons, each drawn by a team of horses, conveyed the wives and children, the small store of goods and provisions, and the indispensable implements of warfare with the soil, while we young men followed with the herd.

The trip was without notable incident till Mount Pleasant was reached. There we were detained three days by rains and floods which made the Skunk River impassable. We camped, and one tent and our wagons afforded us shelter. As soon as it seemed reasonably prudent, we attempted the crossing. The river was about 200 yards wide from bluff to bluff and rapid at that place. The ferry was a poor old craft which a short time after this went down and carried some people to watery graves. Each team and wagon with its load was driven on board and ferried across with a cable and pulleys. Mother Cory, who was about the best woman in this world, scented the danger and rebelled against staying cooped up in the covered buggy. But Father Cory, feeling competent to take care of her and steer the craft too, insisted upon her remaining where it was dry, and his strong will prevailed. But her spirit boiled, and to stir it still worse, as we started off, Uncle George Phoebus called out from the bank, "Good bye, Dolly. I expect never to see you again."

When we were safe on shore again, the good mother made us all laughby exclaiming, "Lordy massey, just to think what might have happened if I *had* drowned! For I was just as mad as I could be!"

In swimming the cattle across, four of them were carried by the current a quarter of a mile below where an island and a lot of drift made the passage ugly. "They are goners," the Mount Pleasant men who were assisting us exclaimed, "there never was a dog got out of that drift." But I was strong and daring in those days. I did not know fear, nor hesitate a moment to risk my life when it seemed necessary. One of the steers in danger was mine. I stripped and went after him and he came out and so did the rest of the cattle.

Making a Beginning: The immigrants' choice of location was largely determined by proximity to water and wood. We settled June 22, 1849, in the edge of the timber which skirts the Skunk River in the north part of Polk County. My brother-in-law, Calvin Cory, had already lived there for two years, and the neighborhood had acquired the name of Cory's Grove, the name it keeps yet. I had some acquaintance with the locality having visited my brother-in-law there about eighteen months before. I entered a quarter-section with the government and loaned the money in Des Moines at forty percent interest to pay the government price of $1.25 per acre.

My wife and I had little besides—$5 in cash, 5 head of yearlings, 2 milk cows, 2 yearling colts, 1 small horse, and a little household stuff comprised it all. We, however, got along with a fair degree of comfort there for two and three-fourths years, paid off the loan, and increased our stock. I had a good pair of hands which I turned to whatever I could find to do besides working my land. I thought nothing of walking six or eight miles to do a short job. I remember walking eight miles to do two days' work and nine miles to do a three days' job for Eli Trulinger. To get my first breaking done, I walked three miles and chopped and split rails at the rate of 400 rails for each acre of breaking.

My way of managing worried Father Cory some. Mother Cory told me about it. She said, "Father doesn't like it because you don't do as he advises you." "Well," I answered, "the way it is, I've set my stake, and I have to work to it. When Father's advice helps me toward making that stake, I'm thankful for it and use it, but when it doesn't, I have to let it go. I have to work to my own plan." After that, I was allowed to work out my own ideas without remonstrance.

I had no team, but I had my eye on a way to get one. I saved my dimes and quarters, and with each five dollars thus accumulated I bought a calf till I owned ten. Sometimes it would take a good many miles of walking to find one but I did not care for that. The men around said I was the biggest fool in the country to be investing in those calves that there could never be any sale for. Uncle Wm. Allen asked, "What in the world do you get 'em for?" "O, because I like to see them eat, there such lots [*sic*] of grass," I replied.

The second summer I began to match and break and use them, and in good time I sold each team that I did not need to keep for from $50 to $75.

Coon Hunting: One of my recreations which was likewise a source of income was coon hunting. I would often after working all day, hunt till midnight, and make more from the hunt than from the day's work. Coon skins brought in Des Moines twenty-five cents apiece, and mine paid for our clothing and groceries. It was my habit to go alone with my dog—the good hunter I had brought from Indiana, and I always carried a sharp knife to cut clubs with, but never a gun nor an ax.

One night some of the boys begged to go with me, and we had several dogs along. We treed a coon, cut down the tree, and as it fell the animal jumped and ran a mile or more. A second and a third time we treed and dislodged and chased what we thought was a "might big coon." The second time we treed him, I climbed up within ten feet of him, and he humped himself as though intending to drop down on me when the dogs seemed to make him change his mind and he sprang to the ground instead. One of the boys nearly lost his life in swimming a bayou after him. We did not secure our game and knew before the chase was done that it was a wildcat.

Going to the Mill: By the latter part of 1849, provisions had become very scarce in Iowa by reason of the demand to supply emigrants to California. Corn commanded from $2 to $2.50 per bushel. The nearest mill was Duncan's Mill four miles north of Oskaloosa and eighty miles from Cory's Grove. The last day of November, I set out in company with James and Walker Cory and Abram Byers to get my grinding done for the year. We were gone eleven days. I lived on corn bread and boiled meat, slept in my wagon every night and nearly froze. The mill was thronged and we had to wait almost a week for our turn at the grinding. A part of my grist was eight bushels of wheat which my work had earned, and it proved to be the only wheat used in my family for eighteen months. The scarcity made rogues desperate, and we had to guard our property every minute. One night as I lay on my sacks, I felt the one at my feet move a little, then a little more. I raised up and a man stepped along to the next wagon and gave a pull at a buffalo robe there. Jim Cory saved that. I was fully awake by that time and freed my mind to the would be thief, and we had a rather lively time. On the way home the boys got into a bad scrape. They wished me to go with them by way of Oskaloosa. It would necessitate four miles extra travel and I said, "No, I'll keep straight ahead, camp at the end of the cut off, and you can find me there." Walker and Byers spliced teams and took the roundabout way, and James staid [*sic*] with me. We didn't have a restful night for the fellow who had tried to steal from us at the mill was camped close by. His morals had not improved any, and the excitement began by that affair at the mill continued decidedly brisk. About midnight Byers came with the word that Walker had met with a mishap in driving and had broken his arm badly. I could not leave my property while night lasted, but at daylight, James remaining on guard, I went back with Byers. We had the broken arm fixed up at Oskaloosa and then went home.

The Indians: We suffered occasionally from Indian alarms. Indians had headquarters down at Tama, but roamed as they pleased and now and then got pretty saucy. Word was brought to us in Cory's Grove [near the Skunk River in northeast Polk County] in '49 that they were coming to massacre us all. Father Cory had been at Fort Des Moines and he came back with the opinion that we should all go to the Fort for safety. It would necessitate the removal of our stock or the desertion of it, and we younger men said no, we'd stay and guard what we had. We gathered our families at the best house, Jeremiah Cory's, quartered our stock close by, and guarded it nights, then went to our work days. It was not supposed that the women folks were in an entirely tranquil state of mind while we were away. After a few days "dragoons," as we called the troops, were sent out to remove the Indians. They were taken to Kansas or Indian Territory, and then we returned to our homes.[1] William Elliot of White Oak Grove south of Cambridge had meanwhile carried his family to Oskaloosa and was returning to White Oak Grove for some of his property when he suddenly came upon the camp of the Indians and soldiers over this side of Mitchellville. He mistook it for a hostile camp, and thinking that the red men had massacred everybody thereabout, he turned, whipped up his team, and ran it wildly to Mitchellville.

Planting a Permanent Home: I was not satisfied at Cory's Grove, and took occasion to make a number of trips around with others who were prospecting for land, and in this way, I first saw the locality which includes my present home farm. One of these excursions was in January of '51 when four of us were north of Skunk four days and slept on the ground nights with one blanket between us. The only settler in Story County was William Parker. He lived near the edge of Jasper [County]. I selected a quarter-section of school land (a part of the sixteenth section). I could not enter it with the government, nor was the authorized agent of the school lands accessible then, but I liked the land and took my chances with it. I had peaceable possession for a few years, then spurred by the boasts of a scallywag a few miles away that he would dispossess me of my home and earnings, I had the land appraised according to the law, went over to the new commissioner, Stephen O'Brien beyond Ames, paid the amount at which it had been appraised plus fifty cents per acre, and secured my title.

A Moving Over: I helped Adolphus Prouty move over to Iowa Center in February of '52—he was the second settler in this county. Then I built a three-sided slab shanty on my place for a temporary shelter for my family and fixed a big bonfire against a felled tree to constitute the fourth side. The last of March, I brought my wife and part of our belongings, and we became the third family in the county. Directly after our arrival, there came a heavy snow, and I hurried back to Cory's Grove to transport our provisions before the thaw should come. But the thaw got the start of me. It made the snow and ice slump and the Skunk a sea. But I got around all right till I was this side of the river. It took me all night to make the distance from there home. The oxen could hardly get along. I had to unload and pull my wagon out several times, and I was in snow water from ankle to hip all the way.

But I could not tarry at home. Soon after breakfast, I started back to the Grove after my brother, Jesse. His leg had been badly injured by a kick from a horse. I borrowed Mr. Prouty's horse for Jesse to ride. On the return I had trouble in getting my horse to swim the Skunk, and when we reached the Calamus, I carried Jesse across on my back. Twelve days later I made another trip over to look after my stock. The Skunk was as high as ever, the raft was on the opposite side, and the icy temperature of the water made swimming risky. I remembered an upturned tree a quarter of a mile below, found it by the few of its roots that remained above water, took off my pants and tied them around my neck, crawled out on the submerged log as far as possible, gave the best jump the circumstances allowed, and landed in water up to my neck. It was just dark when I emerged from my bath and ten o'clock when I reached Cory's Grove, but I was none the worse for the episode.

The New House: I built a good log house pretty soon, pinned together, pointed, and with a puncheon floor. There was not a nail about it nor a stick of lumber except what I had hewed. I made wooden hinges for the door and the chimney was cribbed with sticks and mortar built up outside the house. All the old settlers knew how it was done.

The First Baby: Our first child, Cory Wood, was born in this house February 17th, 1853, and he was about the first child born in these parts.

The First Death: The first death was that of a Norwegian, a stranger who was crossing the prairie. We heard of him, found him dead under his wagon, cared for him, and buried him. His was the first grave in the present cemetery at Iowa Center. We failed to mark the grave carefully, and its location is lost. Those who were with him went on to the north part of the county.[2]

Getting the Plow Mended: Men think it a great task now-a-days to go to the blacksmith shop and have a little work done. In '52, I broke the point of the plow and it took me three days to have it mended. I put a pole to the hind wheels of the wagon, tied the plow on, hitched the oxen to the rig, perched myself on it part of the time—walked the rest, and made the trip to Des Moines and had it mended. The oxen crossed the Skunk willingly when southward bound because they were going to their old home pastures, but on the return it was different. They did not like to forsake the Polk County blue stem. I drove them into the river, but they turned, floundered, and as one of them began to drown, I had to swim in and unyoke them, get them back to the shore, and fish the cart and plow out with a grapevine. Twice I went through this process. Finally, I hitched a grapevine to the leader, went ahead and pulled, while a friend from Cory Grove drove, and the crossing was effected.

We Wanted More Neighbors: I cannot tell you how glad we were to have neighbors come. We were ready to give time, effort—in fact, anything in our power to make settlers welcome. We were poor, but we gladly shared our fare with them, and our little cabin sometimes sheltered as many as could be bestowed on the floor. One time two men from above Des Moines came over prospecting. A flood detained them at my place two days. They became uneasy and wanted help homeward. I knew a place two miles below where I could cross the Indian [Creek] with my horse, for he was a good swimmer. We found the place, but the boat was on the other side. I started across on horseback, the other two horses following, but soon the two unaccustomed to swimming became frightened and scared my horse so that I was obliged to draw his head under water that I might slide off of him and get away from the floundering of the three animals which threatened to drown me.

As the horses all drifted down stream and became tangled in grapevines, I had to swim and release them, bring them one by one ashore, get the boat, and row the men across, they leading the horses. I went on with them and helped them across the Skunk, and we arrived at Cory's Grove at dark. We had been out since an early dinner, and I had spent five hours in the water. The travelers gave me a dollar. Luckily, I was not working for money entirely.

New Houses: We thought nothing of going a dozen miles to lend a hand. I carried up a corner of the first house built in Nevada—T. E. Alderman's—in September, '53, and the next summer helped build the second one—John McLain's log hotel.

The first framed house built at Iowa Center was William Brodie's. It is still standing. Mr. Brodie drew the lumber for it from Iowa City.

The First Mill and the Money of the Fifties: The first mill in the county was built by John Parker in 1856, just north of Iowa Center on a springy place near East Indian [Creek]. My cousin, Christopher C. Wood, Nathan Webb, and myself bought it a little later, and after eighteen months we added to the saw mill a grist mill comprising two sets of burrs. We sawed the lumber for the subsequent buildings in this vicinity, and did a good business in grinding flour and feed.

Every old settler knows that '57 was the hardest year this country has known. Those who find fault with our money now ought to have had a little of the financial experience of that time. One who receives a bill in any part of this country today glances at it to see whether it is a one, a two, a five, or a ten dollar bill, then stuffs it into his pocket and keeps it there without inquiry or anxiety till he is ready to use it. In those days, if he did business of any account, he carried a Bank Note Detector[3] around with him, examined every bill as he received it to ascertain the probability of it being good for something, and didn't stop to feed his horses till he had paid it out again, lest the next mail announce that it was worthless. If he started to go back east with the bills on the State Bank of Iowa, he was shaved on them when he passed over into Illinois, still more when he crossed into Indiana, again in Ohio, and by the time he reached the Atlantic Slope his money was of small account.[4]

B. F. Allen & Stevens had a private bank in Des Moines and issued bills which they called Nebraska money. When that bank failed, men hereabout lost a great deal. Some men I knew lost several hundred dollars apiece—a heavy blow in those times. There was little money to be had, harvest hands commanded but 50 cents a day, payments on homes were coming due, and meantime families must be fed.

I had saved $400 in gold to make the last payment on the mill. This I took over to Polk and Marshall Counties and bought up the loose wheat at $1.00 per bushel. My partners did not wish to share in the deal, so I carried it myself. Wheat went up in a few days to $1.50 per bushel and soon after to about $2.00 and flour was $9 a hundred. Contractors from Webster City and other places at some distance came on and were ready to take away all my flour at a big profit to me. I liked money pretty well but I didn't like to have Story County starved out, so the contractors did not get my flour. I sold it all about home on time. The pay was to come in at harvest. Well, some of it did come, but $500 of it failed for good. Too many claims pressed. However, I had cattle to turn off and was able to make my payment all right when it came due.

The Coldest Days: The coldest days I ever knew were the last day of 1863 and the first day of '64. The old court house at Nevada burned on the intervening night. I went many times to my cattle shed 200 yards south of the house. I thought there was no cold I could not face for that distance, but I was mistaken. I would have to turn my back some when coming north. With the best care I could give my cattle, one steer froze to death. F. M. Baldwin was dealing in hogs then and had driven 300 head over to State Center for shipment. That was as far west as the railroad came. The storm caught them, heaped the snow over them, and nearly all perished. I had intended going with him with my own drove, but the weather indications not just suiting me, I declined to start out. I saved my herd by cuddling the animals in the barn. Baldwin tried to dress the frozen carcasses of his hogs before shipping them. He managed to heat water for the purpose, but each would be encased in ice almost as soon as drawn from the scalding water, and he was forced to send them on just dug out of the snow. A shipper named Killen at State Center lost 600 head in the same storm.

A Court Episode: A pretty rough set used to visit the Center [Iowa Center] some times. One day a trial was being held there and J. L. Dana was the attorney on one side. He took his revolver out of his pocket and laid it on the table indicating his intention to enjoy peace even if he had to fight for it. During the trial a fracas occurred outside and I could see that a little fellow was being foully dealt with; hence, I stepped out to haul off the big bully who was getting the better of him. Just as I stooped over in the interest of fair play somebody seized me by the seat of my pants, gave me a half swing and a throw, and I picked myself up from the other side of the road. It was quite a throw considering that I weighed 150 pounds or more. I allowed scrappers to settle their own hash after that. That was before the population was civilized.

The Lowell Trial: It was in 1854, I think, that old man Lowell choked his wife to death over on the East Indian. His preliminary trial was before Justice Joseph P. Robinson on what is now the Finlay place. I was there. There weren't many settlers here then and not folks enough present to make a decent jury. The case was clear—the actions of the old man, the testimony of the children, and the appearance of the body. The body had been exhumed, and the prints of fingers on the woman's throat told a plain story. Justice Robinson did not believe in wasting time, nor words, nor proceedings, so he sentenced the prisoner on the spot. These, as I remember them, were his words, "Hang him till he's dead, dead,

dead, and may God have mercy on his soul!" However, we concluded we had better proceed according to law, so we took the scared old fellow over to Judge Evans west of Ames, thence he was sent to Des Moines and there tried and sentenced to life imprisonment. I followed the proceedings all through.

Oak from Acorns: One of the small chaps who came in the caravan to Cory's Grove was William J. Venneman. He was a little six year old then, bright, cheery, good humored, and spry as a quail. We all thought a sight of him—just as we have ever since. He grew up at the Grove, and about '62, when he was hardly twenty-one, he enlisted and went to the war. He had a good taste of the hard fortune of the soldier, for he was captured at Allatoona and sent to Andersonville where the prisoners were herded like cattle, and during a rain of three days when they had not a spot to be down except in the mud and water, he, like the rest, had not a bite to eat during the entire time. Luckily, after a month or two he was able to slip in with a lot of older prisoners that was [*sic*] being exchanged. He returned to his regiment—the 39th Iowa—and served till the war closed. He married a good woman, moved to Indian Creek, has reared a nice family, accumulated a comfortable property, and is now the honored representative from this county for the second term. His career illustrates the possibilities of the little fellow out on the frontier—the humblest one doesn't know what opportunities and duties lie before him.

First Election in Story County: I voted at the first election held in Story County. It was in August 1852 over in the Sam McDaniels shanty on the East Indian. Col. Scott owns the place now, I believe. There was only a handful of voters. The second election was held in April of the next year ('53) over on the Brouhard place, and the third one at Adolphus Pronty's. The Story County History published in 1890 locates those elections differently, but my recollection of them is as I have stated. I have failed to vote at but one election since I was twenty-one.

Locating a County Seat: I was one of the three commissioners chosen to decide the location of the county seat of Marshall County. Marietta had precedence, but the location was low, and at times was accessible only by boats. It was at a time of high water that we went over and examined sites. We had to swim streams. We decided on the present site of Marshalltown. There were only a few houses about there. There was war between the people of the two little huddles, and Marietta folks slept on their arms to defend against the removal of the records, but they had to go.

I have always been a radical Republican as was my father before more from the death of the old Whig party. I have not jumped at conclusions, for I have seen abundant demonstrations of the value of Republican principles. About half of my life has been passed under Democratic rule, but the development of the country and the prosperity of the country have plainly been the product of Republican principles and policy.

• • •

In his 1911 *History of Story County: A Record of Settlement, Organization, Progress, and Achievement*, William O. Payne, assistant editor and later editor of the *Nevada Representative* newspaper from 1882 to 1917, also wrote about the first settlers in the county. Below are excerpts from Chapter IV, "The Early Settlement," about the early settlers beside the Skunk River in western Story County where Norwegian immigrants founded settlements in the mid-1850s.

• • •

William O. Payne's History of Western Story County

Of the permanent settlement, the earliest is now definitely understood to have been that of Dan W. and Mormon Ballard on the east side of Palestine Township on the 8th of March 1848. They gave their name to Ballard Grove and Ballard Creek. They built them homes, occupied land, and remained there in the locality for about 30 years. They were not the sort of men to harmonize with the Norwegian settlement which, in time, completely surrounded them, and ultimately they sold out and went farther West. As has been before noted, they were not directly followed by any number of other settlers coming, like them, from Des Moines, but they were first in the county of permanent settlers and the fact has to be recognized and recorded. The next settler, and the one who for a quarter of a century was supposed to have been the first in the county, was Wm. Parker. He located on the southern edge of Collins Township, and there established the homestead upon which he lived and died. Writing under date of June 23rd, 1876, for the purpose of establishing his record of settlement, he said, "In the fall of 1848, I came to Story County and built me a log cabin, size 12 X 14 feet. April 12,

1849, I came to my cabin. It had no opening for door or window. I cut out a door with my ax so I could carry my goods in, and moved into the pen without roof or floor. I cut a tree for boards to cover the cabin, took my wagon bed apart to make a floor in my mansion to keep the two little babies off the ground, and being root hog or die, my better half and I went to work. Some people say it is hard times now. They do not know hard times when they see them. Let them take it rough and tumble as I did, and they may talk. We lived in this hut till the next August when I put me up what was called a good house in those days. I went 60 miles to mill, took me about a week to make the trip. We had a cast iron mill in the neighborhood that we used to run by hand. We were often glad to get a peck of corn cracked on this mill. Now I can go to mill and return in half a day. I have now 230 acres of land, all fenced except 11 acres. Collins Township has improved in proportion."

The first of the settlers on Skunk River [in western Story County] was John H. Keigley. He located in the northeastern part of Franklin Township, west of Skunk, and near the stream which is known as Keigley's Branch. He lived there for many years and spent his old age in Ames where he died. He was a man of much force and was always prominent in the affairs of his portion of the county. It happens that in 1869, someone writing to the *Story County Ægis* concerning some matters of early history, invited by his narrations some correction, which Mr. Keigley, in a note to the then editor, made the following statement, "In company with Nathaniel Jennings, I landed in Skunk River, Franklin Township, November, 1851, and erected a cabin on the farm where I now reside. Then as Alexander Sellkirk, 'I was monarch of all I surveyed.' The next to locate on Skunk River was Jesse Hussong[5] and William Arrasmith[6] and families who came in the fall of 1852. Next came Franklin Thompson, William D. Evans, E. C. Evans and families. Then the following February 1853, James Smith and sons located in Lafayette Township, his being the seventh family to locate on Skunk River, and not the first. I could give the settlement of each further if necessary. It was not my intention to write a full history of our county but to correct an error."

The last of Mr. Keigley's observations suggests how some of the difficulties of compiling the earliest history of the county might have been obviated, for, in fact, there was none of the earlier settlers better qualified than himself to have written a full history of the county any time, and if he had done so instead of excusing himself for not doing so, we should now be very glad.⁷ It will be noted that Mr. Keigley in this statement, while he denies to James Smith the credit of being the first settler on Skunk, which credit we think was never really claimed for him, fixed him definitely as the first settler in Lafayette.⁸ Also, contemporaneous with Mr. Keigley, was his brother-in-law, Nathaniel Jennings, a bachelor, who never married, but who made his home with the Keigleys until the call for arms in 1861. Then he went out with Company E of the Third Iowa Infantry, of which company he was defeated for a Lieutenancy by one single vote, and he died in the service at Memphis in August 1862. Other testimony concerning the first settlers on Skunk is offered by Stephen P. O'Brien. He came to the county in October 1852, and is the sole present day survivor of these men who settled in that locality before the organization of the county. He cites that in November 1852, a presidential election was held for the settlement on Skunk River and Squaw Fork and returns made to Boone (or Polk) County. This was the first election to be held in the county or at least in that part of the county, and it appears to have been held for the west part of the county. The election was held at the home of Shadrick Worrell in Worrell's Grove near the old time village of New Philadelphia, and probably a dozen votes were cast. Those now recalled who supposedly participated in this election are John H. Keigley, Nathaniel Jennings, Samuel Hiestand,⁹ John Wheeler, John T. Wheeler, Thomas Vest, Shadrick Worrell, Eli Dean, Sr., and John Hussong.

From the Conclusion of Chapter IV: This year of 1852 is the one in the course of which came in the most of the settlers who were to have the honor of participating in the organization of the county [on April 4, 1853]. Prior to this year, the number who had found their way into the county was so small and their locations as a rule were so remote from each other, that anything in the way of the formation of a unit was out of the question even if there had not been the very great troubles before mentioned relating to Skunk River 'the almost impassable bogs that bordered it' and nameless but numerous sloughs. But Boone and Marshall Counties [the counties bordering the west and east sides of Story County] had both been properly organized in 1849 and Polk and Jasper [counties on Story's southern border] some time before. The skirmishers of the advancing line of migration had already reached the intervening county, and it was evident that the influx of the human tide was close at hand. In all of the new settlements, the very first occupations of the country were the squatters who expected by occupying the land to be able, when the lands should be opened to entry, to make the most advantageous selections. But with the opening of the lands for entry, there was always a new tide of people seeking to possess the new country at government prices for land. Story County at this time had the skirmishers already within its borders; and its lands had become, in spite of sloughs and of Skunk River, the most attractive that there were left.

Those who were on the ground were confident that the next year [1853] would bring a very material change, and these conclusions appear now to have been fully warranted. Of course, Skunk River continued to be bad for a dozen or 15 years, but the sloughs, however disagreeable, were only an incident to the country and were not, in fact, its dominating feature; nor did the rush ponds spread so wide but that there was between them a very large amount of upland such as would be the most attractive to the settler when once means of communication and transportation should be provided, or the prospective number of settlers should be such as to promise early unity of action in the matter of providing such means of transportation and communication. The time had come to make a county, and notwithstanding the meager means which the emigrants were bringing into the county, there was manifest confidence in the future. Those who were here and coming in and getting possession of the land were sure that there would be an early rise in values, and the spirit of hopefulness appears to have been about as high as it well could be in the frontier settlement. The time for the making of Story had been a little slow in its arrival, but the delay meant nothing of loss in the matter of ultimate prospects, and incentive for moving in, establishing homes, and building up the county was abundant.

• • •

Story County completed its organization by electing county officers on April 4, 1853, under an Act of the Iowa General Assembly approved January 1853. After a Federal Land Office opened in Ft. Des Moines, Iowa, in June of that same year, there was a rapid influx of settlers into the county. State censuses conducted in 1854, 1855, 1856, and 1859 enumerated 836, 1,568, 2,868, and 3,826 people respectively in the county.

The 1860 Federal Census for Story County enumerated 4,051 people which included 388 Norwegian immigrants. The first caravans of Norwegian families arrived in 1855 and 1856 and founded two settlements, the first near where the Ballard brothers settled in 1848 on the west side of the Skunk River in southwestern Story County and a second on the east side of the Skunk River in the northwestern part of the county near where the James C. Smith family settled in 1853.

About the Authors and Transcriber
by the Compiler

John Manor Scott was born in Ohio in 1824. He taught school in Ohio and Kentucky, explored the eastern border of the Iowa Territory with a friend in 1843, and returned to Ohio where he resumed teaching and the study of law. He was admitted to practice law in Ohio in 1845, but at the outbreak of the Mexican-American War in 1846, Scott enlisted in a regiment of Kentucky volunteers. He was held as a prisoner of war in Mexico City for eight months. From 1852 to 1854, Scott owned and edited the *Kentucky Whig* newspaper before deciding to return to Iowa in 1856 and settle in Nevada, Iowa. In 1859, Scott was elected to the Iowa Senate, but when the Civil War broke out in 1861, he resigned his seat and became a Captain in the 3rd Iowa Volunteer Infantry, later being promoted to Lieutenant Colonel. In August 1862, Scott was commissioned Colonel of the 32nd Iowa Infantry. That same month, 11 Norwegians from the Story City area volunteered for the unit. In 1867, Scott was elected Lieutenant Governor of Iowa, and in 1870, he was appointed Assessor of Internal Revenue. He was again elected to the Iowa Legislature as a senator in 1885. Col. Scott died in Des Moines, Iowa, in 1903, and is buried in the Nevada Municipal Cemetery, Nevada, Iowa, beside his third wife, Mary S. Wright, whom he married in 1863. His first wife died of cholera while he visited Iowa for the first time in 1843, and his second wife died while he was serving in the Mexican-American War.

"**William Kennison Wood**, son of John and Anna Wood, was born in Logan County, Ohio, April 19, 1823. He died at Iowa Center, Iowa, March 21, 1917, at the age of ninety-three years, eleven months and two days. His boyhood was spent in Ohio and Indiana. His schooling was that offered by the district schools of the times, which, whatever their shortcomings, seem to have produced a splendid, rugged, and enterprising type of alumni. He was married on October 17, 1847, to

Melinda Cory. In 1849, on the 22d of June, the 'Cory Clan' made settlement in Polk County, Iowa, at Cory Grove. It is seldom that so many forceful characters are found in so small a group of people. From this little caravan of five families have come a large number of noteworthy descendants, most prominent among who is Wm. A. Sunday, the evangelist, whose mother was a cousin of Mrs. Wood. Early in 1851, Mr. Wood acquired from the government the land near Iowa Center which has been his home for sixty-six years. Here he wrought out his life work. He was a natural leader of his community. The first sawmill and gristmill in the county was built on his initiative. He represented the county in the state legislature from 1868 to 1872. He owned 1,300 acres of land eventually, although he had entered the state with but five dollars capital. Besides his energy and industry, he had a name for honesty and integrity which he valued very highly. In boyhood, he had been converted and had united with the Baptist church. He was one of the most active members of the Iowa Center Baptist church...."[10] Wood's first three wives preceded him in death, and he was survived by a fourth wife, Sarah Griffith Davis, whom he married in 1876. He and his four wives are buried in Woodland Cemetery, Iowa Center, Iowa.

Adaline M. (Brown) Payne was born in South Champion, Jefferson County, New York, in 1834. She graduated from the State Normal School at Albany, New York, in 1854, and taught school until 1859 when she married William P. Payne. In 1874, they moved to Mitchellville, Iowa, where William was principal and Adaline was matron of the Mitchell Seminary. In 1875, Adaline began teaching high school at Nevada, Iowa, where her husband had accepted a position as school principal and Adaline became an assistant in the high school. In 1880, they moved to Boone, Iowa, where William worked for the newspaper for two years before they purchased the original newspaper in Story County, the *Nevada Representative*, in 1882. While they lived in Boone, Adaline taught school for one year, and after they returned to Nevada, she taught in teacher institutes in Story, Boone, and other counties for 10 years plus taking an active part in the publication of the newspaper. Her work for the newspaper included a column, "Words From Busy Women," where she published her transcription of William K. Wood's pioneer story about his early life in Story County. Adaline was a charter member of the Nevada Woman's Club and a frequent delegate to state conventions of the Iowa Federation of Women's Clubs. She and her husband were ardent supporters and workers on behalf of the Nevada Public Library. Adaline is buried in the Nevada Municipal Cemetery, Nevada, Iowa, beside her husband, William P. Payne.

William O. Payne, an only child, was born in Massachusetts in 1860, and came to Mitchellville, Iowa, with his parents, William P. and Adaline M. Payne, in 1874. In 1877, William was among the first nine students to graduate from Nevada High School. Upon completing his undergraduate degree at the University of Iowa in 1882, he entered the university's law school and received his degree the following year. Although he was admitted to the Iowa Bar, Payne never practiced law. Instead, he began assisting in the publication of the *Nevada Representative* which his parents purchased in 1882 and over which he gradually assumed editorial responsibility. While editing the newspaper, Payne was elected to local positions as justice of the peace and member of the city council, and he also attended many political conventions. His interest in public affairs led him to become a prolific writer of political editorials that were quoted widely. After the family sold the newspaper in 1917, Payne became the editor and publisher of the *Iowa Forum*, a weekly political journal published in Des Moines, Iowa. He was active in the Republican Party and was an unsuccessful candidate for the nomination as a U. S. congressman in 1914 and U. S. senator in 1930. Payne died in Des Moines, Iowa, in 1935 and is buried in the Nevada Municipal Cemetery, Nevada, Iowa, along with his wife, Jessie Dickins Payne, whom he married in 1886.

Acknowledgement

The compiler gratefully acknowledges Geoff Schumacher, Publisher, *Nevada Journal*, for permission to reprint "How Story County Got Its Name."

A Brief History of the First Norwegian Settlement of Story and Polk Counties, Ia. 1855–1905

by Oley Nelson, 1905
Translated by Oley Nelson in 1930[1]

A short history of the first Norwegian Settlement of Story and Polk Counties, Iowa, including Palestine Congregation and Soldiers enlisted in the Civil War

The original Norwegian History of the Settlement in Polk and Story Counties was compiled by Oley Nelson of Slater, Iowa in 1905 and is now translated by Mr. Nelson into English.

A Brief History 1855 to 1905

In 1848 to 1854 there was a large emigration from the three parishes in Norway, known as Etne, Skaanevik and Fjeldbergs parishes, to America, Lisbon, Illinois. The emigrants came from Norway to seek and acquire a home for themselves and their families and they expected to find government land at a government price on which to make their permanent homes in the world. They had bid goodbye to relatives and friends in Norway and had prepared for the long voyage in their sailing ships to America, with provisions for their families that would last them from seven to ten weeks on their slow sailing vessels.

When they came to Lisbon, Illinois, it was a great disappointment to them to find that there was no government land to be had. This disappointment was especially great to the mothers, and many of them shed a silent tear and said, "How can I with my family acquire a permanent home here in America?" These mothers could not sing when they were plying their shuttles in the looms nor when they were treading their spinning wheels or when they were rocking their babies in their cradles, thinking of the future. Here was a new language to learn. Climatic conditions were much different from those to which they had been accustomed and where could they think of getting a permanent home when there was no government land to be had at $1.25 an acre.

In early fall of the year 1854 a man by the name of Nils Olsen Naes, who was employed by a Bible Society, traveled in the western settlements of Iowa and Minnesota, selling Bibles, printed in English and the Scandinavian languages. He came to Lisbon, Illinois, and there told them that in Iowa, there was government land to be had for $1.25 an acre, fine prairie with timber along the streams—a large area of land. This made a great stir among the emigrants at Lisbon. They called a meeting and selected a committee to go to Iowa to investigate the land, which was nearly three hundred miles west from Lisbon.

They selected four men, Osmund Sheldahl, Ole Fatland, Osmund Johnson and Ole Apland as a delegation to go to Iowa and investigate this land, and, if it was found to be as described by Nils Olsen Naes, they should secure enough for the colony. These four men left Lisbon, Illinois, the 25th of September 1854 and came back in about thirty days, reporting that they had secured land for the colony and found it very good. This brought cheer to all, especially to the mothers, and they considered this delegation had done a very heroic act and it was like a magnetic inspiration to the whole colony.

They commenced to prepare to immigrate to Story and Polk counties, Iowa, three hundred miles away. What a change! Sadness gave way to joy and the mothers sang songs of cheer while plying their shuttles in the looms or while at their spinning wheels and the winter months were miraculously shortened with the thought of going to new homes in Iowa. The men made ready the covered wagons in which the journey would be made, and when the sixteenth day of May, 1855, arrived word went forth that all those who wished to emigrate from Lisbon to Iowa should congregate at Holdeman's Prairie, a short distance west of Lisbon. And so, on the seventeenth day of May, 1855, they proceeded westward to Iowa—their future homes.

These emigrants had taken with them from Norway, their parishes, a heritage; they were God fearing and respected the teachings of God's word. So at the start of the journey they organized themselves into a tentative congregation by electing Ole Anfinson as their pastor, Knut

Bauge as a teacher and Erick Sheldahl as a chorister. They would not undertake the emigration to Iowa as a colony without it a churchly colony.

The scene can better be imagined by us at this day what this tentative organization meant to this colony. We, who are present and are now celebrating the seventy-fifth anniversary of the event, have the blessings that have come to us, their descendants, during the last seventy-five years.

Let us picture the scene. The order comes to start; one hundred and six souls, twenty-one families, five young men and one widow, were transported by eighteen covered wagons, drawn by ox teams; six covered wagons drawn by horses and one single spring wagon. Their names are as follows:

• • •

Compiler's note: In 1945, Anfin Apland, son of scouting party member Ole Apland, published a "re-compiled, corrected, and added to" version of Nelson's 1905 history which included a list of 108 members of the caravan.[2] Based on my research of Norwegians who lived in central Iowa from 1855 through 1860, Apland is correct about the total number of members in the caravan. However, his list does not include a son of Rev. Ole and Ingerie Anfinson, Ansen, and a daughter of Engebrit and Sarah Heggen, Susana L. Additionally, it includes two people who were not members of the caravan, Anna Larson who was a member of the caravan that arrived in September,[3] and Torger and Gertrud Olson's daughter, Martha, who was not born until 1856. My revised list of names follows:

Rev. Ole Anfinson and wife Ingerie and children, Carine and Ansen
Osmund and Anna Sheldahl and children, Caroline, Erick, Halvor, Henry, and Randy
Erick and Margaret Sheldahl and children, Betsy, Randy, Erick, and Martha
Ole and Carrie Fatland and children, John, Elie, Britt, and Henry
Knute and Carrie Ersland and children, Hactor, Madts, Anna, Anfin, Martha, Elias, Carrie, Engeborg, and Amos
Knute and Carrie Boug [Bauge]
Ivor and Malinde Tweet and daughter, Martha
Barney and Sarah Hill and daughter, Betsey
Peter Christian and Serina Heggem

Lars and Martha Tesdahl

Wier and Martha Weeks and children, Anfin, Halvor, Torres, Wier, Engeborg, Martha, and Hans

Severt and Allis Gravdahl and children, Julia and Andrew

Askel and Golla Larson and children, Lars, Thomas, and Charls

Orga and Ragna Hauge and children, Severt, Sarah, and Lars

Torbjorn and Madela Houge and children, Sarah and Guste

Ole and Valbor Hauge and son, John

John and Brita Severson and children, Mary, John, and Severt

Salemon and Sarah Heggen and children, Andrew, Nels, and Ole

Ole and Anna Heggen

Engebrit and Sarah Heggen and daughter, Susana L.

Torger and Gertrud Olson and children, Cecelia, Ole, and George

Mrs. Julia Shaw and children, Betsy, Thomas, and Erick

Mrs. Torres Olson and children, Hellen and Rasmus

Five young men: Lars Thompson, Ole Apland, Ole Tesdahl, Erick Johnson, and Eivin Olson

• • •

As has been stated before, these emigrants came from a constitutional form of government [in] Norway and they respected their adopted country by becoming citizens of the United States. Not only that, they did not want to make this westward emigration without respecting the Sabbath by holding services. So they held religious services every Sunday during the journey. The three hundred mile trip was covered without any mishap. They arrived on the land that had been selected for them, the seventh day of June 1855. This is now known as the land southeast of the town of Huxley, Iowa.

On reaching their destination they made a ring with their wagons, removed their camp utensils and commenced to prepare the food for the first meal on the piece of land that had been selected by the four men the fall before, September 1854. On the following Sunday, June 10, 1855, in this enclosure of covered wagons, they held their first service and thanked God for bringing them safely through their journey into the new land and asked God's righteous blessing on the new colony. The first Sabbath day Service under roof was held on Ole Fatland's land, under the shelter of a hay shed. Under the roof of the same hay shed the first confirmation class was organized. The members were as follows: Torres Weeks, Viar Weeks, Engebor Weeks, Anfin Ersland, Anna Vee, and Betsy Shaw. These confirmands were confirmed in the spring of 1856 in Rev. Anfinson's home.

Lars Tesdahl, Knut Ersland, and John Severson were the first to erect their own homes. The first three children born to the colony were: Anna, daughter of Mr. and Mrs. Solomon Heggen, born July 4, 1855; Ole, son of Ole and Anna Heggen, born August 14, 1855; and Halvor, son of Lars and Martha Tesdahl, born September 15, 1855. The first wedding was Ole Apland and Anna Ersland, who were married by Ole Anfinson in Ole Fatland's house. The first adult deaths in the settlement were the wife of Knut Ersland and the wife of Erick Tesdahl.

On the 30th day of September, 1855, the colony was increased by thirty-two souls from Lisbon, Illinois, five families and one young man, who emigrated in their covered wagons, drawn by four ox teams and one horse team. They had been six weeks on the road. It was a very rainy season and on a cold rainy day Gunder Madskaar died at Iowa Center, the 29th of September, 1855, and was buried at the same place.

The following are the names of the souls who joined the colony:

• • •

Compiler's note: I have added a family, the Ole Nernes family, to Nelson's and Apland's list of caravan members. The Nernes family is also not on K. (Knut) B. Thompson's list.[4] Thompson was a member of the caravan and four years old when he journeyed with his parents. The Lars Sheldall family was also in the caravan but did not join the others in the new settlement, so they are not included on the list. The Sheldall family continued on to Hamilton County, Iowa, where they settled on land northeast of Story City and became the first Norwegian family to live in that area. Lars Sheldall's son, Rasmus, a young boy of age eight at the time, states, "Fifteen wagon outfits started out from Lisbon at one time, together with a herd of about 150 head of cattle."[5] If there were 15 wagons in the caravan, Nelson, Thompson, Apland, and I have not been able to identify all the families in the caravan as most families likely had only one wagon.

• • •

Benjamin and Engeri Thompson and children, Thomas, Knut, Ceceliafi, and Sarah
Mrs. Carrie Madskaar and children, Engeborg and Erick
Wier and Carrie Johnson and children, John, Ole, Sarah, Julia, Anna, Elie, and Simon
Nels and Carrie Christofison and children, John and Emelia
Erick and Barbero Tesdahl and children, Anna, Seveart, Aamon, Sarah, and Bertha
Ole and Margretha Nernes and son, John
Anna Larson
Thomas Berhow

In the summer of 1857 they erected their first schoolhouse. It was built by private subscription and served also as a church. It was located across the road from where the Palestine church now stands. The first election of a new pastor was in the spring of 1859. They agreed to elect a pastor by lot. They had two candidates, Ole Anfinson and Osmund Sheldahl, the lot falling on Osmund Sheldahl. He was ordained by Rev. Haselqvest of the Augustana synod.

At a meeting on the 3rd day of Christmas, December 28, 1860, a very stormy winter day with zero weather, it was proposed to subscribe for the erection of a church building in the colony. The work was started, but on account of the great national disaster, the Civil War, and as twenty-one of the youngest and best men enlisted in the service of the Union from this colony alone, the church was not finished and dedicated till in August, 1866. It was dedicated by Haselqvest. This church has been remodeled but stands on the same spot as the original building.

The following are the names of the young men who enlisted from the colony:

In the 10th Iowa Infantry: Ivar Tvedt, Ole Anfinson, Torres Scott, Erick Egland, J. O. Johnson, J. W. Johnson, Soren Olson, Henry Egland, Haldor Johnson
In the 91st Illinois Infantry: Lars Bouge, Anfin Ersland, Torres Weeks, Viar Weeks
In the 23rd Iowa Infantry: Elias Ersland, Halvar Weeks, Severt Tesdahl, Andrew Gravdal
In the 47th Iowa Infantry: Thor Holland, Thom Shaw
In the 96th Illinois Infantry: Lars Olson[6]

The following are the names of the charter members of the Palestine Congregation:

Osmund Sheldahl and family, Ole Anfinson and family, Erick Sheldahl and family, Askel Larson and family, Ole Fatland and family, K. A. Bauge and family, Wier Weeks and family, Knute Ersland and family, John Severson and family, Ingebrit Olsen and family, Ole Apland, Ivar Tvedt and family, Torbjorn Hauge and family, Ole Heggen and family, Mrs. Torris Olsen and family, Mrs. Ragna Larson, Peder Christian, Barney Hill, Ole Houge, Salve Heggen.

The above names are the ones who left Lisbon, Illinois in May, 1855.

The following are the ministers that had served this congregation:

Ole Anfinson, 1855–1858
Osmund Sheldahl, 1859–1876
J. H. Myhre, 1876–1880
H. C. Holm, 1881–1893
N. B. Thvedt, 1894–1897
A. L. Huus, 1897–1902
Axel Shefveland, 1902–1903

The Congregation belonged to the Swedish Augustana Synod. In 1873 they joined Konferensen and in 1890 the United Norwegian Lutheran Church of America. The Palestine Congregation today has two daughter descendant congregations. These two congregations were considered auxiliary congregations, but are now independent.

A parsonage was erected in 1876 across the road from the church. This was re-modeled and enlarged in 1894. In 1891, the Bergen congregation of the *Anti-Missouriske Broderskab* [Anti-Missouri Brotherhood] was accepted into the congregation and made a part of it.[7]

During the first fifty years of the congregation there were 1,258 baptisms, 475 marriages and 208 deaths from 1875. Previous to that there are no records.[8]

The Fjeldberg Congregation

The Fjeldberg congregation was organized in either May or June, 1865, in Torres Skarveland's house, half a mile south from what is now Huxley, by Rev. N. Amlund of Story City at the request of several families who had no church affiliation. Prof. F. A. Schmidt and Rev. P. A. Rassmussen, who were visiting at Amlund's home, were also present. The original members were as follows: Jacob Stensen and family; Jacob Jacobson and family; Knudt Toft and family; Anders Toft and family; Ole M. Helland and family.

The congregation had a healthy growth from the first till 1885 when a large number left on account of *"Naadevalg" striden* [the predestination controversy].[9] From then on there were no further divisions and the church continued to prosper, the membership being increased to include 80 families, with 400 souls and 200 confirmed members.

In July 1866, steps were taken to build a church. The building was completed and dedicated November 10th, 1867, by Rev. P. A. Rasmussen. He was assisted by Rev. N. Amlund and Rev. O. G. Jukam. In 1871, the congregation got its first resident pastor, Rev. Sauer. This year also marked the building of a parsonage, east of the church on an acreage which the congregation had bought.

Shortly after the congregation was organized, the question of joining the Norwegian synod came up for consideration. While there was no opposition to the move, it was not till in 1874 that definite steps in that direction were taken. The congregation was accepted into the synod at the annual meeting held in Goodhue County, Minn., that summer. It has ever since been affiliated with that body.

Pastors that have served the congregation up till this writing, 1905, are as follows: N. Amlund, 1865 to 1869; O. A. Sauer, 1869 to 1872; N. Amlund, 1872 to 1874; M. Fr. Wiese, 1874 to 1890; K. L. Guttebo from 1890.

During the first forty years of the congregation there were 1,100 baptisms, 626 confirmants, 178 marriages, and 347 deaths.

Bethlehem Congregation

The Bethlehem congregation was organized January 12th, 1878, as an annex to the Palestine congregation and continued as such till in 1880 when it became an independent congregation. The charter members were as follows: Elling Halverson and family; Lars Thompson and family; Kolben Askeland and family; Halvar Warren and family; Henry O. Hendrickson and family; T. Skola and family, John Stenberg and family; Elias Fronsdahl and family; Torres Simonson and family; Hemming Romsa and family; J. Mickelson and family; Oley Nelson and family.

The congregation has been served by the following pastors: J. H. Myhre, 1878 to '80; H. C. Holm, 1881 to '93; N. B. Thvedt, 1894 to '97; A. L. Huus, 1897 to 1902; H. J. Holman from 1903.

In 1903, the members living in the vicinity of Kelley were privileged to form an independent congregation, served by the same pastor as the Bethlehem congregation. It was named the Bethania. A church had previously been built there.

From 1881 till 1905, the present writing, there were 432 baptisms in the congregation, 350 confirmants, 92 weddings, and 115 deaths.

The Lincoln Congregation

The Lincoln congregation, first known as the Polk City Congregation, was organized at the home of Peter Johnson by Rev. E. Johnson.[10] The first members were as follows: Peder Johnson and family; Torbjorn Nervig and family; Ole Halvorson and family; H. Skarhaugen and family; G. Annon and family; N. Askerson and family; H. Erickson and family; Hans Stenberg, Sr. and family; Hans Stenberg, Jr. and family; Ole Jorgenson and family; Lars Stenson and family.

The congregation has been served by the following pastors: P. Solberg, E. Johnson, N. G. Peterson, E. Estenson, O. P. Svingen, H. Hendrickson, G. C. Gjerstad, N. J. Lohre.

At this writing, 1905, no records are available, showing the number of deaths or other statistics.

Dedicated

This booklet is dedicated to the memory of our pioneer fathers and mothers that came to Story and Polk Counties in 1855 and their descendants. It is easy to obliterate the footprints in the sands of time, footprints that blazed the pioneer trail and should be remembered—handed to the coming generations.

About the Author
by the Compiler

The Honorable Oley Nelson, affectionately known to his Slater friends in his later years as the Grand Old Man, was a man of varied interests and talents. Farmer, soldier, businessman, postmaster, banker, politician, director on national church and higher education boards, and historian are some of the many responsibilities he assumed during his long and active life.

He was born in Rock County, Wisconsin, in 1844. When Oley was three years old, his parents moved to Primrose Township in Dane County where they farmed 160 acres of land. In 1861, his father enlisted in the Civil War and died of illness during a furlough trip home. Motivated by a desire to take his father's place, Oley enlisted in the spring of 1864.[11] He assisted with the capture of Memphis, but afterwards he became seriously ill and was sent home, receiving an honorable discharge in December 1864.

After hearing "that the soil was richer and the corn grew taller in Iowa than in Wisconsin,"[12] Oley and his mother joined a caravan of Norwegian immigrants that moved to southern Story County and northern Polk County in 1867. He and his mother settled on land two miles south of the present town of Sheldahl. When they were unable to make payments on the farm after losing their crop to grasshoppers in 1867, they moved to Des Moines in 1869 where Oley took a job hauling bricks. Later that year, he obtained a position in a mercantile store, the start of his business career. This same year, he married Lizzie Ersland of Cambridge, and together they had 10 children.

In 1873, Oley Nelson was hired by two Des Moines businessmen to help lay out the town of Sheldahl.[13] He moved there, opened the first store, started a grain buying business, and became its most prominent merchant. In 1887, he moved his businesses a mile and a half north to Sheldahl Crossing where the Chicago, Milwaukee and St. Paul Company had completed a railroad depot in 1884.[14] Sheldahl Crossing later was renamed Slater, and Oley became a leading businessman there, organizing the Farmers Savings Bank and becoming its first president. Among his civic projects in Slater was the planning and establishment of the city park which bears his name.

Oley Nelson was interested in state and national affairs, too. He was an active member of the Republican Party and elected to the 1882 and 1884 Iowa Legislatures, the first Story County Norwegian to serve in the state legislature. Later, he was sergeant-at-arms at the statehouse for 14 years, until 1937. He was also a member of the Grand Army of the Republic and served in many capacities including state commander and then national commander during 1936–37 when he was over 90 years old. Additionally, he served as vice-president for the national board of the United Lutheran Church and as a board member for St. Olaf College, Northfield, Minnesota.

Proud of his Norwegian heritage, Oley Nelson seldom passed up an opportunity to talk about it as evidenced by the following news item: "Hon. Oley Nelson of Slater appeared on the program at a meeting of the Luther League of Salems [sic] church Sunday evening. Mr. Nelson gave an instructive and interesting address on the subject, 'The Early Immigration of the Norseman, his loyalty to his church, his adopted country and his sacrifices.' Mr. Nelson commenced his discourse by giving a brief history of Norway and its people and continued with the trials and tribulations of the early immigrants to this country. He recited several personal experiences that he encountered in his service in the Civil War and portrayed the important part the Norwegians played in that conflict. In his closing Mr. Nelson dwelt for a time on the history of the Norwegian Lutheran church up to the present time."[15]

In his 1945 update of Nelson's history, Anfin Apland describes Oley Nelson as "a very bright man, well educated, well read, and well posted on all topics. He had a clear voice and could speak on any subject. He had a strong personality, lots of friends, and was a natural leader. He was good hearted and always wanted to help the needy; too good hearted for his own good."[16] Maury White, former reporter for the *Des Moines Register* and page at the state house when Oley was sergeant-at-arms, remembered this small man as having "a presence, and a stentorian voice. Lord, did he have a voice! The high point of any day's work as a page came when our mentor would square his frail shoulders, march to the center of the aisle and boom out: 'Mr. Speaker, a message from the Senate.'"[17]

Oley Nelson died in 1938 and is buried in the Bethlehem Cemetery, Slater, Iowa.[18]

Compiler's Notes

Oley Nelson's history of the first Norwegian settlement in Story and Polk Counties has become the most often cited history of the central Iowa Norwegians in general histories about Norwegian immigration to the United States.

The idea to write a history originated at a meeting held in Huxley during May 1904 to discuss celebrating the 50th anniversary of the settling of Story County by the Norwegians.[19] The planning group which elected A. L. Kloster chairman and Oley Nelson secretary decided to begin collecting material for a historical sketch of the settlement for the last 50 years. They also decided to hold a celebration during June 1907. Kloster and Nelson were appointed to the history committee along with Revs. Guttebo, Shefveland, and Holman. Other committees selected were: Program—L. O. Larson, Tom Weeks, Anfin Ersland, K. B. Thompson, and John Fatland; Arrangement—Andrew Nelson, W. Weeks, Sivert Tesdahl, Henry Fatland, and Henry Sheldahl.

Readers who are familiar with Nelson's history may wonder why I did not select Anfin Apland's 1945 "re-compiled, corrected, and added to" version of Nelson's history for inclusion in this volume. I considered this possibility, but decided the best way to honor the memory of Oley Nelson was to use the account he wrote about the first Norwegians in Story and Polk Counties.

Nelson's account of why the Lisbon settlers decided to send a scouting party to Iowa has always intrigued me. Surely there had been previous reports about land opportunities in Iowa. Why would the word of one person, Nils Olsen Naes, cause such a stir? It was many years after first reading Nelson's history that I understood why people listened to him. Nils Olsen Naes, also known as Nils Olsen and Nils Olsen Fjeld, was a person many of the Lisbon settlers knew well and obviously respected because he and his family were passengers on the *Kong Sverre* in 1847. Soon after his arrival in Lisbon, his wife died. A year later he married Siri Sjursdatter Matre and a year after that four of his five children died of cholera.[20] Nils continued to work as a farm laborer in Big Grove Township until 1851 when he became a Bible salesman. In 1853, Nils began lay preaching in northern Illinois, southern Wisconsin, northeast Iowa, and southeast Minnesota, and was ordained in 1857 when he became a supply pastor in Preston, Minnesota. From 1870 until his death in 1884, Nils Olson Næs was a pastor in Owatonna, Minnesota, and nearby communities.[21] He is buried in the Highland Cemetery in Dakota County, Minnesota.

Another interesting footnote to Nelson's history is how the scouting party came to find land in central Iowa. According to Carrie O. Larson, granddaughter of Osmund Sheldahl, the scouting party was authorized to go as far as Lincoln, Nebraska (other sources say they were authorized to go as far as Omaha, Nebraska[22]). Outside of Newton, Iowa, they lost their way. After much deliberation, they decided to take a road they thought would head them west again, but instead it headed them north. Larson states, "This led them to Story County, Iowa, indeed destined by God, as the land there was far better than it was in western [eastern] Nebraska."[23]

Acknowledgment

The compiler gratefully acknowledges Mike Nelson for permission to reprint his great great grandfather's history.

A Little About
the First Settlers in Story County

by Erik Arnesen Travaas, 1888
Translated by Ardis N. Petersen & Arlen Twedt

From *Hjemve: Norske Digte og Fortællinger* [Homesickness: Norwegian Poems and Stories] by Erik Arnesen Travaas, collected and published by his daughter, Anna Travaas Gilbert, Minneapolis, Minnesota, 1925

Compiler's note: Erik Travaas' historical narrative is, to my knowledge, the first recorded account of the central Iowa Norwegians. While there are a few factual errors in it which are explained in endnotes, Travaas' narrative is based on real people and real events, and it gives an interesting glimpse into the minds and hearts of these early settlers. Before reading his narrative, it is helpful for the reader to know that the year before the main characters, Lars and Per, made their scouting trip to central Iowa, a scouting party from Lisbon, Illinois, purchased a large amount of land in and around the present day town of Roland.[1] In June 1856, a caravan of 17 families and three single people arrived to begin the new settlement. When Lars and Per moved their families to Iowa in 1857, they settled on land four miles northwest of Roland in southern Hamilton County.[2]

• • •

It is truly easy for everyone to see the progress the first settlers have made since they came here around 40 years ago. When one looks at the prosperity they have achieved, and at the same time looks back on their first days as immigrants, one cannot keep from wondering about the tremendous change that has taken place. But during this time, they have had to struggle and endure the hardships that all immigrants faced.

In order for us to understand the total perspective, we will go back to the time when they lived at home in Norway and follow them in their wanderings. Many of them scarcely thought when they dreamt about America as a land where they could truly accomplish their most fantastic dreams of riches and success, that so many hardships, so much trouble, and all sorts of want should await them. But when the home where one is born is poor, and the house with its low roof has become too cramped, and when all possible ways out for the future seem to be closed, then it is not strange if one feels a longing and desire to leave that place. Many of our Norwegian settlers were precisely like that; they thought that home had become for them too cramped. In the same way, when they looked toward the future they always ran into the same impenetrable fog that seemed to be characteristic of the poorer part of the Norwegian population and has made it so impossible, even for the most industrious one, to create independence for himself.

We think of these emigrants as they go around at home and contemplate the future, about the poverty and destitution that meets them from all directions. We see them in their energetic youth, with courage in the heart and a firm will that seeks to build a path to independence, but always the same obstacle, the same fog, certainly always the same enormous wall there, as a bondage drags the future's comfortable thoughts away and fills the soul with emptiness and longing.

What a miracle then if they let their longings fly up and over the wall of bondage to America, to the land of freedom. The thoughts from their flight came back as a benevolent sunbeam and placed in the soul an infinite abundance of brilliant conception. Most people knew this by experience. Moreover, one or another teasing report comes telling how people over there can come to abundance and fortune in a hurry. All this appears as enchantment to our poor emigrants who now no longer have any misgivings about traveling to *Vinland* [North America] to the golden paradise in the west. What a daring thought, what bold decision!

Ready they stood now and cast one last glance over the meager earth, over the barren rocks that in their hopeless condition had nothing to tempt them anymore. The gray, gloomy mountaintops stood speechless and looked down on them; it was as if they would say, "Sure enough, we are proud of our age, and it flatters us to hear people praise us, and it is also a real joy to carry rich travelers, rich tourists on our shoulders, but to see such a crowd of healthy, happy sons and daughters leave us, that makes us pretty sad. But when we stand here naked and poor and have nothing to offer, so will we silently receive your farewell."

Afterwards they wrapped themselves in the mist that now spread itself over mountain and valley, where it held on to the last ray of sun in its lap. Then it was so sad, so melancholy and dismal. The songbird sat and shook his wings. Every time a puff of wind came by, large sparkling teardrops fell from the buds of the birch tree branches and hid themselves in the grass where they, weak and sparse, peeped forth from the field. The flowers stood sorrowful and closed their blooms, sighing for sunshine. The only one who seemed to be in good spirits was the brook that was frolicking down by the bare rock, doing small wheeling leaps up under the heather. Wandering and looking for the way down toward the ocean the brook sang:

Hurry, hurry, I'm running along,
Come you poor one and follow my step,
I will go out to the free, mighty ocean,
You come also, take your hiking stick.

I will no longer quarrel with the mountain water,
I will go out on the big, wide open plain,
Come with me also, we have the same longings,
The same situation that holds us prisoner here.

So the brook set off for the unknown. The poor emigrants did the same, but a strange feeling gripped them when they looked back, looking at their dear but poor home lying there in the steep slopes surrounded by some barren site as always. It wasn't easy to tear themselves away; they had to fight to get loose from these many strange memories that tied them to these poor homes that they possibly will never see any more. But the struggle for existence is often hard enough to chase and drive away even the most tender feelings, and it is like that here also.

The emigrants had set themselves a goal. They should and must struggle to reach it, and many bitter tears were suppressed and stifled. Worst was when the last decisive moment came, when the anchor was lifted and the sailors joined in song; when father and mother or sister and brother ran around and waved the last good-bye, then it was as all the restrictive ties dissolved in a ceaseless cry of tears.

The song from the merry sailors seemed to the poor emigrant as one exceedingly long funeral hymn. It is painful at such a time of departure to see so many waving hands and handkerchiefs from a large mass of people. At the moment it seems to one as if he would really be buried alive.

Now the course was set over the roaring ocean to America. Up on the deck one sees them standing in groups supporting themselves at the railing in a row while the ship began to move at full sail.

With a certain repressed feeling they stood and looked back towards land, as if once more to cast one last glance toward the bluish coast of the fatherland. A strange sensation of hopelessness, a hidden emptiness gripped them for a moment, until they finally were awakened to consciousness by the ship's violent heaving from the powerful motion of the waves.

The fatherland, with its proud nature and sparkle, has disappeared. The home and all that ties them there begins somehow to be a weak glimmer that shows itself through memories' rays.

The surroundings seem gloomy and monotonous. Just a big, turbulent sea meets your eye which confronts you from one horizon to the other, with gigantic waves that arrive breaking in greenish foamy reflection, and whose breaking can make even the bravest to shudder and tremble.

All this is for a poor emigrant not daily accustomed to being out on the large high seas—nothing pleasant to see. Therefore, one sees also how quickly one after another disappears down under the deck. It is as they found comfort to now see the appalling contest among the towering waves.

We also step down below deck, but what in the world? What sight meets us here? From every bunk vomiting, voices retching in excruciating pain. We see one after the other hanging his head over the bunk, retching and screaming.

In those days it was not so comfortable to travel to America as it is now. Now one can come on board a splendid steamship where all goes as in a merry game and where one gets food and drink, I almost said in bed. At that time one had to provide his own food, cook and take care of his food, which was not always so simple a thing to get done. The cookhouse stood on the deck with a very poor stove where one must wait for the others for hours. Often brawls and fist fights broke out because all wished to be the first to get their food cooked.

It is strange to see how on a really stormy day they had difficulty keeping their footing on the rolling deck. Often it happened that the fat roast, the delicious soup that they had made with great difficulty, in an unguarded moment, finds its place on the deck in between the rope work and other objects lying around. Almost ready to cry, the cook gets up from falling, holding on to the empty plate or the empty pot in his hand, looking over at the delicious soup, the cooked peas, or the unforgettable roast that now can no longer comfort his greedy appetite. Bracing and holding on to all he can get hold of, he has to recover and go into the cookhouse to attempt it again. He now feels certain that it is no longer the solid ground he is moving on, and he shows a little more caution. But splash, there lies another one holding the empty coffee pot in his hand while the contents go all over the deck. Those who have made the trip to America aboard a sailing ship know by experience what unpleasantness people are exposed to.

One week after the other slowly sneaks by. In the end, life on board gets ghastly. Imagine about three or four hundred people packed together in a one dark, dirty place where all kinds of filth and nastiness grow and thrive. Under such circumstances one cannot but wonder why the number of immigrants increases so rapidly. After such a voyage we are sure that our poor pioneers were truly happy, but also very tired when they finally reached Quebec after the long, difficult trip. But with this the journey was not over. Once more they were packed into a kind of ferryboat to go to Montreal. From here they went by train through the country until they finally reached their destination in Lisbon, Illinois.

Here they were welcomed and treated in the best manner by their local countrymen. No doubt they had at the time no splendid farmhouses like they have now to offer the newcomers who were tired from their journey. Their intentions were good, and no one asked about splendid houses and places. At that time people didn't have the love of display as now, nor did they suffer from luxury fever, but knew much more about ague and other unpleasantries that went with the life of the immigrant.

A simple and in many respects a poor log house was what settlers also had to be satisfied with. It was not uncommon that four or five families slept under one roof. There prevailed more brotherhood and confidence among the settlers at that time than has, unfortunately, been shown later. This was probably because of:

> *After work and sweat,*
> *Then comes selfishness,*
> *That pushes friendship to the door,*
> *And the relationship will never be as before.*

About a couple years later, our newcomers were still at this place. They had now seen for themselves the local situation; had learned to guide the plow and drive oxen because the settlers knew little about horses at that time. Now they thought it could be interesting to go out on an adventure and try something for themselves. It looked as if they didn't like it where they were. In Story County, Iowa, they had heard there should be an endless amount of arable land, preferably prairie land, and it seemed most wanted to move there. So it was decided that two of the newcomers should undertake a trip there with the goal to find the best place for a new Norwegian settlement.

They chose Lars Vestland, and *Store* [big] Per, as he was usually called. Both were from Western Norway. Lars was a small, strong, well-built man, but Per was a very gigantic figure. When one saw him one could not other than be reminded of an old Norwegian giant with steel in arm setting out on a Viking expedition. Per was a good-natured fellow, but woe if one came into his disfavor. Then a bear hug would be much more preferred than a hug with him.

Then oxen were hitched to the wagon and all the necessary things for the journey were brought with them. As protection against weather and wind, they placed a kind of tent over the wagon. This rested on three arches that were fastened to the wagon's frame. The tent or canvas fitted together in both ends and gave what one might say a rather comfortable shelter. A crack with the whip and the oxen moved out with an even, slow stride. It takes patience to drive with oxen. One must take care that they don't all of a sudden make some unexpected turns and get stuck in a slough.

It is now long past spring, the grass is vigorous and green, and the same goes for the maize on the large extensive fields. Here and there are woods showing their light green foliage where the delightful singing of songbirds is heard. Also, the whippoorwill now and then lets its charming voice be heard.

Lars drove the oxen while Per stared out over the landscape whistling an old sad tune. It is so lovely, so refreshing, to breathe the fresh air, so stimulating to look out over the fertile fields. He thinks about his poor home in Norway, makes comparisons, but finds that it is infinitely poorer than the rich earth he can see here. Even though he feels a good deal of loneliness in his heart, he can not but feel thankful that Providence has brought him so well and so surely to this fertile land whose richness, by diligence and work, will be inherited from generation to generation.

The further west they come, the wilder and more desolate the country looks. Often it seems they never will arrive at their destination. The obstacles caused by the difficulties of travel have already lengthened their trip, but Lars and Per are still in good spirits. From their earliest childhood they have gotten in the habit of waiting for everything with patience, and that helps them. A trip over the wild prairie demands patience like nothing else.

Finally they reach as far as the border of Story County. Here the wild prairie begins to show its impressive expanses. When one looks out over the endless plains, it appears as a troubled sea where the waves begin to subside after a storm. They were very surprised about all the uncultivated land which lay here waiting to be changed to productive acres and meadows.

Both Lars and Per were filled with hope that in this country they could find a place where they could build and live in the future. "Just look," said Lars, "Here it's possible to get yourself a very large farm, very much larger, I should think, than the one we had at home which we called large." Per thought the same way. "And just imagine how we can reap with long handled scythes," continued Lars. "It will certainly be better than puttering along with a short handled sickle and cutting every little straw among the stones as we had to do back home."

"Yes," said Per and laughed a little, "Here the *husmands'* [tenant farmers'] wives should soon get their sack filled, for you know, they always carried their sickle and sack along the rivers and up in the marshes where they knew there would be a few untouched straws. Poor creatures, it was certainly not so good for them, but were they perhaps not pleased? Oh, certainly it did not look any worse. They sang while the sweat was streaming down their faces as they carried soil to cover the bare rocks. In the long winter evening they would sit and tell about new and old things, about wood nymphs and *nisser* [elves], and all kinds of troll people, and with such apparent cheerfulness as if they didn't lack for anything, yet as you know, there was little food in their house."

"Certainly," said Lars, "I think that the poor people at home were just happy to be alive, even though they hardly had food or other resources. I really wish they had been here. I am sure that they would have gotten pay for their toil and drudgery."

The sun was now about to go down; therefore, they had to hurry on if they were to reach Nevada before it got too dark. A strong crack with the whip, and the oxen lunged ahead, panting and groaning and tossing a wistful glance at the attractive green grass that stood tempting them by the wayside. While Lars was chewing on a large plug of tobacco and while his thoughts dwelt on the large expanse of beautiful prairie which lay stretched out before his view, he cared little about the wishes of the oxen. Per sat and imagined the beautiful settlement that the Norwegian settlers, in a short time, would establish in this country. He thought about how nice it would be when they could come so far that they could together build a church, call a pastor, and have it just like it was at home where they could go to church and hear God's word, hear the lovely old hymn tunes that could, so wonderfully, dispose one to devotion and holy sadness. By these reflections he began to hum an old hymn tune, one that he had heard so often in his ears that his old mother frequently had sung for him when he was very little. He drew a deep sigh because he thought about her who sat at home on the bare, stony ground surrounded by sorrow, loneliness, and poverty. It was as if something strange sat in his throat when he thought about his brothers and sisters, his old father there anxious and worried, toiling and laboring from early morning to late evening, and yet he could hardly provide bread and sustenance for himself and his family. If they only had had such beautiful, rich land as here. But it could not be otherwise, and so he sighed deeply and prayed to God in his quiet mind that He would give him good fortune and blessing in this rich, strange country. Then he could in time be able to help his brothers and sisters and his poor parents out of their needy condition.

Finally they had reached Nevada. Here they made camp. It had already begun to get dark, but they could still see some pitiful shacks which, upon closer look, turned out to be the beginnings of a town.[3] Here they found a sort of general store that sold all kinds of things that lay scattered around in a mess. Here was also a post office, but quite plain, I understand.

The inhabitants appeared to Lars and Per to be Americans, and they found them difficult to understand. Still they got enough out of them that if they set the course toward the north and west, ten or fourteen miles from there, they would find all the land they wished to inspect. Satisfied, Lars and Per went back to their camp where they unhitched the oxen. While the oxen gorged on the green grass, the two lay down to rest under the canvas of the wagon where they soon fell in a deep sleep under which they had the most wonderful dreams. They dreamed they saw the widespread prairie changed to golden productive acres, where the ripened wheat and the vigorous maize waved in the wind. They dreamed about filled granaries, about teeming herds of horses and cattle, about mile long pigsties, and about chickens and wild turkeys.

But when they awakened in the morning they remembered very little of their nice dreams. They saw their own oxen grazing at some distance in this big herd, and they saw the same golden acres waving in the prairie. But it was nothing but a dream, and they couldn't imagine that this dream could come true in the future. Therefore, they walked rather carelessly and again hitched the oxen to the wagon. Before the sun rose they were already a long way on the north road. In the beautiful sunshine we see them coming over the prairie by Nevada, talking about this and that, about their dear sweethearts from their youth, who now in their white blouses, their red bodices, and silver-lace trimmed caps, go plodding along at home as usual. It seems like a hidden pleasure on Lars' and Per's smiling hearts when they now, in peace and quiet, think about the time when their dear sweethearts will be in their arms. It is as if they are floating on clouds from east to west, receiving greetings from their loved ones far away.

A little before the sunset they had reached the area where Roland was later built. Also, here the same empty landscape was spread before them.[4]

Here they began to look around really well. The country was beautiful and had a deep rich soil. If they could just find some wood for fuel for building a house and such, they thought then they might be all right.

The day after that, a man told them that five or six miles to the west there was a little stream where there was a good-sized woods. Hearing this, they decided at once to go investigate if it was really so. Again they hitched the wagon, and along in the afternoon they reached the splendid woods along the Skunk River. Their joy was great to see the richness of the woods which in the future would be of much benefit to them and other settlers.

Here along the Skunk River and by the edge of the timber, individual Americans had settled. Their poor log cabins didn't look very inviting, but Lars and Per wished they had one of them. At least it was a roof over their heads, they thought.

Not far from here was the place where Story City was later built.[5] After they had looked over the surroundings and satisfied themselves that this part of the county which they now had traveled through would be best suited for beginning a Norwegian settlement, they started back again. Without hindrance and any unusual happenings, they reached Lisbon.

As anyone might guess, they were asked unending questions about how things had gone on the trip; if they had found fine and good land, if they had found woods in the area, and about everything else possible and impossible. A crowd of settlers had gathered when they heard Lars and Per had come back. They wanted to hear them tell about the trip across Iowa's wild prairies. With liveliness and confidence, Lars and Per sat down and told clearly about all they had seen and experienced. In a delightful manner, they told about the lovely landscape in Story County, about the beautiful woods that grew by the Skunk River, and about the gigantic prairie grass that stood like a little forest and waved in the wind. When they were through telling it, all went home.

When the next spring came, one could see them in one moving wagon after the other going west to Story County all packed with household goods, with old plows, and other things that the settlers must have in order to manage. That Lars and Per were first in the wagon train is not so strange. They had traveled the same way before and now must help the others find the landmarks. They rode together with the same oxen and the same wagon as the first time. In the wagon, one saw their Norwegian trunks, with their large strange *rosemaling* [rose painting] peeking out in the sunshine. In these they kept their most precious treasures, their most holy treasures. There lay the Bible, the New Testament, and hymn book which was given at confirmation. And there was kept also other precious things that dear hands had given them in the moment of departure that the old simple people called a love gift.

That doesn't belong to our time any more. Now we are so educated that we don't need more experience about affairs of the heart. Engagement and the rite of marriage can now be done on the same day, so to speak, and therefore it's not so strange if divorce comes the day after.

All goes well according to expectations. When darkness falls, encampment is made where all sit in an intimate circle and talk until far into the night. And so the travel goes until they finally reach their destination.

As time went on, a new way of life was changing the previously empty prairie. The plow with two or three span of oxen begins to make furrows here and there over the prairie. In the woods by the Skunk River is heard the sound of the ax. The old mighty trees, which for hundreds of years have been good friends with other trees in the woods, must now fall as an offering for man's tyrannical hand. Across the prairie we see team after team hauling loads of timber from the woods.

The settlers need houses in a hurry, so we see one after another chopping away at the huge oak trees, two sides taken off, thereafter laid in place and so on until the log house is finished. When one after the other is built, and the grass roof with its sod has been put on, one might find it difficult to believe that civilized people would want to live there since both sun and moon on occasion can show themselves through the meter-long spaces that can be seen between each log. The settlers have already learned some Yankee tricks, among others that they fill the large spaces with kneaded soil and later the whole inside is white washed. One must not suppose that such houses are warm and comfortable during the winter. On the contrary, the opposite is often the case. Therefore, it takes a strong character to live your life in such poor cabins when the really harsh winter cold sets its icy seal on the cups and bowls and everything else.

Life became very busy on the prairie now. The prairie chickens, which had enjoyed peace and quiet for many years, cackled and courted each other in the tall prairie grass. They could not understand what all this commotion should mean. Wandering, they stood and looked at the man behind the plow. They must have thought that now the redskins are after us, and in that thought they stole away through the grass.

The man behind the plow is Per, big and broad shouldered and with an expression on his face that witnesses to joy and inner happiness. He takes long thoughtful steps and shouts now and then a haw and gee to the oxen who obediently must go according to his thundering voice. Over on a little hill stands his new log house, really quite simple, but inside is Per's sweet girl. Like the friendly sun in May, she goes here, spreading sunshine and coziness for her good Per because she has now become his wife. No wonder that Per, who goes behind the plow, looks both glad and pleased because he is very happy.

A little ways off we see another new log house. Here we find Lars with his beloved wife. Both seem to be glad and happy. Here and there over the prairie new log cabins are seen erected every year. Relatives and friends from Illinois as well as from the fatherland stream in great numbers to the new Norwegian settlement.

They are hard and difficult times which they have to struggle through. To begin with, resources are small and insignificant, and the roads often impassable. The closest market place at first was in Iowa City. It took many days to travel that long way. Later they got a new market place in Marshalltown. That seemed to them to be a big relief even though they still had almost 30 miles to transport their products.

With regard to school and churches, it was not so easy either. Everyone must help themselves as best they could. When Sunday came, they had to be satisfied with the father in the house reading the text out of a sermon book. It went this way for many years. But when the number of people increased every year, a measure of success, they agreed to build churches and call a pastor. A few of those who had settled near Roland made the suggestion that they should form a congregation that is on the east prairie, as they called it. At the west prairie by Story City, they made the same decision, and then the east prairie and west prairie were put together as one call.[6]

It happened that a young student from *Kristiania* [Oslo] came and took the call. Now Per had his wish fulfilled. Now he, as well as all the other settlers, could go to church, be along and sing the same lovely old hymns as before, sit with attention, and listen to the blissful words that streamed from the young pastor's lips.

To be sure, their churches weren't as ornate, as decorated as one now sees them. But frugality always finds enough in a little.

In the same way, it was also strange to see how simple and modest people at that time came to church: twill trousers, twill skirts generally, and the men with simple straw hats and women with bonnets and head scarves. Their looks were in truth not very charming. But what did one care about it at that time. They didn't think they were better than they were—namely poor settlers. They had other things to think about at the time than finery and foolery.

Often they had to fight against the hard times, bad years, little earnings, and many other troubles in various ways as people nowadays know nothing about. When the harsh winter came and when the icy cold from the northwest stole bitterly over the open prairies, it would be no fun to sit in the cold, poor log cabin where you had to keep firing the stove constantly. When sticks of wood from the timber were used up, and they had nothing to burn, it was no laughing matter, you can be sure. Then father must take his oxen to the timber and often it could happen that a raging snowstorm overtook him on the way, so then he had to fight and struggle through the snow and the cold. At that time you could not wrap yourself into a fur coat and inch thick woolen socks with overshoes on as we see people do nowadays. No, they certainly did not know of such foolishness and neither did they sit inside growling about all the things to be done outside.

The settlers had a good reputation among the few Americans who were there, especially for their honesty, diligence, and industry. It happened not seldom that they could borrow both money and other things from the Yankees when they were in a pinch. But they were always punctual to pay back their debt. The Yankees paid attention to that, and they remember to this day that the Norwegians are an honest and peace-loving people who want to follow with the times and work their way forward.

Finally, the settlers' long-time wish for a closer railroad became fulfilled in that Chicago & Northwestern built a branch line from their big network that should go through Nevada westward to Ames.[7] That became a great relief for them. Now they had only ten or fifteen miles to market. Before they had twice as far.

After that time, it went steadily forward for them. Now Lars and Per could see the beginning of their dreams realized. The settlers had already gotten a lot of livestock. The swineherds, if not just a mile long, looked large and included many fat hogs. The log cabins were now replaced by the more modern farmhouses. Schoolhouses were built here and there all over.

In Story City, or Fairview as it was called at that time, one could now see the beginnings of a town when a couple of stores, a blacksmith shop, and a shoemaker's shop already were erected. There was also a post office where one of the settlers became postmaster.[8]

With great difficulty, the storekeepers had to transport their wares from Nevada or Ames. Even though much of what the settlers had wished for had come true, it seemed as though there was one wish left and that was that they could get themselves an even closer market. They had to struggle with that need for many years. In the meantime, the terrible Civil War broke out where many of our strapping brave settlers took part. It was moving to see them say good-bye to their loved ones at home before they left for the field of battle from which they might not ever come back alive. Many a home became a house of sorrow, where one report after the other told about death and killing by the thousands.

During the terrible war the settlers had to struggle against the hard time. Money lost a great deal of its value. All they needed to buy rose in price. But finally the war came to an end after thousands had offered their lives on the field of battle to bring victory to the North. Though many of the settlers had gone to war and offered their lives, there were also some who fortunately came back. But among the others there were some who received lifetime disabilities. Among those could be mentioned N. Erickson who, as far as I know, was in the biggest and most violent battles and until recently as a reminder has carried a bullet in the knee. It is appalling and at the same time interesting to hear him tell about the war, how they had to suffer and withstand all kinds of tortures and troubles. But the best of all is when he tells about the battle at Gettysburg—how they furiously, with red soldiers' courage, pressed with force and might up on the hill and captured the flag. There could be much to tell about his many strange adventures in the war, but since I am no writer I will let that go.

Now after the war was over came better times. The settlers were well paid for their goods and products. That gave them a good start. There still lay large areas of unplowed prairie, here and there, that permitted the settlers to find both fields and grazing land. This contributed to the increase of their already large herds of livestock. Now the wild prairie had in many places gotten an entirely different look. Instead of the tall prairie grass, now we could see golden fields with their ripe golden wheat, and their tall maize whose soft silk in the lovely sunshine peeked out from each ear.

Instead of the old log cabins and the old-time frame houses could be seen every year new splendid houses arising, surrounded by lovely groves planted by the settlers which now had grown into the large leafy trees in whose shade the oftentimes tired settlers now could find rest and refreshment. Not to mention the beautiful, graceful willow trees that lined both sides of the road, their shade making great splendid avenues.

Now Per's most fervent wish had been fulfilled. God had given him both happiness and blessing, and so had caused him to be able to help his poor parents and his siblings out of the straitened circumstances. He had now gotten them all here, his old father and mother, who now went around as they pleased thanking God for the great things he had done for them in their old age. His siblings had taken land not far from there. All felt satisfied and happy and made surprising progress every year.

Of course, Per had now gotten older but had not lost his strapping figure. He didn't waste his superior strength on unnecessary things, and therefore his many neighbors had great respect for him and regarded him as a really good-natured giant among them. When some arrogant Yankee acted smart, people just called on Per, and then the Yankee tramped away.

As proof of his superior strength, it can be told that one time when his oxen were stuck and the one ox couldn't pull anymore, he unhitched it and put himself in the yoke, and now it could happen the load moved forward. And another time a German or a Yankee, or whatever he was, came and was going to give Per a thrashing. Per was in the field plowing. He didn't worry that he might get a beating. Calm, as he always was, he knelt down on one knee, put his left hand behind his back, and then with his big calm eyes fastened on the Yankee said, "In this position you may have permission to challenge me, and I shall never be worth being called a Norwegian if I can't, with one hand, throw you dead to the ground. Try now if you will." Frightened over Per's calm demeanor, the scoundrel ran as fast as he could with the understanding that Per must be a dreadful guy whom no one should have anything to do with.

We come so far along in time as to the year 1876 when Story City still hasn't gotten a railroad. There began to be rumors that in the near future a narrow gauge branch would be built from Ames north past Story City. As a result of such a rumor, the people in Story City and the surrounding area began to look forward to such an undertaking because if it came to pass it would ease and help many of the inconveniences. Thus it would not be necessary any longer to keep a mail route going from Story City to Nevada. There were many reasons that a railroad to here would in all ways be a great advantage. The next spring it was already said that the new railroad was begun, and great was the joy when along in the summer they saw it come closer to town.

But when it looked as if it would come a ways outside of town, it was seen as necessary for the sake of the transportation to establish a new town beside the old one. This was done, and in that way the town got the name Story City. Now there came a great upheaval. Every house had to be moved and repaired, new houses were built, all pointed to a new beginning. Saloons and gambling houses seemed now more than ever to thrive and flourish, to the harm and shame for many of the settlers' children who liked to indulge.

In 1879, the first brick block building was erected. Here was established an Opera Hall where one from time to time had the opportunity to see and hear the many entertaining pieces that the traveling companies presented. Yes, it was strange what progress the town made after the railroad came. Workers streamed in from all sides. One store after the other was built, the traffic increased, the farmers earned money, and store keepers no less. In 1882, the railroad from Ames to Story City was converted from narrow gauge to wide gauge, which now would be continued and go directly to St. Paul.[9] At the same time, there was a railroad built from Marshalltown through Roland ending in Story City. Now it seemed that every wish was being fulfilled. The farmers, or as we here have called them, settlers, have now gotten their wish. They had achieved prosperity, many even wealth. They were close to markets and had everything.

But just ask them if they really are happy. Then you will get the answer in the form of a prolonged "No!" They will still be able to answer you and say, "When I had my log cabin and the first forty acres I was really happier than I have been since." I can't explain why that is, but that is the way it is.

Yes, it is strange when we look out over the settlement where proud, splendid buildings cover the landscape with all their wonderfully carved decorations and all their varied colors that, so to speak, include all the colors of the rainbow, and then think back to the first poor cabins we saw over the open prairies. The change is really great.

Now when we come into the present time, if we would think about all the hard work, the many hardships that the first settlers had to struggle through, then we would certainly have reason to call ourselves fortunate. But how often don't we hear the opposite said since many say, "No, if we had been here when Per, Lars, and Sjur and all the others came and could have gotten our land for almost nothing as they did, then we could also have gotten to be somebody. But as it is now, nobody can get anywhere." This is what we can often hear.

They argue over conditions as they were then and as they are now.

Many of the first settlers have already found peace for their dust and are gathered to their forefathers.

The present generation takes their place and will, as it seems, continually keep on building what the old ones have begun. That is true in the temporal as well as the spiritual respect, and we dare hope the old Norwegian in us long will live and witness to the inheritance our fathers gave us.

Herewith ends my simple and incomplete account of the first settlers, their life and further progress.

About the Author
From the Foreword to *Hjemve: Norske Digte og Fortællinger*
by Mrs. Anna Travaas Gilbert, daughter of Erik Travaas
Minneapolis, Minnesota, August 3, 1925
Translated by Hans Gangstø

My father, Erik Arnesen Travaas, was born [in 1855] at the Travaas farm in Valestrand parish in Hordaland County. He was the son of farmer Arne Nilsen and wife Kari Helgesdaughter.

When he was 17 years old, he immigrated to America and stayed there for a few years. He returned home and a short time later married Elen Marie Knutsen. Then he went back to America and came to Albert Lea, Minnesota. He stayed there for a while before continuing on to Story City, Iowa, where he lived for 14 years. He then went to Minnesota, living at different locations, such as Kandiyohi County, Little Falls, Wilmar, Cottonwood County, Revere, and close to Walnut Grove. At last he settled in the beautiful woods at Moose Lake.

The earliest memories I have of my father from my childhood years are that he, in the evenings after work, brought out his violin and started to play—playing and dreaming. I would then bring a chair and sit next to him, and in blessed joy listen to him play the most wonderful music he magically conjured on his instrument, until I slumbered and fell into sweet dreams.

The musical notes seemed to soothe my father's spirit and help him to relive his pleasant childhood days.

I was too young at the time to understand his longings for everything that his heart held dear on the other side of the great ocean.

I did not understand my father until after his death, when I found these poems in an old suitcase.

These poems were a revelation to me; in them he so beautifully and emotionally interprets his innermost thoughts and feelings.

A feeling of deep despair overwhelms me, and I think of how misunderstood and lonely he was during his life. He was very reserved by nature, so few knew his innermost thoughts.

By profession he was a plasterer and greystone mason. He also tried his hand at farming, but this was not for him. He did not succeed and gave up farming.

He did not like the cold winters in Minnesota, but dreamt of going to a warmer climate. In 1907, he left for Idaho and later for Portland,

Oregon, where he felt comfortable. But due to his failing health, he had to seek a climate with thinner air. So in 1914, he went to Spokane and later to Springdale, Washington, where he lived until the fatal illness forced him to stay at Edgecliffe Sanatorium in Spokane. He died of tuberculosis there on September 24, 1916.

From the narrative above, one will understand that my father was a restless soul and had a hard time finding a place where he could be comfortable and settle down. He was a dreamer, with a poet's and artist's soul that did not fit in the practical life. He always dreamed of the old country, Norway, and his poems on Norwegian nature and daily life are declared by connoisseurs as remarkably beautiful and well written. His other poems and prose as well are, as far as I can judge them, too valuable to be lost and deserve to be widely known.

For this reason, and in memory of my dearly misunderstood father, I publish his poems.

About the Translators
by the Compiler

Ardis N. Petersen was born in Upland, Nebraska, in 1912. Her grandfather helped found a Danish settlement in east central Nebraska where he lived in a dugout along Turkey Creek his first year on the prairie. When his dugout flooded the next spring, he built a sod house on drier land. During her long life, Ardis lived in several of the well-known Danish settlements in the Upper Midwest as the daughter of a teacher turned businessman and as the wife of a pastor who served Danish congregations in Kansas, Iowa, and Minnesota and another congregation in Nebraska. In 1966, I became her son-in-law, and it is my honor to write this biographical sketch about her.

Among Ardis' varied interests were the language, history, and culture of Denmark and of Danish-Americans. After her husband's death in 1980, she became coordinator of an annual four-day meeting at the Danebod Folk School in Tyler, Minnesota, which she continued to coordinate for 20 years. Modeled after the Gruntvigian folk school movement in Denmark, the meetings are a blend of stimulating lectures, joyful singing, thoughtful devotions, entertaining story telling, lively conversation, delicious food, and evening folk dancing. Ardis was also an active contributor to Danish literary publications and to historical museums in Tyler and the Museum of Danish America in Elk Horn, Iowa.

A visit to Ardis' home was never complete without one game of *Scrabble*, usually three or four. She loved words and language, so it was easy for her to say yes when asked to translate this important historical narrative. We worked on it during visits to each others' homes over the course of three or four years during the late 1990s. Her knowledge of *Bokmål*, or Dano-Norwegian which came into use while Norway was under Danish rule from 1397–1814, was invaluable. She made every effort to maintain the integrity of the author's eloquent, and sometimes lofty, writing style and yet translate it into today's language. While she insisted that I include my name as co-translator of this narrative, it is truly her creation.

At age 90, Ardis also translated Knut Takla's newspaper reports that were written from central Iowa. This was while she was still writing a weekly column for her hometown newspaper, participating in a writers' group, playing piano dinner music at the nursing home once a week, accompanying a singing group, and leading morning exercises at the retirement village where she lived in Tyler, Minnesota. She continued writing her weekly newspaper column until shortly before her death in 2007 at the age of 95. To be as alive in mind, body, and spirit as Ardis always was should be the hope of us all.

Hans Gangstø, who translated the foreword to Travaas' book of poems and prose, is a friend I met on the Internet in 1997 when I was devoting most of my historical research to identifying the farms where the 395 Norwegians who were living in central Iowa by the end of 1860 had emigrated from in Norway. Hans responded to a request for information I posted on the Internet. When he discovered I had posted another request, he wrote and said he enjoyed doing look-ups and asked me to send further requests directly to him.

Hans and his wife, Kirsten, live in Haugesund, Norway, where Hans retired as sales manager for an automobile dealership. His leisure time interests include genealogy and family history and documenting gravesites in and near Haugesund. He is also very interested in emigration history, especially from the Rogaland *fylke* [county] where he lives and the Hordaland *fylke* which borders Rogaland to the north. His knowledge of these two counties is invaluable to my research because almost all of the central Iowa Norwegians who emigrated came from these areas. Hans is an avid reader of American literature, and he is equally comfortable at conversing and writing English, so we enjoy carrying on lively correspondence.

In 2003, my wife, Asta, and I had the pleasure of welcoming Hans and Kirsten as guests to our home. Having gotten to know each other very well through our email correspondence, we knew we would enjoy each other's company, and we did. In preparation for their visit, I assembled a guidebook which I entitled "A Guide to Central Iowa's Norwegian Historical Attractions." We spent a very long day using the guide to see the oldest Norwegian settlement areas in central Iowa. Along with us was my mother-in-law, Ardis, who conversed with Kirsten in Dano-Norwegian. While Hans and Kirsten were in Iowa, they also visited relatives of Kirsten's whose ancestors had immigrated to the Eagle Grove, Iowa, community. In 2006 and 2016, we had the pleasure of being guests in Hans and Kirsten's home in Haugesund.

Compiler's Notes

Lars, or Lars Vestlandet as he is often referred to in the narrative, is Lars Henderson (Håvig). He was born in 1825 on the Håvig farm in Bømlo, a municipality south of Bergen, Norway. In the late 1840s, Lars was the first person from his community to immigrate to America. He returned to Norway, and when he came back to the United States in 1856, he had a family, and they were accompanied by other families from Bømlo. The following year, 1857, Lars, his wife, Anna, and their three children were among 16 families who moved from the Lisbon Settlement southwest of Chicago to central Iowa. Lars died in 1908 and is buried in Fairview Cemetery in Story City, Iowa.

Per is Peder Larson Tjernagel also known as "Store Per" or "Big Peder" because of his size and strength. Peder and his wife, Malena, were also among the families in the 1857 caravan. Peder was born in 1826 on the Tjernagel farm in the Sveio municipality which is just across the fjord from Bømlo where Lars was born. Peder emigrated in 1851. Whether he knew Lars in Norway is not known, but it was natural for them to be friends in their newly adopted country since they had grown up close to one another. Peder died unexpectedly in 1863 and is buried in Boe

Cemetery south of Randall, Iowa. *Store Per: Norwegian-American "Paul Bunyan" of the Prairie* is a biography about his life.[10]

Erik Travaas was born in the same municipality as Store Per. He was born in 1855 and emigrated in 1873. He returned to Norway where he married Elen Marie Knutsen, and they emigrated in 1876. Erik and Elen settled in Albert Lea, Minnesota, but by 1880, they were living in Story City, Iowa, where Erik worked on the railroad. His daughter, Anna Gilbert, states they lived there for 14 years which indicates they moved back to Minnesota in the early 1890s.

Travaas may have penned the name Lars Vestlandet because in other historical sources he is often referred to as *Tallige* Lars [Patient Lars].[11] Since Store Per died before Travaas moved to Story City, Lars Henderson is obviously the source of Travaas' information about Lars and Per's 1856 scouting trip to central Iowa. Judging from the following newspaper item, Lars enjoyed talking about his first years on the Iowa prairie: "Genuine Hard Times: These are hard times in some respects, but nothing to compare with those endured by the early settlers here. Lars Henderson, of Scott Township, in relating several interesting incidents connected with the early settlement of this county, speaks of his neighbors going to Marshalltown (some 40 miles distant), and making the privilege of sweeping the mill floor to obtain flour enough to keep their families alive until they could procure food elsewhere. Mr. Henderson himself had to pay $1.50 per bushel for half rotten corn, which he washed in Skunk River and had it cracked in the rude corn cracker then in use here; and upon this course meal his family subsisted for many weeks. Mr. H. added: 'Think of that and then talk of hard times.'"—*Hamilton Freeman.*[12]

Two other characters Travaas mentions by name are N. Erickson and Sjur. There is not enough information in the narrative to know for sure who Sjur was, but N. Erickson is undoubtedly Nils Erickson Severaid who was born in Skånevik, Norway, in 1839. In 1858, Nils and two brothers immigrated to Lisbon, Illinois, where two other brothers and a sister had previously immigrated in 1854. In 1861, Nils enlisted in the 91st Illinois Infantry and served until 1865 after which he moved to central Iowa where the rest of his siblings settled except for a brother who settled in Minnesota. Nils died in 1895 and is buried in the Fairview Cemetery in Story City, Iowa.

Acknowledgment

The compiler gratefully acknowledges Shirley Frandson for giving him a copy of Erik Travaas' historical narrative. Shirley is a grandniece of Erik Arnesen Travaas. Her grandfather, Jonas Arneson Travaas, was Erik's brother. Jonas [1851–1892] and his wife, Barbar [1852–1889], immigrated to Story City, Iowa, where Jonas was a stone mason. They are buried in the Fairview Cemetery in Story City.

Big Norwegian Settlement, Roland, Iowa

by Knut Takla, 1900
Published in *Skandinaven*, Chicago, July 13, 1900
Translated by Ardis N. Petersen

"Central Iowa has one of the largest in America"

In central Iowa is one of the largest connected Norwegian settlements in the state, yes perhaps one of the largest in the Northwest.

The story of this settlement is much like the stories of the other older Norwegian settlements. In the early fifties around Lisbon, Illinois, there were a number of young, ambitious Norwegian men, some of them married and some single, who wished to get a piece of land to work and to live on. Land prices around Lisbon had begun to rise considerably, and since many of the men had rather thin purses, they needed to look around for cheaper land. The choice fell on Iowa. A committee was chosen and was sent west to look into the conditions before the whole group should make the move.

In June of 1855 the following persons went: Jonas Duea, Mons Grove, Paul Thompson, Lars Shjeldal, Jacob Erickson, John Nelson Tarvastad, Torris Mehus [John Mehus], and Ola Øine all joined in the discovery expedition. They went in two prairie schooners and followed the so-called Overland Trail [aka California Trail]. They stopped when they came to Newton, Iowa, and began to look around after land. There was a lot of good land around there, but there was a dearth of trees, and trees were much prized by the first settlers. So they traveled farther north past Iowa Center and up to the northwestern part of Story Co. where they found what they sought. Here was good fertile prairie land which could be bought from the government for $1.25 an acre and also good water and trees at a reasonable distance. The future has shown that these settlers knew how to judge land.

After they had chosen land for themselves and for many of their friends in Illinois and made the necessary arrangements concerning the purchases of same, they traveled back to Lisbon. The whole trip took only the surprisingly short time of barely four weeks.

In the fall of the same year, Thor O. Hegland and Lars Grindem [aka Lars Sheldall] moved here from Kendall Co., Illinois, where they bought land and settled on it over winter. Thus they became the first permanent residents in this big Norwegian settlement.

But the actual migration to this place happened first in the summer of 1856 when the following persons moved west: Jonas Duea, siblings Erick, Lars, Rasmus and Anna Shjeldal—later Mrs. Mons Grove, the brothers Jacob and Rasmus E. Aske along with the son Mickel E. Aske, Larson Larsen Tungesvik, Haavard Thompson, Hans Pedersen, Sjur Britson, Jacob J. Østiven, Jacob N. Meling, Ole Rasmussen Tysdal, Erick Jacobsen, Hans Tvedt, Sjur Opstvedt, and Lars Hegland.

Almost all of them were fathers of families, and as they traveled westward they made up a train of 24 immigrant wagons of which 20 were drawn by as many pairs of oxen and the other four by horses. They also had with them a herd of 150 cows, in other words, a fully equipped immigrant train.

On the journey westward, which took three weeks, they lost a man by the name of John Nes who drowned in the Iowa River close to Marengo while he was trying to drive some cattle over the river.[1] Other than that, everything went well. They arrived at their destination on the 15th of June.

It didn't look very bright for them. Not a house, not a settler to be seen. The only neighbors they had were, besides the two aforementioned Norwegian families who came the previous fall, three or four American families who had settled on some wooded land by the riverbank. Otherwise the land was completely empty.

But the company was made up of hardy men and women who were used to working and used to handling their tools without gloves on their fingers. "They took their God in their hearts and put their life on the line" to build their future home for themselves and their families. The first thing was to break a piece of land and build a home before winter came. The land or the farm often came first, and the prairie schooner had to be, for the time being, kitchen, dining room, living room, and bedroom, for some clear into November.

Concerning the housebuilding, they followed the good old custom of helping one another. Most of the first settlers bought a larger or smaller piece of wooded land which they could buy the first year for $10.00 an acre. The following year it cost $50.00 an acre. Now it can likely be bought a good deal cheaper.

On this land they got timber for a log house and whatever else was needed. When five or six neighbors had gotten a house built for one, they would go to the next, and that way all around. These houses were not very big, usually just one room of 14–16 or up to 18 feet square. But they had both one or two and sometimes three families within the four walls. That is one of the many ways to prove that where there is heartroom, there is also houseroom.

One day I asked one of those people if they hadn't suffered greatly in body and soul when they thus found themselves in the wilderness without house and home. The old man sat and thought a bit and then he smiled and looked in my face as he answered, "Oh yes, we worked very hard, you can be sure, but we also had fun. I lived in the prairie schooner until the middle of November."

These were for the most part young, strong, and vigorous people who didn't occupy themselves with worrying about the many ups and downs of life. They looked on the bright side and met every mishap with laughter and a lively joke.

The most difficult time for them was the first winter that began with bitter cold and a lot of snow. As an example of the amount of snow can be told that one man drove a considerable load of timber over the roof of his own cowbarn without noticing it until he was well over it. Anyone can understand the situation when we realize that they had 30 miles to the nearest flour mill in Marshalltown and 120 miles to the nearest railroad station in Iowa City. But the requirements of the settlers were not great. However, there were some things they needed, such as flour, salt, etc. If they should try to travel the long way to town, they had a good chance to get lost or to get stuck in the snow drift and so freeze to death on the way.

Winter went and spring came with flowers and sunshine. Everything looked brighter because with the warmth of summer came not only the scent of flowers and mild winds, but also there came more new settlers from Illinois. In 1857, came Sam Haaland, Ola Ritland, John Pederson Bjørka, John Christian, Andrew and Anderson Tjernagel, and Ola Breiland.

In 1858, again came the following: Mons Grove, Paul Thompson, Lars Bøe, Lars Hendrickson, Tjerand Halsnes, Ole Hegland, and Mickel Hegland.

In 1859, came Abel Olsen and in 1860, Ole Veierson, Knut Thompson,[2] Thom Lien, and Joakim Evensen.

These are the men who have laid the foundation to the Norwegian settlement in central Iowa, a settlement which from a very small beginning has grown to become one of the largest in the country reaching over large sections of Story, Hardin, Hamilton, and Boone Counties with a population of many thousand souls. These old settlers had a reason to be proud of their work. A stranger who comes after an absence of 45 years will not get lost. One farm lies next to another all over the previously empty prairie. The little log houses have given way to beautiful large homes. Neither will one see the long-horned oxen come patiently pulling their heavy loads to town. Now it is only spirited horses, often hitched to splendid wagons, coming speeding over the country roads. Here, as so many other places, it was in the log house and with the faithful and strong work animal, the ox, that many of these old settlers laid the foundation for their considerable fortunes which for most of them is counted in the thousands of dollars.

One thing the old Norwegian settlers never forgot to take with them in their wanderings over America's plains. That was our heritage, God's Word! Their old father and mother gave them the Bible at their departure, and it followed them as their most precious treasure. Among the first things they always thought of when they were settled was to get a pastor and build a church. Thus also here. In the first years, they were served by Pastor P. A. Rasmussen who came several times a year the long way from Lisbon, Ill., to baptize, confirm, marry, and bury the dead in addition to preaching God's Word. Some of the time they were served by Pastor Osm. Shjeldal. Already in 1859 [1860], they got their own pastor when Pastor N. Amlund came from Norway to serve the congregation as well as other congregations which might be organized later. In 1860 [1865], they built the first church on Baar H. Børoens farm, barely a mile east of Story City. It was a relatively large and nice wooden church which later was moved into town. Today within the bounds of the settlement, there are 19 large Norwegian churches which are served by eight Lutheran pastors who belong to the Norwegian Synod, the United Church, or Hauge's Synod's Association.

The ranks of these old settlers are thinning out little by little. One after another moves every year to their last resting place. The last one to leave us is Abel Olsen who died the 29th of May and was buried the 31st with a great many people in attendance. Those who are still here carry the mark of old age. For most of them, the back is bent, the fingers are crooked, and the limbs shake. But there are also a few who still, in spite of their age and their hard life through many years, can work as fast as any youth.

When the first settlers began farming here, they raised a little of each of these: wheat, buckwheat, oats, corn, and livestock. Over the course of time, they have gone more and more to raising of just corn and livestock. The best area for corn is said to be Story Co., and proof that this claim is not just taken out of the air is that, in spite of the terrible drought, we will still get an excellent corn crop if no misfortune strikes. The soil is so rich that it can withstand the worst strain.

Some years ago, they mostly raised fat cattle for butchering, and the farmers around here have taken in many shining dollars for the loads of fattened cattle sent to Chicago. In the later years, it has become more common to raise good dairy cows for the sake of the creamery business. There are creameries all over, and a number of them are judged to be among the best in the state. The Roland creamery thus received a prize of 55 dollars at a butter exhibition in Lincoln, Nebraska, if I remember right, and several others have also been fortunate in competition.

It isn't just little things a farmer takes in for his milk during the year. A medium sized farmer told me that he had in a year taken in over 600 dollars for his milk. If we add this sum to the other income he had from the farm, it gets to be quite a good annual income off 160 acres of land even if many people have to be hired to work the farm.

It is a matter of course that in such a large Norwegian settlement that there must also be a number of little towns with a Norwegian population. Thus we have Story City, Randall, Jewell, Ellsworth, Radcliffe, McCallsburg, and Roland where we can always find a larger or smaller group of Norway's sons and daughters. The most Norwegian of them all, and likely the one that according to its size is the most Norwegian town in America, is Roland. Of all its 600 people, only the doctor, the editor, and an old retired railroad man are Americans. Also, there is a Danish family and two Swedes who shall become one family. Otherwise all, big and little, old and young, are Norwegian men and women.

Roland lies in the heart of the oldest settlement, but the town is much younger than the settlement. It is one of these quiet and peaceful country towns which old farmers like so well to live in. Here is no noise of freight wagons and no noisy machines. Even a tramp is a rarity so that the children of the town at once announce this great happening when such a person shows himself in town. Besides, the town lies quite high and is healthful, and it is close to church and school, things which the farmers like.

About the Author
by the Compiler

Knut Knutson Takla was born in 1857 near Voss, Norway. He immigrated to the United States in 1885, and the next year he was hired by the Norwegian-American newspaper, *Skandinaven*, as a "traveling agent and money collector."[3] *Skandinaven* was owned by John Anderson whose publishing company was the leading publisher of Norwegian books, especially books of fiction. For the next 22 years, Knut traveled to Norwegian communities in Wisconsin, Minnesota, Iowa, and South Dakota selling books and newspaper subscriptions and renewals.

Occasionally, Knut wrote reports about the communities he visited for *Skandinaven*. Eleven of his reports were written from central Iowa.[4] Some time during or after 1895, Knut found another reason for spending time in central Iowa, especially Roland. Her name was Anna Karina Kessel, a widow who moved to Roland from Chicago in 1895 with her two daughters.[5] Knut and Anna Karina were married in Roland in 1897. After living in Chicago for a few months, they returned to Roland and rented a home.

In July 1901, the *Roland Record* reported, "Knut Takla and family left Roland Monday for a trip to Norway Europe. Mrs. Takla and children will remain there for four years for the benefit of two of the children. Mr. Takla will return and resume his business as traveling agent for *Skandinaven* in September."[6] Knut had inherited land in Norway that year,[7] and according to Norwegian inheritance laws, he had to live on the land to keep possesion of it.

Knut's last visit to central Iowa may have been in 1906. His report, "A Little from Central Iowa," written in Story City on October 30 concluded with a very long list of names under the caption, "Some Old Friends."[8] Whether or not he informed his friends that he would not be returning to central Iowa, it seems like this was his way of saying goodbye to people he had known for many years.

In July 1908, Knut returned to Norway to live and complete a book about Norwegian immigration to the United States. *De norsk folk in De Forende Stater: dere dalige liv and økonomiske stilling* [The Norwegian People in the United States: Their Daily Lives and Economic Conditions] was published in Kristiania (Olso), Norway, in 1913. After its publication, Knut began traveling around Norway giving lectures and showing movies he had taken from his travels in the United States. He was a member of *The Norwegian Society for the Restriction of Emigration*, an organization that "believed that the main problem facing agricultural production in Norway was the extreme labor shortage, a result of the heavy emigration to America."[9] His membership in the organization suggests the point of view in his book and lectures.

Odd Lovoll, former chair of Scandinavian American studies at St. Olaf College, Northfield, Minnesota, begins his review of the book this way: "In his critical essay on the Norwegian-American experience, Knut Takla traced a physical degeneration from the day the immigrants landed in the New World—a development that continued in the later generations."[10] Lovoll then quotes Takla: "The descendants of these giants, men and women, who emigrated 40–50–60 years ago, are pale, anemic, and weak individuals, who cannot endure any real exertion and are susceptible to all kinds of diseases." Another reviewer summarized Takla's point of view this way: "Emigration should have been shut off at 1890 and that should have been the end of it.… The many opportunities that had been in the United States, and that some people here in Norway still believe are there, are now pretty much all exhausted and very few more opportunities can be had."[11]

Anna Karina died in 1916. Her daughters from her first marriage and Anna and Knut's younger son, Knut Ingemann, returned to the United States, but their older son, Karl Gustav, stayed in Norway. Knut continued to live in their home, but as he got older, it was difficult for him to read or write due to failing eyesight. School children often read the newspaper to him, but he could still take long walks with his dog and go fishing down by the river. During his last years, he became totally blind. His last years were spent in a nursing home where he died in 1950 at the age of 93.

About the Translator

See Erik Travaas' "A Little About the First Settlers in Story County" for a biography of Ardis N. Petersen.

Acknowledgments

The compiler gratefully acknowledges Ardis N. Petersen for translating Knut Takla's 1900 report from Roland, Iowa. In addition, he is grateful to Daron W. Olson for sharing his paper, "Thoralv Klaveness and Knut Takla: Travel Writing and The Norwegian-American Identity, 1904–1913" and introducing the compiler to Takla descendant, Karen Takle Quinn; Hans Gangstø for his genealogical research on Knut Takla; Kaare Mehl for translating Borghild Dale's biography of Knut Knutson Takla; and Anne Carina Takla Haugen and Anne Haugen, granddaughter and daughter of Knut Takla, for reviewing the biography.

The Early History of the Norwegian Settlement in Howard Township

by John M. Mason, Editor, 1902 & 1903
and M. O. Rod, Editor, 1909

Obituary of John Michaelson [1831–1902]
Published in the *Roland Record*, June 18, 1902

It is impossible to write a history or biography of John Michaelson without giving the early history of the Norwegian settlement of Howard Township. He was one of the first ones who tracked their way across the prairies of Illinois and half of Iowa to found a new settlement when Story County land sold for $1.25 an acre from the government of the United States of America.

John Michaelson (Grindem) was born on the place of Grindem in Etne, Norway, March 25, 1831 and died at his home in Roland June 9, 1902; leaving four children: S. J. and M. J. Michaelson and Mrs. G. S. Mason and Mrs. E. F. Bell, all of Roland. Mr. Michaelson grew to young manhood in Norway. In the year 1853 he left his native country to try his fortune in the United States. He had no money but a strong right arm and an indomitable will. With a party of others he arrived at Lisbon, Grundy County, Illinois where he sought and found work. Here he was married in the year of 1855 and it is worthy of notice that five couples were married on the same day by the same preacher in the same church. Among those others who were married that day we have our towns people Mr. and Mrs. Erick Sheldahl and Mrs. Anna Haaland still living.

It is a characteristic feature of the Norwegian that he is anxious to have a home of his own. So these people in Illinois heard of the rich prairies of Iowa and in the spring of 1855 Mons Grove, Paul Thompson,

Jacob Erickson (Ashe), John Mehus, Ole (Aine) Thompson, Erick Sheldahl,[1] Jonas Duea, Lars Grindem [Sheldall], and John Tarvestad went west to buy land. They came as far west as what is now Howard Township where they decided to locate. They were laughed at for settling in the frog ponds of Story County but their good judgment has since been proved. These men bought an "eighty" for John Michaelson which he retained till his death and is located a mile south of town.

The following year Ole Rasmusen (Tisdal), Lars Hegland, Jonas Duea, Erick Sheldahl, Sam Britson Sr., Hans Twedt, Jacob and Mike Erickson came out here and settled on their farms. The first summer they lived in their wagons and broke the sod of their farms and built houses for the coming winter. Mrs. Erick Sheldahl's and Mrs. Haaland's brother was drowned in the Iowa River on this trip.[2]

Two years later John Michaelson, M. C. Grove, Paul Thompson, Lars Henderson, Knut Twedt and B. Henderson (Boroien) came out. John Michaelson borrowed $30 from his brother-in-law, B. Simmons. This was his capital during the journey of 6 weeks and 4 days from Big Grove, Illinois, to Howard Township. The spring and summer was terribly wet. Lars Henderson and John Michaelson had horses while the others had oxen. Mr. Michaelson's team was used times innumerable to pull others less fortunate out of the mud and mire. In crossing the Wapsipinicon River the water was high on account of the heavy rains. A yoke of oxen became entangled in crossing and sank. John Michaelson swam the river to save the oxen and went down with them but managed to save himself and the oxen, a feat he has always considered the work of God Almighty. They arrived on a Sunday and Mr. and Mrs. John Michaelson and two children, Mrs. Bell and Mrs. Mason, received shelter in the hospitable hut of Mr. and Mrs. Erick Sheldahl, where they lived one year, their first in Story County. He had $6.00 when he came and no work to be had. This year was a bad one. Many were sorely disappointed. Erick Sheldahl sowed 8 bushels of wheat in the spring and reaped 8 bushels in the fall. This first summer Mr. Michaelson plowed up the sod on his eighty and in the fall he and Mr. Sheldahl husked corn for one John Smith southwest of here for which they received each a bushel of corn a day and one bushel for the use of the team. They divided the salary and so they each had a bushel and a half a day for their labor. Mr. Michaelson had a dog with him from Illinois which he traded for a pig when he got out here. This was his real start. He was always successful with hogs. When he left the house of Erick Sheldahl, Mr. Sheldahl refused to receive pay for sheltering him and his family for a year and so Mr. Michaelson gave him a young pig which Mr. Sheldahl later sold for $15. In the meantime John Michaelson had bought an old log house of "Doc" Ballard's and had moved it to his eighty. Into this he moved the next spring and in this little hut four families with children have lived for a year at a time without trouble or grumbling. It was a characteristic of these early settlers that if one had food they all had and no one suffered from hunger unless all did. They always helped each other. John Michaelson, Paul Thompson and Mons Grove were neighbors and were almost always together in their work during these early days. Mrs. Michaelson had no stove when they began housekeeping in the old log house but cooked outdoors on a contrivance of stone. In the fall she had made enough butter to buy a stove and Mr. Michaelson went to Des Moines and got her one.

$1.25 an acre was paid for prairie land and $10 an acre for timberland. Grandpa Michaelson has told us that when he bought the farm where E. F. Bell is now living, he broke up the sod south of the creek and sowed wheat for which he received $2 a bushel and the first crop paid for the land. He moved from the eighty to this quarter section and here he lived till he moved to town. About this time his father died and John's sole inheritance was an old fashioned flint lock shotgun which was remodeled to use percussion caps and tons of wild game did he bring home in his time. He used his old gun only two weeks before his death on a couple of rabbits that were eating his garden. These rabbits will never eat any garden anymore.

These early Norwegian pioneers carried their love for education and religion with them across the waters and across the wild prairies. Their Bible and prayer book was always at hand. The first school was held in a little barn belonging to Jonas Duea who was also the postmaster. But the barn could not always be used for schoolhouse purposes so these fellows went to work and borrowed money from H. J. Wulfsberg and built a schoolhouse very nearly on the spot where Dr. Rice's house is standing now. The first church was built on the farm of B. Henderson, and N. Amlund, only recently dead, was the first pastor. Marengo, Marshalltown, Des Moines, Boone, Alden and Iowa City were the early trading points. When the Grange movement began a store was put up here by the old settlers and it was built on the site of the old school house.³ Paul Thompson, Jonas Duea, John Evenson and Abel Oleson were the managers of this store and changed about in taking care of it.

People were coming in fast now, land went up in value and old settlers became prosperous. The prairies they had never expected to be taken up soon became dotted with farmhouses, schoolhouses and churches. John Michaelson went into the mercantile business with Iver Johnson and continued this until three years ago when he sold to his sons S. J. and M. J. Michaelson and the firm became Johnson & Michaelson Bros. About 14 years ago he moved to town and later went into the lumber business, first alone but later in company with S. O. Hegland, the firm still remaining Michaelson & Hegland.

Three years ago his wife died and he never fully recovered from this. They had tried the hardships of frontier life together, had seen the small log huts give away to the present palatial residences, had weathered the storms of poverty and adversity together with the peculiar good fortune and composure of Grandma Michaelson. Never a day passed but that he alluded to "Betsey" in some way or other the last three years of his life. He suffered much lately and was eager to get his leave of absence. His life, common with all the early settlers, had been an eventful one. He was ready to go. He died in the afternoon of Monday, June 9, 1902, surrounded by his folks. He was buried from Salem's church Thursday following carried to his grave by his old comrades, Paul Thompson, Mons Grove, Erick Sheldahl, J. J. Sevde, Jonas Duea and Ole Langland. The church was nicely decorated, as was his grave. Revs. Smedal and Whitman conducted the funeral. Rev. Sandven of Salem's church, of which he was a member, could not be present because of washouts on the railroad. These are the main facts of his life as well as the writer has been able to gather them. The early history of the settlement and the pioneers we have tried to get correctly. If any mistake has occurred it is unintentional.

Grandpa Michaelson leaves 4 children, 18 grandchildren and 1 great-grandchild. He was the writer's grandfather and a good one. We have known him from infancy, have lived with him when we reached maturity and early learned to love him.

Obituary of Mons Grove [1830–1903]
Published in the *Roland Record*, May 27, 1903

Another of Howard Township's most respected pioneers has gone to his eternal rest. One by one these *"banebrydere,"* way breakers, give way to old age and death. They leave us, but the evidences of their work while with us remain. Our well-improved farms, beautiful little cities, schools and churches stand as imperishable monuments to their greatness. M. C. Grove was born in Voss, at Grove, Norway, June 12, 1830. At the age of 20 he left his fatherland for America in 1850. He settled in Kendall County, Illinois, where he hired out and worked by the month and did anything that would procure him clothing and bread. In 1859 he was married to Miss Anna Sheldahl by Rev. O. Sheldahl. He died at his home in Roland, May 22, 1903 and was buried from Salem's church Sunday, May 24, Rev. Sandven officiating. He left at death, a wife, and 6 children. M. N., O. M. and E. R. Grove and Misses Lorenda, Mary and Emma Grove, all of this place. He was 72 years, 11 months and 10 days old. He was a quiet man. No one can remember him in controversy with any man. He was truly one of God's noblemen, honored and respected by all who came in contact with him and loved at home by the members of his family. He was always faithful in his church attendance as well as attending to his civic duties. M. C. Grove is a part of the early history of Howard Township. He was with the first nine men who drove across the prairies of Illinois and Iowa in 1855 to buy land. They were M. C. Grove, Paul Thompson, Jacob Erickson, John Mehus, Ole Thompson, Eric R.[4] Sheldal, Jonas Duea, Lars Grindem and John Tarvestad. They bought land for themselves and for their friends in Illinois. In the year of 1856 Ole Rasmusen, Lars Hegland, Jonas Duea, Erick R. Sheldahl, Sam Britson Sr., Hans Twedt, Jacob and Michael Erickson came west and broke their farms, living in the wagons. Mons Grove did not come out until in 1858 when he and Paul Thompson and John Michaelson and several others came out and settled on their farms. Mons had bought 200 acres embracing the 160 acres one mile south of town and including 40 acres that he later traded to Oliver Thompson for a horse. This forty is part of the farm now owned by M. O. Anderson. Here he worked as best he could using oxen to haul his wagons and plows. Here he married the faithful woman who lived with him till his death. Together they labored in these early days when often all they had to eat was a little corn meal and bacon. But hard work and persistent faith in a better future crowned their labor with success. The nearest market places were Marengo, Alden, Marshalltown, Boone, Iowa City and Des Moines. To these places they had to haul their butter and eggs and dressed pork where they received but little in return. After a while the county settled up, towns rose up all around, markets became better and were nearer and prosperity came as a welcome guest after years of toil and privation. These early pioneers had also the love of the God of their fathers in their hearts and a deep respect for education. They built a church on B. Henderson's farm and a schoolhouse very nearly on the spot where Dr. Rice's house now stands. It is worthy of notice that they borrowed the money themselves from H. J. Wulfsburg with which to build the first schoolhouse.

In the year 1891 he and his son Martin bought the hardware business of Duea & Stole and conducted it for a number of years until a few years ago Oscar and Martin bought it and the business in now called Grove Bros. When too old to manage his farm he moved to Roland where he has lived in peace and quiet these last days of his life.

He died surrounded by his family who sincerely mourns his death. He was carried to his grave by old time friends who were: Paul Thompson, Eric R. Sheldahl, Oliver and Torres Thompson, Oscar Thompson and Jonas Duea. His work is done and soon the last one of these pioneers will lie down and die and be carried away to the cemetery and the last chapter of the first Norwegian settlement in this part of the county will be closed.

We of the younger generation are reaping the benefits of our fathers. Let us not forget the heritage they left us: honesty, sobriety, hospitality, love of education and sincere religion.

About the Author
by the Compiler

Editor John M. Mason, who was ordained Rev. John M. Mason when he was 31 years old, was born on a farm in Howard Township in 1878, the first child of George and Malinda Mason. Rev. Mason's maternal grandparents, John and Betsey Michaelson, moved from Lisbon, Illinois, to Howard Township in 1858. His paternal grandparents, Mads and Anna Sandvik, immigrated to Lisbon in 1861. From Lisbon they moved to Clinton County, Iowa, where they lived until 1865 when the family moved to Benton County, Iowa.[5] In the early 1870s, the family moved to Story and Hamilton Counties, and by this time Rev. Mason's father was using Mason as his surname rather than the Sandvik surname. George married Malinda Michaelson in 1877.

After completing his public school education in Howard Township, John M. Mason attended Jewell Lutheran College in Jewell, Iowa, from 1894 to 1896. He then taught country school for two years, attended seminary the following year (1898–1899), and returned to teaching as head of the grammar department at Roland High School. In 1900, he decided to try the newspaper business as editor of the *Roland Record* which he did for the next three years. During his teaching and publishing days, he was active in the Roland Home Literary Society, often participating in their debates.

While editor of the *Roland Record*, John M. Mason married Martha Boyd, whose maternal grandparents, Jonas and Martha (Sheldahl) Duea, were members of the first Norwegian group who settled in the Roland area. Martha's father, J. H. Boyd, was an early settler, too, immigrating to Story County in 1871 and marrying Julia Duea the next year.

Mason purchased a farm one mile south of Roland in 1903. His successor at the newspaper, another son of a Howard Township Norwegian immigrant, wrote, "John M. Mason, ex editor of the *RECORD*, has at last seen his long cherished hope realized. He is now feeding hogs, milking cows, assorting chickens, and setting up his 'straight line' sticks for spring plowing."[6] While farming, Mason also became a charter member and the secretary of the Story County Poultry Association and member of the first Board of Directors for the Roland Canning Factory established in 1904.

John M. Mason's father was "a deeply religious man and his home was a Christian home where family devotion was the order of the day and going to church on Sunday was taken for granted."[7] John M. Mason was baptized and confirmed in the Salem Lutheran Church in Roland, but the Mason family began attending Trinity Lutheran Church in Roland when it was established in 1900.[8] Mason was the Trinity church secretary until 1906 when he decided to resume his theological study at United Church Seminary in St. Paul, Minnesota. Late that fall, he had a farm sale, and the following year he moved his family to St. Paul.

Shortly after Rev. Mason was ordained at the 1909 United Synod Assembly in Des Moines, Iowa, the Mason family, which now included four children, was on a train to central Saskatchewan, Canada, where Rev. Mason had accepted a call to a Norwegian Lutheran congregation at Watrous in central Saskatchewan. He conducted church services and weddings in homes and sometimes under the shade of a tree, tended the 160 acres he homesteaded near Watrous, hunted and fished with his brother, William, who also settled on a farm near Watrous purchased by their father, and added to his Indian artifact collection.[9]

In 1915, Rev. Mason became the pastor of three congregations in Chippewa County, Minnesota: Our Savior's in Montevideo and the Mandt and Brono rural congregations. Except for a year's leave of absence during WWI to serve as a chaplain, he and his wife served Our Savior's congregation for the next 33 years. The congregation recognized his dedicated service by giving him a pension and a home to live in while he remained in Montevideo. Rev. Mason died in 1947, and almost 60 years later, he was still remembered as a "kindly and quiet man who made daily visits to the hospital"[10] and "a saint who would do anything for anybody."[11]

Compiler's Notes

Rev. John M. Mason was the first Norwegian editor of the *Roland Record*. Having grown up in a community his grandfather helped found, he was especially sensitive to the oral history being lost with the deaths of the founders of the Howard Township Norwegian settlement. The next time a similar review of Howard Township's history appeared in the *Roland Record* was in 1909. Again, it was part of an obituary of yet another of the early settlers, Ole Rasmusen. His obituary follows these notes.

The history contained in Ole Rasmusen's obituary is noteworthy in that it highlights the fact that the founders of the Northern Settlement followed in the footsteps of their friends, family, and acquaintances who began the Southern Settlement southwest of Cambridge, Iowa. Most church and community histories in the Northern Settlement fail to acknowledge their settlement was not the first colony of Norwegians in central Iowa. The Southern Settlement had already been selected by a scouting party in September 1854 and founded in June 1855.

By omitting any reference to the Southern Settlement, local histories about the Northern Settlement lead the reader to believe that the Northern Settlement was the only Norwegian colony in central Iowa. However, the early pioneers of the Northern Settlement were well aware of the earlier settlement south of them where some had friends and relatives. Ivar Havneros, author of the 1907 history of the St. Petri congregation, states there was already a Norwegian settlement in southern Story County, but he does not mention that many of the people in both settlements came from the same area near Lisbon, Illinois. In contrast, in the brief historical sketch of Howard Township included in Ole Rasmusen's obituary, the author points out that reports from Lisbon settlers who purchased land to begin the Southern Settlement encouraged other people in Lisbon to investigate central Iowa. This led to a scouting party purchasing land in Howard Township in June 1855 and founding the Northern Settlement in June 1856.

The name of the author of the obituary was not printed in the newspaper, but it was presumably written by the then editor, M. O. Rod. Editor Rod was the eldest of Erick and Julia Rod's 11 children. Erick M. Rod emigrated from Saude, Norway, in 1879 and lived in Nevada, Iowa, until 1884 when he moved to Roland to work in the Johnson & Michaelson mercantile store. Two years previously, he had married Julia Jacobson, who was born at Lisbon, Illinois, and came to northern Story County with her parents in 1865.

Mikkel Olai (M. O.) Rod was born on a farm south of Roland in 1882. He attended Iowa State Normal School at Cedar Falls and taught in country schools near Roland until 1905 when he purchased the *Roland Record*. In 1913, he sold the newspaper and began following in his father's footsteps, first as a partner in a general store in Roland and later succeeding his father as secretary of the Farmers Mutual Insurance Association in Roland, a position he had until 1931 when he went into business for himself in the insurance, real estate, and tax business. M. O. was very active in his church and community, teaching Sunday school for 20 years and serving in many capacities in the Bergen Lutheran Church and serving on the Roland Town Council and later as Mayor of Roland for 14 years. He was also active in politics at the county and state levels.

Obituary of Ole Rasmusen [1831–1909]
Published in the *Roland Record*, April 15, 1909

Ole Rasmusen (Tysdahl) was born in Norway, Europe, July 13, 1831, and died at his home in Roland on Tuesday, April 6, 1909, being 77 years, eight months and 23 days old when called by the Angel of Death. When still a young man, he left Norway to seek a new home in the new country and he came to Lisbon, Ill, where he lived a few years. It was at this place that he was married to Anna Aske by Rev. Rasmussen April 22, 1854, to which union eleven children were born, nine of whom survive their father. They are Mrs. Malinda K. Michaelson, of Rushville, Neb; B. M. Rasmusen, United States Consul at Stavanger, Norway; H. M. and Andrew, of this place; Mrs. Mattie Henderson, of Story City; R. O. Rasmusen, Mrs. Raney Grindem, J. V. and S. T. Rasmusen, all of this place. All the children were at his bedside when death claimed him, except B. M. and H. M. Rasmusen.

In the death of Mr. Rasmusen the older citizens of our community recall some of the early history of the township of which the deceased took a share. In 1854 [1855], a few families moved from Fox River, Ill. to Huxley, Iowa, where they formed the first Norwegian colony in Story County. The people living around Lisbon, Ill, hearing of what these people had found, decided that they too wanted homes of their own, where land was cheap, and so in the spring of 1855, they sent eight men to Iowa to investigate and to purchase land for several of these men if they found the country suitable. The men who made this trip were Jonas Duea, Mons Grove, Jacob E. Aske, John N. Tarvestad, Paul Thompson, Lars Sheldahl, Ole Eino and John Mehuus. These men went about twenty miles north of Cambridge, where they found land that suited them and they proceeded at once to buy farms. These men returned at once to their homes, told their neighbors about the fertile land that could be had at $1.25 per acre. The same fall two men, Lars Sheldahl and Thor Hegland, and their families moved to Howard Township and to them belongs the honor of being the first Norwegian settlers in the township. The next spring, a large number left Illinois to find homes in the far west and among these were Mr. and Mrs. Rasmusen. The others in company were Jacob E. Aske, Rasmus E. Aske, Jonas Duea, A. B. Jacobson, Lars Ness, Mikkel E. Aske, Sjur Britson, Lars Hegland, Jacob Meling, Bertha Ness, Hans Pederson, Erick Sheldahl, Torkel Opstvedt, Hans Twedt, John N. Tarvestad, Rasmus Sheldahl, Erick Sokten, Hover Thompson and Rasmus Tungesvig.

Mr. and Mrs. Rasmusen settled on the farm which they bought and lived there until nine years ago when they moved to Roland to enjoy the fruits of their labors. Only a few now remain of the first company who moved here that year. They are as follows as far as we have been able to learn: Mrs. and Mrs. Erick Sheldahl, Mesdames Ole Rasmusen, John N. Tarvestad and Torkil Opstvedt and Messrs. Jonas Duea and Lars Hegland, and of course the children of many of the above people. Since these people came here they have seen the country transformed so that there is no resemblance to what it was when they settled here.

The funeral of Mr. Rasmusen was held from Bergen Church last Saturday afternoon, a large number of people being present to pay a last tribute to a friend and old settler. Rev. G. Smedal preached the funeral sermon after which the remains were laid to rest in the Roland cemetery.

The sorrowing family is extended the sincere sympathy of their friends in the hour of their bereavement.

Acknowledgment

The compiler gratefully acknowledges his friend, Jim Mason, grand-nephew of the Rev. John M. Mason, for sharing information about his uncle and for reviewing Pastor Mason's biography.

The Stavanger and Hordaland Colony in Central Iowa: Chapter 54 from *Det Norske Settlementers Historie*, 1908

by Hjalmar Rued Holand
Translated by Jacob Hodnefield[1]

Old Fox River in Illinois has always been the great gathering place for emigrants from Stavanger, Hordaland, and Hardanger. In the forties and fifties many hundreds of these came hither every year. But Fox River was only the portal to America. They stopped here for a short time and worked for their acquaintances, whereupon they later journeyed farther west in order to found their own homes.

Among these early immigrants may be mentioned the brothers Sheldahl. Their names are Lars, Rasmus, Erik, Haldor, and Osmund Sheldahl. They were sons of a bailiff [*lensmand*] in Norway and all were schoolteachers. They went to America in 1846 and became leading men in Illinois and Iowa among the people from their home districts, and they did much to promote emigration. Another man, also from Etne, who deserves to be mentioned, is Torkel Henryson, who occupies a position of special esteem among his fellow countrymen in the vicinity of Story City, Iowa. In 1847 he, together with Lars Sheldahl, and on the encouragement of the Sheldahl brothers, organized an emigration society of 165 persons, hired a ship ("Kong Sverre") on his own account in Bergen, and arrived safe and sound in New York.

One of the leading men in the Lisbon and Fox River colony in Illinois in the fifties was Erik Nilsen, the first to emigrate from Sigdal. Although he was one of the very few from the east country in Norway in this large settlement of people from the west country, he was by no means the only one. Old pioneers in various places in Iowa and Illinois remember, with cordial affection, his genial and cheerful character and great helpfulness. He was an enlightened and experienced man, and he was well-to-do and became poor more than once through his willingness to help needy fellow countrymen. But he was none the less cheerful. Nor did his need ever become so great, nor his house so crowded, but that he made room, with board and lodging, for a homesick immigrant. He gave them food and shelter and good advice and shared his work and his shillings with them. He was a good man to discover in a strange land.

> *Vis i raad*
> *Og rask i daad*
> *Var han den første mand.*
> *I lag og kirke*
> *Og nabovirke*
> *Han var en hædersmand.*

> *Wise in counsel*
> *and quick in deed,*
> *he stood first.*
> *In society and in church*
> *and in neighborly activity,*
> *he was a man of honor.*

When one shipload after another of people from Stavanger and Hordaland were dumped down on the prairie at Lisbon, times soon became hard. The prices on land went up, and hundreds of poor and bewildered immigrants went about discouraged and without work. In Norway they had heard that in America,

> *"Der the og kaffe og melk og rømme*
> *vil kolonisterne oversvømme;*
> *der flesk og hvede or daglight brød,*
> *der vugges hver mand i lykkens skjød."*

> *"Where tea and coffee and milk and cream*
> *are sufficient to flood the colonists;*
> *where pork and wheat are daily bread,*
> *there every man is cradled in the lap of luck."*

Now they found out that conditions in America could be fully as strait as in Norway and even more so. They then regretted bitterly that they had permitted Mammon's empty promises to tempt them to leave the estates of their fathers. There they had the one thing needful in rich measure; what more was lacking?

Then Erik Nilsen told them about Iowa's wide expanses. "There, beyond the Mississippi River, lies a land as rich as Egypt's flesh pots," he said. "There are billowing plains with here a river or a grove. The hills are as fertile as the Mount of Olives, and the lowlands as rich as the meadows of Goshen. And the land is so large than one could place all of Norway, with Buskerud, Hordaland, and Finmark both crosswise and lengthwise in it and still have room for mountain pastures on all sides. Go there and obtain land, as there are as yet hardly any settlers."

This was advice which had pith and substance to it. It was weighed and discussed endlessly, for in the beginning, the idea found little adherence. "Go to Iowa! What an insane idea! Did not the large rainless desert begin on the other side of the Mississippi River, where there are only cactuses, rattlesnakes, and volcanic mountains? That would be only to tempt Providence. Better than that would be to go back to Norway." Others, on the contrary, were of the opinion that the extent of the desert was not so great after all. It undoubtedly did not begin before one arrived at the other big river, which was called the Missouri River, where the water ran yellow and muddy from all the fine sand, which the hurricanes of the desert blew into it. Moreover, would not Erik Nilsen know; for had he not been all the way to California?

This view of the affair received unexpected support by the chance arrival of Nils Olson Næs, a lay preacher, who had been in northeastern Iowa. He related that there was a superabundance of both forest and prairie land, which could be bought from the Government for $1.25 per acre. After weighty and extended discussions, it was agreed to send four men to inspect the land and also to give them power of attorney to buy a tract of land, in case it was suitable for agriculture.

The Haugians took no part in this. Elling Eielsen, who did not like to see his large congregation at Fox River weakened by emigration, expressed the opinion that such unsteady desire to wander and desire for worldly gain was only an outcropping of the old heathen Viking blood. He warned against tempting the Lord by resorting to the wilderness, where, far removed from the loving communion with the believers and with those rich in grace, the faith of their childhood might suffer wreckage. Fallen to the lusts of the flesh and to Mammon's greed, they would be surrendered to the devil, who goes about like a roaring lion seeking whom he may devour.

The four men, who were sent out, were Osmund Sheldahl, Ole Fatland, Ole Apland, and Osmund Johnson. Osmund Sheldahl later became the new settlement's minister of many years' standing. They started on the 24th of September, 1854. In those days the California trail crossed Iowa from Davenport to Omaha, strewn with thousands of remains from the forced marches of the gold diggers. They followed this trail, on the advice of Erik Nilsen. They made rapid progress in a light buggy over this road till they came to Story County. Here they found a superabundance of all sorts of good land. They selected what they wished, and then they went to Des Moines, where papers were issued to them by the Government Land Office. Four weeks after their departure they were back in Lisbon.

Expectation was great when the people heard that the four emissaries had returned. All at once these rose to an eminence a head higher than all other men in the settlement. A meeting was immediately called, and the composed and sensible Osmund Sheldahl acted as chairman.

"We have carried out our mission," he said, "and found a region which surpasses our greatest expectations in beauty and fertility. There are smooth, sunlit hills, but no stones; and rich, juicy meadows, but no floods. There is good water and sheltering woods along all water courses. It is surely a land which, like Caleb's Canaan, flows with milk and honey. But, unlike yon lauded land, we have here no enemies to fear. There were dark Jebusites and Amasites and the large sons of Anak, who barred the way for God's chosen people. There were here indeed at one time perhaps red Indians galloping in the hunt after the big buffaloes, but now they have departed for distant hunting grounds. Now the land lies quiet and inviolate and waiting for us. Brothers, it is a land which the Lord has prepared for us. We came from Norway's mountain nooks, where we had to break the ground on stony tracts and on steep slopes between floods and slides and where our pastures lay in the shadow of glaciers. Now we can stretch our limbs in an easy walk with plow or scythe, and the rich soil will richly reward our labors. And we have obtained papers from the Government, whereby our right to the land is secured for all time."

Ole Fatland and Ole Apland fully agreed to this. Osmund Johnson on the other hand was a little doubtful. While he would not deny the correctness of what Sheldahl had said, he would nevertheless doubt that the land ever would be settled that far west. It was after all 300 miles from Lisbon. It would in any case take four or five hundred years. In the meantime there would not be any railroad, and it would be a long time before any kind of Government and civilized manners would find their way that far. He believed, therefore, that he would not go.[2]

The winter passed quickly with all sorts of expectant preparations. Among other things, those who made preparations to go to Iowa organized a congregation. As an expression of its great expectations, it was called the Palestine congregation. Ole Anfinsen was chosen minister, Erik Sheldahl was chosen precenter [*klokker*], and K. A Bauge was chosen teacher. The following, with their families, joined the congregation and went along on the trip:

Ole Anfinsen	Ole Apland
K. A. Bauge	Knut Ersland
Severt Gravdahl	Ole Fatland
Ole Hauge	Torbjørn Hauge
Ole Heggen	Salve Heggen
Christian Heggen [Heggem]	Engebret Heggen
	Axel Larsen
Barney Hill	Erik Sheldahl
Torger Olson	John Severson
Osmund Sheldahl	Ivar Tvedt
Lars Tesdahl	Wier Weeks
Guro Shaw	

There is only another instance, the Herrnhuter congregation at Ephraim, Wisconsin, in the history of the Norwegian people in this country, where an entire congregation, with a minister in the van, has thus migrated. It is also one of the largest groups which has set out to clear new land.

Finally the day dawned, which had been decided upon as the day of departure, the 17th of May, 1855. They were then all gathered on Holdeman's prairie, half way between Lisbon and the Fox River, ready to move. The company consisted of 106 people, 25 teams of oxen and horses, together with a large number of cattle. They broke up with many wishes of good luck and well-being on the part of the large crowd which had gathered to bid them farewell.

Smoothly and quietly they moved on, with their thoughts full of plans for their future homes. The children especially thought it was a glorious trip, as they drove the cattle day after day and saw changing scenes. They rested three Sundays on the trip; and each Sunday they conducted divine services in the open. On the 7th of June they reached their destination.

Many an adventurous train has winged its way over the western plains; zealous and patient Jesuit missionaries proclaiming Virgin Mary's mother love for the red sons of the prairie; ambitious Spaniards seeking a short passage to India's pearls; fearless discoverers; intriguing politicians; and fool-hardy adventurers. Only nine years before our immigrants, Brigham Young and his company journeyed the same way, with fanatical dreams about a priestly empire on the other side of the mountains. Only five years before, there stormed over the same path a continuous army of excited men towards California's distant valleys with the thirst of gold in their hearts, while back of them, like blood-thirsty hawkers, followed sly gamblers and daring criminals. At the very same time armed men rode off to Nebraska and Kansas in order, by murder and lawlessness, to maintain the stand taken by their parties on slavery or not slavery.

How different was not this company of Norwegian pioneers? These did not set out for the purpose of subjecting new kingdoms, dig the alluring gold, nor by force and intrigue to procure political power. Their goal was to open a way and build a settlement, till the soil, and make the wilderness blossom like the rose. The minister rode at the head, who, with a Bible in his hand, pointed from the temporal to the eternal. Their swords were mattocks and their spears were sickles. Their chests admittedly were empty of fine clothes, golden ornaments, and weapons. Instead there were to be found only sacks of barley and wheat, oats and corn. But the little seed, which these pioneers brought along, has grown into a large field of grain, which now furnishes sustenance for millions. Each year Iowa's crops represent more than double the value of all our country's world-famous gold and silver mines, and the year's corn crop alone would easily be able to pay off the national debt of half a dozen European countries.

This was the beginning of the so-called Southern Settlement, which is situated in the vicinity of Cambridge and Slater. Here dwell now about 3,000 very well-to-do countrymen. The greater number of Norwegians in this part of the State, however, live about 25 miles farther north, in the so-called Northern Settlement, which begins east of Roland and extends far west of Jewell Junction, including large parts of Story, Hamilton, and

Hardin counties. Here dwell now more than 9,000 Norwegian people; and the beginning of this settlement is as follows:

When the Haugians at Lisbon heard about the beautiful land in Iowa and how easy it was to get a hold of, they, too, decided to seek their fortune there. But to do all things in proper order and be doubly sure, they chose eight men to go out and investigate conditions. These men were Jonas Duea, Mons Grove, Jacob E. Aske, John N. Tarvestad, Paul Thompson, Lars Sheldahl, Ole Eino, and John Mehuus. These started out in the spring of 1855, soon after the large company under Osmund Sheldahl, and found excellent land on the prairie, where the town of Roland is situated.

Many pioneers out there have wondered why this second group did not go to the southern part of Story County, where their countrymen from Lisbon had settled the same year. The soil is of the same quality, and the vast spaces were as yet unoccupied. There would have then been formed a continuous Norwegian settlement instead of, as now, two. The reason, however, is not difficult to understand. The first group was Synod-Lutheran,[3] while the other was Haugian. Moved by the same kind of cordial love which separated Lot and Abraham, and with thoughts of peace in matters of the church, they put a distance of 25 miles between them. [This analysis is factually inaccurate. See Compiler's Notes for correct information.]

A large company, of which most were Haugians, now made preparations to go to Roland the next year. However, there were two men who already the same year moved out. These were Lars Sheldahl and Thor Hegland, and to them belongs the honor of being the very first Norwegians in this mighty colony, which now is 25 miles long and 20 miles wide and peopled by only Norwegians.

The large company, which went out the next year, consisted of the following and their families:

Jacob E. Aske	Hans Pederson
Rasmus E. Aske	Erik Sheldahl
Jonas Duea	Torkel Opstveit
A. B. Jacobson	Hans Tveidt
Lars Næss	John N. Tarvestad
Mikkel E. Aske	Ole Rasmussen
Sjur Brictson	Rasmus Sheldahl
Lars Hegland	Erik Søkten
Jacob Meling	Hover Thompson

Bertha Næss   Rasmus Tungesvig

They had 24 wagons and a couple hundred cattle.

But although they now had found excellent land at a low price, their troubles were not on that account over. The first winter out there will not soon be forgotten by the old pioneers. It was one of the worst winters that history knows anything about; and, since most of the new settlers had not procured for themselves comfortable houses, they suffered severely. The enormous masses of snow made roads almost impassable, and many a discouraged poor wretch feared that he had gone entirely astray in an ice desert. During the entire winter they had to melt snow for water for both people and stock; and when all pots and pans were full of half-melted snow, there was little warmth in the house. Once that winter, several of the pioneers set out for Marshalltown, a distance of 45 miles. Wrapped in a bearskin coat with a pair of fast horses, such a drive is not so bad, even if the snow cuts pretty sharply. But at that time there were not many fur coats in the settlement. One had to be content to wrap oneself up in all the old rags and scarfs which could be spared and depend upon body warmth. Unacquainted with the terrain as they were, they lost their way, and when night came they were forced to stop on the open prairie. It was piercing cold with a northwest wind, and it was disagreeably dark. Some of them scraped snow from the ground till it was bare, and then they stood and stamped all night to keep awake. For a change they threw the sacks off and on, turned the sleigh around, and carried on other fooleries hour after hour, until the first light of morning appeared. That, however, was a joyless jest.

Later there followed the hard times which preceded the Civil War. Never has our country had such hard times as then. Marengo, a distance of 110 miles, was the nearest railroad station, and thither they often drove live hogs. But the prices were so low that it was clearly something which would cause them to lose courage. Pork was one cent a pound, butter four cents; and one had to give ten dozen eggs for a spool of thread. Calico was 25 cents and sheeting 75 cents a yard.

Another thing that reminded the pioneers that this world is really a vale of tears was the condition of the roads. Iowa's roads are still mud trenches, on account of which the State ought to hide its face in shame. But at that time, before the land was drained, they were indescribable. About a third of Story County at that time consisted of stretches of bog, which now at a great cost have been drained. At that time the low places were most often under water, and the old pioneers relate that they generally got stuck in the mud ten to twenty times if they drove across the county. They had to carry their planks and wheat sacks across the soft marshes and then push and wriggle the wagon, with diverse appeals to various higher powers. Under such conditions it was not strange if the first love some times became a bit lukewarm. Worst were the "Skunk River bottoms" right in the middle of the settlement. Here it became routine to pay certain Hordaland men for piloting one through, the water being two to four feet deep. The passengers had to splash through afterwards. The men often had to go ahead with an axe to break the ice, while the horses struggled and pulled to the utmost.

One thing which will surprise a stranger is that there are no Norwegian place names in these large settlements. No one would know from the names of towns that Norwegians ever lived here. Skonevik, Etne, Fjeldberg, Stavanger, and Bergen are surely as pretty and useful names as Jewell Junction, Story City, McCallsburg, Ellsworth, and Radcliffe. But our Haugian pioneer had no thought for such patriotic vanity. He bustled and struggled with the mortgage, disciplined his children with conscientious zeal, and let the Yankees have their way with such nonsense as the names of towns and local politics. Doubtless he did not keep many newspapers; but then he had so much greater spiritual refreshment in the prayer meetings.

About the Author
by the Compiler
Based on the author's autobiography, *My First Eighty Years*

Hjalmar Rued Holand was born in southeastern Norway in 1872. In 1884, two years after his mother died, he immigrated to Chicago with a sister. He lived with a brother and his wife in Chicago, taking care of their children and attending school through the seventh grade before getting a full-time job. After two years on his own, he decided to go Wautoma, Wisconsin, to visit another sister and her husband and to see his father who had now immigrated.

In Wisconsin, Hjalmar made a friend who persuaded him to sell books so they could attend college. Hjalmar had always been a bookworm and had accumulated a library of over 200 books before selling them to pay a medical bill. By selling books in the summer and working other jobs during the school year, Hjalmar finished Battle Creek College, and then he attended the University of Wisconsin at Madison where he completed his B.A. in 1898 and M.A. in 1899.

Holand's book customers were Norwegian farmers in western Wisconsin and Minnesota. Whether he sold a book or not, he usually found a meal and lodging among the people he met. One summer, he was offered a bowl of blueberries by a woman he refers to as "The Blueberry Lady." During the course of their conversation, she asked him how he liked his work, and he told her it was okay except for the evenings. Being city-reared and not knowing much about farming, he found conversation awkward. She suggested he ask his hosts about their early immigrant experiences, and from then on Hjalmar made it a point to find lodging with older Norwegian settlers. Later in the evenings, he recorded these conversations, and so began Hjalmar's career as a historian.

When he started at the university, Hjalmar's ambition was to complete a Ph. D. and move to New York to become a literary person, a novelist, or a historian. In the summer of 1898, he made a bicycle trip to explore the peninsula north of Green Bay, Wisconsin. He fell in love with the natural scenery and decided to purchase 57 acres where he could live during his retirement years. Upon his return to Madison, however, he learned that his land was an ideal place to grow fruit. He changed his plans and built a home there where he and Evelyn, then his fiancé, eventually raised a family, and the city boy became a fruit tree farmer.

After completing his M.A., economic necessity required Hjalmar to seek work. Since he had also always loved maps, he took a traveling sales job with Rand McNally & Co. In 1902, he attended a meeting in Minneapolis, Minnesota, to discuss the possibility of starting a Norwegian cultural society. By this time, several of his articles had been published, and he was working on a book about Norwegian immigration. Holand was elected archivist and historian for the society. He began traveling around to Norwegian settlements to enroll members, presenting talks to provide financial support for his travels. He would spend several days in a settlement interviewing old settlers and writing an article for publication in Norwegian-American newspapers and other Norwegian publications. It was from this material that his *De Norske Settlementers Historie*, the first comprehensive history of Norwegian settlements established prior to the Civil War, was published in 1908.

The challenges of developing his fruit farm and pursuing his historical interests were keeping Holand fully occupied by this time, but another challenge awaited him, one that would consume the rest of his life and be the subject of four books. During a 1907 visit to Douglas

County, Minnesota, he was told about a stone, the now famous Kensington Stone, unearthed by a farmer near Kensington. After visiting with the farmer, Holand became the owner of the stone, and soon he was immersed in the fields of philology and archaeology, leading him to the conclusion that the writings on the stone were runic characters carved by Vikings on an expedition in Minnesota in 1362. Later his interest turned to mooring stones, boulders by lakeshores and rivers used to moor large boats. Holand identified 10 mooring stones in Minnesota which he believed marked locations of campsites used by the Vikings during their expedition and provided further evidence of the authenticity of the Kensington Stone. He believed this proved the Vikings had been in America long before Columbus.

The last chapter of Holand's autobiography published in 1957 is entitled, "How to Stay Young." In it he states his belief that the secret to a prolonged and healthy life is to find an occupation for which one has a native aptitude and to follow it diligently. He contended this leads to a life rich in contentment and to a sensation of victory when one's purpose is accomplished. "These two feelings—contentment and victory—are both conducive to a long life."[4] His life was an example of following one's passions, and it undoubtedly helped keep him in good health to the age of 87.

Hjalmar Rued Holand published 12 books plus many newspaper and magazine articles. He died in 1963 and was buried near his Ephriam, Wisconsin, home.

About the Translator
by the Compiler

Jacob Hodnefield was born in 1877 on his parents' farm southwest of Roland, Iowa. In 1881, his parents, who emigrated from Norway in 1872, moved to a farm southwest of Radcliffe, Iowa. After attending Jewell Lutheran College in nearby Jewell from 1894 to 1898, Jacob enrolled in the University of Minnesota where he graduated in 1902, the same year he was married to Alma Thompson. In 1905, he completed a Master's degree at the University of Minnesota and worked as a university librarian until 1914 when the family returned to Radcliffe, Iowa, to farm. Jacob accepted a position as head of the accession department for the Minnesota Historical Society in 1921, and from 1929 to 1932 he headed the reference department of the James Jerome Hill Reference Library in St. Paul. The following year, Jacob began working with state and federal projects, most of them connected with the Minnesota Historical Society, later becoming curator of newspapers for the society until his retirement in 1946.[5]

Jacob Hodnefield's interest in Norwegian immigrant history is well known to members of the Norwegian-American Historical Association established in 1925 of which he was a charter member. Through his efforts, the association began publishing "Some Recent Publications Relating to Norwegian-American History" in *Norwegian Studies and Records*. Jacob's first annotated bibliography appeared in the 1930 edition, and his final bibliography was published in 1954 along with this acknowledgement from the editor, Carlton C. Qualey, "Mr. Hodnefield's bibliographies have become a fixture in these volumes, and the association is very much in debt to him for his continued invaluable services."[6] In addition to serving as Chairman of the Board of Archives for the Association, Jacob also published two articles in *Norwegian Studies and Records*, "Erik L. Peterson" in 1949 and "Norwegian-American Bygdelags and the Publications" in 1954.

During his retirement, Jacob Hodnefield also began contributing to the historical record of central Iowa by translating Holand's 1908 history of the central Iowa Norwegians and Oley Nelson's "A Brief History of the First Norwegian Settlement of Story and Polk Counties, Ia. 1855–1905" and writing "The Story County Colony of 1855" which was published in *The Annals of Iowa* in 1955. His seminal contribution to central Iowa, however, is an unpublished 225-page manuscript, *Iowa Life 1875–1925: The Story of a Central Iowa Community of Norwegian Immigrants and Their Descendants*. It was given to the Norwegian-American Historical Association along with a letter to Dr. Theodore C. Blegen, managing editor of the Norwegian-American Historical Association since its inception, stating, "You may do with it what you wish."[7] After Blegen resigned this position in 1960 due to illness, he forwarded the manuscript to the Association stating, "I think the narrative has distinct possibilities for publication, but I was not able to do anything with it during the past few years."[8] The first two chapters of Hodnefield's unpublished manuscript, "The Land" and "Those Who Came," will be published in Volume 3 of *The Central Iowa Norwegians*.

Jacob Hodnefield died in Glendale, California in 1960.

Compiler's Notes

Hjalmar Rued Holand's history, originally published in the February 6, 1906, edition of *Decorah-Posten* [The Decorah Post], is noteworthy because it is the first historical account that combines early histories of both the southern and northern settlements into a general history of Norwegian settlement in central Iowa. It was published soon after two events celebrating the 50th anniversary of the coming of the Norwegians to central Iowa. The first event was held in Cambridge, Iowa, on June 7, 1905, and the second event was the triennial convention of the Norwegian Pioneer Association of America held in Story City, Iowa, on October 11–12, 1905.

The publication date of Holand's history in *Decorah-Posten* suggests Holand was present at the Story City celebration.[9] Oley Nelson was a speaker at that celebration, and likely Holand received a copy of his history since it appears that he drew his information about the Southern Settlement exclusively from Nelson's history. However, he must have interviewed pioneers familiar with the early history of the settlement in northern Story County to obtain information about the Northern Settlement. There is no evidence Holand used the two histories of the Northern Settlement that had appeared in newspapers before 1905, Knut Takla's 1900 history in *Skandinaven* (Chicago) and John M. Mason's 1902 history in the *Roland Record*, and he had to have interviewed people to learn stories such as Torkel Henryson's and the Sheldahl brothers' involvement as promoters of emigration from Etne, Skånevik, and Fjelberg.[10]

Holand is the only historian who explains Erik Nilsen's involvement in encouraging Lisbon settlers to investigate Iowa as a possible settlement location, advice that was based on Nilsen's experience traveling across Iowa during the time of the California Gold Rush. Nilsen also accompanied Torkel Henryson and two other men to Iowa in the fall of 1855 to inspect the settlement location chosen by the June scouting party.[11] Henryson was still living in 1905, so he could have been Holand's source regarding Nilsen's involvement. However, as Oley Nelson's 1905 history states, it was not until the Bible salesperson, Nils Olsen Næs, returned to the Lisbon Settlement with the same advice about Iowa, that the settlers organized a scouting party to investigate land in Iowa.[12] Næs was someone many of the Lisbon settlers knew from Skånevik, Norway, so his advice may have been given more credence.[13]

While it is evident that Holand interviewed pioneers living in the Northern Settlement, he was either misinformed about two important points or reached conclusions without talking to enough people. Holand states, "Many pioneers out there have wondered why this second group did not go to the southern part of Story County, where their countrymen from Lisbon had settled the same year. The soil is of the same quality, and the vast spaces were as yet unoccupied. There would have then been formed a continuous Norwegian settlement instead of, as now, two. The reason, however, is not difficult to understand. The first group was Synod-Lutheran, while the other was Haugean." There are two factual inaccuracies in this part of Holand's history; one pertains to the availability of land in southern Story County and the other concerns the synod affiliation of the Palestine congregation.

When the eight-member scouting party left Lisbon in late May 1855, two members of the scouting party, Jonas Duea and Lars Sheldall, had already been to central Iowa. They came in March 1855 and purchased land northeast of Fairview (Story City).[14] They were experienced pioneers, and although Haugeans, their reason for purchasing land in northern Story County was probably not because of religious preference. The likely reason is settlers and land speculators had already purchased much of the government land in southern Story County and northern Polk County, especially land near timber resources.[15] When the two men returned to Iowa in June as part of the eight-member scouting party, there was still a large amount of government land available at $1.25 per acre on the open prairie east of Fairview (Story City), and the other members of the scouting party must have agreed that it was a better settlement location than southern Story County.[16]

Regarding synod affiliation, it is not true, as Holand states, that the settlement in southern Story County was Synod-Lutheran, that is, affiliated with the Norwegian Synod established in 1853. Norwegian Synod pastors were required to complete seminary education before ordination and this was not the case for Palestine's first two pastors, Ole Anfinson and Osmund Sheldahl, who were former lay preachers ordained by the Northern Illinois Synod established in 1851.[17] In 1860, the Norwegians and Swedes withdrew from the Northern Illinois Synod and organized the Scandinavian Evangelical Lutheran Augustana Synod of North America, also known as the Scandinavian Augustana Synod or simply Augustana Synod. Pastor Sheldahl, who had been elected pastor of the Palestine congregation in January 1859, was re-ordained into this new synod at its organization meeting at Jefferson Prairie, Wisconsin, in June

1860. The Palestine congregation had not joined any synod up to this time, but in 1860, they decided to join the newly formed Augustana Synod.[18] Theologically, the Augustana Synod stood in the middle ground between the Eielsen Synod, a synod re-constituted in the mid-1870s as the Hauge Synod, and the Norwegian Synod.[19] The leader of the Eielsen Synod was Pastor Elling Eielsen whom Holand refers to in his history. Pastor Eielsen was an itinerant Haugean lay preacher who was the first ordained Norwegian pastor in the United States.

A more plausible conclusion for Holand to have reached about religious differences is that the scouting parties chose different settlement areas out of a sense of loyalty to the pastors serving them in Illinois. Pastor Ole Andrewson was serving many of the first settlers in southern Story County,[20] and Pastor P. A. Rasmussen was serving many of the first settlers in northern Story County.[21] Pastor Andrewson was ordained in 1846 and joined the Eielsen Synod that same year. Two years later, he left the Eielsen Synod over disagreements with Pastor Eielsen and affiliated with the Franckean Synod until 1851 when he joined the Northern Illinois Synod.[22] Pastor Rasmussen was ordained in 1854 and joined the Eielsen Synod the same year.[23] Even though he left the Eielsen Synod two years later over disagreements with Pastor Eielsen, Pastor Rasmussen as well as Pastor Andrewson could not be described as Synod-Lutheran in 1854 and 1855 when the scouting parties were making decisions about central Iowa settlement locations. The fact remains, however, that the availability of land seemed to be the overriding consideration regarding where to purchase land. With little desirable land left in southern Story County and northern Polk County, the June 1855 scouting party was forced to look elsewhere for a settlement location, and they chose northern Story County.

Acknowledgments

The compiler gratefully acknowledges the Norwegian-American Historical Association for permission to reprint Jacob Hodnefield's translation of Holand's 1908 history of the central Iowa Norwegians. The compiler also gratefully acknowledges comments received from Jim Mason, Steve Sheldahl, and Peter Harstad regarding the compiler's analysis of the inaccuracies contained in Holand's history.

Notes

The Settlement Period 1855–1880
by Arlen Twedt

[1] Carlton C. Qualey, *Norwegian Settlement in the United States* (Northfield, Minnesota: Norwegian-American Historical Association, 1938), 94.

[2] O. E. Rølvaag, "The Vikings of the Middle West," *The American Magazine*, October 1929, 46.

[3] Fairview was the name of the town platted in 1855 in the eastern part of present-day Story City. When it was discovered there was another Iowa town with the same name, the name of the post office for Fairview was changed to Story City. In 1878, the town's name was officially changed to Story City when Fairview's businesses moved approximately one mile west to be close to a new depot built for a narrow gauge rail line completed from Ames to Story City.

Emigration from Skånevik, Etne, and Fjelberg

[4] For more information about the passengers on the four emigrant ships, see "Four Immigrant Shiploads of 1836 and 1837" by Henry J. Cadbury in *Norwegian-American Studies* (Northfield, Minnesota: Norwegian-American Historical Association, 1927), 2:20–22.

[5] In 1964, new administrative districts were created which assigned Fjelberg to the Kvinnherad *kommune* and the Skånevik district was split between the Kvinnherad and Etne *kommuner*.

[6] Knud Langeland, *Norwegians in America, Some Records of the Norwegian Emigration to America:* A transcribed and translated version of the 1888 *Nordmændene i Amerika, Nogle Optegnelser om De Norskes Udvandring til Amerika* (Waukon, Iowa: Astri My Astri Publishing, 2012), 31.

[7] Jim Mason, "Biography of Nils Hanson Veste also known as Nelson Hanson," an addendum to "Why Lisbon, Illinois" by Arlen Twedt, Steve Sheldahl, and Jim Mason (n.p. 2010) in the archives of the Norwegian-American Historical Association, Northfield, Minnesota.

[8] For more information about the Sugar Creek Settlement, see "The Beginnings of Norwegian Settlements in Iowa" by I. Rudolph Gronlid (master's thesis, State University

of Iowa, 1928), 12–22, and "The Norse in Iowa to 1870" by H. Fred Swansen (PhD diss., State University of Iowa, 1936), 25–28.

[9] Mason, "Biography of Nils Hanson Veste also known as Nelson Hanson."

[10] The Norwegian was John Hill, aka Johannes Johannessen [1819–1893], who emigrated from the Hidle farm in Strand, Rogaland, in 1839 and settled in Lisbon the same year. Reference: *A History of The Norwegians of Illinois* by A. E. Strand, comp. & ed. (Chicago: John Anderson Publishing Company, 1905), 355 & 444.

[11] When the 1850 Census was taken, there were 10,541 Norwegians living in Wisconsin compared to 2,788 in Illinois. Reference: *Digitalarkivet* [The National Archives of Norway], "Norwegians in the US 1850 Census," accessed March 23, 2004, http://gda.arkivverket.no/cgi-win/WebMeta.exe?spraak=e.

[12] Jim Mason, personal correspondence to the author, February 3, 2006.

[13] A. E. Strand, comp. & ed., *A History of the Norwegians of Illinois* (Chicago: John Anderson Publishing Company, 1905), 69, 118, and Maxine Mess, email message to author, July 4, 2000. I visited Lisbon, Illinois, for the first time in 1978 to gain a firsthand perspective on the Norwegian settlement area, but I am grateful to the late Maxine Mess for giving me a better understanding of the geography of the settlement and for answering many questions about the Lisbon area.

[14] Steve Sheldahl, email message to author, June 19, 2007. The 80 acres was located in N½SE¼, Section 27, Township 35N (Big Grove), Range 6E.

[15] Ingvald Skålnes, *"Utvandringa frå Skånevik"* ["The Emigration from Skånevik: A 150-year Anniversary"], trans. Anne S. Helvik and Jarle Steinkjer, in *Etne Sogelag Årsskrift 1986* ([Etne, Norway]: n.p., 1986), 101.

[16] "Norway-Heritage Hands Across the Sea" forum, accessed April 8, 2009, http://www.norwayheritage.com/.

[17] "Cost of passage, Norway—America," accessed November 14, 2003, http://www.norwayheritage.com/ships/cost.htm.

[18] Ibid.

[19] Steve Sheldahl, email message to author, October 16, 2003. Another source shows the Larson and Sheldahl farmsteads in northeast Nettle Creek Township, but Sheldahl's review of the Grundy County land records did not confirm ownership of land in this location. Reference: Esta Freeland & Gladys B. Willert, comp. & ed., *The Huxonian: Huxley Centennial, 1882–1982* (Ames, Iowa: Sigler Publishing, 1982), 4, map.

[20] Gerhard B. Naeseth, *Norwegian Immigrants to the United States: A Biographical Directory, 1825–1850* (Decorah, Iowa: Vesterheim Norwegian-American Museum, 1997), 2:223–225, 314.

[21] Ivar Havneros, *History of St. Petri Congregation from its foundation June 1857 to its 50th Jubilee, June 1907*, trans. Rachel Vangness (Story City, Iowa: n.p., 1907), 1.

[22] Hjalmar Rued Holand, *"Stavanger og Hordaland Kolonien i Midtre Iowa"* ["The Stavanger and Hordaland Colony in Central Iowa"], chap. 54, trans. Jacob Hodnefield, in *De Norske Settlementers Historie* (Ephraim, Wisconsin: *Forfatterens Forlag*, 1908), 458. This history first appeared as a newspaper article in *Decorah-Posten* [The Decorah Post], February 6, 1906. Holand's 1908 history of Norwegian settlement has also been translated by Malcom Rosholt and Helmer M. Blegen and published in 2006 by Astri My Astri Publishing, Waukon, Iowa.

[23] Naeseth, *Norwegian Immigrants to the United States*, (2000), 3:23, and *"Litt om utvandringa frå Etne til USA kring midten av 1800-talet"* ["A little about emigration from Etne to the United States around the middle of the 1800s"] by Marcelius Helleland, *Haugesunds Avis*, April 3 & 6, 1970.

[24] The route they walked was part of a postal road from Bergen to Stavanger opened in 1785. In 2016, during a visit with my second cousins who live near Skånevik, I hiked this portion of the road (7.0 kilometers) with our daughter, Karla, and her husband and my two grandchildren. Prior to hiking this portion of the road, I also hiked a portion of the road with relatives who live near Herøysundet.

[25] Ståle Dyrvik, *"Den Tidlege Utvandringa Frå Indre Sunnhordland"* ["The Early Emigration from Inner South Hordland"], trans. Lambrecht Haugen, 73, 75–76.

[26] Halle Steensland, "Recollections from My Journey to America and My First Years in America," trans. Odd S. Lovoll, in *Norwegian-American Studies* (Northfield, Minnesota: The Norwegian-American Historical Association, 1992), 33:235–242, accessed December 3, 2003, http://www.naha.stolaf.edu/pubs/nastudies.htm. For more accounts, see volumes 1, 3, 8, & 12 of *Norwegian-American Studies*.

[27] Havneros, *History of St. Petri Congregation*, 3.

[28] *Biographical and Historical Memoirs of Story County, Iowa* (Chicago: Goodspeed Publishing Co., 1890), 420–421.

[29] Mathilde Rasmussen, *A Brief History of the P. A. Rasmussen Family* (Minneapolis, Minnesota: n.p., 1945), 5–6.

[30] Naeseth, *Norwegian Immigrants to the United States*, (2004), 4:1–8.

[31] Ibid., 44–51.

[32] "Norway-Heritage Hands Across the Sea," accessed January 23, 2013, http://www.norwayheritage.com/.

[33] Theodore C. Blegen and Martin B. Rund, *Norwegian Emigrant Songs and Ballads* (Minneapolis, Minnesota: The University of Minnesota Press, 1936), 165.

[34] Ibid & M. L. Michaelsen, *Stavanger Sjøfarts Historie: Seilskibene og Seilskibsfarten i Aarene fra 1600 til 1922* [Stavanger Navigation History: Sailing Ships and Sailing Ships' Trade in the Years from 1600 to 1922] (Stavanger, Norway: n.p., 1927).

[35] Skålnes, *"Utvandringa frå Skånevik,"* 101.

[36] Anders Haugland, *"Den tidlege utvandringa frå Skånevik"* ["The Early Emigration from Skånevik"], trans. Anne S. Helvik and Jarle Steinkjer, in *Etne Sogelag Årbok 1988* ([Etne, Norway]: n.p., 1988), 71. For a more thorough discussion of the causes of emigration, see "Emigration Causes and Controversy" by Theodore C. Blegen, chap. 7 in *Norwegian Migration to America 1825–1860* (Northfield, Minnesota: Norwegian-American Historical Association, 1931; New York: Haskell House Publishers Ltd., 1969), 154–176.

[37] Naeseth, *Norwegian Immigrants to the United States*, (2004), 4:x.

[38] Yngve Nedrebø, "A Century of Norwegian Emigrant Routes," (Slightly altered version of the original, printed in *The Norseman*, March 1988), accessed November 22, 2007, http://home.online.no/~fndbred/emirou.htm.

[39] "Norwegians in the US 1850 Census" accessed March 23, 2004, *Digitalarkivet* (http://gda.arkivverket.no/cgi-win/WebMeta.exe?spraak=e).

[40] This figure is based on a review of Gerhard Naeseth's *Norwegian Immigrants to the United States*, volumes 2, 3, and 4; the "Norwegians in the US 1850 Census" database;

bygdebøker (farm history books) from Skånevik and Etne; and Arlen Twedt's unpublished "Early Settler Database," Central Iowa Norwegian Project, Ankeny, Iowa, 2017).

The First Central Iowa Norwegian Settlement: 1855–1860

[41] J. H. Battle, "Nettle Creek Township," & "Saratoga Township," chap. 12 & 14 in *History of Grundy County, Illinois* (Chicago: O. L. Baskin & Co., Historical Publishers, 1882), 287, 300–301.

[42] Charles E. Rosenberg, *The Cholera Years: The United States in 1832, 1849, and 1866* (Chicago: The University of Chicago Press, 1962), 4. For information about cholera in Norwegian settlements, see "Health Conditions and the Practice of Medicine Among the Early Norwegian Settlers, 1825–1865 by Knut Gjerset and Ludvig Hektoen, *Norwegian-American Studies* (Northfield, Minnesota: Norwegian-American Historical Association, 1926), 1:1–60.

[43] Naeseth, *Norwegian Immigrants to the United States*, (2000), 3:24–34.

[44] Lowell M. Volkel, transcriber & indexer, *1850 Illinois Mortality Schedule* (Thomson, Illinois: Heritage House, 1972–1973), 1:68–70 & 2:20, 22, 29, 31–33, & 36–37.

[45] Ibid., 32–33.

[46] Ibid., 29.

[47] *The Slater News*, October 31, 1912.

[48] *The Cambridge Leader*, October 31, 1912.

[49] *The Story City Herald*, January 9, 1930.

[50] A. M. Henderson, *Historical Events and Reminiscences of The St. Petri Lutheran Congregation, Story City, Iowa. And its Present Day Activities* (Story City: n.p., 1932), 16.

[51] In 1978 when the author visited this small cemetery which is located in Section 17 of Nettle Creek Township, it was surrounded by newly tasseled corn stalks. The only evidence it was a cemetery was a small pile of broken gravestone markers piled at the back of an open space within the cornfield that a farmer had mowed with a haymower.

[52] Odd S.Lovoll, *The Promise of America: A History of the Norwegian-American People* (Minneapolis: University of Minnesota Press & Norwegian-American Historical Association, 1984), 28, table.

[53] Anders Haugland found the same phenomenon. See *"Til Amerika"* ["To America"] in *Skåneviksoga: I gode og vonde dagar frå 1750 til 1965* (Skånevik, Norway: Skånevik bygde-boknemnd, 1998), 6:138.

[54] John M. Armstrong, M.D. "The Asiatic Cholera in St. Paul," *Minnesota History Magazine*, September 1933, accessed December 1, 2014, http://collections.mnhs.org/MNHistoryMagazine/articles/14/v14i03p288–302.pdf. Dr. Armstrong states, "In 1848, another visitation took place. The disease broke out almost simultaneously in New York and New Orleans, and in 1849 it overran the entire country east of the Rocky Mountains and was reintroduced through Canada. By 1850, it had spread throughout the entire Mississippi Valley and had appeared in San Francisco where it was introduced by way of Panama. In 1851, the epidemic began to abate, but in 1854 cholera was again imported from Europe and the West Indies. It prevailed generally throughout North America and particularly in the basins of the Mississippi and Ohio rivers. After 1855, only scattered cases occurred till 1866, when the disease was again introduced at Halifax, New York, and New Orleans."

55 *Encyclopedia of Chicago*, "Epidemics," accessed December 1, 2014, http://www.encyclopedia.chicagohistory.org/pages/432.html.

56 The number of cholera deaths was compiled from biographical profiles of the families who lived in central Iowa prior to 1861 which will be published in Volume 2 of *The Central Iowa Norwegians*.

57 Oley Nelson, *En kort historie af det forste norske settlement i Story og Polk counties, Iowa* (Chicago, n.p., 1905), republished in English by the author under the title *A Brief History of the First Norwegian Settlement of Story and Polk Counties, Ia. 1855–1905* (Slater, Iowa: The Slater News [Press], 1930), 1–2.

58 "A fatal epidemic of cholera in the middle States" is one of the reasons Goodwin identifies for the increase of immigration into Iowa beginning in 1850 and "particularly during the years 1854 to 1856." Reference: "The American Occupation of Iowa, 1833–1860" by Cardinal Goodwin, *Iowa Journal of History and Politics*, 17 (January 1919): 97, accessed November 14, 2015, http://penelope.uchicago.edu/Thayer/E/Gazetteer/Places/America/United_States/Iowa/_Texts/journals/IaJHP/17/1/American_Occupation_of_Iowa*.html.

59 Scott Crosier, "John Snow: The London Cholera Epidemic of 1854," Center for Spatially Integrated Social Science, accessed December 1, 2014, http://www.csiss.org/classics/content/8.

60 Kathleen Tuthill, illustrated by Rupert Van Wyk, "John Snow and the Broad Street Pump: On the Trail of an Epidemic," *Cricket*, November 2003, reprinted by permission by UCLA Department of Epidemiology, School of Public Health, accessed December 1, 2014, http://www.ph.ucla.edu/epi/snow/snowcricketarticle.html.

61 Anfin Apland in Oley Nelson's *En kort historie af det forste norske settlement i Story og Polk counties, Iowa* (Chicago, n.p., 1905), republished in English by the author in 1930 under the title, *A Brief History of the First Norwegian Settlement of Story and Polk Counties, Ia. 1855–1905*; and re-compiled, corrected and added to by Anfin Apland in 1945 under the same title, 3.

62 Carrie O. Larson, "Reverend Osmund Sheldahl 1824–1900" in *Larson Family History 1830–1980*, Carrie O. Larson, ed. (Des Moines, Iowa: n.p., 1980). Larson states the following about her grandfather, "Word came to them that land was available farther west. In the winter of 1853, a group of 30 families organized to set out for this area. In early August 1854 he [Osmund Sheldahl] was sent, as a leader of four men, to make a pre-journey to this territory near Lincoln, Nebraska." Other sources state they were authorized to go only as far as Omaha, Nebraska, in search of land (see Pastor Olaf Holan, *"Noen Minneord Om Etnesbuen Pastor Osmund Sheldahl"* ["Some Commemorative Words About Etne's Pastor Osmund Sheldahl"] in *Etne Sogelag Årsskrift 1986* ([Etne, Norway]: n.p., 1986), 91, and Don Fatka, "From Norway to Story County" in *History Book, Sheldahl, Iowa* (n.p., n.d.). Omaha was the more likely boundary of their instructions because Lincoln did not exist in 1854. Land west of the Missouri River was opened for settlement with the passage of the Kansas-Nebraska Act on May 30, 1854, and Omaha City was founded on July 4 of the same year. The village of Lancaster, which later became Lincoln, was not founded until 1856.

63 Holand, *"Stavanger og Hordaland Kolonien i Midtre Iowa,"* 460.

64 Ibid., 459–460.

65 Ibid.

⁶⁶ Holand, *Stavanger og Hordaland Kolonien i Midtre Iowa*, 460. Holand states, "This view of the affair received unexpected support by the chance arrival of Nils Olson Næs, a lay preacher, who had been in northeastern Iowa."

⁶⁷ Nelson, *En kort historie af det forste norske settlement i Story og Polk counties, Iowa*, 2.

⁶⁸ Naeseth, *Norwegian Immigrants to the United States*, (1993), 1:20.

⁶⁹ Tuttle purchased land at the Federal Land Office in Iowa City, Iowa, on June 1, 1854 (Federal Land Records, SHSI microfilm ARC-34). According to a family history written by his grandson, Royal Tuttle, Osmund's first wife died in 1852, and after purchasing land in Benton County, Osmund returned to Norway. He married Helen Sophia in 1855, and they returned to Benton County in 1859 (Benton County Records, SHSI microfilm BEN-54).

⁷⁰ *The Slater News*, January 15, 1914.

⁷¹ John A. T. Hull, Secretary of State, *Census of Iowa for 1880* (Des Moines: F. M. Mills, 1883), xliv.

⁷² Apland, in Nelson's *En kort historie af det forste norske settlement i Story og Polk counties, Iowa*, (1945), 3.

⁷³ Chapter VI of Harry E. Downer's *History of Davenport and Scott County, Iowa* (Chicago: The S. J. Clarke Publishing Company, 1910), 1:197.

⁷⁴ *The Slater News*, January 15, 1914. This information is contained in an obituary for Anna Apland, wife of Ole Apland, who was a member of the scouting party. The area "near Cedar Rapids" referred to in the obituary is likely in southeastern Benton County where Osmund Tuttle, aka Osmund Tøtland, an 1836 Norwegian immigrant to LaSalle County, Illinois, purchased land in 1854.

⁷⁵ Nathan H. Parker, *Iowa as it is in 1855; A gazetteer for citizens, and a hand-book for immigrants, embracing a full description of the state of Iowa* (Chicago, Illinois: Keen and Lee, 1855), 62.

⁷⁶ Ibid., 69.

⁷⁷ Ibid., 70.

⁷⁸ Larson, "Reverend Osmund Sheldahl 1824–1900," *Larson Family History*.

⁷⁹ Allen states, "Josiah Chandler was the pioneer in this village, building a saw mill on Skunk River in 1853, which was the nucleus of this town," and "J. C. Sladden opened a store [in present-day Cambridge] in 1854." The Goodspeed account records, "J. C. Sladden did business in an early period at Cambridge and Iowa Center," and "During the fall of 1854, George Childs built a residence.... The flooring was from the first log sawed at Josiah Chandler's mill at Cambridge." This source also states, "In 1851, however, a Maine man ... came to [the] Story County site prospecting. This was Josiah Chandler. He looked over the Skunk bottoms, then water covered, and selected an elevated site, which was then surrounded by water, but above high-water mark, as that on which he should settle.... It is not known just when Josiah and Jairus, with Mr. Alexander, secured the site of the present town as above entered, but it may have been as late as 1854. Josiah concluded he would plat a town of about square dimensions, with its streets running parallel to the river instead of in cardinal directions. He did so, and named the new town Cambridge, and, of course, the plat is like the old French surveys.... The plat was not recorded, however, until November 1856, although it is Dr. Grafton's opinion that it was laid out probably three years before." References: *A History of Story County Iowa from the Earliest Settlement to the Present* by William G. Allen (Des

Moines: Iowa Publishing Co., 1887), 52, and *Biographical Historical Memoirs of Story County, Iowa* (Chicago: Goodspeed Publishing Co., 1890), 118, 133, & 207.

[80] Story County was a young county at the time. White settlement had been slow because of the poor drainage of the Skunk River watershed. Although the county was opened for settlement in 1846, it was 1848 before the first white settlers built cabins in Story County. When the 1854 Iowa Census was taken, there were only 836 people living in the county. See "Story County in the Early 1850s" in this volume of *The Central Iowa Norwegians* for more information about this period of Story County's history.

[81] Larson, "Reverend Osmund Sheldahl, 1824–1900," *Larson Family History*.

[82] Leola Nelson Bergmann, "Scandinavian Settlement in Iowa," *The Palimpsest* 37, no. 3 (1956): 156–159.

[83] Larson, "From Whence We Came," *Larson Family History*.

[84] Holand, *"Stavanger og Hordaland Kolonien i Midtre Iowa,"* 462.

[85] Larson, "Askel Rabbin Stole Larson," *Larson Family History*.

[86] Apland in Nelson's *En kort historie af det forste norske settlement i Story og Polk counties, Iowa*, (1945), 5.

[87] Haugland, *"Den tidlege utvandringa frå Skånevik,"* 72.

[88] Federal Land Records, microfilm ARC-19, State Historical Society of Iowa Research Center, Des Moines, Iowa.

[89] Story County Land Records, Book B, 68.

[90] Esta Freeland & Gladys B. Willert, comp. & ed. *The Huxonian: Huxley Centennial, 1882–1982* (Ames, Iowa: Sigler Publishing, 1982), 4, map.

[91] Nelson, *En kort historie af det forste norske settlement i Story og Polk counties, Iowa*, 3.

[92] Ibid.

[93] Apland in Nelson's *En kort historie af det forste norske settlement i Story og Polk counties, Iowa*, (1945), 4–5.

[94] In 1929, Sarah aka Siri [1835–1931] was the only living member of this group. Reference: "An Historical and Sociological Study of a Rural Town in Central Iowa" by Minnie Elisabeth Allen (master's thesis, Iowa State College, 1929), 55.

[95] When Anfin Aplin updated Oley Nelson's 1905 history of the settlement, he added this family to the list of families who began the settlement in June 1855. When they emigrated and from what parish is unknown.

[96] Mary Qualley, "Largest single group of Norwegians to come to Iowa found Huxley and 'Flowing with Milk and Honey,'" *Des Moines Tribune*, May 28, 1955.

[97] Based upon a review of the maps available at the State Historical Society of Iowa Research Center in Des Moines, Iowa, the 1853 map was probably a township map of the United States published by J. H. Colton, No. 86 Cedar St., New York.

[98] Goodwin states, "The decade beginning in 1850 was to witness a migrating tide which was to sweep over the waste places of the State and to inundate the valleys and hills with more than sufficient human energy to build up a Commonwealth of the first rank. ... During the fall and early winter of 1854 there was an almost uninterrupted procession of immigrants crossing on the ferries at Prairie du Chien, McGregor, Dubuque, Burlington, Davenport, and Keokuk. Sometimes they had to wait in camp two or three days for their turn to cross. ... During the two years from 1854 to 1856 there was an increase of more than one hundred and ninety thousand in Iowa's population. That is, the number of settlers who came during those two years almost

equaled the total population of the State in 1850." Reference: "The American Occupation of Iowa, 1833–1860" by Cardinal Goodwin, *Iowa Journal of History and Politics*, 17 (January 1919): 96–99.

[99] *The Weekly Rock Island Republican*, May 23, 1855. For more information about ferries at Rock Island, see *Historical Encyclopedia of Illinois and History of Rock Island County*, edited by Newton Bateman, LL. D. and Paul Selby, A. M. (Chicago: Munsell Publishing Company, 1914), 1:635–636.

[100] Malinda Ann Thompson, "Biography of Peder Christian Heggem and His Wife Anna Serina," (n.p.: Thompson, 1926).

[101] Minnie Elisabeth Allen, "An Historical and Sociological Study of a Rural Town in Central Iowa" (master's thesis, Iowa State College, 1929), 55.

[102] Apland in Nelson's *En kort historie af det forste norske settlement i Story og Polk counties, Iowa*, (1945), 5.

[103] Parker, *Iowa as it is in 1855*, 25.

[104] Anna Apland's obituary states, "The colony pitched their tents in the vicinity of what is now the Apland school house where they commenced to share life's joys and sorrows." *The Slater News*, January 15, 1914.

[105] Ibid.

[106] In 1846, Ft. Des Moines' population was 127, in 1850 it was 502, and after a United States Land Office was opened in the city in 1853, it grew rapidly to a population of 3,965 in 1860. Reference: *The History of Polk County, Iowa* (Des Moines: Union Historical Company, Birdsall, Williams & Co., 1880), 677.

[107] Swedish immigrants began settling at Swede Point in 1846.

[108] The owner of the store was J. C. Sladden. According to Allen, J. C. Sladden opened a store in Cambridge in 1854. Reference: *A History of Story County Iowa from the Earliest Settlement to the Present* by William G. Allen (Des Moines: Iowa Publishing Co., 1887), 52. Sladden was not enumerated on the 1854 Iowa Census for Story County, but he may have arrived after the census was completed as of June 1, 1854.

[109] Apland in Nelson's *En kort historie af det forste norske settlement i Story og Polk counties, Iowa*, (1945), 9.

[110] Ibid., 6.

[111] Anna is not on Apland's list of members of this group, but her obituary states, "While she was not a member of the first colony, she came to Iowa shortly afterwards." Reference: *The Slater News*, November 2, 1927. Anna's mother, Ragna Hauge, was a member of the first caravan that arrived June 7, 1855.

[112] Minnie Elisabeth Allen, "An Historical and Sociological Study of a Rural Town in Central Iowa," 55.

[113] Only seven families and one single person have been identified as members of this caravan. Assuming Rasmus Sheldall was correct in his recollection of there being 15 wagons in the caravan, other unidentified people must have come on this journey.

[114] Nehemias Tjernagel, "Rasmus Sheldall's Pioneer Story," *The Story City Herald*, June 8, 1922. See *History of Story County* by W. O. Payne, 1911, 1:32–34, also where Payne recounts recollections of William K. Wood who settled near Iowa Center in 1852. Regarding Wood's early experience near Iowa Center, Payne states, "It was in this time that occurred the first death in that quarter, being that of a Norwegian stranger, who was crossing the prairie. Settlers heard of him, found him dead under his wagon and buried

him, and his grave was the first in the present cemetery." Gunder Madskaar would surely have been buried by his friends, but stories can change over time, so Wood's recollection could be referring to Gunder's death.

[115] A biography of Andrewson, *Ole Andrewson: Crofters Boy and Pioneer Pastor* by Leif Skoje, translated by Roger Bond, 2004, is available online @ http://www.hjartdal historielag.no/emigr/andrewson.htm.

[116] J. C. Jensson, Rev. *American Lutheran Biographies* (Milwaukee, Wisconsin: A. Houtkamp & Son, 1890), 36.

[117] O. [Ole] Andrewson to the corresponding secretaries of the American Home Mission Society, September 14, 1855, American Home Missionary Society Papers, Billy Graham Center Archives, Wheaton, Illinois.

[118] *The Cambridge Leader*, July 1, 1920.

[119] Deeds for 15 tracts of privately owned land purchased before 1865 show they paid $1.25 to $4.16 per acre for what is assumed to be unimproved land, i.e., virgin prairie land, at least one mile away from timber resources with an average price paid of $2.56 per acre.

[120] Deeds for 23 timber lots purchased before 1865 show they paid $4 to $25 per acre for timber lots with an average price paid of $14 per acre.

[121] *The Cambridge Leader*, July 1, 1920.

[122] Apland in Nelson's *En kort historie af det forste norske settlement i Story og Polk counties, Iowa*, (1945), 6.

[123] Story County Land Deeds, Book B, 66–67.

[124] Ibid., Book H, 524.

[125] Will Porter, *Annals of Polk County, Iowa, and City of Des Moines* (Des Moines, Iowa: Geo. A. Miller Printing Company, Printers and Publishers, 1898), 172.

[126] The acres not shown in Figure 5 are 400 acres in Palestine Township and 146 acres in Lincoln Township.

[127] *The Nevada Representative*, January 1, 1874. For another letter from a Norwegian correspondent from Cambridge about an upcoming church convention to be held at the Palestine church, the newspaper used the heading, "Norway, South," apparently to distinguish it from the Norwegian settlement in northern Story County (see *The Nevada Representative*, June 9, 1880).

[128] Nehemias Tjernagel, *The Passing of the Prairie by a Fossil: Biographical Sketches of Central Iowa Pioneers and Civil War Veterans*, ed. Margaret Harstad Matzke (AuthorHouse, Bloomington, Indiana, 2009), 174.

[129] A record of people who moved to the settlement during this time has not been found. This information might be part of the early church records, but the Palestine Lutheran Church does not have them. They are in the possession of a descendant of Osmund Sheldahl, the second pastor of the Palestine congregation.

[130] *The Story City Herald*, October 26, 1922. Their son, Thomas, was born in Hamilton County on January 23, 1859, so Erick and Britha likely moved to the Southern Settlement in 1859 or 1860.

[131] As can be seen in Figure 5, a few parcels of government land were purchased after 1854, but otherwise the only land that could be purchased for $1.25 per acre was swamp or overflow land. This was land the federal government designated unfit for cultivation and deeded to the state of Iowa under the Swamp Land Act of 1850. The

state of Iowa in turn deeded the land to the counties who sold it to purchasers holding certificates of pre-emption who agreed to drain the land and convert it to agricultural and other uses.

[132] Norway Heritage, "Index of Departures 1825–1925," http://www.norwayheritage.com/.

[133] Mrs. E. L. Severeid, "Reminiscences of Pioneer Life by an Old Settler," *The Story City Herald*, May 30, 1940.

[134] *I Remember Slater, Iowa, 1889–1989* (Lake Mills, Iowa: Graphic Publishing Company, Inc., 1989), 178.

The Second Central Iowa Norwegian Settlement: 1856–1860

[135] Local histories of churches and communities in the Northern Settlement seldom refer to the Norwegian settlement founded in southern Story County, Iowa, in 1855. Unfortunately, this leads readers to believe the June 1855 scouting party that decided to begin a Norwegian settlement in northern Story County discovered cheap government land in central Iowa on their own. The most complete reference to the Southern Settlement the author has found was published as part of an obituary in the *Roland Record*, April 15, 1909, and was likely written by the editor of the newspaper, M. O. Rod, who grew up in the Roland community and purchased the newspaper in 1905. The obituary states, "In the death of Mr. Rasmusen the older citizens of our community recall some of the early history of the township of which the deceased took a share. In 1854 [1855], a few families moved from Fox River, Ill. to Huxley, Iowa, where they formed the first Norwegian colony in Story County. The people living around Lisbon, Ill., hearing of what these people had found, decided that they too wanted homes of their own, where land was cheap, and so in the spring of 1855, they sent eight men to Iowa to investigate and to purchase land for several of these men if they found the country suitable. The men who made this trip were Jonas Duea, Mons Grove, Jacob E. Aske, John N. Tarvestad, Paul Thompson, Lars, Sheldahl, Ole Eino and John Mehuus. These men went about twenty miles north of Cambridge, where they found land that suited them and they proceeded at once to buy farms. These men returned at once to their homes, told their neighbors about the fertile land that could be had at $1.25 per acre."

[136] Explorations in Iowa History Project, "Tips to Stagecoach Travelers" (Malcolm Price Laboratory School, University of Northern Iowa, 2003), accessed June 5, 2010, http://www.uni.edu/iowahist/Frontier_Life/Stagecoach/Stagecoach.htm. For information about Iowa's stage trails, see *Stagecoach Trails in Iowa* by Inez E. Kirkpatrick (Crete, Nebraska: J-B Publishing Company, 1975).

[137] Porter, *Annals of Polk County, Iowa, and City of Des Moines*, 172.

[138] Biography of Miles White in *History of Baltimore, Maryland from its founding as a town to the current year, 1829–1893* (Baltimore: S. B. Nelson, Publisher, 1893), 649–651.

[139] United States Department of the Interior Bureau of Land Management Web site @ http://www.glorecords.blm.gov/default.aspx.

[140] Hamilton County Land Deeds, Book 1, 414 (Lars) and Book 14, 446 (Jonas).

[141] *Roland Record*, October 19, 1911.

[142] The author has found six different sources listing the members of the June 1855 scouting party. The sources are: Knut Takla, *"Stort norsk Settlement"* ["Big Norwegian Settlement, Roland, Iowa"], *Skandinaven*, July 13, 1900; John M. Mason, Editor, [obituary of John Michaelson], *Roland Record*, June 18, 1902; H. Rued Holand, *"Lidt Nybyggerhistorie"* ["A little history about a new colony"], *Decorah-Posten* [The Decorah Post], February 6, 1906; Ivar Havneros, *History of St. Petri Congregation from its foundation June 1857 to its 50th Jubilee, June 1907*, trans. Rachel Vangness (Story City, Iowa: n.p., 1907), 3; M. O. Rod, Editor, obituary for Ole Rasmusen, *Roland Record*, April 15, 1909; and M. O. Rod, Editor, "60th Wedding Anniversary," *Roland Record*, October 19, 1911.

[143] When Oliver Thompson left the Etne parish on April 21, 1854, to immigrate to the United States, the name recorded in the Etne Grindheim *Klokkerbok* was Halvor Tollefson Øyne (p. 80) and in the Etne *Ministerialbok* it was Halvor Tollefson Øien (p. 241). The six different lists of scouting party members (see previous note) refer to him as Ole or Ola, but when he married Caroline Simmons on July 1, 1862, in Grundy County, Illinois, his name was recorded as Oliver Thompson which is an Americanized version of Halvor Tollefson.

[144] Holand, *"Stavanger og Hordaland Kolonien i Midtre Iowa,"* 464–465.

[145] Havneros, *History of St. Petri Congregation*, 3.

[146] Nathan H. Parker, *The Iowa Handbook for 1856: with a new and accurate map* (Boston: John P. Jewett and Co., 1956), 95–96.

[147] Ibid., 96.

[148] Havneros, *History of St. Petri Congregation*, 3.

[149] William G. Allen, *A History of Story County Iowa from the Earliest Settlement to the Present* (Des Moines: Iowa Publishing Co., 1887), 65.

[150] The route of the Iowa Central Air Line Railroad began appearing on maps of Iowa in 1854 (see Historic Maps of Iowa @ http://alabamamaps.ua.edu/historical maps/us_states/iowa/index.html).

[151] Another researcher who reached the same conclusion about the lack of government land in southern Story County being the reason a second Norwegian settlement was founded in northern Story County is Julian E. McFarland. In *A History of The Pioneer Era on the Iowa Prairies*, 1969, McFarland describes the founding of the Southern Settlement using Oley Nelson's 1905 history as his source and then on p. 144 he states, "When more land seekers came the next year, 1856, they found government land in the Palestine area all gone. Again, a party of four decided to go up the Skunk River looking for unclaimed lands. ... One may guess at their route, via Ballard's Grove and past G. W. Kelley's place near Walnut Grove. They would have been welcomed at the Squire Cory cabin and further upstream by William Arrasmith and John H. Kiegley. They probably crossed the Skunk on the limestone ledge where Sopher's Mill was later built and kept on north. Between present Story City and Roland they found the numerous Smith family trying to start a mill and found the town of Smithfield. But there was plenty of unoccupied land and they staked their claims nearby." McFarland was apparently not aware a scouting party had purchased land for a second settlement in Howard Township the previous year (1855), and based on other information McFarland found on p. 66 of William G. Allen's *A History of Story County, Iowa*, 1887, he must have erroneously concluded the group that founded the Howard Township settlement in 1856 did not purchase land until after they arrived in Story County.

152 Holand, *"Stavanger og Hordaland Kolonien i Midtre Iowa,"* 465.

153 Ibid., 460.

154 William J. Peterson, *Iowa: The Rivers of Her Valleys* (Iowa City, Iowa: The State Historical Society of Iowa, 1941), 165.

155 See Samuel Augustus Mitchell's 1854 "A New Map of the State of Iowa," and J. H. Colton's 1855 "Colton's Township Map of the State of Iowa" @ http://alabama maps.ua.edu/historicalmaps/us_states/iowa/.

156 Parker, *The Iowa Handbook for 1956*, 95–96.

157 See S. F. Baker's 1857 "Iowa" map and Joseph H. Colton's 1859 "Iowa" map @ http://alabamamaps.ua.edu/historicalmaps/us_states/iowa/.

158 Havneros, *History of St. Petri Congregation*, 4.

159 Two members of the scouting party, Erick Nelson and Hans Pederson, had been in Iowa before when they were lured west during the California Gold Rush. Erick Nelson is the person Hjalmar Rued Holand credits with suggesting Iowa for a new settlement location and Hans Pederson's obituary states, "He came to this country in 1849, stopping in Grundy County until 1852, when he joined the gold rush for California. He drove an ox-team from Illinois to the far western gold field." References: Holand, *"Stavanger og Hordaland Kolonien i Midtre Iowa,"* 460, and *Story City Herald*, June 25, 1908.

160 Havneros, *History of St. Petri Congregation*, 4.

161 *The Story City Herald*, July 8, 1922.

162 The list of caravan members was initially compiled from lists in Knut Takla's article about the Northern Settlement in *Skandinaven*, July 13, 1900; Ivar Havneros' 1907 history of the St. Petri congregation; Hjalmar Rued Holand's 1908 history the Stavanger and Hordaland colony in central Iowa; and Ole Rasmusen's obituary in the *Roland Record*, April 15, 1909, likely written by the editor, M. O. Rod. It has been confirmed and added to by the author's analysis of the 1856 Iowa Census for Lafayette and Howard townships, land records, biographies, obituaries, and family histories.

163 Two other sources state the drowning occurred in the Iowa River. One is in John Michaelson's obituary written by his grandson, Editor John M. Mason, where Mason states, "Mrs. Erick Sheldahl's and Mrs. Haaland's brother was drowned in the Iowa River on this trip (see *Roland Record*, June 18, 1902)." The second is in a brief sketch of the life of Sjur Britson recorded by Nehemias Tjernagel where Tjernagel recorded, "On a visit to his home [Sjur Britson's home] he told me among other things … In coming across the prairie from Illinois (there were twenty families in the party) the Britsons were witnesses of another tragedy, viz, the drowning of John Ness in the Iowa River. He and Christen Peterson had gone out to bathe, but John never came back; it was thought he had gotten beyond his depth and was seized with the cramps. It was said that Michael Erickson tried to rescue him, but nearly lost his life in the attempt. John left a widowed mother and two brothers, Lars and Christopher, to mourn his untimely death. The gloom occassioned by this grevous occurrence was partly offset by the arrival of a little daughter in the family of Hans Twedt. They set out from Illinois with but one child and when they came to Iowa they found they had two (see "Little Stories of Pioneer Days," *The Story City Herald*, August 17, 1922)."

164 Havneros, *History of St. Petri congregation*, 4–5.

[165] An obituary for Mike Erickson published in the *Roland Record*, August 4, 1910, states, "They arrived at their destination on the fourteenth of June and at once proceeded to break the sod on which to raise a crop." Another source states they arrived the next day, June 15, 1855 (See "Big Norwegian Settlement, Roland, Iowa" included in this volume of *The Central Iowa Norwegians*).

[166] Steve Sheldahl, "Sheldahl Ancestors and Story City, Iowa," November 30, 2007, addendum to *Searching for Roots: A Study of Ancestors* by Stephen A. Sheldahl, 2nd ed. (Northglenn, Colorado: Scudder Press, 2010).

[167] Peder Gustav Tjernagel, *The Follinglo Dog Book: From Milla to Chip the Third* (Ellsworth, Iowa: Ellsworth Printing Company, 1909), 11. Reprinted as *The Follinglo Dog Book* with prologue and epilogue by Peter Tjernagel Harstad (Iowa City: University of Iowa Press, 1999).

[168] Story County Land Deeds, Book 31, 26.

[169] W. O. Payne, *History of Story County, Iowa: A Record of Settlement, Organization, Progress and Achievement* (Chicago: The S. J. Clarke Publishing Co., 1911), 1:51.

[170] *The Nevada Representative*, November 5, 1878.

[171] Erik Arnesen Travaas, *"Litt om de første settlere i Story County, skrevet i 1888"* ["A Little About the First Settlers in Story County, written in 1888"], trans. Ardis N. Petersen & Arlen Twedt, in *Hjemve: Norske Digte og Fortællinger*, comp. Anna Travaas Gilbert (Minneapolis, Minnesota: Anna Travaas Gilbert, 1925), 214–237. Travaas was born in 1855 and emigrated from the Travaas farm in Valestrand parish in Hordaland in 1873. He returned to Norway where he married Elen Marie Knutsen, and they immigrated to Albert Lea, Minnesota, in 1876. By 1880, they were living in Story City, Iowa, where Erik worked on the railroad. They lived in Story City for 14 years before moving back to Minnesota in the early 1890s. Travaas' historical narrative is included in this volume of *The Central Iowa Norwegians*.

[172] Story County Land Deeds, Book D, 396.

[173] Hamilton County Land Deeds, Book I, 412–413.

[174] Ruth Ritland and Mrs. O. E. Ritland, compilers and editors, "Ritland Family History," (n.p., n.d.), 1.

[175] They are listed as "Knud Helvig and family" in Ivar Havneros' *History of St. Petri Congregation*, but a family historian believes they did not have their first child, Caroline 1860–1860, until after they moved to Story County. Reference: Email from Richard Holtman to author, December 12, 2010.

[176] A Lars Bouge family is on Havneros' 1907 list of families (see *History of St. Petri Congregation*) who moved to central Iowa in 1857; however, the author has not found any trace of a Lars Bouge family in Iowa or Illinois. Lars Bouge is believed to be Lars J. Boyd [1829–1912] who emigrated from the Bauge farm, Skånevik, Hordaland, to Lisbon, Illinois, in 1858. In August 1862, he volunteered for the 91st Illinois Infantry, but he could have been in central Iowa before that time. He is buried in the Ames Municipal Cemetery, Ames, Iowa.

[177] Hamilton County Land Deeds, Book I, 369.

[178] *A Biographical Record of Hamilton County, Iowa* (New York: The S. J. Clarke Publishing Company, 1902), 349.

[179] Ritland & Ritland, "Ritland Family History," 1.

[180] *Biographical Record and Portrait Album of Hamilton and Wright Counties, Iowa* (Chicago: Lewis Biographical Publishing Co., 1889), 281.

[181] Havneros, *History of St. Petri Congregation*, 7.

[182] This is a combined list drawn from Havneros' 1907 *History of St. Petri Congregation*, Paul and Enger Thompson's list (see *Roland Record*, October 19, 1911), and an obituary for Tjeran and Borghild Halsnes' daughter, Anna Kathrine (see *The Story City Herald*, June 11, 1925). Christian Erickson appears only on Thompson's list.

[183] A biography of Mons Grove is included in this volume of *The Central Iowa Norwegians* (see "The Early History of the Norwegian Settlement in Howard Township" by John M. Mason and M. O. Rod).

[184] *Roland Record*, October 19, 1911.

[185] *Roland Record*, June 18, 1902.

[186] Story County Land Deeds, Book D, 121.

[187] J. W. Lee, *History of Hamilton County, Iowa* (Chicago: The J. S. Clarke Publishing Company, 1912), 2:414.

[188] Michael D. Green, "'We Dance in Opposite Directions': Mesquakie (Fox) Separatism from the Sac and Fox Tribe" in *Iowa History Reader* by Marvin Bergman, ed. (Ames, Iowa: Iowa State University Press, 1996), 28–33.

[189] For more specific information about the return of the Meskwaki tribe to Tama County, see *Iowa: A Bicentennial History* by Joseph Frazier Wall (Nashville, Tennessee: American Association for State and Local History, 1978), 59–61.

[190] Havneros, *History of St. Petri Congregation*, 7.

[191] Nehemias Tjernagel, "Little Stories of Pioneer Days," *The Story City Herald*, October 26, 1922.

[192] Erik and Guro's son, Erick, and his wife were presumably living in the settlement, too, when Erik and Guro arrived, but they moved to the Southern Settlement before June 1860 where they were enumerated on the 1860 Census. Living near Erick in the Southern Settlement were his sister, Engebor Charlson, and his brother, Peter. Another brother, Henry, was, presumably, living near him, too, because he volunteered for the 10th Iowa Infantry, Company K, in December 1861, the same unit Erick had joined in October 1861.

[193] The author has not found a list of families in this caravan.

[194] Isabelle Lein Coats, "Life History of Thomas A. Lein, 1831–1907" (n.p.n.d.).

[195] In Havneros' *History of St. Petri Congregation*, the Knud Aske, aka Knudt Thompson, family is on a list of families who arrived in 1857, but obituaries for Knudt's wife, Christena, and their son, Henry, state the family came in 1860. Knudt purchased 180 acres of land near the Skunk River in Howard Township on July 6, 1857, so he was likely a member of the 1857 caravan, but he apparently returned to Illinois and stayed there until the family moved to Iowa in 1860.

[196] Knut Takla, *"Stort norsk Settlement"* ["Big Norwegian Settlement, Roland, Iowa, June 1900], *Skandinaven*, July 13, 1900. This history is included in this volume of *The Central Iowa Norwegians*.

Making Farmsteads on the Prairie

[197] Parker, *Iowa As It Is in 1855*, 203.
[198] *Biographical and Historical Memoirs of Story County, Iowa*, 321.
[199] *A Biographical Record of Hamilton County, Iowa*, 344–349.
[200] Payne, *History of Story County*, 1:30–31.
[201] 1852 Iowa State Special Census.
[202] Hull, *Census of Iowa for 1880*, 583, table.
[203] 1856 Iowa Census.
[204] 1858 Story County Census Returns, filed April 18, 1859, and published with the Iowa Census returns for 1859.
[205] Hull, *Census of Iowa for 1880*, 583, table.
[206] Centennial History Committee, *A History of Roland, Iowa, 1870–1970* (Roland, Iowa: The Record, 1970), 96.
[207] This information is based on 16 land deeds for Norwegians who moved to the Southern Settlement before 1861 and presumably purchased virgin prairie land. For the 16 deeds, the average price paid was $2.53, the range was $1.00 to $3.75 per acre, and the median price was $2.80 per acre.
[208] This information is based 32 land deeds for Norwegians who moved to the Northern Settlement before 1861, 15 deeds for land purchased at least two miles away from the Skunk River and 17 deeds for land purchased within one mile of the river. For the 15 deeds, the average price paid per acre was $3.09, the range was $1.25 to $5.62 per acre, and the median price paid was $3.00 per acre. For the 17 deeds, the average price paid per acre was $6.67, the range was $1.75 to $18.75 per acre, and the median price paid was $5.26 per acre.
[209] Ibid.
[210] Hamilton County Land Deeds, Book 1, 369.
[211] "Norwegians in the US 1850 Census," *Digitalarkivet* (http://gda.arkivverket.no/cgi-win/WebMeta.exe?spraak=e).
[212] 1860 United States Census, Schedule 4.
[213] *Biographical and Historical Memoirs of Story County, Iowa*, 115.
[214] Ibid., 115–116
[215] This information is based on 52 timber lot deeds for Norwegians who moved to central Iowa before 1861, 28 deeds for the Southern Settlement and 24 deeds for the Northern Settlement. In the Southern Settlement, lots were purchased west of Cambridge in Ballard Grove, north of Cambridge beside the Skunk River, and southeast of Cambridge in White Oak Grove. The average lot size was 5.13 acres, and the average price paid per acre was $13.16 with a range of $1.63 to $25.00 per acre and a median price of $12.00 per acre. In the Northern Settlement, all timber lots purchased were beside the Skunk River. The average lot size was 7.26 acres, and the average price paid per acre was $15.65 with a range of $1.75 to $30 per acre and the median price of $15.00 per acre. Generally, the most expensive timber lots were north of Story City in southern Hamilton County, and the least expensive lots were south of Story City in southern Howard Township and northern Milford Township.
[216] *Record of Surveys made by County Surveyor of Story County*, Story County Recorder's Office, 54.
[217] Ibid., 57, 93–94, 106, 109.

[218] David N. Ballard, Jr. "Nineteenth-Century Mills and Milling Industries in Story County, Iowa," *Journal of the Iowa Archeological Society* 31 (1984): 164 & 180.

[219] Ibid., 166.

[220] W. A. Weir, "Lafayette: Past and Present," in *Atlas of Story County, Iowa, containing maps of cities, villages, and townships of the county* (Davenport, Iowa: The Heubinger Surveying and Map Publishing Co., 1902), Part I—6.

[221] Ibid. & Ballard, "Nineteenth-Century Mills," 178.

[222] Ibid.

[223] Nehemias Tjernagel, "Little Stories of Pioneer Days," *The Story City Herald*, January 4, 1923. A photograph of the house is in Payne's *History of Story County*, 1:28.

[224] Julian E. McFarland, *A History of The Pioneer Era on the Iowa Prairies* (Lake Mills, Iowa: Graphic Publishing Company, Inc., 1969), 146. For more detailed information about constructing log cabins, see "Early Cabins in Iowa" by Mildred J. Sharp in *The Palimpsest* 2, no. 1 (January 1921).

[225] Ibid., 151.

[226] *The Cambridge Leader*, July 1, 1920.

[227] Severeid, "Reminiscences of Pioneer Life by an Old Settler."

[228] Carrie Knutson, "Pioneer Days" in *Jewell: The Gem, 1881–1981* [The Centennial History for Jewell, Iowa] by Keith Peterson, Chairman, et. al. (n.p., 1981), 77.

[229] Havneros, *History of St. Petri Congregation*, 5.

[230] Nehemias Tjernagel, "H. B. Henryson's Pioneer Story," *The Story City Herald*, February 23, 1922.

[231] *Biographical and Historical Memoirs of Story County, Iowa*, 392.

[232] Nelson, *En kort historie af det forste norske settlement i Story og Polk counties, Iowa*, 6.

[233] *Roland Record*, June 18, 1902.

[234] *Roland Record*, February 6, 1913.

[235] Arlen Twedt, "Early Settler Database" (unpublished), Central Iowa Norwegian Project, Ankeny, Iowa, 2017.

[236] They were the Ole Apland and John Larson families.

[237] For the 1850 Census, 12 of the 20 families reported owning real estate valued from $200 to $800 with the average real estate owned of $338. The 1855 Illinois Census required the value of livestock to be reported, but not the value of real estate owned. The Kendall and Lafayette County censuses are water damaged and undecipherable, but on the Grundy County census, five families who moved to central Iowa were identified. The value of livestock owned ranged from $100 to $600 with an average of $440.

[238] See Appendix F for the author's thoughts on why established farmers in Illinois might have chosen to move to central Iowa.

[239] Morris is 11 miles southeast of Lisbon and a slightly longer distance from the northwest area of Nettle Creek Township where many of the early central Iowa Norwegian families lived prior to moving to Iowa.

[240] See the histories by Oley Nelson, Erik Travaas, Knut Takla, John M. Mason, M. O. Rod, and Hjalmar Rued Holand in this volume of *The Central Iowa Norwegians*.

Farming on the Frontier

241 The moldboard is the curved metal plate in a plow that turns over the earth from the furrow.

242 Hon. L. S. Coffin, "Breaking Prairie," *Annals of Iowa* 5, no. 6 (July, 1902): 450.

243 John Lamb states, "Lane was advised many times to record his plow with the patent office, but he declined to do so. He explained that his only desire was to benefit others with his ideas and asked for no special recognition or remuneration." Reference: "Lockport, Home of the First Steel Plow" by John Lamb, *Graphic Newspapers*, March 14, 1968, 14.

244 Hiram M. Drache, "The Impact of John Deere's Plow," Illinois Periodicals Online, accessed November 17, 2015, www.lib.niu.edu/2001/iht810102.html.

245 Ibid.

246 Daryl D. Smith, "Tallgrass Prairie Settlement: Prelude to Demise of the Tallgrass Ecosystem." Paper presented at the Twelfth North American Prairie Conference: Recapturing a Vanishing Heritage, University of Northern Iowa, Cedar Falls, 1992, accessed November 14, 2015, http://tallgrassprairiecenter.org/pdf/Recapturing_A_Vanishing_Heritage.pdf.

247 *Biographical and Historical Memoirs of Story County, Iowa*, 377–378.

248 Ritland and Ritland, "Ritland Family History," 1.

249 *Biographical and Historical Memoirs of Story County, Iowa*, 302.

250 Haugland, *"Den tidlege utvandringa frå Skånevik,"* 72.

251 *Roland Record*, August 4, 1910.

252 1856 Iowa Census, table showing the population, agricultural statistics, number and value of hogs and cattle sold, etc. of Story County for 1856.

253 Agricultural product information was obtained at 44 dwelling houses in Story County, four dwelling houses in Polk County, and four dwelling houses in Hamilton County. The names and year of settlement of the 29 families in the Southern Settlement were: Osmund Anfensen ca. '57, Ole Anfinson '55, Ole Apland '55, Knut Bauge '55, Erick Egland '57 or '58, Knut Ersland '55, Oley Fatland '55, Severt Gravadahl '55, Salamon Heggen '55, Severt Hellend '57, Barney Hill '55, Thomas Houg '55, Wier Johnson '55, Ole Johnston, Oscar Larson '55, Ole Nernes '55, Ober Oleson, Engebrit Olson '55, Thor Olson, Torger Olson '55, Ole Olston, John Severson '55, Osmund Severson '56, Erick Sheldahl '55, Osmund Sheldahl '55, Lars Tesdahl '55, Ole Thompson, Iver Twedt '55, and Wier Weeks '55. In the Northern Settlement, the names and year of settlement for the 23 families were: Baard Henryson Beroen '58, Sjur Britson '56, Jonas Duea '56, Jacob Erickson '56, Rasmus Erickson '56, Ole T. Hegland '57, Lars Henderson aka Henryson '58, Osmund Henryson '57, Erick Jacabson '56, Jacob B. Jacobson '56, Peder Larson '57, Jacob Nelson '56, John Nelson '56, Lars B. Olson '57, Torkel Opstvedt '56, John Pierson '57, Ole Rasmusen '56, Ole Ritland '57, Erick R. Sheldahl '56, Lars Sheldall '55, Paul Thompson '58, Rasmus Larson Tungesvik '56, and Hans Johnson Twedt '56.

254 Nelson, *En kort historie af det forste norske settlement i Story og Polk counties, Iowa*, 3.

255 Nehemias Tjernagel, "Rasmus Sheldall's Pioneer Story."

256 Havneros, *History of St. Petri Congregation*, 4.

257 Nehemias Tjernagel, "H. B. Henryson's Pioneer Story."

[258] A. B. Caine, "Horses Pull Iowa Into Prominence," in *A Century of Farming in Iowa: 1846–1946* (Ames, Iowa: The Iowa State College Press, 1946), 141. Caine further states, "... by 1880, the ratio was 335 horses and mules to each ox."

[259] "Draft Animal FAQ," Tiller's International, accessed February 16, 2016, http://tillersinternational.org/resources/draft-animal-faq/.

[260] "Trail Basics: Supplies," *National Oregon/California Trail Center*, accessed December 2, 2015, http://www.oregontrailcenter.org/HistoricalTrails/Supplies.htm.

[261] Mildred Throne, "'Book Farming' in Iowa 1840–1870," *Iowa Journal of History* 45 (April 1951): 120.

[262] *The Prairie Farmer*, May 10, 1860, 301, accessed from the Illinois Digital Newspaper Collections @ http://idnc.library.illinois.edu/.

[263] Story County Land Deeds, Book C, 634, $1,000 on February 19, 1857, in the N½ SE¼, Section 30, 85-23, plus 12 acres in SW¼ of same section. An 1883 plat map of Howard Township shows the N½SE¼ without trees and containing 92 acres.

[264] According to Carl Kurtz, prairie seed grower, the prairie was three and one-half to four feet tall by the end of July and by late August or early September the yellow-flowered compass plants would be seven and one-half feet tall and the big blue stem grass would be about nine feet tall. Conversation with Carl Kurtz on January 5, 2016.

[265] Payne, *History of Story County*, 1:157.

[266] Sina Kloster Moran, "Pioneer Days in Southwest Story County," *Nevada Evening Journal*, June 13, 1953.

[267] For Schedule 4 of the 1860 Census, enumerators were required to record information for the year ending June 1, 1860, which meant the bushels of grain and tons of hay reported were harvested in 1859. Families who settled in central Iowa in 1855 were reporting information about their third harvest, those who came in 1856 were reporting information about their second harvest, and those who moved to central Iowa in 1857 were reporting information about their first harvest. This explains why agricultural product information was only collected at 52 of the 81 dwelling houses owning real estate in 1860.

[268] Apland in Nelson's *En kort historie af det forste norske settlement i Story og Polk counties, Iowa*, (1945), 5.

[269] Nehemias Tjernagel, "Rasmus Sheldall's Pioneer Story."

[270] Havneros, *History of St. Petri Congregation*, 4.

[271] The child was Ole T. Hill, son of Thor and Malinda Olson (Hill) who was born east of Nevada, Iowa, on June 28, 1858.

[272] Nehemias Tjernagel, "H. B. Henryson's Pioneer Story."

[273] Payne, *History of Story County*, 1:156.

[274] Ibid., 1:154.

[275] Ibid., 1:160.

[276] Nehemias Tjernagel, "Rasmus Sheldall's Pioneer Story."

[277] *The Prairie Farmer*, April 1, 1854, 151, accessed from the Illinois Digital Newspaper Collections @ http://idnc.library.illinois.edu/. For more information about kitchen gardens, see "Pioneer kitchen gardens: How the pioneers planned and planted," accessed December 9, 2015, http://littlehouseontheprairie.com/.

[278] Payne, *History of Story County*, 1:169.

²⁷⁹ *The Prairie Farmer*, November 29, 1860, 345, accessed from the Illinois Digital Newspaper Collections @ http://idnc.library.illinois.edu/, in a report from a farmer living in Van Buren County in southeastern Iowa.
²⁸⁰ Payne, *History of Story County*, 1;160.
²⁸¹ McFarland, *A History of The Pioneer Era on the Iowa Prairies*, 153–154.

The Frontier Economy

²⁸² Tacitus Hussey, "History of Steamboating on the Des Moines River from 1837 to 1862," *Annals of Iowa* 4, no. 5 (April, 1900): 331–333.
²⁸³ *Roland Record*, June 18, 1902.
²⁸⁴ The towns are listed chronologically according to their plat date. Regarding Cambridge, Rev. Konkel states, "The plat was not recorded, however, until November 1856, although it is Dr. Grafton's opinion that it was laid out probably three years before." Reference: *Biographical Historical Memoirs of Story County, Iowa* (Chicago: Goodspeed Publishing Co., 1890), 207.
²⁸⁵ *Biographical and Historical Memoirs of Story County, Iowa*, 205.
²⁸⁶ See note #107 for more information about J. C. Sladden.
²⁸⁷ Andrew Maland, comp. *Eighty-fifth Anniversary of the Palestine Lutheran Congregation: Historical Souvenir* (Slater, Iowa: The Slater News Press, 1940), 4.
²⁸⁸ [W. H. Gallup, editor & proprietor], "Story County: Past and Present," *The Story County Representative*, January 5, 1871.
²⁸⁹ Payne, *History of Story County*, 1:113.
²⁹⁰ Ibid., 1:55, 133, 136, 140, 153.
²⁹¹ McFarland, *A History of The Pioneer Era on the Iowa Prairies*, 77.
²⁹² 1856 Iowa Census, table exhibiting the professions, trades, or occupations of the inhabitants of Story County for 1856.
²⁹³ Allen, *A History of Story County, Iowa*, 13–14.
²⁹⁴ 1858 Story County Census Returns.
²⁹⁵ Payne, *History of Story County*, 1:116.

Volunteering for War

²⁹⁶ Skånevik 1828–1848 *Ministerialbok*, 86, #9, Anders Nielson Tveito, born February 11, 1844, baptized February 18, 1866, accessed @ http://www.arkivverket.no/eng/Digitalarkivet.
²⁹⁷ *The Slater News*, August 17, 1939.
²⁹⁸ William H. Silby, Lt. Col. Commanding Regiment, "Regimental History of the 10th Iowa Volunteer Infantry," March 30, 1865, in *1866 Report of the Adjutant General of the State of Iowa*, 184–193, accessed February 9, 2016, http://iagenweb.org/civilwar/regiment/infantry/10th/10_iowa.htm.
²⁹⁹ Severt Tesdahl, translated by Sanford Tesdell, "The Civil War Letters of Private Severt Tesdall, Company 'A', 23rd Iowa Volunteer Infantry Regiment," accessed February 20, 2016, http://www.iowavalor.com/e107_files/downloads/the_civil_war_letters_of_private_severt_tesdall.pdf. Another set of letters written by a member of the 23rd Iowa Infantry from Story County are contained in *Dear Companion: The Civil War Letters of Silas I. Shearer*, ed. Harold D. Brinkman (Ames, Iowa: Sigler Printing &

Publishing, Inc., 1995). For another history of Company A, see *History of Story County* by W. O. Payne, 1911, 1:226–237, and Guy E. Logan's historical sketch of the 23rd Iowa Infantry @ http://iagenweb.org/civilwar/books/logan.htm.

[300] Payne, *History of Story County*, 1:237.

[301] Jens Ritland, "Jens Ritland's War Story," transcriber Nehemias Tjernagel, *The Story City Herald*, March 9, 16, 23, & 30, 1922. This history is also available online @ http://www.ritland-32nd-iowa.com/. For another history of Company K, see *History of Story County* by W. O. Payne, 1911, 1:238-249, and Guy E. Logan's historical sketch of the 32nd Iowa Infantry @ http://iagenweb.org/civilwar/books/logan.htm.

[302] In the "Life History of Thomas A. Lein, 1831–1907" by Isabel Lein Coates (n.p.n.d) received from Arvid Lein on March 29, 1985, Coates states, "Father, Jens Ritland, and Henry Henryson Berhow [Beroen] were comrades and pals in the army, in Story County, and in Norway where they were neighbors and friends. At the battle of Shilo, Henry Berhow [Beroen] was shot and killed at father's feet; Henry seemed to have a premonition that something would happen to him; he seemed so nervous and that was not like him; he had always been so fearless and brave; they noticed him tremble, so they suggested he get down at their feet, so he got down at father's feet; a few minutes later a bullet hit him and he died a short time after. The others were not hurt. Father took charge and looked after the burial and sent word to his folks."

[303] Meridian, Mississippi, was an important railroad center and the location of a Confederate arsenal, military hospital, and prisoner-of-war stockade.

[304] In Peder Gustav Tjernagel's memoir, *Follinglo Dog Book: From Milla to Chip the Third* (Elsworth, Iowa: Elsworth Publishing Company, 1909), 29, Tjernagel recalls the following conversation he had with Baar Beroen, Henry B. Henryson's father, "Then he told us about his son, Henry, who enlisted and went to the war and was killed on the battlefield. The poor old man was moved to tears while relating this sad story yet so fresh in his memory."

[305] In the *Story of the Thirty Second Iowa Infantry Volunteers*, compiled and published by John Scott in Nevada, Iowa, 1896, Scott states, "Oliver Johnson, died July 7, 1864, on the road home, on furlough."

[306] J. L. Anderson, "The Vacant Chair on the Farm: Soldier Husbands, Farm Wives, and the Iowa Home Front, 1861–1865," *The Annals of Iowa* 66 (Summer 2007): 242, accessed February 26, 2016, http://ir.uiowa.edu/cgi/viewcontent.cgi?article=1139&context=annals-of-iowa.

[307] Ibid., 258.

[308] *The Slater News*, August 7, 1918. An obituary for Torkel Romsa's wife, Martha, states, "After two years' residence in Iowa came the death of her husband as the result of an accident. Most of the men folks having gone to war, much of the work of the neighborhood fell upon the shoulders of Mr. Romsa and it was while thus employed, falling trees for wood, that he accidentally cut himself in the leg with an axe. He persisted working with the result that infection and blood poison set in and his death followed leaving the widow with four [three] children to provide for." In January 1863, their daughter, Josephine, was born, and now Martha had four young children to care for. Her obituary further states, "She mastered the situation and with help came through the multiplied duties. She again married [in December 1863], her second husband being Hemming Romsa [her brother-in-law]."

309 *The Story City Herald*, August 11, 1938.

310 Prior to moving to central Iowa in May 1862, Henry purchased 80 acres in Section 28 of Howard Township and a 6.6-acre timber lot in Section 6 of Milford Township on April 19, 1862. Reference: Story County Land Deeds, Book G, 510.

311 Erik Evans, also known as Erik Erickson Skoge, emigrated from Skånevik, Norway, on April 13, 1863. Reference: Skånevik *Ministerialbok* 1848–1869, 350, #7 accessed @ http://www.arkivverket.no/eng/content/view/full/629.

312 *The Roland Record*, August 15, 1934.

Railway Service Arrives

313 "Baltimore and Ohio Railroad," *Wikipedia*, accessed December 13, 2015, https://en.wikipedia.org/wiki/Baltimore_and_Ohio_Railroad.

314 *The Cambridge Leader*, December 14, 1911.

315 Havneros, *History of St. Petri Congregation*, 3.

316 Odd S. Lovoll, *Across the Deep Blue Sea: The Saga of Early Norwegian Immigrants* (St. Paul, Minnesota: Minnesota Historical Society Press, 2015), 146.

317 William H. Thompson, *Transportation in Iowa: A Historical Summary* (n.p.: Iowa Department of Transportation, 1989), 23.

318 See *A History of Iowa* by Leland L. Sage (Ames, Iowa: Iowa State University Press, 1974), 108–115, for a concise summary of the construction of the four rail lines.

319 "Iowa Central Air Line Railroad Report and Maps," from the *First Annual Report of the President and Directors to the Stockholders of the Iowa Central Air Line Railroad Company*, Chicago: Daily Press & Tribune Printing Establishment, 1858, 1–8, accessed December 30, 2015, http://publications.newberry.org/k12maps/module_11/images/Graff 2151.pdf.

320 For historical maps of Iowa, see http://alabamamaps.ua.edu/historicalmaps/us_states/iowa/index.html.

321 Allen, *A History of Story County, Iowa*, 314. For more information about Story County's efforts to obtain its first rail line, see Allen, 220–222 & 314–315, *Biographical and Historical Memoirs of Story County, Iowa*, 178–180, and W. O. Payne's *History of Story County, Iowa*, 1:263–268.

322 *The Story County Ægis*, June 22 & July 6, 1864.

323 The depot name, Ames Station, is included in the following news item from the November 23, 1864, edition of the *Story County Ægis*: "We learn that the Cedar Rapids and Missouri River company are about the surveying a line to determine the practicability of building a branch from Ames Station in this county to Des Moines."

324 C. E. Turner, Esq. *A History of the Town of Ames, Story County Iowa* (Ames, Iowa: Office of the Ames Intelligencer, 1871), 13. From the Ames Historical Society Web site, Ames, Iowa: "The first business in Ames, begun in the summer of 1865, was operated out of the railroad depot. Tradition has it that H. F. Kingsbury, station agent, express agent, and postmaster, added a small stock of groceries in the depot, thus becoming the earliest merchant in town. N. A. Rainbolt soon joined Mr. Kingsbury and after a short time became sole owner, moving the business to the corner of Onondaga and Duff." accessed April 29, 2016, http://ameshistory.org/.

325 *Story County Ægis*, December 14, 1864.

[326] Barbara Mask, "The first railroad bridge did not go all the way across the river," accessed December 19, 2015, http://www.cityoffulton.us/images/stories/pdf_files/historical_articles.

[327] See Lovoll, *Across the Deep Blue Sea*, 46–50, for further information on this topic.

[328] *Biographical and Historical Memoirs of Story County, Iowa*, 210.

[329] *Story County Ægis*, December 14, 1864.

[330] *The Nevada Representative*, January 5, 1874. For more information about the efforts of Ames citizens to obtain the narrow gauge rail line, see "Ames and the Narrow Gauge," cha. 32 in Payne's *History of Story County, Iowa*, 1:341–348.

[331] L. F. Andrews, *Pioneers of Polk County, Iowa, and Reminiscences of Early Days* (Des Moines: Baker-Trisier Company, 1908), 2:248–250, accessed January 2, 2016, http://iagenweb.org/polk/biographies/POPCI_Vol_2/F_M_Hubbell/F_M_Hubbell.pdf.

[332] In 1879, the Chicago & North Western Railway Company purchased the narrow gauge line and broadened it to a standard gauge railway.

[333] Story County Land Deeds, Book U, 640.

[334] Apland, in Nelson's *En kort historie af det forste norske settlement i Story og Polk counties, Iowa*, (1945), 14–15.

[335] *Biographical and Historical Memoirs of Story County, Iowa*, 216.

[336] Although the town of Roland traces its beginning to June 1873 when a Grange store was opened in the township, the town was not platted until 1881 when rail service reached Howard Township.

[337] *The Nevada Representative*, June 9, 16, 30, August 25, September 15, & December 8, 1875.

[338] *The Nevada Representative*, January 24, 1877.

[339] L. J. Ternagel, "More Light on Randall History," *The Story City Herald*, January 4, 1940.

[340] Ibid.

[341] Sheldahl, "Sheldahl Ancestors and Story City, Iowa." The Rasmus Larson family was among the families who founded the Norwegian settlement east of Fairview in Howard Township in June 1856.

[342] *The Nevada Representative*, July 10, 1878. On December 18, 1878, another letter from this person was published which describes all the businesses on main street.

[343] F. Q. Lee, "The New Courthouse—Principal Events Occurring During the 'Seventies,'" cha. 5 in *History of Hamilton County, Iowa* by J. W. Lee (Chicago: The J. S. Clark Publishing Company, 1912), 1:178.

[344] For more information about Callanan, see "History of Ellsworth, Iowa," accessed January 19, 2016, http://www.ellsworthia.us/callanan.htm.

[345] L. J. Tjernagel, "More Light on Randall History."

[346] Steve Sheldahl, "Lars Henryson, Pioneer of RFD?" January 1, 2001, addendum to *Searching for Roots: A Study of Ancestors* by Stephen A. Sheldahl, 2nd ed. (Northglenn, Colorado: Scudder Press, 2010).

[347] The town of Randall was platted when the Toledo & Northwestern Railroad originating in Tama, Iowa, completed its line to Randall in 1883. The town the railroad company platted was on land Lars Henryson purchased in 1874 located in the northeast quarter of Section 26, Ellsworth Township, but in 1864, Lars Henryson had also purchased land in the northwest quarter of Section 25 where he had platted and sold

lots. These lots were incorporated into the town of Randall when it was platted in 1883, but no homes were constructed on the lots until J. P. Anderson built a home on one of them in the early 1880s. For more information, see *Searching for Roots: A Study of Ancestors* by Stephen A. Sheldahl, 2nd ed. (Northglenn, Colorado: Scudder Press, 2010), 33; the 1896 plat map of Randall; and a "Short History of the Town of Randall" by G. O. Paulsrud, *The Story City Herald*, November 30, 1939.

More Glimpses of Pioneer Life

[348] Some of the memoirs will be published in Volume 2 of *The Central Iowa Norwegians*.

[349] *The Passing of the Prairie by a Fossil: Biographical Sketches of Central Iowa Pioneers and Civil War Veterans*, edited by Margaret Harstad Matzke, was published in cooperation with the Story City Historical Society (Bloomington, Indiana: AuthorHouse, 2009).

[350] Reprinted as *The Follinglo Dog Book* with prologue and epilogue by Peter Tjernagel Harstad (Iowa City: University of Iowa Press, 1999).

[351] Peder Gustav Tjernagel, *The Follinglo Dog Book: From Milla to Chip the Third*, 29–30.

[352] "An Old Setter and Union Soldier Passes Away," (n.p; 1898).

[353] Severeid, "Reminiscences of Pioneer Life by an Old Settler."

[354] Apland in Nelson's *En kort historie af det forste norske settlement i Story og Polk counties, Iowa*, (1945), 7.

[355] Takla, *"Stort norsk Settlement."*

[356] The Old Brick Capitol building was located where the Soldiers and Sailor's Monument now stands south of the present capitol. Completed in 1857, it was used until the Golden Dome Capitol was completed in 1884.

[357] Thompson, *Biography [of] Peder Christian Heggem and wife Anna Serina*, 8.

[358] Malinda Ann Heggem Thompson, "A Little History of the Family for the Relatives," *circa* 1930.

[359] Moran, "Pioneer Days in Southwest Story County."

[360] Mrs. Erick Johnson, "Reminiscence," *Story City Herald*, September 29, 1938.

[361] Payne, *History of Story County, Iowa*, 2:158.

[362] Nehemias Tjernagel, "Little Stories of Pioneer Days," January 4, 1923.

[363] Apland in Nelson's *En kort historie af det forste norske settlement i Story og Polk counties, Iowa*, (1945), 7-8.

[364] Severeid, "Reminiscences of Pioneer Life by an Old Settler."

[365] Nehemias Tjernagel, "H. B. Henryson's Pioneer Story."

[366] For more information on Story County mills, see "Nineteenth-Century Mills and Milling Industries in Story County, Iowa" by David N. Ballard, Jr., *Journal of the Iowa Archeological Society* 31 (1984).

[367] "Ole Braland's Pioneer Story" states, "… and he immediately hitched up his easygoing oxen and made for Marshalltown, where he hoped to be able to buy flour. It took him about three days to reach his destination. There were no speed limits in those days. The oxen set the pace." Reference: *The Story City Herald*, February 16, 1922.

[368] The author has not found any accounts of families living in the Northern Settlement milling wheat in Cambridge.

369 *The Cambridge Leader,* July 1, 1920.

370 Lee, *History of Hamilton County, Iowa,* 1:47–48. J. W. Lee was born in Tuscarawas County, Ohio, in 1845, and moved to Iowa with his parents in 1872.

371 Knutson, "Pioneer Days," 77.

372 McFarland, *A History of The Pioneer Era on the Iowa Prairies,* 153–154.

373 Apland in Nelson's *En kort historie af det forste norske settlement i Story og Polk counties, Iowa,* (1945), 9.

374 Nehemias Tjernagel, "H. B. Henryson's Pioneer Story."

375 Moran, "Pioneer Days in Southwest Story County."

376 Johnson, "A Reminiscence."

377 Arlen Twedt, comp. *Meskwaki Along the Upper South Skunk River: Pioneer References of Their Presence in Hamilton, Story, and Polk Counties* (self-published, Ankeny, Iowa: The Copy Shop, Ankeny, Iowa, 2012).

378 Lee, *History of Hamilton County, Iowa,* 1:402.

379 *Roland Record,* May 27, 1903.

380 Severeid, "Reminiscences of Pioneer Life by an Old Settler."

381 Thompson, "A Little History of the Family for the Relatives."

382 Payne, *History of Story County,* 1:112.

383 Knut Gjerset & Ludvig Hektoen, "Health Conditions and the Practice of Medicine Among the Early Norwegian Settlers, 1825–1865," *Norwegian-American Studies* 1 (1926), accessed April 1, 2016, http://www.naha.stolaf.edu/pubs/nas/volume01/vol1_01.htm.

384 Ibid.

385 Thompson, "A Little History of the Family for the Relatives." See "Little Stories of Pioneer Days" by Nehemias Tjernagel, *The Story City Herald,* January 4, 1923, for his comments about ague and malaria.

386 Larson, "Reverend Osmund Sheldahl, 1824–1900," *Larson Family History.*

387 *Biographical and Historical Memoirs of Story County, Iowa,* 207, 333–335.

388 *I Remember Slater, Iowa, 1889–1989,* 178.

389 The Branjord family forms the basis of a historical novel by Jerry L. Twedt, *Land of Promise, Land of Tears* (Bloomington, Indiana: AuthorHouse, 2012).

390 L. J. Tjernagel, "Scott Township History," *The Story City Herald 1940: Anniversary Number* (Story City, Iowa: The Story City Herald), 125.

391 Apland in Nelson's *En kort historie af det forste norske settlement i Story og Polk counties, Iowa,* (1945), 7.

392 Nehemias Tjernagel, "Little Stories of Pioneer Days," *Story City Herald,* April 5, 1923.

393 This information is from Arlen Twedt's unpublished "Early Settler Database," Central Iowa Norwegian Project, Ankeny, Iowa, 2017. Some death dates were estimated because the author was unable to confirm death dates.

394 Nehamis Tjernagel, "Angels of the Sick Room," *The Palimpsest* 23 (September 1942): 298. This journal article was based on an article Nehemias published in *The Story City Herald* on March 29, 1923.

395 Ibid., 299.

396 Elizabeth Y. Enstam, *Technical Leaflet: Using Memoirs to Write Local History* (American Association for State and Local History, November 1982, Leaflet #145).

397 An extensive bibliography of resources concerning the history of the central Iowa Norwegians will be published in Volume 3 of *The Central Iowa Norwegians*.

Organizing Church Congregations

398 Theodore C. Blegen, *Norwegian Migration to America: The American Transition* (Northfield, Minnesota: Norwegian-American Historical Association, 1940; New York: Haskell House Publishers Ltd., 1969), 100. For a brief review of this topic see "The Norwegian Immigrant and His Church" by Eugene L. Fevold, *Norwegian-American Studies*, 23 (1967): 3, http://www.naha.stolaf.edu/pubs/nas/volume23/index.htm. For more information see *The Lutherans in North America* edited by E. Clifford Nelson (Philadelphia: Fortress Press, rev. ed., 1980).

399 Travaas, "A Little About the First Settlers in Story County," 223–224.

400 Holand, *"Stavanger og Hordaland Kolonien i Midtre Iowa,"* 463.

401 Rev. Hans O. Oppedal, "History of St. Paul's Church Near Rosendale," *The Story City Herald*, July 9, 1936.

402 Ole Anfinson was ordained in the Northern Illinois Synod in 1855, Osmund Sheldahl was ordained in the Northern Illinois Synod in 1859 and in the Scandinavian Augustana Synod in 1860, and Nils Amlund was ordained in the Norwegian Synod in 1860.

403 Both pastors also helped organize other congregations in central Iowa before 1880 which were outside the settlement areas described in this history.

404 Pastor O. M. Norlie, *Norsk Lutherske Menigheter i America: 1843–1916* (Minneapolis, Minnesota: Augsburg Publishing House, 1918), 1:342–350, 387–393. J. H. Myre served the Palestine congregation from 1876 to 1880 and the Bethlehem congregation from 1878 to 1880. O. A. Sauer served the Fjeldberg congregation from 1869 to 1872. M. Fr. Wiese served the Fjeldberg congregation from 1874 to 1890. Endre Johannessen served the Salem congregation from 1870 to 1873 and the Bethel and Lincoln congregations from 1871 to 1875. Ingvald Eisteinsen served the Bethel and Lincoln congregations from 1875 to 1878 and the Salem congregation from 1874 to 1883. H. Hendrickson served the Bethel, Salem, and Lincoln congregations from 1878 to 1882. J. J. Tackle served the Trinity congregation from 1876 to 1879, the St. Paul congregation from 1876 to 1878, and the Mud Lake congregation from 1877 to 1879 when it dissolved. Neh. Christensen served the Trinity and St. Paul congregations from 1879 to 1882.

405 The other congregations they helped organize up through 1880 were located in Homer 1869, Webster City 1870, Nevada 1870, Brushy Creek 1872, Tipton 1872, Hamilton *circa* 1874, Des Moines 1876, and Mud Lake 1877. Reference: Norlie, *Norsk Lutherske Menigheter i America*, 348-349, 387–388, 399, 404, 428.

406 See "Processes of Modernization in Norway in the 19th Century: 1814–1884," chap. 2 in *Multiple Modernities: A Tale of Scandinavian Experiences* by Gunnar Skirbekk (The Chinese University of Hong Kong: The Chinese Press, 2011), 19–44, for a discussion of the Haugean movement in Norway during the late 17th and early 18th centuries. Skirbekk states, "Haugianism was at once a religious movement (with Lutheranism, but against official Lutheranism) and a class movement (against Lutheran state officials....). Haugianism combined charismatic leadership and a national network of solidarity

(between 'brethren and sisters,' not individualistically). The Haugians promoted modernizing activities and learning processes on a broad scale: economic activities, sociopolitical organization, training in public speaking in assemblies (women were welcome both as speakers and leaders), promoting literacy and thereby creating an alternative public sphere—for instance, presumably as many as one in four Norwegian citizens, inclusive of new-born infants and the elderly, bought a copy of Hauge's writings at a time of hunger and hardship."

[407] Norlie, *Norsk Lutherske Menigheter i America*, 320, map.

[408] Nelson's 1905 history states this shed was constructed on Oley Fatland's land. Anfin Apland's 1945 re-compiled, corrected and added to edition of Nelson's 1905 history also states it was on Fatland's land. Oley Fatland's land was one mile north of the Palestine Lutheran Church, the NW¼ of Section 30, Union Township.

[409] An 1883 platmap of Union Township shows the school building one mile east of the church in the southwest corner of Section 29 in the middle of school district No. 2. It was known locally as the Apland school house. References: *Cambridge, Iowa: The First 150 Years*, 44 (includes photograph of the school) and *Cambridge, Iowa: 150 Years of Education in Cambridge and Union Township, Story County, Iowa*, 112 (includes the same photograph and a remembrance of the school by a former student).

[410] Maland, *Eighty-fifth Anniversary of the Palestine Lutheran Congregation*, 4.

[411] Havneros states, "In the second year when the pastor came to visit the congregation, it had the joy of celebrating a festive occasion, namely confirmation. Rasmus Larson Tungesvig, one of the settlers in Fairview, had built a large roomy barn, and in it the first confirmation service was held." Reference: Havneros, *History of St. Petri Congregation*, 6.

[412] The Sheldall School house has been preserved as a museum in Story City, Iowa.

[413] Havneros, *History of St. Petri Congregation*, 9.

[414] *The Story City Herald*, January 4, 1923.

[415] The original location was close to where the stop sign at the end of the I-35 southbound exit ramp to Story City is located today.

[416] *Brief Centennial History of the Fjeldberg Lutheran Church, Huxley, Iowa* (Huxley, Iowa: n.p., 1965), 2.

[417] Havneros, *History of St. Petri Congregation*, 7.

[418] Ibid., 12.

[419] *Salem Lutheran Church: Seventy-fifth Anniversary 1868–1943* (Roland, Iowa: n.p.), 17.

[420] The *Decorah-Posten* newspaper was founded in Decorah, Iowa, in 1874.

[421] Maland, *Eighty-fifth Anniversary of the Palestine Lutheran Congregation*, 19.

[422] Sheldall School, Story City Historical Society, *Information Sheet* [available at the schoolhouse located at the northwest corner of Broad and Hillcrest in Story City, Iowa], n.d.

[423] Pastor Paulsrud may have been referring to Ole J. Olson's support of Jewell Lutheran College founded in 1893 by the Jewell Lutheran College Association. In 1897, the college and all of its property was transferred to the Iowa District of the Hauge Synod of which Pastor Paulsrud was a member. In 1905, Pastor Paulsrud was president of the college's Board of Trustees and a member of the Executive Committee. The college was closed in 1925, and the property was purchased by the local school district.

The South Skunk River Watershed

424 Information about the history of the bridge built in 1876 is contained in a National Register of Historic Places Inventory Nomination Form prepared by Sven B. Cafvert, Ames Audubon Society, n.d., found in the David Gradwohl Papers, Box 5, Folder 9, Special Collections Department, Parks Library, Iowa State University, Ames, Iowa.

425 Larson, "From Whence We Came," *Larson Family History*.

426 Johnson Brigham, *Des Moines: The Pioneer of Municipal Progress and Reform of the Middle West together with the History of Polk County, Iowa* (Chicago, The S. J. Clarke Publishing Company, 1911), 1:115. Johnson states, "Fort Des Moines then had a population of about 650 or half that of Iowa City, the State Capital." In June 1853, a Federal Land Office was opened in Ft. Des Moines, and its opening combined with the decision to move the state capital to Ft. Des Moines and the anticipation of railway service arriving later, the city and county was destined to grow quickly. Later in Chapter XII, "Looking Backward on Fort Des Moines in the Fifties," Brigham states, "In 1857, when Des Moines became the State Capital, it had grown to nearly 5,000, and the county had a population estimated at over 10,000."

427 On January 25, 1855, the Fifth General Assembly approved moving the state capitol to a site "within two miles of the junction of the Des Moines and Racoon rivers in Polk County."

428 Marshall, the orginal name of the town, was platted in August 1853, and the next year the first house was erected in the new town. See *Description and History of Marshall County, Iowa, 1862* (Marshalltown, Iowa: Taylor & Barnhart, Publishers, Chapin & Co., Printers, 1862), and *The History of Marshall County, Iowa, A History of the County, its Cities, Towns, Etc.* (Chicago, Western Historical Company, 1878) for more information about Marshalltown.

429 Within Lafayette Township is a 40-acre tract of prairie wetland, Doolittle Prairie State Preserve, containing nine prairie potholes. The preserve is located two and one-half miles south of Story City and is open to the public. An excellent aerial view of the potholes can be seen at http://www.igsb.uiowa.edu/Browse/landscap/landscap.htm, and information about the preserve can be found by searching for "Doolittle" at http://www.storycountyiowa.gov/. The prairie pothole characteristics of Lafayette Township can also be seen using Google Earth.

430 *South Skunk River Watershed Rapid Watershed Assessment* (United States Department of Agriculture, May 2008), accessed May 2, 2016http://www.nrcs.usda.gov/Internet/FSE_DOCUMENTS/nrcs142p2_007355.pdf.

431 The South Skunk River watershed covers most of Story County. The southern one-third of Palestine Township in the southwest corner of the county is outside of the watershed, and a larger area in the northeast corner of the county including Middle Minerva Creek is also outside the watershed.

432 H. D. Ballard, "Early Days in Howard," in *History of Story County, Iowa: A Record of Settlement, Organization, Progress and Achievement*, (Chicago: The S. J. Clarke Publishing Co., 1911), 2: 157.

433 H. H. Boyes, "Early Days," in *Atlas of Story County, Iowa* (Davenport, Iowa: The Huebinger Surveying and Map Publishing Co., 1902), part I-4.

434 Swamp or overflow land is land the federal government designated unfit for cultivation and deeded to the state of Iowa under the Swamp Land Act of 1850. The state of Iowa in turn deeded the land to the counties who sold it to purchasers holding certificates of pre-emption who agreed to drain the land and convert it to agricultural and other uses.

435 *Biographical and Historical Memoirs of Story County, Iowa*, 118.

436 Ibid., 119.

437 J. H. Frandsen, "J. H. Frandsen Tells of School Experiences at County School" in *The Story City Herald Anniversary Number: A Quintuplet Celebration, 1940* (Story City, Iowa: Paul A. Olson & Sons, Publishers, 1940), 47, supplement to *The Story City Herald*, October 24, 1940.

438 Phillip E. Frandson, "Lafayette Township: The Geography of a Portion of Central Iowa" by Phillip E. Frandson (master's thesis, University of Nebraska, 1948), 68.

439 Leslie Hewes & Phillip E. Frandson, "Occupying the Wet Prairie: The Role of Artificial Drainage in Story County, Iowa," *Annals of the Association of American Geographers* 40, no. 1 (March 1952): 41.

440 Larson, "Reverend Osmund Sheldahl 1824–1900," *Larson Family History*.

441 Peterson, *Iowa: The Rivers of Her Valleys*, 165.

442 *The Story County Ægis*, July 12, 1865.

443 *The Story County Ægis*, September 9, 1865.

444 *The Story County Ægis*, November 9, 1866.

445 "Oley and Ingeborg Nelson" in *I Remember Slater, Iowa* (Lake Mills, Iowa: Graphic Publishing Company, Inc., 1989), 157.

446 *The Story County Ægis*, January 23, 1868. The January 9, 1868, report from the supervisors' meeting stated, "On Tuesday they arranged a tariff for the Skunk River Bridge at Cambridge which it is hoped will 'give greater satisfaction than that' heretofore existing. In consideration of three hundred dollars from the county treasury to Mr. Billings, the proprietor under license, this gentleman is to issue family passes good for one year to *bona fide* residents of the county at the rate of $1.00. This ticket will allow the head of a family, and all its members, free passage on presentation across the bridge. Transient travelers will pay the same toll as heretofore established." In the January 30, 1868, issue of the newspaper, the following letter from the *Marshall Times* appeared: "Out in Story County, at the famous crossing of the 'Skunk Bottom,' where so many of us have waded to the armpits, or 'got slewed,' the Supervisors are attempting to build a substantial crossway, or series of bridges and embankments. Lately, it was determined to change the toll in order to eke out the building fund. In pursuance of this, a sign was set up indicating the various amounts assessed upon all who pass that way. From this bill of fare we copy the following item, and if we haven't got it right, bro. Brainard, of the *Ægis* can correct it: '*Four horse mule or ox buggy or wagon 50 cts.*' If that isn't 'a legend strange and vague,' the Court fails to understand herself!"

447 Ballard, "Nineteenth-Century Mills," 139.

448 During their June 1866 meeting, the Board of Supervisors passed the following resolution: "That the sum of three hundred dollars be appropriated out of the Bridge Fund for the purpose of building a bridge over Skunk River on the S. line of Sec. 12, T 85, R 24, said bridge to be supported by two stone abutments and one pier in the middle and to be completed by Jan. 1st 1867 …" It was, apparently, not completed during 1867

because at the board's January 1868 meeting, the following resolution was passed: "That the sum of one hundred dollars be appropriated out of the Bridge Fund and placed in the hands of W. A. Wier to be expended in the completion of the bridge across Skunk River near Story City and that he make report, under oath, of his proceedings at the June session of this Board, 1868." References: *Story County Ægis* June 22, 1866 & January 16, 1868. Copies of Nevada's newspaper from June 1868 through April 1870 were not preserved, so it is not known when the bridge was completed. Many years later, H. B. Henryson recalled the following memory from 1858 when his parents moved to Story County: "Mr. Henryson remembers that the first time he crossed the Skunk River, July 2, 1858, it by boat, and the stream was swollen to a width of 83 rods." Reference: *The Story City Herald*, February 23, 1922.

[449] "Rasmus Sheldall's Pioneer Story" recorded by Nehemias Tjernagel (*The Story City Herald*, June 22, 1922) states, "The big bridge across the river near-by [the Sheldall farm] was always called Grindheim Bridge." Earlier in the article it states, "Though the elder Sheldall [Rasmus' father] was born on the gaard Sheldall in Norway, and used the name in writing, he was commonly called Lars Grindheim because of his residence for a period at the gaard Grindheim. Both are 'gaarde' (farms) in the immediate vicinity of each other in the eastern Etne, Norway."

[450] Nehemias Tjernagel, "Little Stories of Pioneer Days," *The Story City Herald*, October 12, 1922, "A few yards north of the old Grindheim bridge was situated the ford where early settlers used to cross the river."

[451] Members of the scouting party are listed in six different sources (see note #141), and John M. Mason is the only author who includes Erick Sheldahl as a member of the scouting party.

[452] *Roland Record*, June 18, 1902.

[453] The author visited Lisbon, Illinois, for the first time during the summer of 1978 and was struck by the similarity of the area to where he had grown up south of Roland, Iowa.

[454] Battle, "Nettle Creek Township," 285.

[455] Isaac Hoge, "History of Nettle Creek Township" in *History of Grundy County* (Munsell Publishing Company, 1914), accessed December 3, 2007, http://grundycountyil.org/history/nettlecreektwp.php.

[456] *Roland Record*, October 19, 1911.

[457] *Biographical and Historical Memoirs of Story County, Iowa*, 223, "Very soon a Grange store was proposed, and in June, 1873, Jonas Duea & Co. built the store on the site of the present schoolhouse. The associates of Mr. Duea were John Evenson, Paul Thompson, and Abel Oleson. After several changes in the firm, a new building was erected opposite the Norwegian Lutheran Church for the store in which Mr. Evenson and Mr. Duea were the active spirits." The church was built in 1874, so Thompson was apparently only a partner in the Grange store for a short time.

[458] Allen, *A History of Story County, Iowa*, 381.

[459] Ibid., 340.

[460] Ibid., 339.

"it was a matter of deliberate colonization"

[461] Payne, *History of Story County*, 1:23.
[462] *The Story County Aegis*, June 15, 1866.
[463] Hull, *Census of Iowa for 1880*, 583, table.
[464] Blegen, *Norwegian Migration to America: 1825–1860*, 350.
[465] All of the 382 emigrants whose parishes are listed in this table have been documented in parish records, farm history books [*bygdeboker*], or other sources.
[466] *Emigranter pr år* 1814–1929, chart from "Norway The Crossing: USA Statistics," accessed May 23, 2016, http://digitalarkivet.uib.no/utstilling/eng/usa.htm.
[467] *The Story County Representative*, June 25, 1874.
[468] Twedt, "Early Settler Database."
[469] Apland, in Nelson's *En kort historie af det forste norske settlement i Story og Polk counties, Iowa*, (1945), 10.
[470] "Walnut Grove Community" (n.p.,n.d.), received from Maxine Thomason, niece of Glen Severson, July 2003.
[471] *The Slater News*, April 9, 1924. Erasmus immigrated in 1856 and Jonas immigrated in 1864. Erasmus purchased an 11-acre timber lot northwest of Cambridge on June 29, 1864, and Jonas purchased 60 acres of land in the same section on July 20, 1864. Reference: Story County Land Deed Index, Book K, 514 & 516.
[472] *The Cambridge Leader*, September 27, 1934.
[473] Glen Severson, "Rasmus Jonsen and Anne Margrethe Berentsen: My Norwegian Grandparents," probably written before 1929, received with correspondence from Joyce Walker, daughter of Glen Severson, August 1, 2013.
[474] Larson, Fred W., *The Story of the Larson Clan* (1936); additions by Silas B. Larson January, 1972; and edited by Darryl D. Larson, June 1988. Later in the biography it states, "On July 10, 1866, Jonas and one of the other wagons drove into the yard of Erasmus Lewis, a friend of Jonas' from Norway. But scarcely had they gotten their families into the cabin and the teams unhitched when a fierce storm and severe wind struck the place, thus giving them an early introduction to what the storms over the bleak and bare prairies of the early days here could do to the pioneers."
[475] Bertha Barnes Peterson, "Introduction," in *History of the Lande Clan* [1968 ed.], (n.p., 1932).
[476] *The Nevada Representative*, April 2, 1879.
[477] The families may have moved to central Iowa at the encouragement of H. O. Hendrickson who moved to Des Moines in the spring of 1866. Hendrickson was a boyhood friend of Oley Nelson who along with his mother was one of the families who moved from Wisconsin to the Southern Settlement in 1867. Reference: *The Slater News*, November 28, 1934. Another family who could have encouraged the families to move is Thomas and Elizabeth Nelson who purchased land in Lincoln Township in June 1866. References: Polk County Land Deeds, Book W, 600 & *The Slater News*, April 30, 1903.
[478] Some of the families who moved to central Iowa may have been members of a church congregation Pastor P. A. Rasmussen from Lisbon, Illinois, helped organize in 1854, the Primrose congregation which Pastor Rasmussen served until 1860. Reference: Norlie, *Norsk Lutherske Menigheter i America*, 102–103. In 1859, Pastor Rasmussen went to Norway and met two recent seminary graduates, John Fjeld and Nils Amlund, who were willing to become pastors in the United States. Fjeld accepted a call to Dane County

where he served the Primrose congregation from 1860 to 1883. Amlund accepted a call to Story County, Iowa, where he served a congregation Pastor Rasmussen helped organize in 1857, the St. Petri congregation, and served until Pastor Amlund became its pastor in 1860. Since Pastor Rasmussen served the Primrose and St. Petri congregations up until 1860, he could also have informed families in the Primrose congregation about settlement opportunities in central Iowa.

[479] Four of the families were the Halvor Erickson, Elling Halverson, Ole Halverson, and William Oskerson families. References: *A Partial Genealogy of the Family of Ben and Lisa Erickson of Huxley and Eagle Grove, Iowa* by Paul J. Hermann (Ames, Iowa: n.p., March 1972), 56–62, and email messages from Paul Hermann to the author June 17 & 18, 2002. Other Wisconsin families who purchased land in Lincoln Township, Polk County, in 1867 and who were likely in the caravan were the Helga Helgeson, Oley Nelson, Thomas Nervig, and Anon T. Nervig families. There could have been other families, too, based on a review of the 1870 Census and land records for Lincoln Township. Hermann's genealogy contains the following information about Ole Halverson: "The story is told about Ole coming to Iowa in a covered wagon and pulling onto his land, there was not a tree on the place and no house. It was necessary to live in the covered wagon until some kind of shelter could be erected. That first shelter was a log cabin built from trees that were cut from the creek area miles to the west of the farm. They had to travel seven or eight miles to Polk City, the nearest town, to buy supplies and sell produce."

[480] John P. Herrick, "Oley Nelson—An Unforgettable Character," *Annals of Iowa* 25, no. 2 (1943): 118. This article also contains an interesting stenographic report of an extemporaneous talk Oley Nelson gave at a meeting of the Pioneer Lawmakers Association of Iowa in Des Moines on March 17, 1921.

[481] Twedt, "Early Settler Database."

[482] Knutson, "Pioneer Days," 75.

[483] Havneros, *History of St. Petri Congregation*, 16.

[484] Nehemias Tjernagel's list of pioneers was published in *The Story City Herald* on July 20 & 27 & August 3, 1922.

[485] John Fardal, "The 'Sognings' came to Hamilton County 80 years ago this month: And three of original party are still living," transcriber Mrs. Odean Monson, *The Story City Hereald*, June 2, 1949.

[486] J. O. Ringstad, "History of Trinity Lutheran Church," *The Ellsworth News*, June 25, 1925.

[487] Arlen Twedt, "Emigration From Helvik," in *Emigration from Helvik: Descendants of Anders Axelson (Mowat) Helvik Who Emigrated to Iowa 1852–1892* (Ankeny, Iowa: n.p., 1993), 1–7.

[488] *Digitalarkivet* [The National Archives of Norway], "Norwegians in Iowa in United States 1880 Census," accessed June 2, 2016, http://gda.arkivverket.no/cgi-win/WebMeta.exe?spraak=e and 1880 Census for Hardin County.

[489] Qualey, *Norwegian Settlement in the United States*, 228–229.

Becoming a Settled Prairie

[490] *The Story County Aegis*, August 10, 1866.

[491] A. T. Andreas' *Illustrated Historical Atlas of the State of Iowa, 1875* (Chicago: Lakeside Press, 1875), 65.

[492] Payne, *History of Story County, Iowa*, 2:160.

[493] Margaret Nelson & Jeffrey Freeland Nelson, untitled article submitted for the *Iowa Barn Foundation Magazine*, received in email correspondance from Margaret Nelson, September 3, 2009.

[494] *Biographical and Historical Memoirs of Story County, Iowa*, 279. See Ronna Lawless's article in *The Tri-County Times*, September 24, 2015, for more information about the Apland barn which has been featured on the Iowa Barn Foundation's barn tour, accessed June 9, 2016, http://tricountytimes.com/news/five-story-county-barns-featured-tour-weekend.html.

[495] Allen, *A History of Story County, Iowa*, 380.

[496] *The Nevada Representative*, July 30, 1879.

[497] In an annual report to the Circut Court of Story County in November 1880, the administrator of Ole Apland's estate reported $59,000 for mortgage and contract notes. Reference: Ole Apland's Probate Record, Story County Courthouse, Nevada, Iowa.

[498] Paul Haugland to Hans Kjærland, January 17, 1876, in *Kvinnhers-minne: Årbok for Kvinnherad VIII*, ed. Ivar Vaage (Husnes, Norway: Kvinnherad Sogelag og Husness Mållag, 1996), 104–106.

[499] Peder Gustav Tjernagel, *The Follinglo Dog Book: From Milla to Chip the Third*, 58.

[500] *The Nevada Representative*, May 26 & June 2, 1880.

[501] Ibid., May 26, 1880.

[502] Ibid., May 19, 1880.

[503] W. C. B. Allen & W. A. Stinchcomb, "Resources & Wealth of Story County," *The Nevada Representative*, May 26, 1880.

[504] *Digitalarkivet* [The National Archives of Norway], "Norwegians in Iowa in the United States 1880 Census," accessed March 23, 2004, http://gda.arkivverket.no/cgi-win/WebMeta.exe. The 1880 Federal Census was reviewed for Concord Township because the *Digitalarkivet* database does not include Hardin County.

[505] Hull, *Census of Iowa for 1880*, 583–584, table.

"good loyal citizens"

[506] Ballard, "Early Days in Howard," 2:162.

Appendix A

[507] In addition to Naeseth's *Norwegian Immigrants to the United States*, the following sources were used for reference: *"Den Tidlege Utvandringa Frå Indre Sunnhordland"* by Ståle Dyrvik, *Etne Sogelag Årsskrift 1986* [Etne, Norway], 69 (Table 1), and "The Digitized Parish Registers" @ http://www.arkivverket.no/. In Table 1, Dyrvik shows 40 people emigrated from Etne, Skånevik, Fjelberg, and Kvinnherad during 1836–1844, but only 23 of these people are on passenger lists in Naeseth. In the Skånevik parish records, Amund Johanneson Sævereid and Ingebor Ericksdatter and their four children are

recorded as immigrating to the United States, but they are not reflected in Table 1 nor are they on a passenger list in Naeseth. Also, Torbjørn Larsen Tungesvik and Kari Eriksdatter and daughter are not recorded as immigrants to the United States in the Skånevik or Etne parish records or by Dyrvik, but they are on a passenger list in Naeseth. They moved to the Stavanger parish in 1842 and emigrated in 1843.

[508] Mason, "Biography of Nils Hanson Veste also known as Nelson Hanson."
[509] Ibid., 14, note 38.
[510] Ibid., 2–5.

Appendix B

[511] George T. Flom, *A History of Norwegian Immigration to the United States: From the Earliest Beginning down to the Year 1848* (Iowa City, Iowa: Privately Printed, 1909), 355 & 93.

[512] Hans Gangstø, email to the author, February 10, 2005. Gangstø states, "The *bygdebook* for Strand, volume 3, page 1,307, has a listing of Johannes Johannessen Hidle. There is no mention of him going to Fjelberg, and, as far as I can find, there is no connection in the family to Fjelberg."

[513] Martin Ulvestad, *Nordmændene i Amerika* (Minneapolis, Minnesota: History Book Company's forlag, 1907), 18.

[514] Haugland, *Skåneviksoga*, vol. 3, 71, and 1900 United States Census.

[515] Arlen Twedt, Steve Sheldahl, and Jim Mason, "Why Lisbon, Illinois?" (n.p., 2010), an unpublished paper in the archives of the Norwegian-American Historical Association, Northfield, Minnesota.

[516] Mason, "Biography of Nils Hanson Veste also known as Nelson Hanson."
[517] *The Story City Herald* (Story City, Iowa), February 16, 1928.
[518] *Clay Center Times* (Clay Center, Kansas), October 3, 1901.
[519] *Clay Center Times* (Clay County, Kansas), October 6, 1904.
[520] *Morris Daily Herald* (Morris, Illinois), October 13, 1942.
[521] *Biographical and Historical Memoirs of Story County, Iowa*, 420–421.

Appendix C

[522] Osmund emigrated in 1845, Lars, Erik, and Rasmus emigrated in 1847, and Haldor emigrated ca. 1869.

[523] Holand, *"Stavanger og Hordaland Kolonien i Midtre Iowa,"* 458.
[524] Larson, "Reverend Osmund Sheldahl 1824–1900," *Larson Family History*.
[525] Dyrvik, *"Den Tidlege Utvandringa Frå Indre Sunnhordland,"* 75.
[526] Flom, *A History of Norwegian Immigration to the United States*, 52, 56, 61–62.
[527] Skålnes, *"The Emigration from Skånevik,"* 100.
[528] Anders Haugland, *Skåneviksoga: Gardar og ætter Sævareid-Skånevik*, vol. 3 (Skånevik, Norway: Skånevik bygdeboknemnd, 1988), 167, and Ståle Dyrvik, *Etnesoga: Folket i Stødle sokn*, vol. 4 (Etne, Norway: Etne Kommune, 1995), 272.
[529] Payne, *History of Story County, Iowa*, 2:160.
[530] Henderson, *Historical Events and Reminiscences of the St. Petri Lutheran Congregation*, 16.
[531] Larson, "From Whence We Came," *Larson Family History*.

532 *The* [Des Moines] *Register and Leader*, October 13, 1905.

Appendix D

533 Original Patents of Land, Fort Des Moines, Vol. 8, 1849–1859, Microfilm ARC #19, State Historical Society of Iowa Research Center, Des Moines, Iowa.

534 Story County Land Deeds, Book S, 579. According to the deed filed October 30, 1871, Enoch Johnson received ownership to the 40 acres on December 10, 1869 under the Homestead Act of 1862, Homestead Certificate Number 33, Application 80. This is the only example the author has found of a central Iowa Norwegian receiving land under the Homestead Act.

Appendix F

535 Morris is 11 miles southeast of Lisbon and a slightly longer distance from the northwest area of Nettle Creek Township where many of the early central Iowa Norwegian families lived.

536 See the histories by Oley Nelson, Erik Travaas, Knut Takla, John M. Mason, M. O. Rod, and Hjalmar Rued Holand in this volume of *The Central Iowa Norwegians*.

537 Ole E. Rølvagg, *Concerning Our Heritage*, trans. Solveig Zempel (Northfield, Minnesota: The Norwegian-American Historical Association, 1998), 41.

538 Blegen, *Norwegian Migration to America: The American Transition*, 480–481.

539 See "Hans Nielsen Hauge: His ethics and some consequences of his work" by Sigbjørn Ravnåsen, 2004, for more information about Hauge's life, accessed March 20, 2016, http://www.disciplenations.org/article/pdf-hans-nielsen-hauge-ethics-consequences-work/.

540 Blegen, *Norwegian Migration to America: The American Transition*, 132.

541 For information about Hans Nielsen Hauge and Eielsen, see "Hans Nielsen Hauge: His ethics and some consequences of his work" by Sigbjørn Ravnåsen, 2004, accessed March 20, 2016, http://www.disciplenations.org/article/pdf-hans-nielsen-hauge-ethics-consequences-work/; *Norwegian American Lutheranism Up to 1872* by J. Magnus Rohne (New York: The Macmillan Company, 1926), 35–41; and Chapter 5, The Emerging Church, by Theodore C. Blegen in the *Norwegian Migration to America: The American Transition* (Northfield, Minnesota: The Norwegian-American Historical Association, 1940), 131–137.

542 E. Clifford Nelson & Eugene L. Fevold, *The Lutheran Church Among Norwegian-Americans: A History of the Evangelical Lutheran Church* (Minneapolis, Minnesota: Augsburg Publishing House, 1960), 1:18.

543 Larson, "From Whence We Came," *Larson Family History*.

544 For background on the settlement of the frontier, see: "The Significance of the Frontier in American History" by Frederick Jackson Turner, 1893, accessed March 25, 2016, http://www.gutenberg.org/ebooks/22994; Chapter 3, Immigration & Expansion, in *The Immigrant in American History* by Marcus Lee Hansen (Harvard University Press, 1840, 53–76; and Chapter 7, "They rushed from place to place," in *From Peasants to Farmers* by Jon Gjerde (Cambridge University Press, 1985), 137–167.

Lisbon, Illinois: A Gateway to the West
by Jim Mason

[1] A. T. Andreas, *History of Cook County, Illinois, From the Earliest Period to the Present Time* (Chicago: A. T. Andreas, Publisher, 1884); Bessie Louise Pierce, *A History of Chicago, Volume I. The Beginning of a City, 1673–1848* (New York: Alfred A. Knopf, 1937); Odd Lovoll, *A Century of Urban Life. The Norwegians in Chicago before 1930* (Northfield: The Norwegian-American Historical Association, 1988).

[2] C. A. Clausen, translator and editor, *A Chronicle of Immigrant Life. Svein Nilsson's Articles in Billed-Magazin, 1868–1870* (Northfield: Norwegian-American Historical Association, 1982), 128.

[3] *Ibid.*, 79.

[4] Gunnar J. Malmin, ed., *America in the Forties. The Letters of Ole Munch Raeder* (Minneapolis: University of Minnesota Press, 1929), 43–44.

[5] E. Clifford Nelson, ed., *A Pioneer Churchman. J. E. C. Dietrichson in Wisconsin, 1844–1850* (New York: Twayne Publisher, Inc., 1973), 117.

[6] References on Hallstein Torrison are Lovoll, *A Century of Urban Life*, 12, 15; Rasmus B. Anderson, *The First Chapter of Norwegian Immigration, (1821–1840). Its Causes and Results* (Madison, Wisconsin: published by the author, 1896), 194–195; George T. Flom, *A History of Norwegian Immigration to The United States* (Iowa City: Privately Printed, 1909), 94–95; Anders Haugland, *Skåneviksoga* 6 (Skånevik Bygdeboknemnd, 1998), 135–140.

[7] Milo M. Quaife, *Chicago's Highways Old and New. From Indian Trail to Motor Road* (Chicago: D. F. Keller & Company, 1923), 72–86.

[8] Kerry A. Trask, *Black Hawk. The Battle for the Heart of America* (New York: Henry Holt and Company, 2006); R. David Edmunds, *The Potawatomis. Keepers of the Fire* (Norman: University of Oklahoma Press, 1978).

[9] Lois Kimball Mathews, *The Expansion of New England. The Spread of New England Settlement and Institutions to the Mississippi River 1620–1865* (1909, 1936) (New York: Russell & Russell, Inc., 1962), 261.

[10] *Ibid.*, 211–214; Herman R. Muelder, *Fighters for Freedom. The History of Anti-Slavery Activities of Men and Women Associated with Knox College* (New York: Columbia University Press, 1959), 84–114.

[11] Mathilde Rasmussen, *A Brief History of the P. A. Rasmussen Family* (Minneapolis: privately printed, 1945), 9.

[12] Muelder, *Fighters for Freedom*, 100–101.

[13] Ruth Clark May, "Abolitionists and The Underground Railroad" in Kathy Farren, editor, *A Bicentennial History of Kendall County, Illinois* (Yorkville: Kendall County Bicentennial Commission, 1976), 125–145; Muelder, *Fighters for Freedom*, 192–220.

[14] May, "Abolitionists and the Underground Railroad," 131, 150, 151; Anderson, *The Firest Chapter of Norwegian Immigration*, 109–127.

[15] E. W. Hicks, *History of Kendall County, Illinois...* (Aurora: Knickerbocker & Hodges, 1877); Newton Bateman and Paul Selby, *Historical Encyclopedia of Illinois and History of Kendall County* II (Chicago: Munsell Publishing Company, 1914); Farren, *A Bicentennial History of Kendall County*.

[16] Mrs. John L. Shufelt, *When Lisbon Was a Prairie* (Yorkville, Illinois: The Kendall County Record, 1917), unpaged.

[17] Helen Stine Ullrich, *This is Grundy County its History from Beginning to 1968* (Morris: Grundy County Board of Supervisors, 1968); Bateman and Selby, *Historical Encyclopedia*; Farren, *A Bicentennial History of Kendall County*; Special Authors and Contributors, *History of Grundy County Illinois* (Chicago: Munsell Publishing Company, 1914); Carl Ortwin Sauer, *Geography of the Upper Illinois Valley and History of Development* (Urbana: Illinois State Geological Survey, 1916), 144 ff.

[18] Charles H. Brown, *William Cullen Bryant* (New York: Charles Scribner's Sons, 1971), 205–207; 217–218; 323–324; Keth Huntress and Fred W. Lorch, "Bryant and Illinois: Further Letters of the Poet's Family," *The New England Quarterly*, 16 (December, 1943), 634–647.

[19] William Cullen Bryant, "The Prairies," in F. O. Matthiessen, ed., *The Oxford Book of American Verse* (New York: Oxford University Press, 1950), 61–65.

[20] William Cullen Bryant, *Letters of a Traveller; or, Notes of Things Seen in Europe and America* (London: Richard Bentley, 1850), 262–263.

[21] Henry Wadsworth Longfellow, "The Song of Hiawatha," *The Poems of Henry Wadsworth Longfellow* (New York: Random House, The Modern Library, n.d.), 259. For an exploration of this theme in early nineteenth century American literature see Roy Harvey Pearce, *The Savages of America. A Study of the Indian and the Idea of Civilization* (Baltimore: The Johns Hopkins press, 1953), 169–195.

[22] Malmin, *America in the Forties.*, 103–104. For a discussion of Norwegian immigrant attitudes concerning the displacement of indigenous peoples in nineteenth century landtaking, see Betty A. Bergland, "Norwegian Immigrants and 'Indianerene' in the Landtaking, 1838–1862," *Norwegian-American Studies* 35 (Northfield: The Norwegian-American Historical Association, 2000), 319–350.

[23] Sauer, *Geography of the Upper Illinois Valley*, 163–178.

[24] United States Census, Population, 1850, 1860; Helen Rankin Jeter, *Trends of Population in the Region of Chicago* (Chicago: The University of Chicago Press, 1927), 53–54. For the early settlement history of Norwegians in the Lisbon area see Carlton C. Qualey, *Norwegian Settlement in the United States* (Northfield: Norwegian-American Historical Association, 1938), 17ff; and Flom, *A History of Norwegian Immigration*, 354–361.

[25] United States Census, Population, 1850.

[26] "Historical Sketch of Grundy County," *Holiday Supplement, The Morris Herald* (Morris: The Morris Herald, E.B. Fletcher, Publisher, 1888), 9.

[27] Donald Wray, "The Norwegians: Sect and Ethnic Group," 168ff; and Evon Z. Vogt, Jr., "Town and Country: The Structure of Rural Life," 236ff., in W. Lloyd Warner, *Democracy in Jonesville. A Study of Quality and Inequality* (New York: Harper & Brothers, 1949).

[28] Evon Z. Vogt, *Fieldwork among the Maya. Reflections on the Harvard Chiapas Project* (Albuquerque: University of New Mexico Press, 1994), 39.

[29] U.S. Census Bureau, Census 2000, *DP-2 Profile of Selected Social Characteristics: 2000, Grundy County, Illinois; Kendall County, Illinois*.

[30] Michael Gambone, "The Immigrant Presence in Grundy County, 1850–1860: Directions, Developments, and Consolidation," in Michael P. Conzen and Melissa J. Morales, eds., *Settling the Upper Illinois Valley. Patterns of Change in the I & M Canal Corridor*,

1830–1900 (Chicago: Committee on Geographical Studies, The University of Chicago, 1989), 65–66.

[31] Nelson, *A Pioneer Churchman,* 118–119.

[32] *Ibid.,* 119.

[33] For background on Elling Eielsen and other lay preachers, see Olaf Morgan Norlie, *Elling Eielsen. A Brief History* (Norway, Illinois: The Elling Eielsen Centennial 1839–1939, 1940); Theodore C. Blegen, "The Emerging Church," *Norwegian Migration to America. The American Transition* (Northfield: The Norwegian-American Historical Association, 1940), 131–174; Laurence M. Larson, "The Lay Preacher in Pioneer Times," *The Changing West and Other Essays* (Northfield: Norwegian-American Historical Association, 1937), 147–170; E. Clifford Nelson and Eugene L. Fevold, "Haugeanism Organizes: Eielsen's and Hauge's Synods," *The Lutheran Church Among Norwegian-Americans, Volume I, 1825–1890* (Minneapolis: Augsburg Publishing House, 1960), 126–150.

[34] *Eightieth Anniversary Program of Lisbon Evangelical Lutheran Church* (Lisbon, Illinois: Lisbon Evangelical Lutheran Church, 1934), 5, 18; J. C. Jensson (Roseland), *American Lutheran Biographies* (Milwaukee: Jens C. Roseland, 1890), 35–37. In 1846, Andrewson joined with Eielsen and others in the organization of the "Evangelical Lutheran Church in America," otherwise known as the "Eielsen Synod," and was a signer to the statement of beliefs, known as the "Old Constitution," of the Synod, that was composed by Eielsen and his followers. Several years later, Andrewson withdrew from the Eielsen group. In 1851, Andrewson participated in the formation of the Northern Illinois Synod, an organization of Norwegian, Swedish, and English churches in Illinois.

[35] J. C. Jensson (Roseland), *American Lutheran Biographies,* 602–603; Rasmussen, *A Brief History of the Rasmussen Family.*

[36] *Eightieth Anniversary,* 17; A. E. Strand, ed., *A History of Norwegians of Illinois* (Chicago: Anderson Publishing Company, 1905), 67–70. Algot Strand's history includes an account of Eielsen, in 1846, bringing Viar and Synneva Tendalsvikjo (Wier and Synneva Weeks), recently arrived in Muskego, to the Lisbon home of Rasmus Larson Tungesvik, who previously had known Wier Weeks in Norway. Tungesvik encouraged Weeks to build a cabin on Tungesvik's land. In 1849, Weeks converted the house into a meeting place for the Lisbon Lutheran congregation when Weeks moved to his own farm on the prairie north of Lisbon village (later known as North Lisbon or Helmar).

[37] For a discussion of these issues, see Blegen, *Norwegian Migration to America,* 241–276, 418–453; and Nicholas Tavuchis, *Pastors and Immigrants. The Role of a Religious Elite in the Absorption of Norwegian Immigrants* (The Hague: Martinus Nijhoff, 1965).

[38] J. Magnus Rohne, *Norwegian American Lutheranism Up to 1872* (New York: The Macmillan Company, 1926), 48–49.

[39] *Ibid.,* 49–51.

[40] Marcus Lee Hansen, *The Immigrant in American History* (Cambridge: Harvard University Press, 1942), 62.

[41] Flom, *A History of Norwegian Immigration,* 355; United States Census of Population, Kendall County, Illinois; Grundy County, Illinois, manuscript reports, 1850 Federal Census.

[42] United States Census of Population, Saratoga Township, Grundy County, Illinois, manuscript reports, 1850 Federal Census.

[43] Strand, *A History of Norwegians of Illinois*, 67–70; *Kendall County Record*, October 8, 1890; *Kendall County Record*, February 14, 1900; Flom, *A History of Norwegian Immigration*, 358–359.

[44] Sauer, *Geography of the Upper Illinois Valley*, 161–189; James William Putnam, *The Illinois and Michigan Canal. A Study in Economic History* (Chicago: The University of Chicago Press, 1918); Harold W. Mayer and Richard C. Wade, *Chicago. Growth of a Metropolis* (Chicago: University of Chicago Press, 1969), 39; Michael P. Conzen and Kathleen A. Brosnan, "The Geographical Vision and the Reality of the Illinois & Michigan Canal," *Bulletin of the Illinois Geographical Society* XLII, Number 2 (Fall, 2000), 5–19.

[45] *The Free Trader* (Ottawa, Illinois), March 23, 1850. See also Theodore Calvin Pease, *The Story of Illinois* (Chicago: The University of Illinois Press, 1949), 136.

[46] Theodore C. Blegen, ed., and trans., *Ole Rynning's True Account of America* (Minneapolis: The Norwegian-American Historical Association, 1926), 79.

[47] Clarence A. Clausen and Andreas Elviken, eds. and trans., *A Chronicle of Old Muskego. The Diary of Soren Bache, 1839–1847* (Northfield: Norwegian-American Historical Association, 1951), 15.

[48] Malmin, *America in the Forties*, 138.

Story County in the Early 1850s
by Col. John Scott, William K. Wood, and William O. Payne

[1] The Sauk and Fox (Meskwaki) tribes ceded central Iowa to the U. S. Government in 1842 in order to pay their trading debts and agreed to move to a reservation in Kansas in the fall of 1845. The Meskwaki were reluctant partners in this agreement, and some of them refused to leave central Iowa and others returned to central Iowa because they were unhappy in Kansas. This is the reason William K. Wood and other families living in the Cory's Grove area would have had Indian scares in 1849. The tribes' permanent settlement area was along the Iowa River in Tama County where they planted and harvested crops during the growing season. During the winter months, families moved to nearby rivers and creeks including the Skunk River and its tributaries where they hunted, fished, and trapped. Through the help of friendly white residents in Tama County and the Iowa Governor, a special legislative session passed a law in 1856 allowing Meskwaki to purchase land in their former permanent settlement area where they resumed their former lifestyle. In 1900, there were approximately 360 Indians living in the Meskwaki Settlement in 65 households, most of them living in wickiups with only a few living in frame houses (see "Meskwaki History" CD, State Historical Society of Iowa, 2004). It was common for people living near central Iowa's rivers and creeks to see Meskwaki up into the early 1900s. For information about their camping locations near the central Iowa Norwegian settlements, see *Meskwaki Along the Upper South Skunk River: Pioneer References of Their Presence in Hamilton, Story, and Polk Counties* compiled by Arlen Twedt and self-published in 2012 (available in central Iowa county libraries and the State Historical Library of Iowa) and "Meskwaki Sites Along the Upper South Skunk

River" by Cynthia L. Peterson, *Newsletter of the Iowa Archeological Society*, Summer 2013, Issue 226, Vol. 63, No. 2, which is also available at the Web site of the Office of the State Archaeologist @ http://archaeology.uiowa.edu/meskwaki-sites-along-upper-south-skunk-river.

² The Norwegian was Gunder Madskaar [1809–1855] who emigrated from Etne, Norway, to Lisbon, Illinois, in 1854 with his wife, Kari Anfinson [1812–1856/57], and their two children. In August 1855, they were members of a caravan of 15 wagons that moved from the Lisbon Settlement to central Iowa where others from the Lisbon area had founded a Norwegian settlement southwest of Cambridge on June 7, 1855. Reminiscences of the trip state, "They reached Iowa Center during a snow-storm and were obligated to stay there for several days as they could not get across the swollen Indian creek. They finally rafted their wagons across, carrying the freight by hand over a foot-log. In order to get the cattle over, the bell-cow was wheedled into crossing first, and then only were the rest willing to come. Gunder Madskaar was taken sick with typhoid fever and died while they were at Iowa Center." Reference: *Story City Herald*, 6/8/1922. Wood's recollection of this event is only partially correct. There was one family and a single man in the caravan, the Lars Sheldall family and Thor Hegland, who were headed to northern Story County where land was purchased east of Story City earlier in the summer for a second central Iowa Norwegian settlement, but the destination for the other families in the caravan was the Cambridge settlement in southern Story County. In addition, there is no documentation that Gunder Madskaar's body was left under a wagon as Woods tells in his story. The caravan arrived in this settlement on September 30.

³ A bank note detector is a pen designed to identify counterfeit paper money. It applies a small amount of iodine to paper money, and if there is no color change or if the paper turns yellowish, the money is supposedly genuine. Bank note pens were not, however, a foolproof method of identifying counterfeit money.

⁴ For information about this period of Iowa's history, see "Early Banking in Iowa" by Major Hoyt Sherman, *Annals of Iowa* V, no. 1 (April 1901): 1–13.

⁵ Jesse Hussong [1819–1954] was likely a brother of Amanda Jane Hussong [1826–1919] who came to Story County in 1852 with her husband, Henry Cameron, but likely after Jesse had arrived earlier in the year. Jesse and Amanda's parents must have come with Jesse because the father, John Hussong [1797–1862] who died in Story County, is likely the "Grandpaw Hussong" referred to in a memoir, "The Boy on Kiegley Creek" by Guy D. Johnson [1895–1986], a grandson of Amanda and Henry Cameron. A copy of Johnson's memoir, self-published in 1976, is in the Bertha Bartlett Public Library, Story City, Iowa, and it was also serialized in *The Story City Herald*, January 25-September 6, 1978. Johnson began his memoir with the story about how his grandparents met and about their arrival and settlement in Story County: "Amanda Jane Hussong traveled up to Terre Haute, Indiana, to visit some of her friends that had moved up there from Kentucky. While she was up there the girls got together and had a party. They invited in some of the boys, and one of the neighbor boys, Henry Cameron, met Jane for the first time. They struck up a friendly acquaintance and before the evening was over, Henry told Jane that he was running away the next day. His father had bound him out to a blacksmith for seven years or until he was twenty-one years old. The blacksmith was to learn (*sic*) him a trade and give some schooling, but he never got to go to school. Schools

were private and high priced in those days. Henry figured that he was close to twenty-one years old, so now was the time to get out and join the Army. He told Jane, 'I'll be gone for a year. Will you wait for me?' Jane said she would. They were married on August 12, 1847. The Camerons made their home in Terre Haute for about five years.... In 1852, they made the trip in the covered wagon to Iowa. It was late fall when they pulled into the little village of Bloomington on the east side of Skunk River in Story County, Iowa. They were tired and worn out. The trail was heavy and long and there were many creeks and ditches to ford. Their children were sick. They were happy when they looked and found Grandpaw Hussong's cabin in the edge of the woods. There they stayed over winter. The next spring they found a place they liked on the west side of Squaw Creek and started a home there. They first built a shed type shelter to live in while Henry built a log house. They lived on this same place for many years. The neighbors called Mrs. Cameron, Aunt Jane, but when I came along many years later, I found out that these folks were Grandpaw and Grandma Cameron.... Mother told me a lot of things about the Cameron family. Grandpaw Cameron and his family came to Iowa in 1852....Grandpaw and his family landed in Story County and stayed the first winter at Bloomington, a small village on the east side of Skunk River about two and a half miles north of where the city of Ames is now located. There was not a mark or a dot on the map to show that there might be a city there someday. The 1849 map of Iowa said, 'Story County, no population.' Grandpaw looked the lay of the land over but he could not see that there would someday be a state college [Iowa State University] right near where he settled. Next spring, he moved west across Skunk River and Squaw Creek, and on a hill just west of the creek he built a shed type log shelter. There they spent the next winter. He cut logs and poles, hauled and pulled them up on a hill a little south of his shed house and there he built a big log house. My mother was born in this log house in 1865. She told me the old log house was nice and warm on cold winter days. They sat and played on the floor in front of the big rock fireplace."

[6] Their pioneer story, "Arrasmith Family On One Story Co. Farm Since 1852," was published in the Nevada-Story County Centennial Edition of the *Nevada Evening Journal*, June 13, 1953. Soon after William and Alvina Arrasmith were married in Clay County, Indiana, they joined other friends and headed for Iowa. Their pioneer story, written by their youngest daughter, Edith Miriam, in 1946, states, "Progress was, of course, very slow, and when they reached Madrid, Iowa, they stopped there for a time with some acquaintances who had moved there previously. They entered a few acres of land there and put in a crop of corn. After the corn was laid by, Father and the other men of his friends, went up to the farm in Story County. He cut trees and made a one room cabin with a fireplace. This cabin continued to be the home of the Arrasmith family until 1860 when four rooms were built a few rods southeast of the cabin.... In August 1852, the cabin now being completed, Father and Mother moved from Madrid into their new home. There they lived until the corn was ripe. In the months they had been living in Iowa, Grandfather and Grandmother Arrasmith had also moved to Iowa. So when the time came for Father to husk the corn, Uncle Dudley Arrasmith, one of his brothers age 10 years, came to stay with mother who was but 17 years of age on January 25 before she was married on March 4, 1852. Father went down and husked the corn staying at Madrid from Sunday night until Saturday when he would drive to the new home with a load of corn. It was a long lonely week for those two youngsters for they usually saw no

one but each other during the time father was gone. There were sometimes Indians traveling through, but I do not remember of hearing that any came during the time they were alone. Mother said that on Saturday night she would hear the wagon rattling long before father arrived with his load of corn.... Mother said that before they had lived in the cabin many days, she looked out the door and there was a woman and two children on horseback. This woman was Mrs. Keigley who lived northeast about two or three miles. She had seen smoke down that way for several mornings. That was the beginning of a life-long friendship."

[7] In their histories of Story County, W. O Payne and Col. John Scott both attempted to account for all of the early settlers to the county. Another source for information about the early settlers is William G. Allen's *A History of Story County, Iowa* published in 1887. Concerning settlement beside the Skunk River upstream from Keigley's settlement location in northeastern Franklin Township, Allen states on p. 65, "The first men looking for a location above John H. Keigley's were in the spring of 1852 from Appanoose County, Iowa, (but formerly from Indiana, as most of the early settlers were) were Robert Bracken, George and Daniel Prime, John, Jesse and Samuel Smith, and viewing the county up near what is now Story City. Mr. Bracken and George Prime liking it well thought they would move in the fall, but the Smiths and Daniel Prime thought they would look farther, consequently went west into Kansas and Nebraska, and not liking the west as well as they did here, returned late in the fall to find their claims (as Bracken and Geo. Prime made claims) taken possession of by three families of Quakers who came in the last of August. They came from the south, stopping over a few days with Wm. Arrasmith who lived where he now does, he being the only settler between Squire Corey's [who settled at Ballard's Grove in Palestine Township in 1850, per obituary, *Story County Watchman*, October 13, 1882, and purchased government land four miles north of Ballard Grove and close to the Skunk River in Washington Township in 1851] and Keigleys, there being too many for the Quakers and being non-residents they left, and leaving the first settlement to be made by Robert and William Bracken, George and Daniel Prime, John, Jesse and Samuel Smith, all men of families who located in what became Lafayette Township, this county, none of them living here at present, and only Robert Bracken residing here till death...."

[8] The Smith family settled in Howard Township which was part of Lafayette Township until it was organized as a separate township in 1859.

[9] In "Nineteenth-Century Mills and Milling Industries in Story County, Iowa" by David N. Ballard, Jr. (*Journal of the Iowa Archeological Society* 31 (1984): 164), Ballard states, "Heistand was one of the first settlers in Story County. He entered the county in 1848 and, after developing his farmstead, returned to Indiana in the winter of 1851/1852 for more supplies and to collect his daughter and her husband, Stephen O'Brien. On the return trip Heistand brought to his farmstead saws for a sawmill and wheels for a carding mill." Ballard's reference for this information is the *Ames Daily Tribune and Evening News*, Diamond Jubilee Edition, September 29, 1928. The microfilmed copy of the newspaper is too blurry to read, so Ballard's information about Heistand entering Story County in 1848 could not be confirmed.

[10] "Passing of W. K. Wood Story County Pioneer," *The Maxwell Tribune*, March 29, 1917.

A Brief History of the First Norwegian Settlement of Story and Polk Counties, Ia. 1855–1905
by Oley Nelson, 1905

[1] Oley Nelson, comp., *En kort historie af det forste norske settlement i Story og Polk counties, Iowa* (Chicago, n.p., 1905), translated and republished by the author under the title *A Brief History of the First Norwegian Settlement of Story and Polk Counties, Ia. 1855–1905* (Slater, Iowa: The Slater News, 1930).

[2] Anfin Apland, comp., *A Brief History of the First Norwegian Settlement of Story and Polk Counties, Ia. 1855–1905* [a re-compiled, corrected and added to edition of this history by Oley Nelson, originally published in Norwegian in 1905 and translated into English by Oley Nelson in 1930] (Des Moines, Iowa: n.p., 1945), 4–5.

[3] *The Slater News*, November 2, 1927. Anna's obituary states, "While she was not a member of the first colony, she came to Iowa shortly afterwards."

[4] *The Cambridge Leader*, July 1, 1920.

[5] Rasmus Sheldall, "Rasmus Sheldall's Pioneer Story," transcriber N. Tjernagel, *The Story City Herald*, June 8, 1922.

[6] Lars Olson's identity is unknown. He is not on the roster for the 96th Illinois Infantry @ http://civilwar.illinoisgenweb.org/r100/096-k-in.html. On the Norwegians in the Civil War Web site @ http://vesterheim.org/collections/civil-war-database/ there is a Lars Olsen from Etne., Hordaland, Norway, who lived in Story County, but further information about this Lars Olsen could not be found.

[7] More information about the Bergen congregation is contained in note #9.

[8] There are church records for the previous years, but they are in the possession of Pastor Osmund Sheldahl's descendants.

[9] This controversy in the Lutheran church began in the 1870s and led to the withdrawal of one-third of the membership of the Norwegian Synod membership by 1888. Pastor O. M. Norlie's *Norsk Lutherske Menigheter i America: 1843–1916*, vol. 1 (Minneapolis, Minnesota: Augsburg Publishing House, 1918), 344, indicates the group that left the Fjeldberg congregation organized themselves into an anti-Missouri congregation in 1888. This was the Bergen congregation that joined the Palestine congregation in 1891. For information about the predestination controversy, see E. Clifford Nelson's *The Lutherans in North America* (Philadelphia: Fortress Press, rev. ed. 1980), 313–325.

[10] Rev. E. Johnson was Rev. Endre Johannessen, the first pastor of the Lincoln congregation, 1871 to 1875. For more information, see O. M. Norlie, *Norsk Lutherske Menigheter i America*, 345.

[11] W. O. Payne, *History of Story County, Iowa: A Record of Settlement, Organization, Progress and Achievement*, vol. 1 (Chicago: The S. J. Clarke Publishing Co., 1911), 431.

[12] John P. Herrick, "Oley Nelson—An Unforgettable Character," *Annals of Iowa* 25, no. 2 (1943): 118. This article also contains an interesting stenographic report of an extemporaneous talk Oley Nelson gave at a meeting of the Pioneer Lawmakers' Association of Iowa in Des Moines on March 17, 1921.

[13] "Oley Nelson," *The Slater News*, April 20, 1938.

[14] James A. Storing, "A Town That Moved." *The Palimpsest* 20 (February 1939): 60–61.

[15] *The Roland Record*, November 17, 1921. Some of Oley Nelson's remarks were, in all likelihood, similar in content to a pamphlet he published entitled, "The Early Norwegian Immigrant: From 1840 to 1860" (Minneapolis, Minnesota: Augsburg Publishing House, 1906) that he used as an address at the reunion of the 15th Wisconsin Regiment in Minneapolis, Minnesota, on August 14, 1906.

[16] Apland, *A Brief History of the First Norwegian Settlement of Story and Polk Counties, Ia. 1855–1905*, 15.

[17] Maury White, "Oley Nelson was an Institution," *Des Moines Register*, March 23, 1997. A similar recollection was described in 1935 by George Mills, long-time political reporter for the *Des Moines Register*, when he wrote, "Pick out a rocking chair and retire when you are over 90? Not Oley Nelson. Despite his age, he again served as sergeant-at-arms of the house in the forty-sixth Iowa general assembly. For seven sessions, since 1923, he has filled the post. Many a time in the last session was the house debate broken by a loud voice saying, 'Misss-teer Spea-ker!!' ... 'Mr. Sergeant-at-arms.' ... 'Message ... from the senate.' ... Whereupon the suddenly hushed house would of necessity have to pay attention while the youthful senate minion read his message with the veteran leaning on a cane at the boy's side." (press release from the *Iowa Daily Press* bureau published in the *Ames Daily Tribune and Times*, November 2, 1925).

[18] For a more thorough biography of Oley Nelson, see "Oley and Ingeborg Nelson," in *I Remember Slater, Iowa* (Lake Mills, Iowa: Graphic Publishing Company, Inc., 1989), 156–159.

[19] *Story City Herald*, June 3, 1904 (Reprinted from the *Slater News*)

[20] Anders Haugland, *"Den tidlege utvandringa frå Skånevik"* ["The Early Emigration from Skånevik"], trans. Anne S. Helvik and Jarle Steinkjer in *Etne Sogelag Årbok 1988* ([Etne, Norway]: n.p., 1988), 72.

[21] Rasmus Malmin, O. M. Norlie, and O. A. Tingelstad, *Who's Who Among Pastors in all the Norwegian Lutheran Synods of America: 1843–1927* (Minneapolis, Minnesota: Augsburg Publishing House, 1927), 435.

[22] Pastor Olaf Holan, *"Noen Minneord Om Etnesbuen Pastor Osmund Sheldahl"* ["Some Commemorative Words About Etne's Pastor Osmund Sheldahl"] in *Etne Sogelag Årsskrift 1986* ([Etne, Norway]: n.p., 1986), 91 and Don Fatka, "From Norway to Story County," in *History Book, Sheldahl*, Iowa (n.p., n.d.).

[23] Carrie O. Larson, "Reverend Osmund Sheldahl 1824–1900," in *Larson Family History: 1830–1980*, Carrie O. Larson, ed. (Des Moines, Iowa: n.p., 1980).

A Little About the First Settlers in Story County
by Erik Arnesen Travaas, 1888

[1] On June 8 & 14, 1855, the scouting party from Lisbon, Illinois, purchased 2,560 acres in Howard Township, and all but 200 acres was in and around the future town of Roland. The land was purchased for $1.25 per acre at the Federal Land Office in Ft. Des

Moines, Iowa. On September 27, 1855, a second Lisbon scouting party purchased an additional 1,600 acres of government land in both Howard and Lafayette Townships, and on October 27 & 29, 1855, a third Lisbon scouting party purchased another 556 acres of government land in the two townships at the Federal Land Office in Ft. Des Moines.

[2] There was only one Norwegian family living in southern Hamilton County when Lars and Per settled there, the Lars Sheldall family. Lars was a member of the June 1855 scouting party, and he moved his family there in the fall of 1855. They lived close to the Skunk River two miles west of where Lars and Per settled.

[3] The village of Nevada began in 1853 when it was selected as the site for the county seat for Story County.

[4] Travaas states, "It is now long past spring...." when Lars and Per began their trip to Iowa. If he is correct about this departure time, Lars and Per would have found the 17 families and three single people who left Lisbon, Illinois, in May on their 300-mile trip to Story County to begin the new settlement. They arrived at their destination in the middle of June 1855.

[5] This statement implies there was not a town nearby, but in June 1855, a town named Fairview was platted close to where the city park is located in Story City. The next year, Fairview's first three businesses opened, and in 1857, a portable steam-powered sawmill began operation. However, according to Goodspeed's *1890 Biographical and Historical Memoirs of Story County, Iowa*, p. 202, "there was little or no business by 1860, and during the war the mill was removed."

[6] Travaas did not move to central Iowa until the late 1870s, so it is understandable he did not know the church history of the area very well. It is true the earliest settlers worshiped in their homes, but they also organized a church congregation, the St. Petri congregation, in June 1857 when their pastor from Lisbon, Pastor P. A. Rassmusen, made his first visit to the settlement. Pastor Rassmusen continued to make visits to the settlement until the congregation called Pastor Nils Amlund to be their pastor. Pastor Amlund began his ministry in 1860, and in 1865, the congregation dedicated a church building which was located east of Story City on the east side of the Skunk River. In 1874, a second church building was erected on the east prairie close to where the town of Roland was later platted. That same year, the first church building was moved to the west side of the Skunk River where the present St. Petri Lutheran Church is located.

[7] The Chicago and North Western rail line reached Nevada on July 4, 1864, and Ames the following year.

[8] Story City was known as Fairview until 1878 when a depot was built a few blocks west of the village of Fairview, and Fairview's businesses were moved to be close to the depot. The depot was built for a narrow gauge rail line that had been completed from the Rock Island depot in Des Moines to Ames in 1874 and extended to Story City in 1878. Fairview's post office name had been Story City since 1856 when it was discovered there was another Iowa post office named Fairview. In 1881, the two towns were incorporated under the name Story City.

[9] After the Chicago North Western Railway Company purchased the narrow gauge rail line and made it a wide gauge line, there were plans to extend the rail line to St. Paul. These plans never materialized, and the rail line was only extended two miles north to Randall and then a few miles to Callanan (an abandoned town).

¹⁰ See *Store Per: Norwegian-American "Paul Bunyan" of the Prairies* by Peter Tjernagel Harstad (Lakeville, Minnesota: Jackpine Press, 2011). Other books containing stories about him are *The Follinglo Dog Book: A Norwegian Pioneer Story from Iowa* by Peder Gustav Tjernagel and written in 1909 (Iowa City, University of Iowa Press, 1999) and *The Passing of the Prairie by a Fossil: Biographical Sketches of Central Iowa Pioneers and Civil War Veterans* by Nehemias Tjernagel, edited by Margaret Harstad Matzke (Bloomington, Indiana: Author House, 2009).

¹¹ For references to *Tallige* Lars, see the previously cited *The Follinglo Dog Book*, 84 & 102–104, and for a biographical sketch of him see the previously cited *The Passing of the Prairie*, 178–180.

¹² *The Nevada Representative*, November 5, 1878.

Big Norwegian Settlement, Roland, Iowa
by Knut Takla, 1900

¹ Two other sources refer to the drowning of John Ness. One confirms the drowning took place in the Iowa River and the other states it took place in the Cedar River. In a brief sketch of the life of Sjur Britson recorded by Nehemias Tjernagel, Tjernagel recorded, "On a visit to his home [Sjur Britson's home] he told me among other things ... In coming across the prairie from Illinois (there were twenty families in the party) the Britsons were witnesses of another tragedy, viz, the drowning of John Ness in the Iowa River. He and Christen Peterson had gone out to bathe, but John never came back; it was thought he had gotten beyond his depth and was seized with the cramps. It was said that Michael Erickson tried to rescue him, but nearly lost his life in the attempt. John left a widowed mother and two brothers, Lars and Christopher, to mourn his untimely death. The gloom occasioned by this grievous occurrence was partly offset by the arrival of a little daughter in the family of Hans Twedt. They set out from Illinois with but one child and when they came to Iowa they found they had two (see "Little Stories of Pioneer Days," *The Story City Herald*, August 17, 1922)." However, according to Ivar Havneros, John Ness drowned in the Cedar River. Havneros states, "On the trip to Iowa they were blessed with beautiful weather. Having reached Cedar River where they camped over Sunday, a beautiful baby girl was born to the Hans Tvedts (Mrs. Harlow, Spokane Falls, Washington). Here also, tragedy struck in the drowning of John Naes." See *History of St. Petri Congregation from its foundation June 1857 to its 50ᵗʰ Jubilee, June 1907*, trans. Rachel Vangness (Story City, Iowa: n.p., 1907), 4.

² The St. Petri Lutheran Church history includes the Knud Aske aka Knudt Thompson family on a list of families that arrived in 1857 (Havneros, 1907), but obituaries for Christena Thompson and their son, Henry, state the family came in 1860.

³ Knut Takla, *Det norske folk in De Forenede Stater: deres daglige liv og økonomiske stilling historisk over Amerika-landets fremtids-muligheter for en indvandrer* (Kristiania: J. M. Stenersen & Co., 1913), VII.

⁴ Translations of these reports will be in Volume 3 of *The Central Iowa Norwegians*. For a complete listing of Knut Takla's reports to *Skandinaven* see Norway in America: The bibliographical collections of Thor M. Andersen @ http://www.nb.no/baser/tma/english.html.

⁵ According to the 1900 Iowa Census for Story County, Anna was born in 1863 and immigrated to the United States in 1865.

⁶ *Roland Record*, July 3, 1901.

⁷ Hans Gangstø, email message to author, October 27, 2004.

⁸ *Skandinaven*, December 5, 1906.

⁹ Daron W. Olson, "Thoralv Klaveness and Knut Takla: Travel Writing and The Norwegian-American Identity, 1904–1913" (paper, Society for the Advancement of Scandinavian Study Conference, Minneapolis, Minnesota, May 2, 2003).

¹⁰ Odd Sverre Lovoll, *A Folk Epic: The Bygdelag in America* (Boston: Twayne Publishers for the Norwegian American Historical Association, 1975), 72.

¹¹ Borghild Dale, "Knut Knutson Takla, 1857–1950," in *Gamalt frå Voss*, Hefte XVIII (Voss, Norway: Voss Bygdeboknemnd, 1986), 127–128.

The Early History of the Norwegian Settlement in Howard Township
by John M. Mason, Editor, and M. O. Rod, Editor

¹ Erick Sheldahl's name does not appear on M. O. Rod's list of scouting party members or on the lists of Havneros (1907) and Holand (1908). Biographies of him in Story County histories (Goodspeed, 1890 and Payne, 1911) do not mention him as being a member of the scouting party nor does his obituary. He lived in the same general neighborhood where Editor Mason grew up, so it is strange that Mason listed him as a member of the scouting party.

² Two other sources refer to the drowning of their brother, John Ness. One confirms the drowning took place in the Iowa River and the other states it took place in the Cedar River. In a brief sketch of the life of Sjur Britson recorded by Nehemias Tjernagel, Tjernagel recorded, "On a visit to his home [Sjur Britson's home] he told me among other things ... In coming across the prairie from Illinois (there were twenty families in the party) the Britsons were witnesses of another tragedy, viz, the drowning of John Ness in the Iowa River. He and Christen Peterson had gone out to bathe, but John never came back; it was thought he had gotten beyond his depth and was seized with the cramps. It was said that Michael Erickson tried to rescue him, but nearly lost his life in the attempt. John left a widowed mother and two brothers, Lars and Christopher, to mourn his untimely death. The gloom occasioned by this grievous occurrence was partly offset by the arrival of a little daughter in the family of Hans Twedt. They set out from Illinois with but one child and when they came to Iowa they found they had two (see "Little Stories of Pioneer Days," *The Story City Herald*, August 17, 1922)." However, according to Ivar Havneros, their brother drowned in the Cedar River. Havneros states, "On the trip to Iowa they were blessed with beautiful weather. Having reached Cedar

River where they camped over Sunday, a beautiful baby girl was born to the Hans Tvedts (Mrs. Harlow, Spokane Falls, Washington). Here also, tragedy struck in the drowning of John Naes." See *History of St. Petri Congregation from its foundation June 1857 to its 50th Jubilee, June 1907*, trans. Rachel Vangness (Story City, Iowa: n.p., 1907), 4.

[3] According to Goodspeed, 1890, Norway Grange No. 218 was organized in the early 1870s, and the Grange store was built in 1873.

[4] See note #1 regarding Erick Sheldahl.

[5] The Clinton and Benton County Norwegian settlements in eastern Iowa were established by settlers who had originally settled in the Fox River Norwegian settlement area where the Lisbon settlement is located. There were central Iowa Norwegians who lived in the Clinton and Benton County settlements before moving to central Iowa, but it is unusual to find a family who lived in both settlements prior to moving to central Iowa.

[6] *Roland Record*, February 24, 1904.

[7] *The Roland Record*, September 5, 1946.

[8] The Trinity Lutheran congregation was organized on August 5, 1900, by former members of the Salem Lutheran Church in Roland who left during a controversy over secret societies. Salem's constitution prohibited membership in certain secret societies. At their annual meeting in January 1900, they voted to give congregational members who had joined the newly formed Masonic Lodge in Roland six months to reconsider. Trinity was originally called the English Evangelical Lutheran Church and affiliated with the Iowa General Synod. In 1905, the congregation applied and was accepted into the Norwegian United Church Synod, one of three main Norwegian synods at the time. That same year, the Roland Masonic Lodge was dissolved and its charter moved to Story City. There were approximately 20 members in the lodge at that time. When the three Norwegian synods merged in 1917, the members of Trinity decided to dissolve their congregation. Some of them rejoined the Salem congregation, and others joined the Bergen congregation in Roland.

[9] In a memoir, *Montana Live*, privately published in 2002 by Editor Mason's son, also named John M. Mason, he writes on p. 79, "My father was very much concerned about the way our country was treating the Indians that today we call the 'Native Americans.'… While in Canada my father had become interested in the Indians there where they were not treated so poorly. They had no Reservations. He worked with them and formed strong ties with their leaders and Medicine men. This interest carried over in his work in Montevideo." Editor Mason's son goes on to describe how his father took his family on exploration trips looking for artifacts from a Sioux tribe that had once lived west of Montevideo. He also describes how his father helped build a museum in Smith's Park in Montevideo and donated his entire collection of artifacts to the museum.

[10] Arnold Anderson, telephone interview with compiler, August 31, 2005.

[11] Lois Baker, informal conversation with compiler, Montevideo, Minnesota, September 8, 2005.

The Stavanger and Hordaland Colony in Central Iowa
by Hjalmar Rued Holand

[1] Another translation of Chapter 54 is by Malcolm Rosholt which has been published in *History of the Norwegian Settlements* by Hjalmar Rued Holand, Astri My Astri Publishing, Waukon, Iowa, 2006.

[2] Osmund Johnson was the earliest immigrant in the scouting party, having immigrated to the Muskego Norwegian Settlement in Wisconsin in 1843. According to his son's obituary, the family moved to the Lisbon Settlement a few months later (see *The Cambridge Leader*, December 14, 1911). As the most seasoned immigrant in the scouting party, Johnson possibly expressed some concern about starting a settlement in frontier country. However, Holand's description of Osmund Johnson's doubts are exaggerated in light of his actions: Johnson purchased land on October 9, 1854, at the Federal Land Office in Ft. Des Moines along with the other members of the scouting party, 331 acres in Section 30, Union Township. In his 1945 re-compiled, corrected, and added to version of Oley Nelson's *A brief History of the First Norwegian Settlement of Story and Polk Counties*, Anfin Apland, who was the son of another scouting party member states, "But he did not come with the colony in 1855 because he had some land and livestock to look after in Illinois. He came the next year." Johnson's son's obituary states, "Late in the fifties the family moved to this state settling on a tract of land west of the village which they had purchased a few years previously." If the family came in 1856, they did not arrive in time to be enumerated on the 1856 Iowa Census, but they are listed on the 1860 Federal Census for Union Township, Story County, Iowa.

[3] The members of the Palestine congregation were not Synod Lutherans. See Compiler's Notes for more information about this topic.

[4] Hjalmar R. Holand, *My First Eighty Years* (New York: Twayne Publishers, Inc., 1957), 250.

[5] The information in this paragraph was condensed from a biography in *Families of Hodnefjell of Mosterøy Island, Rogaland District, Norway, and Related Families of Norway and America*, compiled by Wilma (Hodnefield) Trebil (n.p., 1993), 76–77.

[6] Carlton C. Qualey, ed., *Norwegian-American Studies and Records*, vol. 17 (Northfield, Minnesota: Norwegian-American Historical Association, 1952), preface, http://www.naha.stolaf.edu/pubs/nastudies.htm.

[7] Jacob Hodnefield to Dr. Theodore C. Blegen, November 10, 1955. Jacob Hodnefield papers, Norwegian-American Historical Association archives, St. Olaf College, Northfield, Minnesota.

[8] Theodore C. Blegen, no addressee but presumably prepared for his successor, undated and written after Jacob Hodnefield's death. Jacob Hodnefield papers, Norwegian-American Historical Association archives, St. Olaf College, Northfield, Minnesota.

[9] There is no mention of Holand visiting central Iowa in the local newspapers for Cambridge, Story City, or Roland from January 1905 through January 1906 (no issues of *The Slater News* were preserved). Yet, the most likely time for Holand to have visited central Iowa was October 11–12, 1905, when the Norwegian Pioneer Association of America held its fourth triennial convention in Story City. The convention drew delegates and visitors from several states to hear nationally known speakers, and this

would have been of interest to Holand, not only because of his interest in Norwegian immigrant history, but also because of his interest in enrolling members for the Norwegian Cultural Society of which he was archivist and historian. Since Holand is not mentioned in the local newspapers, it seems reasonable to assume he attended the convention but was overshadowed by the many speakers on the convention program.

[10] Another example is the story about northern Story County Norwegians traveling to Marshalltown during the harsh winter of 1856–57. This story appears in Nehemias Tjernagel's "Ole Braland's Pioneer Story" that will be published in Volume 2 of *The Central Iowa Norwegians*.

[11] Ivar Havneros, *History of St. Petri Congregation from its foundation June 1857 to its 50th Jubilee, June 1907*, trans. Rachel Vangness (Story City, Iowa: n.p., 1907), 4. Nilsen purchased 320 acres of government land in Howard Township (160 acres in Section 12 & 80 acres in Section 15) at Ft. Des Moines on September 29, 1855, perhaps for speculation, because he continued to live in Illinois, http:/www.glorecords.blm.gov/ (search for Erick Nelson).

[12] Oley Nelson, *En kort historie af det forste norske settlement i Story og Polk counties, Iowa* (Chicago, n.p., 1905), republished in English by the author under the title *A Brief History of the First Norwegian Settlement of Story and Polk Counties, Ia. 1855–1905* (Slater, Iowa: The Slater News [Press], 1930), 2.

[13] According to Rasmus Malmin et. al, Nils Olsen Næs was a Bible salesman from 1851 to 1853 and an evangelist in southern Wisconsin, Minnesota, northern Illinois, and Iowa from 1853 to 1856, *Who's Who Among Pastors in all the Norwegian Lutheran synods of America 1843–1927* (Minneapolis, Minnesota: Augsburg Publishing House, 1928), 435. The only Norwegian settlements in northern Iowa until 1853 were in northeast Iowa in Clayton, Allamakee, and Winnishiek counties. In 1853, Norwegians began to settle farther west into Mitchell County. When Næs told his friends in Lisbon that government land was available in Iowa for $1.25 an acre, it would, therefore, have probably been based on information he learned from his travels in northeastern Iowa.

[14] Jonas Duea purchased 52.66 acres in Section 31 (SW fractional ¼ SW¼), Township 86, North Range 23, and Lars Sheldall purchased 52.79 acres in the same section (NW fractional ¼ NW¼). Both purchases were made on March 30, 1855, from Miles White, a land agent in Ft. Des Moines, Iowa.

[15] The government land office was opened in Ft. Des Moines in June 1853. A newspaper editor who witnessed this event wrote, "Business was so furious that the great rush was over by 1856," Will Porter, *Annals of Polk County, Iowa, and City of Des Moines* (Des Moines, Iowa: Geo. A. Miller Printing Company, Printers and Publishers, 1898), 172.

[16] The land was purchased in Howard Township which in 1855 was part of Lafayette Township. Howard became an independent township in 1860.

[17] Laurence M. Larson, *The Changing West, and Other Essays* (Northfield, Minnesota: Norwegian-American Historical Association, 1937), 164–165. According to Osmund Sheldahl's granddaughter, Carrie Larson, Osmund received some training in theology at Upsala University in Sweden. In one section of her family history she states, "He had pursued in the study of divinity and engineering, especially in surveying" and in another section she states, "He majored in theology," "From Whence We Came" and "Reverend

Osmund Sheldahl 1824–1900" in *Larson Family History: 1830–1980*, Carrie O. Larson, ed (Des Moines, Iowa: n.p., 1980).

[18] Pastor O. M. Norlie, *Norsk Lutherske Menigheter i America: 1843–1916* (Minneapolis, Minnesota: Augsburg Publishing House, 1918), 342.

[19] E. Clifford Nelson, *The Lutherans in North America*, ed., rev. ed. (Philadelphia: Fortress Press, 1980), 189.

[20] The Lisbon Evangelical Lutheran Church history states, "Elling Eielsen and Ole Andrewson took care of the pastoral work until P. A. Rasmussen became pastor in Lisbon in 1854." The history also lists 19 marriages officiated by Pastor Andrewson from 1847 through 1850, seven in Kendall County and 12 in Grundy County, *Lisbon Evangelical Lutheran Church of the Unaltered Augsburg Confession, 1854–1934* (Lisbon, Illinois: n.p.: 1934), 5 & 13. Further evidence that Pastor Andrewson was serving this group of Lisbon settlers is contained in a quarterly report he submitted to the corresponding secretaries of the American Home Mission Society, September 14, 1855, where he states "In the field where I now labour, things seems about the same. I have formerly informed you of the more awakened interest in the preached word of God, but the main difficulty is now, that the people moves out to Iowa. Oure whole congregation in Lisbon has left, consisting of between 30 to 40 families & by next spring I suppose a good number will start from this settlement," American Home Missionary Society Papers, Billy Graham Center Archives, Wheaton, Illinois. Typed transcriptions of Andrewson's reports to the American Home Missionary Society are in the Oscar Vitalis Anderson papers at the Swenson Swedish Immigration Research Center, Rock Island, Illinois.

[21] Havneros, *History of St. Petri Congregation*, 6.

[22] Pastor O. M. Norlie, *Norsk Lutherske prester i America*, 1843–1913, (Minneapolis, Minnesota: Augsburg Publishing House, 1914), 96.

[23] Ibid., 101.

About the Central Iowa Norwegian Project

Preserving the history of Norwegian settlement in Story, Polk, Hamilton, and Hardin Counties

Established in 1995, the Central Iowa Norwegian Project gathers information for writing and publishing a history about the first 50 years of Norwegian settlement in central Iowa.

Primary research objectives for the project are to:

- Locate existing histories and other resources about the history of the central Iowa Norwegians.

- Learn about the Norwegian families and individuals who lived in Story, Polk, and Hamilton counties from 1855 through 1860.

- Collect stories about life in the settlements from 1855 through 1905.

In 2003, the scope of the project broadened to include publication of previously written histories and memoirs and other research concerning the 1855–1905 time period.

Anyone having information about the early settlers, stories about life in the settlements, and/or resource material is encouraged to contact Arlen Twedt at:

Central Iowa Norwegian Project
509 NE Stone Valley Dr.
Ankeny, Iowa 50021-4113
Email: atwedt@aol.com

The Central Iowa Norwegians Volume 2 Contents

The Early Pioneers: 1855–1860: Biographic & Demographic Profiles by Arlen Twedt. This is the signature piece in this volume. It consists of short biographies of all the families who lived in central Iowa prior to 1861.

"Memoirs of Peder Christian and Anna Serina Heggem" by Malinda Ann Thompson, 1926 & 1930

"Rasmus Jonsen and Anne Margrethe Berentsen" by Glen Severson, ca. 1930

"Reminiscences of Pioneer Life by an Old Settler" by Mrs. E. L. Severeid, 1940

"Pioneer Days in Southwest Story County" by Sina Kloster Moran, 1953

"Introduction to History of the Lande Clan" by Bertha Barnes Peterson, 1968

"60th Wedding Anniversary," a biography of Paul and Enger Thompson by Editor M. O. Rod, 1911

"H. B. Henryson's and Ole Braland's Pioneer Stories" by Nehemias Tjernagel, 1922

"Pioneer Days" by Carrie (Williams) Knutson, 1932

"A Reminiscence" by Mrs. Erick Johnson, 1938

"A Tribute to Pioneers" by Pastor G. O. Paulsrud, 1931

"Rasmus Sheldall's Pioneer Story" by Arlen Twedt, 1999

"Nils Bauge's Pioneer Story" by Arlen Twedt, 2003

"Emigration from Skånevik: A 150-year Anniversary" by Ingvald Skålnes, 1986, translated by Anne S. Helvik & Jarle Steinkjer

"The Early Emigration from Skånevik" by Anders Haugland, 1988, translated by Anne S. Helvik & Jarle Steinkjer

The Central Iowa Norwegians Volume 3 Contents

The Town Building Period: 1880–1905 by Arlen Twedt. This is the signature piece in this volume. Topics include building towns, educating children, mills and markets, communication and travel, political involvement, farms and agriculture, businesses on Main Street, and amusement and culture.

"Reports from central Iowa" published in *Skandinaven* by Knut Takla, 1893–1906, translated by Ardis N. Petersen

"Glimpses from Life in the Norwegian-American Community" published in *Minneapolis Tidende* by Carl G. O. Hansen, 1932–33, translated by Sten Valen

Chapters 1 & 2 from *Iowa Life 1875–1925: The Story of a Central Iowa Community of Norwegian Immigrants and Their Descendants,* unpublished manuscript by Jacob Hodnefield, 1955

"Osmund Sheldahl, Pathfinder and Pastor" by Arlen Twedt

"Fifty Years in Central Iowa: The Celebrations in Cambridge and Story City," 1905, newspaper accounts compiled by Arlen Twedt

"The Central Iowa Norwegians—A Retrospect" by Arlen Twedt

"Selected Bibliography of Norwegian Settlement in Central Iowa" by Arlen Twedt

This volume may also include yet undiscovered histories and memoirs or other studies by the author.

www.ingramcontent.com/pod-product-compliance
Lightning Source LLC
Chambersburg PA
CBHW060108170426
43198CB00010B/812